THE
LORD'S PRAYER
THROUGH
NORTH AFRICAN
EYES

THE
LORD'S PRAYER
THROUGH
NORTH AFRICAN
EYES

A Window into Early Christianity

Michael Joseph Brown

T&T CLARK INTERNATIONAL
A Continuum imprint
NEW YORK • LONDON

T & T Clark International, Madison Square Park, 15 East 26th Street, New York, NY 10010

T & T Clark International, The Tower Building, 11 York Road, London SE1 7NX

T & T Clark International is a Continuum imprint.

Cover design: Corey Kent

Library of Congress Cataloging-in-Publication Data

Brown, Michael Joseph
  The Lord's prayer through North African eyes : a window into early Christianity / by Michael Joseph Brown.
      p. cm.
  Includes bibliographical references and index.
  ISBN 0-567-02670-1 (pbk.)
    1. Lord's prayer—Criticism, interpretation, etc.—Africa, North—History—Early church, ca. 30–600. 2. Clement, of Alexandria, Saint, ca. 150–ca. 215. 3. Tertullian, ca. 160–ca. 230. I. Title.
  BV230.B696 2004
  226.9'606'09397—dc22

2004002822

Printed in the United States of America

04 05 06 07 08 09   10 9 8 7 6 5 4 3 2 1

RETURNS POLICY

Please take a moment to check your order. If something is damaged, defective, or missing, we apologize. Please call our office **within 60 days** of the invoice date at **1-800-406-3627** to report the problem.

You may return items by following these directions:

1. You may return any item within 24 months from the invoice date except dated items, such as calendars, annuals and curriculum. The items must be in saleable condition with no marks or price tags.

2. Please pack items carefully and include a packing slip with a list of the items included, the invoice numbers, and the reason for return. A copy of your original invoice, or a list of your original invoice numbers, date purchased and discount received will ensure that you receive proper credit.

3. We cannot accept collect shipments, but we will be happy to arrange for a pickup if the problem was our error.

4. Please place your name and address on the outside of the box as they appear on the "bill to" section of your invoice.

5. If there is more than one box, please mark each box consecutively. For example: box 1 of 2, etc.

6. Please send your returns, via UPS or the U.S. Post Office to: T&T Clark International, Morehouse Publishing, Continuum, or Living the Good News

   Returns Department
   3101 North 7th Street
   Harrisburg, PA 17110

ACCOUNT NO.	INVOICE NO.	INVOICE DATE	TERMS
50637	3165869	11 FEB 05	Gratis

B I L L T O

DAMON LINKER ASSOC EDITOR
FIRST THINGS
156 FIFTH AVE STE 400
NEW YORK NY 10010

FOLD

SALES AREA	PURCHASE ORDER
	REVIEW COPY+/SB

ISBN NUMBER	QTY.	TITLE	LOCATION CODE	LIST PRICE	%	AMOUNT
0-8264-1623-3	1	1 AMERICAN PROVIDENCE (H)	E353C	24.95	%	Free
		** REVIEW COPY **				

RS

Main Warehse

Quan   1
Weight   .99#

INTEREST CHARGED AT 1.5% PER MONTH

SUB-TOTAL	SHIPPING CHARGE	AMOUNT PAID	INVOICE TOTAL
.00	0.00		.00

SHIP TO

INST OF RELIG AND PUBLIC LIFE
DAMON LINKER ASSOC EDITOR
FIRST THINGS
156 FIFTH AVE STE 400
NEW YORK NY 10010

First Class

Amount Enclosed $ _____
PLEASE RETURN THIS PORTION WITH YOUR CHECK

ACCOUNT NO.	INVOICE NO.
50637	3165869

FOLD

To Imani

Table of Contents

List of Abbreviations

For references to ancient texts, I have generally used the abbreviations of the *SBL Handbook of Style for Ancient Near Eastern, Biblical, and Early Christian Studies* (Peabody, MA: Hendrickson, 1999), and the *Checklist of Editions of Greek and Latin Papyri, Ostraca and Tablets* (4th ed.; BASPSup 7; Atlanta: Scholars Press, 1992; updated: http://scriptorium.lib.duke.edu/papyrus/texts/clist.html). Other commonly used abbreviations in this book include the following:

AE	*L'Année épigraphique* (Paris, 1888–)
CIL	T. Mommsen et al., eds., *Corpus inscriptionum latinarum* (Berlin, 1863–)
CIL²	G. Wilmanns, ed., *Corpus inscriptionum latinarum* VIII (Berlin, 1881).*Supplementa* i–iv, ed. R. Cagnat et al. (Berlin, 1891–1916).*Supplementum* v (Indices) (Berlin, 1942–59).
FIRA	S. Riccobono et al., eds., *Fontes iuris Romani anteiustiniani*, 2d ed., 3 vols. (Florence, 1940–41).
HB	Hebrew Bible
ILAfr	R. Cagnat et al., eds., *Inscriptions latines d'Afrique* (Paris, 1923).
ILAlg	S. Gsell et al., eds., *Inscriptions latines de l'Algérie*, 2 vols. (Paris, 1922–57).
ILS	H. Dessau, ed., *Inscriptiones latinae selectae* (Berlin, 1892–1916).
ILTun	A. Merlin, ed., *Inscriptions latines de la Tunisie* (Paris, 1944).
IRT	J. M. Reynolds and J. B. Ward Perkins, eds., *The Inscriptions of Roman Tripolitania* (Rome, 1952).
LP	The Lord's Prayer
NT	New Testament
SM	The Sermon on the Mount

Preface

This book was supposed to be a revision of my dissertation, a project that appeared simple enough. It ended up being much more than a simple revision. My dissertation, "The Lord's Prayer Reinterpreted: An Analysis of This Cultic *Didachē* by Clement of Alexandria (*Stromateis* VII) and Tertullian (*De oratione*)," looked at both North African thinkers from an essentially intellectual perspective. It probed their philosophical ideas, their relationships to Greek and Roman discourse on religion and prayer, and how these two Christian intellectuals used these ideas and discourse to construct their own presentations of their community's devotional practices. Not an unimportant endeavor in itself, I always felt that the argument lacked a certain *je ne sais quoi*. I was not sure at the time what that "needed thing" was, but the nag was there.

In 1998, thanks to a grant from the National Endowment for the Humanities, I attended a summer institute on the culture and society of Roman Egypt at Columbia University in New York City. It was my first exposure to the discipline of papyrology. Thanks to Roger Bagnall, I learned a lot about life outside of the philosophical and literary aristocracy and its supporters. As I began to read more and dig further, I wondered how such data would influence my own teaching of the New Testament and my study of early Christianity. Yet, I saw what I started at Columbia inject itself repeatedly into my courses. I also began to realize how my traditional historical training had not introduced me to such resources for New Testament study. Once I began to incorporate what is generally called material culture into my research, I saw just how stimulating such data could be for my writing.

At first I thought I would incorporate bits and pieces of my newfound interest in material culture into this revision of my dissertation. As the project progressed, I realized that it would occupy much more than my argument hither and thither. It would be an integral part of my approach to the subject of the Lord's Prayer. Therefore, I revised the chapters to include a vision of the Lord's Prayer through the eyes of an imagined Greco-Roman auditor, as well as extended discussions of Alexandria and Carthage in the

Roman period. These additions allowed me to discuss the theological perspectives of Clement and Tertullian within their particular social contexts. I adopted the term "ethnoreligious" from the work of Christopher Haas because I felt it also fit the type of perspective I wanted to highlight.[1] Christians in Alexandria, for example, formed a group with an arguable ethnic identity. They were Gentiles who inherited a struggling institution from a once-vibrant Jewish community in the metropolis. And yet, Christianity was not really a movement confined to a particular ethnic group. The only real ethnic import for the term *Gentile* is its designation as not Jewish. Christians in Alexandria were Greek, Egyptian, and Roman. What bound these individuals together was a common commitment to this entity, called the *ekklēsia*, which worshipped a deceased Galilean prophet as the Savior of the world.

What the reader finds in the following chapters is a complete reworking of my original project, a renovation of my previous work. And, as some renovations can be extensive, this book represents what amounts to a "gutting" of my original floor plan and a reconstruction of a new one. I thoroughly appreciate the support I received from my colleagues at the Candler School of Theology at Emory University. Luke Timothy Johnson, in particular, has been a great supporter of this project, reading portions of the manuscript and offering cogent suggestions. I thank Dean Russell E. Richey for allowing me a pretenure leave in the fall of 2002 to pursue my writing. Candler also provided me with a travel grant in the summer of 2000 to make my first visit to Alexandria. I also thank the Association of Theological Schools for providing me with a Lilly Theological Research Grant to visit Egypt in the fall of 2002 and for assistance in doing my research. A subsequent ATS Conference in the spring of 2003 gave me the conceptual framework I needed to bring this project to fruition. To be honest, I do not think I could have completed this book without that conference. Finally, I thank Henry Carrigan and T & T Clark International for bringing this book to press. I take full responsibility, however, for any shortcomings found in this book. Although I stand on the shoulders of giants, my ability to extend the larger academic discourse is limited by the problem of my own finitude.

This book begins with the concept of cultic *didachē* (critical reflection upon cultic practices) proposed by Hans Dieter Betz, and extends it in ways that demonstrate the importance of social location and cultural presuppositions in the interpretation of cultic texts and acts.[2] Beginning with an imagined Greco-Roman auditor of the Lord's Prayer, this book demonstrates how a Greco-Roman's understanding of the prayer would have been different from that of a hellenized Jew in Palestine. Drawing upon both material and intellectual resources, I look at the discussions early Greco-Roman Christians had regarding prayer generally and the Lord's Prayer in particular. This leads to a focus on the cultic *didachai* of Clement of Alexandria and Tertullian of Carthage, and offers a window into the turbulent and sometimes confusing world of second-century Christianity in Africa.

Chapter 1 looks at the Lord's Prayer as a form of cultic *didachē* in the early church. It examines in a cursory manner how the Lord's Prayer was used as a means of creating communal identity. It then illustrates how a Greco-Roman Christian of the second century CE might have interpreted the prayer.

Chapter 2 looks at the material and cultural resources that were available in the Greco-Roman world as a means of understanding religion and prayer. First it focuses on the understanding of religion and prayer in the Greek philosophical tradition, a resource used by many early Christians and modern scholars. Then it examines the understanding of religion and prayer represented in the Roman tradition, a resource often underexamined in scholarship on early Christian interpretation. This chapter serves as a basis for the subsequent discussions of Clement and Tertullian.

Chapter 3 reconstructs the environment of Roman Alexandria. It first reconstructs the material environment of Greco-Roman Egypt. Second, it looks at the material environment and cultural exchange that characterized the great Egyptian seaport. This reconstruction by necessity involves discussions of various social, political, and ethnoreligious issues such as population, literacy, educational institutions, economic exchange, social conflict, and governmental oversight. These are used as a basis for highlighting the distinctive material and cultural mix that flourished in the Egyptian city of Alexandria.

Chapter 4 places Clement within the context of the discussion conducted in chapter 3. Further, it looks at the particular Christian theological vision contained in Clement's major writings. Finally, the fruits of this analysis are used in an investigation of Clement's treatise on prayer, *Stromata* 7. In this section I highlight the cultural resources used by Clement in his interpretive analysis of prayer (drawing on the discussion in chapter 2) and how these resources allow Clement to develop his own distinctive cultic *didachē*. I argue that Clement draws primarily from the Greek philosophical tradition in his vision of religion, and that this tradition greatly influences his interpretation of the practice of prayer.

Chapter 5, similar in purpose and scope to chapter 3, surveys similar topics and issues. Chapter 6 places Tertullian of Carthage within the context of the discussion conducted in chapter 5. It also looks at the particular Christian theological vision presented in several of Tertullian's major writings. Finally, the fruits of this analysis are used in an investigation of Tertullian's treatise on prayer, *De oratione*. In this section, I highlight the cultural resources used by Tertullian in his interpretive analysis of prayer and how these resources allow him to develop his own distinctive cultic *didachē*. I argue that Tertullian draws primarily from the Roman religious tradition in his conception of religion, and that, as with Clement, it greatly influences his interpretation of the practice of prayer.

Chapter 7 is a synthesis of the discussion conducted in the prior chapters. It focuses on the theological visions employed by Clement and Tertullian in their analyses of prayer. These two strategies are then posited as trajectories used by later Christian interpreters in their interpretations of cultic *didachai*, especially as it concerns the practice of prayer. I believe that the strategies used by Clement and Tertullian became normative for Christian discussions of devotion and worship. It is my fervent hope that this discussion will provide scholars and students alike with greater insight into the interrelationship between intellectual and material-cultural matters.

As a final expression, I thank Imani Gridiron and Michael Anthony Brown for their patience and support. Because writing has occupied so much of my time, I know I have not been the partner and parent I should have been. From our trips to Egypt to our discussions of large chunks of this manuscript, Imani supported my writing through both elation and despair. More than anyone else, Imani understands how difficult writing this book has been. Although more accommodating, Michael has also suffered through my struggles with this book. I hope that as he grows up he can appreciate what this and other such projects mean to me. I delight in his curiosity repeatedly, and I look forward to having more time to spend with him in the near future.

Notes

1. Christopher Haas, *Alexandria in Late Antiquity: Topography and Social Conflict* (Ancient Society and History; Baltimore: Johns Hopkins University Press, 1997).

2. Hans Dieter Betz, *Essays on the Sermon on the Mount* (Philadelphia: Fortress, 1984); idem, *The Sermon on the Mount: A Commentary on the Sermon on the Mount, Including the Sermon on the Plain (Matthew 5:3–7:27 and Luke 6:20–49)* (ed. Adela Yarbro Collins; Hermeneia—A Critical and Historical Commentary on the Bible; Minneapolis: Fortress, 1995).

I

The Lord's Prayer through Greco-Roman Eyes and Ears

Behind those closed doors before God, we are all equals.
—Chrysostom (*Hom. Matt.* 19.4)

A Myopic Conversation

Prayer among Christians developed in relationship with Greco-Roman and Jewish ideas and models of cultic practice. Still, Christian prayer sought not merely to imitate the prayers of others but to establish for itself something distinctive in the pluralistic environment of the Roman Empire. One of the best ways to manifest that distinctiveness was through a divergent understanding of cultic practice. A distinctive view of cult in turn required a proper rationale. The basic rationale for Christian practice was its being taught or otherwise mandated by the Lord. That is, Christians used both Jewish and non-Jewish models and understandings of prayer, but they reinterpreted them in light of an authority they ascribed to the risen Christ (see, e.g., Heb 4:14–5:10; 7:1–9, 28). In fact, Christianity was unique in that, from the first, it found a way to implement a cultic practice that rendered animal sacrifice unnecessary (e.g., Heb 9:13–14). By contrast, Jewish cultic practice did not preclude animal sacrifice until after the destruction of the Jerusalem temple in 70 CE. Greco-Roman religion, which also relied heavily on animal sacrifice, eventually faded from existence.

That prayer was a part of the cultic practice of the early church is beyond question. The source for the earliest forms of Christian prayer was Judaism.[1] Members of the Jesus movement prayed at the times and according to the rituals established by the practice of Hellenistic Judaism (see Acts 2:46; 3:1, 11; 5:12–21). The available evidence also suggests that Christians

1

adopted the most common position of prayer: standing with arms out-stretched and palms upward (see, e.g., Matt 6:5; Mark 11:25; Luke 18:10–14; 1 Tim 2:8). As the church moved into the wider Hellenistic world, it began to adapt its forms and practices to that of a non-Jewish culture.[2]

In this chapter I outline one way prayer was conceived and used in early Christianity by focusing on the Matthean version of the Lord's Prayer (LP), specifically trying to determine how a Greco-Roman Christian might have heard it. Matthew's version of the prayer—with slight modifications—has been the most taught and thus best known to the majority of Christians. Also, any attempt to isolate and interpret an "original version" of the LP would be fruitless and inconsistent with the aims of this discussion. Focusing on how the prayer was appropriated is a more helpful starting point for this investigation, and the most popular form of appropriation is that found in the Sermon on the Mount (SM).

Other examinations of the LP have looked at its various recensions, possible original form, use in the liturgy of the church, and function as part of a larger cultic *didachē*.[3] Included in many of these discussions have been nearsighted explanations of the Jewish context from which the prayer arose.[4] All of these have been helpful in their own ways, although they are not the focus of this investigation. I have decided to take a farsighted focus on the appropriation of the LP by Greco-Roman Christians because they serve as a sure basis upon which to analyze its form and intent. Scholarship has yet to arrive at a consensus regarding the particulars of many aspects of the LP, but it can be sure regarding its appropriation by Gentile Christianity.

A Broader Vision

If our analysis of the original form and intent of the LP cannot go confidently beyond how it was appropriated by the early Christian community, then this is the most secure place to begin an examination of its functional intent. Early Christians used the LP in their cultic practices because they believed that the Lord had composed and authorized it. In all the written liturgies that have been passed down to us, the place where the LP figures most prominently is in the eucharistic celebration. It is found in the most ancient liturgies we possess, and we can safely assume that it was recited as a congregational prayer. Still, by its inclusion in the liturgy, something both peculiar and obvious occurred. The prayer's meaning was now determined by its placement. Certain phrases and meanings were highlighted by the liturgical context, while others were effectively veiled.[5] In the Eucharist, for example, the emphasis fell on the petitions for daily bread and forgiveness.

In the Eucharist ritual, the meaning of the petition for bread becomes contextualized as the *eucharistic bread* for which the orants are praying.[6] Within the *missa fidelium*, the importance of the petition for daily bread is highlighted in a context-specific sense.[7] Likewise, forgiveness is often highlighted in the Eucharist liturgy.[8] In this case, the petition is understood as a prerequisite for participating in the ritual act itself.[9] Saint Benedict's *Rule* illustrates another selective emphasis of the petition for forgiveness employed in Christian liturgy:

> Assuredly, the celebration of Lauds and Vespers must never pass by without the superior's reciting the entire Lord's Prayer at the end for all to hear, because thorns of contention are likely to spring up. Thus warned by the pledge they make to one another in the very words of this prayer: *Forgive us as we forgive* (Matt 6:12), they may cleanse themselves of this kind of vice. At other celebrations, only the final part of the Lord's Prayer is said aloud, that all may reply: *But deliver us from evil.* (*Monastic Rule* 13 [Fry])[10]

In this instance, the petition is used as a means of reconciling a community that may be experiencing alienation because of interpersonal offenses. In sum, as used in the liturgical and devotional life of the early church, the LP served as an epitome of the gospel. Like the Ten Commandments and the SM, the LP holds a privileged status as one of the touchstones for understanding and living the Christian life.[11]

An Imagined Greco-Roman Hearing of the Lord's Prayer in Matthew

The SM, one of the five major discourses in the Gospel outlining Matthew's theology, is directed to those who would be disciples of Jesus. Part of it comprises a cultic *didachē* on fasting, almsgiving, and prayer (Matt 6.1–18). Scholars generally agree that the LP, part of this *didachē*, was initially a separate entity prior to its inclusion in the SM. Thus, an analysis that seeks to understand the petitions of the prayer without necessary recourse to the other parts of the SM is valid.

The first component of the LP is the ἐπίκλησις (*invocatio*) in Matt 6:9b: Πάτερ ἡμῶν ὁ ἐν τοῖς οὐρανοῖς ("Our father who is in the heavens").[12] This form of address, invoking a god without using the god's name, is generally thought to be one peculiar to Jewish piety.[13] Greco-Romans, however, were often careful to guard the names of their tutelary deities, and orants often used *cognomina* as a means of addressing a deity.[14] This *invocatio* expresses the belief that God, who is in the heavens, is both the Creator and sustainer of the cosmos and, therefore, transcends it.[15] What is distinctive with respect to this *invocatio* is actually what is missing. There are none of the divine epithets found in other contemporary prayers.[16] Greco-Roman prayers often contained epithets.

It must be assumed that the composer felt that the term πάτερ would suffice as a comprehensive metaphor for the deity. The connotations of the term "father" would have been meaningful to persons within the world of the Roman Empire. A Greco-Roman who would have heard this term might have almost automatically thought of the *paterfamilias*; and the majority of the early Christians who appropriated this prayer were precisely of this persuasion. Its meaning would have resonated on at least four distinct levels: (1) the father as head of the household, (2) the patron-client relationship that was part of what was also deemed the household, (3) the emperor as father of the country, and (4) forms of divine address found in Greco-Roman literature.

In the Roman Empire, the *familia* was the locus for understanding the structure of society. In a strict sense, it is a legal term referring to those under the control of a *paterfamilias*, who was head of this social unit.[17] The household was a network of relationships of mutual obligation that were not exclusively based on blood association. Within this framework, the *patria potestas* of the *paterfamilias* was almost absolute (see, e.g., Dionysius of Halicarnassus 2.25–27). He had the authority to sit in judgment of subordinate members of the household, and the almost unlimited ability to discipline them in any way he saw fit. Furthermore, the familial assets were under the control of the *paterfamilias*. All the property of the *familia* was under his legal control, and he was the only member of the household legally capable of making contracts. As the theoretical framework goes, the *filiusfamilias* had little more independence than a slave. In fact, like a slave, the only property a son could own was as *peculium*. This very austere view of a *paterfamilias* might be the first one that would have come to the minds of those invoking the deity as father, but it would not have been the only one.

In the sources one also finds a more tender understanding of the *paterfamilias*. For example, Horace wrote lovingly of his father to whom he gave all the credit for his decency and morality. He spoke of the sacrifices his father made on his behalf, including serving as his *paedagogus*. He maintained that his father deserved unstinting gratitude and praise (*Sat.* 1.6.65–92). Conversely, Quintilian spoke of the grief he felt at the loss of his two sons (*Inst.*, Preface 6–11). Fond paternal feelings did exist in this legally constructed unit, although deference and obedience were also expected (*pietas*). Seneca the Younger highlights this mind-set when he says, "I obeyed my parents. . . . In only one respect was I unyielding: in refusing to let them do me more kindness than I did them" (*Ben.* 3.38.2 [Shelton]).[18] And, parents were expected to raise responsible children, balancing discipline with understanding (see Seneca, *Ira* 2.21.1–6; Pliny, *Ep.* 9.12).[19]

In sum, the *familia* was the central unit of the Roman social system. Its centrality in law and social consciousness made it a model to which thinkers would often appeal in philosophical and religious discourse. By invoking God through the metaphor πάτερ, the composer of the prayer created a situation in which its Greco-Roman auditors would have associated it with the most central element of the social system, the household. In addition, they would have naturally associated the figure of father with the *paterfamilias*, who held an incredible amount of power over the lives of his subordinates in the social hierarchy. Still, the relationship of the *paterfamilias* to the other members of the household was not one predicated merely on the basis of legal authority. As the data demonstrates, the father was also one who held deep-seated affection for his children, and could garner intense loyalty and affection in return. In this admittedly more modern sense of the term *familia*, the relationship between the *paterfamilias* and other family members is based on a legal (or marital) more than blood kinship model. Given the mortality rate in the ancient world, "father" was not understood in an essentially biological sense. A father could be one to whom another was tied by biology, but this was not the only way to conceive of the status designation. A father was one to whom another was bound and subordinated by law, and yet such a relationship was not devoid of affection and feelings of mutual obligation. As official sustainer of the familial unit, the father served an essential praiseworthy role in the structure of the ancient household. The *familia* relied on the *pater* for its continued existence. Thus, this was one of the ways a Gentile Christian might have understood this term of invocation.

The household, in the Roman mind, was not limited to what we would call the nuclear family, although at times it would be more properly termed *domus* rather than *familia*. The Roman understanding of *familia* embraced also slaves and dependents, including persons who had once been slaves in the household (freedpersons). Such a paternalistic relationship could also be initiated when one individual asked someone better educated and more powerful for advice and protection. The "superior" individual was called the *patronus*, and this individual assumed the role of a father of sorts to the newly acquired *cliens.* The client depended on the patron for assistance in a variety of matters, and at times this relationship could be extended over several generations. The relationship was not much different ideologically than that between parent and child: it emphasized deference and obsequiousness on the part of the client toward the patron. Likewise, it carried an expectation of concern and assistance by the patron to his client. According to Dionysius, there were certain rules that prevailed in this relationship, although data on the existence of such is scant (Dionysius of Halicarnassus 2.9–10).

By the time of the empire, the patronage system had garnered for itself a bad reputation (see Seneca, *Ep.* 19.4). For example, the poet Martial complained that dutiful clients often had rude patrons (*Epigrams* 5.22). Thus, this paternalistic institution, an extension of the father's prestige and power, failed to live up to its intent as a means of protection for the weak, at least in the imperial period. In light of this failure on the part of the patricians for the plebeians, the lower classes would have desired some sort of relationship that guaranteed their benevolent protection against the injustices and other incursions into their lives by the influential and powerful.

The father image appealed to in the LP's *invocatio* could have brought this situation of patronage to mind. Its Greco-Roman auditors might have conceived of the paternalism of the prayer as one of benevolence rather than self-aggrandizement. Calling upon the deity as father would have simultaneously provoked an image of this relationship while, at the same time, placing it within its ideal context. God as Father would care for his dependents in a manner consistent with the ideals initially expounded in the patronage system. As "Father" in a context of patronage, God can be called upon to guarantee peace, well-being, and justice in the lives of those who depend on him. As head of the household, a father was expected to use his power and prestige as a means of enhancing the existence of his dependents. Members of the *familia Dei* would also have expected such enhancement in their lives. Thus, one of the meanings of "Father" found in the *invocatio* that might have resonated with its Greco-Roman auditors is that of ideal patron.

The term *father* was not only given to the head of the household unit; it was also given to the emperor as father of the fatherland (*pater patriae*).[20] Initially, this title was given to Augustus, but it was also employed by other emperors with reservation.[21] Dio Cassius in his *History* addressed the use of the term *father* with respect to the emperor and gave some rationale for its use:

> And the title "Father" gives [the emperors] perhaps a certain added authority over us, such as fathers once used to have over their children. Originally, however, the title "Father" was used both as a title of honor and as a warning to the emperors to love their subjects as they would their own children, and to the subjects to respect the emperors as they would their own fathers. (*Hist.* 21.3 [Shelton])[22]

In spite of Dio's rationale for the title of father, the use of the term for the emperor is to be best understood within the context of the ideology of Roman politics. The Romans, traditionally understood the state, or *res publica*, as an extended family. It was an extension of the *familia* (or *domus*) in its largest sense. Members of the aristocracy were called *patres* (fathers), and it was understood that the members of the patrician class were to care for the lower classes in a paternal manner. Similar to the role performed by the *paterfamilias*, the members of the aristocracy were expected to devote time, energy, and money to the welfare of their inferiors, including providing public service without pay (*munera*). In response, the aristocracy expected gratitude, submission, and veneration from the masses. Once the imperial period began, this notion of fatherly concern was transferred to the emperor. Again, the metaphor of the household best describes the ideal relationship between the rulers and the ruled in the Roman political establishment.

The emperors acquired enormous powers and, in effect, resembled the *paterfamilias* in the execution of their duties. As Dio Cassius makes clear, "[The emperors] have control over all things, sacred and profane" (*Hist.* 19.1 [Shelton]).[23] Such an accumulation of power must have appeared on an imperial scale to be similar to the powers held by the *paterfamilias* on a household scale. In fact, even given the apparent criticisms advanced by Dio, he does conclude that this form of government made the Roman Empire better (see *Hist.* 21.6). The Romans saw imperial rule as an advance over the insecurity and instability of the republican period. Such an understanding is found in the writing of Strabo: "It is difficult to control and administer an empire as large as Rome's other than by entrusting it to one man, as to a father. . . . [In fact, the Romans] have never enjoyed such an abundance of peace and prosperity as that which Augustus Caesar provided from the time when he first assumed absolute power, and which his son and successor, Tiberius, is now providing" (*Geogr.* 6.4.2 [Shelton]).[24] In short, the fatherhood of the emperor and the fatherhood of God would have been a natural association to make with respect to the invocation of the Deity in prayer. Deities operate on a cosmic scale, and in the Roman world the only other entity seen to operate on such a scale was the emperor. The emperor, like the *paterfamilias* and the *patronus*, was charged with all the affairs of his household, which in this case was the empire. Like a deity, the emperor was expected to bring peace, justice, and equity to all parts of the empire. In fact, the ideal emperor was to teach his subjects the proper way to live by setting an example (see Velleius Paterculus, *Hist.* 2.126.2–5). It would be natural, then, for a Greco-Roman to associate the fatherhood of God with that of the emperor. Like the head of state, the deity was expected to exemplify the ideals of such a fatherhood, which makes the term "father" appropriate when applied to the deity within the context of imperial control.

The literature of the Greco-Roman world also provided numerous examples of a deity addressed as father. Three prominent literary venues affirm the usage of the term with reference to a deity: (1) plays and other general works, (2) philosophical works, and (3) overtly religious texts. Designating a deity as father appears to be a common feature of many Greco-Roman literary works. In Homer, both humans and immortals often call Zeus father.[25] Polyphemos calls the god Poseidon father (e.g., *Od.* 9.529). One finds the same invocation for Poseidon in Euripides (*Hipp.* 887). Aristophanes has Zeus addressed as father (as in *Nub.* 569), while Aeschylus has both Hermes and Zeus invoked as such (*Cho.* 143, 783; *Eum.* 19, 625). In Latin literature, the gods Jupiter and Mars are invoked as fathers (as in *Agr.* 141, for Mars). One interesting Latin example is found in the oath of Aeneas. It is interesting precisely because, as in the LP, the supreme deity (Jupiter) and also Mars are invoked as fathers:

> Witness my prayer now, O Sun, together with this Earth, for whom I have been able to endure such great toils, also you, *all-powerful father*, and you, his Saturnian wife (kinder now, goddess, I pray), and you renowned Mars, *father*, who direct all wars under your power. I invoke both Springs and Rivers, and whatever divine powers there are in the lofty sky and whatever powers dwell in the blue sea. If by chance the victory goes to Italian Turnus, it is agreed that the conquered will depart to the city of Evander, Iulus will withdraw from the fields and no rebellious followers of

Aeneas will afterwards take up arms again or provoke these kingdoms with weapons. But if Victory grants the battle to us (as I
think more likely; may the gods confirm this with their power), I
will not order the Italians to obey the Trojans nor do I seek kingdoms for myself: let both nations unconquered enter into lasting
treaty with equality. I will bring the sacred rituals and deities; let
my father-in-law Latinus hold the military command and his law-
ful power. The Trojans will build a city for me and Lavinia will
give it her name. (*Aen.* 12.176–194 [Hickson-Hahn]; emphasis
added)[26]

In short, there are many examples from ancient literary works where a
deity is called father. In most of these cases, the reference refers to a perceived or acknowledged relationship with the person speaking, but it is
evoked nonetheless.

The philosophical literature also provides some examples of a deity
being called father. In his famous *Hymn to Zeus*, Cleanthes refers to him as
father (line 33). Also, Diogenes Laertius in his discussion of Stoicism refers
to god as father: "He is the creator of the whole and, as it were, the father
of all, both generally and, in particular, that part of him which pervades all
things, which is called by many descriptions according to his powers"
(7.147 [Long & Sedley]).[27] Although of a somewhat different sort than the
other literary works, the philosophical writings posit a relationship
between the deity and the created entity such that the designation of the
deity as father appears appropriate.

In overtly religious texts, designating a deity as father appears quite
common.[28] In such writings as the *Corpus hermeticum* and NHC, Hermes
(a hellenized version of the Egyptian god Toth) is invoked as father (e.g.,
Corp. herm. 13.17–20 and *Pr. Thanks.* VI,7). In addition, there is the interesting designation of Kronos as father in Orphic Hymn 13. According to
Greek religion, Zeus usurped the place of Kronos. This view is clearly supported in other Orphic writings, but this prayer portrays Kronos as the
creator and ruler of the universe:

Ethereal father of blessed gods and men,
subtle of mind, pure, mighty and powerful Titan:
You who supervise the growth and decline of all things,
unbreakable is your control of the boundless cosmos!
O Kronos, father of all beings and creator of time,
      O Kronos of many voices,

the child of earth and starry sky,
in whom are birth and growth and decline, [you are] the
     husband of Rhea, majestic forethought,
you live in every part of the cosmos [as] the ruler of
     creation,
clever and most brave. Hear my suppliant voice,
and bring a good life to a blameless end. (Alderink)[29]

Add to these examples those from countless papyri and other literary sources, and the practice of designating a god as father in religious texts is seen as quite conventional. As in the case of the literary texts, the overt purpose may be to posit a clear relationship between the orant and the deity, but the ideas evoked in the philosophical texts cannot be entirely excluded. In sum, Greco-Roman literature provided another conceptual basis for the Gentile-Christian understanding of God as father in the LP. Writers, philosophers, and liturgists, as well as other social phenomena described above, provided ample illustrations for the Greco-Roman auditor in her interpretation of the *invocatio*.

As father is a concise descriptive metaphor for god, the human component of the relationship is equally as terse. It is simply designated by the possessive pronoun "our." The *invocatio* places God and humans in a clear *relationship*. Such a relationship is indicative of a fundamental understanding of the sociality of existence. Persons in antiquity understood themselves to be in a socially integrated cosmos. Often these notions of social integration were expressed in household metaphors, which would include the use of household terminology. As indicated above, such an understanding is clearly part of the LP. In this case, the model employed in the prayer serves to highlight a hierarchy that the ancients would have clearly understood.

As a component of creation, humanity stands in a subordinate relation to God and is, it was believed, dependent upon God's continued guidance. As the subordinate member of the metaphorical household, humanity finds itself in the position of having a special relationship to God and the rest of creation. In this relationship the value of the human creature is characterized by this creature's ability to know and know that she knows (*homo sapiens sapiens*). In other words, the human being is distinct from all other created life in that the human can know God, approach God, and address God as God.[30]

Although the human is envisioned by the prayer as being the pinnacle of God's creative endeavor, any possible elitism or egoism in this *invocatio* is transcended by the use of the plural possessive pronoun "our." That is, one must envision oneself not in a solitary relationship to God but corporately.[31] Such an understanding refutes one particular interpretation of the *invocatio*, that the LP reflects Jesus' relationship to God.[32] This understanding must be rejected because the *invocatio* does not highlight the distinctiveness of one human being and his relation to God, but the distinctiveness of a people's relation to God.[33] Such an expansive understanding, however, has interpretive problems.

The LP as the early, and later, church has used it has become a vehicle for distinguishing between insiders and outsiders. Christian interpreters have attempted to redefine "our" to mean "Christian." Though such an interpretive move is understandable, it is theologically problematic for at least a couple reasons. First, it has been a fundamental tenet of Jewish, and later Christian, belief that all humanity derives from God and thus can claim God as Father/Creator (e.g. Deut 32:6; Mal 2:10; Acts 17:28–29; 1 Cor 8:6; Eph 4:6). To interpret the invocation of the LP as an exclusive reference to Christians would be a denial of this tenet and would undermine the doctrine of monotheism.[34] It would also undermine the justness of God because God could be understood to prefer and value some above others (cf. Rom 2:11). Furthermore, the context of the prayer in Matthew (the SM) is not clear as to whether this is a prayer for disciples or everyone.[35] The recensions found in Luke and the *Didache* clearly understand the LP to be for disciples. Such usage notwithstanding, an exclusivist appropriation cannot be considered decisive for interpretation. The prayer itself offers at least two options for meaning. On the one hand, the pronoun could refer to members of a particular group exclusively. This would mean that only certain individuals have sufficient standing before God such that their prayers are addressed to the Father. It would also imply that God favors some over others. On the other hand, the pronoun could be understood universally, which would make the invocation both petitionary and intercessory. When Christians pray the LP, they would then be praying on behalf of themselves and all other human beings. Such an interpretation would indicate that God has this posited relationship with all humanity whether particular human beings acknowledge the relationship or not. This interpretation would keep the theological tenet (God's impartiality) described above intact and further augment the validity of the doctrine of monotheism. In short, the pronoun would acknowledge relationship with God but not indicate exclusive relationship with God. It would also indicate that persons should not pray for "things" for themselves that they would not request for others. "Our" should be understood in the more universal sense.

Its largely Gentile auditors and orantes can also integrate such a universal understanding into the present discussion involving the appropriation of the prayer. As the recipient of the creative activity of God, creation and especially humanity hold a distinctive place in the cosmic household. As Creator of all that exists, God continues to display his benevolence through the preservation of the cosmos. Such an idea might resonate with the Greco-Roman auditor as being similar to the peace established by the emperors, the proper running of the household by the *paterfamilias*, and analogous to the Stoic concept of the deity (see, e.g., Diogenes Laertius 7.147, quoted above). In other words, the pronoun "our" in the LP should be understood in its more universal sense as referring to human beings generally. When a Christian in a Greco-Roman context heard and voiced the words of the prayer, she could have naturally assumed that "our" was to be taken as a corporate affirmation. The LP was generally but not necessarily confined to a particular group of individuals known as the church although, admittedly, this was how many later Christians appropriated it.

The second part of this address to God is properly deemed the *pars epica*, the rationale for approaching the deity.[36] In this case, the deity is identified as the one ἐν τοῖς οὐρανοῖς ("in the heavens").[37] Such a designation means that the god being addressed is the one that controls all. It is an implicit recognition of the philosophical appropriateness of monotheism. Greco-Romans, particularly those who were educated, did not deny the validity of monotheism.[38] A good example can be found in Plutarch's *The E at Delphi*:

> But God is (if there be need to say so), and He exists for no fixed time, but for the everlasting ages which are immovable, timeless, and undeviating, in which there is no earlier nor later, no future nor past, no older nor younger; but He, being One, has with only one "Now" completely filled "For ever"; and only when Being is after His pattern is it in reality Being, not having been nor about to be, nor has it had a beginning nor is it destined to come to an end. Under these conditions, therefore, we ought, as we pay Him reverence, to greet Him and to address Him with the words, "Thou art"; or even, I vow, as did some of the men of old, "Thou art One." (393A–B [Babbitt])[39]

In fact, in light of the contemporary propaganda involving the meaningfulness and importance of monarchical rule in the Roman Empire, the idea of the rule of one supreme god would be eminently logical. Just as there is one supreme ruler on earth, there must be only one supreme ruler in the heavens.

The idea of οὐρανός as the abode of the deity is well attested in Greco-Roman literature.[40] Helmut Traub says that the phrase ἐν τοῖς οὐρανοῖς is meant to emphasize God's "complete lack of any earthly or spatial restriction."[41] In the end, however, this designation serves to locate the deity (in the heavens). Moreover, given the hierarchical structure espoused by most people in antiquity, this locative indication serves to highlight God's status and ability to assist the person praying the prayer. In short, this designation gives the rationale for appealing to this particular deity as opposed to others: only the deity located "in the heavens" is willing and able to assist the orant in his quest for a hearing.

The first petition requests that God's name be hallowed: ἁγιασθήτω τὸ ὄνομά σου (6:9c). One could interpret this petition as an instance of the Greek aorist of prayer, which means the subject of the activity would not be God but the orant.[42] In such a case, the petition would recognize that human beings have a responsibility to sanctify God's name on earth. At the same time, it could recognize that the profanation of God's name has reached a point beyond which mere human capacity to correct it is possible. If true sanctification of God's name is to exist, God must intervene. Following the household metaphor discussed earlier, it was the responsibility of the *paterfamilias* to maintain the *sacra* of the household, the *sacra familiae*.[43] Unfortunately, little evidence exists concerning household religious practices (see, e.g., Cato, *Agr.* 141). Still, a couple examples illustrating the importance of family religion can be gleaned from house-tombs and one Roman's ideal vision of religion. For example, a tomb from the second century CE was inscribed as follows:

> To the spirits of the departed. Quintus Appius Saturninus, son of Quintus, built this for himself and for Annia Donata, his well-deserving wife, and for their children and ex-slaves, male and female, and for their descendants. This tomb shall not follow the heir, and may the right of sale not be allowed to those to whom I have left it, or to Donata. (Beard et al.)[44]

Notice that the inscription designates the *paterfamilias* as the party responsible for the religious practices of the family, even with respect to death. The house-tomb was an important part of the religious activity associated with death in Roman culture. Likewise, Cicero, in describing the religious constitution of his ideal state, says, "[Let] their private worship be for those gods whose worship they have duly received from their fathers. . . . Let them preserve the rituals of their families and of their fathers. . . . Let the religious rites of families be maintained in perpetuity. . . . Let them treat their dead kinsfolk as divine" (*Leg.* 2.19–22 [Beard]).[45] Here Cicero advocates the maintenance of religious practices rooted in the household, specifically highlighting the importance of the father. The familial model was at the core of a Roman understanding of religion. In the case of this petition, the activity of God and the rest of the household would be cooperative. The members of the household would expect the *pater* to serve as the exemplar of one's proper relationship with the divine (e.g., Xenophon points out that it is the father's duty to train a young man's soul; *Mem.* 1.2.20). The same would be true of the emperor as *pater patriae*. With the accession of Augustus to the throne, he and his family became the model of proper religious devotion and practice. As father of the nation, it was understood that part of the emperor's position was to demonstrate to his subjects proper religious devotion. If the *pater* is God, then the interaction of the deity is needed to insure proper *pietas* in the *familia*. In sum, human beings are responsible for recognizing the presence of impiety in the cosmic household, and they must endeavor to act in a manner consistent with *pietas*. In the end, however, only the exemplary intervention of God can fully establish proper practice within the cosmos.

The next petition follows from the first. God's authority is discussed metaphorically as being exercised in his kingdom or rule: ἐλθέτω ἡ βασιλεία σου (6:10).[46] The term βασιλεία is somewhat difficult to translate or properly interpret because of the close connection between the dignity of the ruler and the territory ruled in the ancient mind.[47] Yet, it is precisely this relationship that is important. Zeus, as ruler of the cosmos, was often called king (e.g., Hesiod, *Theog.* 886). Likewise, Hermes was invoked as king by Electra (Aeschylus, *Cho.* 125). They are invoked as kings because they possess the dignity to control certain territories. In other words, character is the basis for their authority, and authority gives them the right to βασιλεία.[48]

The ideology of monarchical rule was promoted and widespread in the first century CE, although it was popular much earlier. The benefits of one-person rule were well-known, *pax* (peace) being the most important of them all. Such stability could only be found within the context of a kingdom, at least in the Greco-Roman mind. This petition for the kingdom implicitly acknowledges that the Deity's rule is not universally evident. As such, the request for the kingdom may have reminded the Greco-Roman auditor of the tumultuous and impious time of the late republic.

The coming of the kingdom then would be analogous to the golden age ushered in by Augustus, although this new golden age would be on a cosmic scale. One could call the kingdom an eschatological symbol. It would represent the time of explicit acknowledgement of God's authority and right to govern the cosmos, which would include the confession that all power flows from and is established by God (see, e.g., Rom 13:1-7; Phil 2:9-11). In its most general sense, this petition stands for God's complete victory over evil.[49] It is the assurance that God will not indefinitely tolerate injustice.[50] Some Greco-Romans, like some Jews, believed that the gods acted on behalf of justice (see, e.g., Cleanthes, *Hymn to Zeus*; Cicero, *Nat. d.* 2.75-76).[51] In fact, as the state could be envisioned along the lines of the household, including its system of patronage, the entire cosmos could be understood in the same manner. However, justice could only be found in areas where the patron's will prevailed. Thus, this petition calls for the expansion of God's realm.

The notion of peace, embedded in the idea of kingdom, did not necessarily preclude an appeal to force (see, e.g., Rom 16:20). The *pax Romana* itself was a peace established and kept in place by force. Such a vision of the kingdom requires the imposition of the divine will and the establishment of *pietas*. As described in the LP, God's kingdom is not "a new heaven and a new earth" (Rev 21:1). It envisions the coming of the kingdom as an annexation of territory and the establishment of just relationships. The exact parameters of such an annexation are not immediately clear in the text. Yet, they can be deduced fairly easily. Since a king reigns in places where his dignity is honored, it would appear that the first place the kingdom must be established is in the thoughts, words, and deeds of human beings. The ruled must acknowledge the dignity and worthiness of the ruler. This is why Augustus says, "I excelled all in authority, although I possessed no more official power than others who were my colleagues in each office" (*Res gest. divi Aug.* 34 [Mellor]).[52] As some emperors discovered, power without dignity could lead to the quick end of one's reign. Likewise, just relationships should be the byproduct of benevolent rule. This is highlighted well in the words of Velleius Paterculus:

> Trust has returned to the Forum; dissension has been removed from the Forum, campaigning from the Campus Martius, discord from the Senate house. Justice, equity, and diligence, long buried and forgotten, have been restored to the state. Magistrates once more have authority; the Senate, honor; the courts, dignity. Riots in the theater have been suppressed. Everyone has either been

inspired with desire, or forced by necessity, to behave honestly. Right is honored, wrong is punished. The humble man respects the man of power, but does not fear him. The man of power has precedence over the humble man, but does not despise him. When were grain prices more reasonable? When was peace more auspicious? The peace of Augustus has spread into the regions of the rising sun and of the setting sun, to the boundaries of the southernmost and northernmost lands. The peace of Augustus protects every corner of the world from fear of banditry. . . . The provinces have been liberated from the outrageous misconduct of magistrates. Honor lies waiting for those who deserve it; and the wicked do not escape punishment. Fairness has replaced influence and favoritism; real merit has replaced clever campaigning. And the best emperor teaches his citizens to do right by himself doing right. Although he is very great in his authority, he is even greater by his example. (*Historiae Romanae* 2.126.2–5 [Shelton])[53]

In short, the coming of the kingdom of God involves not only recognition of God's dignity and worthiness but also the establishment of a just and humane social order. The petition indicates that such an annexation requires the activity of God. Thus, the second petition strengthens, as it were, one aspect of the first, the need for God's involvement in the establishment of just relationships.

The third petition, as well as expanding upon the second, emphasizes both petitions even more. Human beings must participate in the process: γενηθήτω τὸ θέλημά σου, ὡς ἐν οὐρανῷ καὶ ἐπὶ γῆς (6:10b–c). The petition clearly recognizes that it is not the earth itself that is incongruent with the rest of the cosmos (heaven), but it is what is upon the earth, human beings, who oppose God's will. "Human self-will is pitted against God's will, and this rebellion is identical with sinfulness."[54] As *pietas* indicates proper relations in the household and the state, it is likewise characteristic of acknowledging one's proper place in the cosmos.[55] Epictetus sums up such an attitude well:

Remember that you are an actor in a drama of such sort as the Author chooses—if short, then in a short one; if long, then in a long one. If it be his pleasure that you should enact a poor man, or a cripple, or a ruler, or a private citizen, see that you act it well. For this is your business—to act well the given part, but to choose it belongs to another. (*Ench.* 17 [Higginson])[56]

Pietas is a matter of deference and obedience to the divine will according to one's station in the cosmos (see also Epictetus, *Ench.* 31). In this petition there may be a connection—made by some scholars—between the LP and the Gethsemane episode in Matt 26:36–56.[57] Early Christians often made a connection between Jesus' obedience in Gethsemane and the petition for compliance with God's will. In the cosmic household the will of the *pater-familias* must be obeyed if the household is to function properly (see, e.g., Seneca, *De providentia* 1.2, 6).[58] As Menelaus says, "The gods have always desired that their orders be listened to" (Homer, *Od.* 4.353 [Lattimore]).[59] All of nature is subject to the divine πρόνοια (providence), as Plutarch points out ([*Lib. ed.*] 3d). It is human beings who disrupt the functioning of the household. Thus, a Greco-Roman Christian might have interpreted this petition in light of common cultural notions. In this petition the orant confesses the need to be subject to divine providence,[60] and, by analogy, makes this subjection to providence an *imitatio Christi*.[61]

The first three petitions of the LP envision the Deity within the context of a socially integrated universe. This social conception means that both the Deity and creation are in a relationship that requires a giving or enhancement on both sides of the social context. Whether such an interaction is viewed as propitiation or the giving of honor, the implicit assumption is that the Deity needs or requires something for continued beneficence and the proper functioning of the cosmos. Some scholars have identified such an understanding in the LP.[62] Although such a view appears contrary to a philosophical Greek understanding of deity, it is perfectly intelligible within the context of the Roman idea of *pietas*.[63] That is, the proper composition of the cosmos requires proper relations among its constituents. The Deity, who occupies the preeminent position in this social organization, must be properly honored as a *pater* or head of this cosmic household. And although God's giving may far exceed what God receives in the relationship, *pietas* requires that something be given God as an acknowledgement of the superior's gift. In short, although the needs of God may be qualitatively different from those of human beings, they are still valid needs.

The fourth petition shifts the focus away from the needs of God (for God's name to be hallowed, God's kingdom to come, and God's will to be done) to the needs of human beings. Nevertheless, the request for bread has long puzzled scholars. What precisely does the petition τὸν ἄρτον ἡμῶν τὸν ἐπιούσιον δός ἡμῖν σήμερον (6:11) mean? The first place to look is context. Hans Dieter Betz maintains that this petition reflects an older agrarian theology.[64] What "older" is supposed to mean in this context is not clear. Still, the economy of the Roman Empire was reliant on agriculture as its base.[65] Furthermore, the economy of the Roman Empire was such that famine was rare, but malnutrition was widespread.[66] In essence, a Greco-Roman would have understood the fundamental importance of food production and distribution to the preservation of human life.

According to Peter Garnsey, bread was rarely eaten in antiquity, especially in rural areas.[67] Jo-Ann Shelton supports such a statement:

> The poorest Romans ate little other than wheat, either crushed and boiled with water to make porridge or *puls*, or ground into flour and baked as bread—if they were lucky enough to have an oven available. Boiling was probably more common than baking because few poor people would have their own oven. Boiled wheat or bread was not a side dish, as it is today; for many Romans, it was frequently their only dish.[68]

Martial provides an excellent example of a relatively modest meal in which such *puls* is served (*Epigrams* 5.78). Wheat was a relatively expensive commodity (see, e.g., the reference to grain in the statement of Velleius Paterculus quoted above). If information from the fourth century is of any assistance, then one *modius* of wheat was equivalent to four days' wages for a farm laborer (see *CIL* 3.805–6, 808–9). Of course, bread is a finished product, but it still would have been relatively expensive for the average person. Still, such a determination would have to be qualified with respect to urban environments, where the government periodically regulated the price of grain and sometimes distributed it without cost to citizens (e.g., the imperial grain dole). This would mean that access to grain—and subsequently bread—would be more frequent for the city dweller. Thus, this petition for bread may reflect the predominantly urban character of early Christianity.

The key to unlocking the meaning of the petition may lie in understanding the apposite adjective ἐπιούσιος (*epiousios*).[69] Unfortunately, no one is exactly sure what *epiousios* means, and it is doubtful that full scholarly consensus on the term will ever be achieved. Notwithstanding the difficulties, the petition appears to request that God create conditions in which the maintenance of humanity is possible. Some early exegetes understood the idea of bread to be primarily spiritual and not material. The idea of spiritual bread was definitely behind the church's understanding of the petition in the eucharistic liturgy.[70] Yet, the petition gives no clear indication that it is meant to be taken metaphorically, although one must admit that bread in antiquity almost always had symbolic valence. The ancients viewed bread as symbolic of the sedentary production of agriculture, which makes civilization possible.[71] Betz argues that this petition demonstrates that food was still a basic concern in the first century, and that basic survival was uppermost in the minds of individuals.[72] Although this is most certainly true, the poor would be more susceptible to the problems of food distribution than the wealthy; thus, the request for bread could be more reflective of their concerns (see, e.g., Tacitus, *Ann.* 6.13; 12.43).[73] In actuality, people of all statuses recognized the importance of divine intervention in averting famine (e.g., 12.43). Furthermore, the petition for bread reflects a theology that is fundamentally social in orientation. That is, bread is symbolic of divine-human cooperative productivity.[74] For the individual of lower status, it can be interpreted as a request to the Deity to insure that human beings cooperate in a manner that brings about the distribution of food to all.[75] To the person of higher status, this petition could be understood as a form of intercession for those most vulnerable to the vicissitudes of agricultural production as well as an implicit acknowledgement of his need to practice generosity. This is why the bread is identified as "our" bread—the sociality of production and distribution being embedded in the pronoun.[76] At any rate, the Deity is asked in this petition to oversee the social order in a way that brings about the feeding of all. It is an appeal to the Deity to be benevolent to all.

The interesting problem raised by this understanding of the petition is its relation to the idea of divine benevolence. Why would God stop the physical sustenance of believers? If God is indiscriminately good by nature, is it not absurd to ask the Deity to provide something, such as food, which is of unquestionable importance and benefit to humans? If such is the case, God cannot be said to be benevolent by nature. Add in the notion of divine omniscience, and this petition creates a substantial philosophical problem for the potential orant. This issue may lie behind the church's attempt to reinterpret the petition to mean something spiritual.

It must be admitted that modern interpreters are at a disadvantage in their efforts to understand how the ordinary person would have understood this petition. The writings of the early Christians that we do possess are biased because they reflect the interests of better-educated and higher-status individuals.[77] Being somewhat insulated from the vagaries of the production and distribution of food, it is understandable that high-status Christians would be somewhat disinclined to further the idea that a thoroughly benevolent God should be asked for something as necessary to survival as food. They advanced various interpretations of this petition that moved the request away from the obvious to the spiritual.[78] The idea of the cessation of God's physical care for humanity runs contrary to the understanding of God adopted by the early church. This basically Platonic metaphysical view perceived God to be perfect in all respects, which included a perfect will. God was not conceived as willing anything other than the good (see, e.g., Plato, *Resp.* 380c). Divine πρόνοια worked in history to bring this about (see Seneca, *Ben.* 4.5.1ff.; 2.29ff.; *De providentia* 1.1.5). As a strategy for preserving the doctrine of divine benevolence, such an interpretive move by early Christian commentators is eminently intelligible. This is especially true given the discussion of ascetic practices surrounding food in ancient philosophical discourse.[79] Still, such a rationale is fundamentally problematic. Christians of higher status reinterpreted the petition for bread in a manner that made it less material and more symbolic. In one sense, they expanded this petition from being solely about food. In another sense, their interpretations of the petition for bread were problematic in that they implicitly communicated to some that God was not fundamentally concerned with material matters. Moreover, it could turn the daily struggle for existence into something seemingly base and unworthy of intellectual consideration. Such an interpretation could also exclude material concerns from the discourse on justice and equity.[80]

The strategies of Christian interpreters of the petition for bread notwithstanding, this request can be understood within the context of the household. The distribution of food to various members of the *familia* was the province of the *paterfamilias*. It was his job to determine the just distribution of goods, which sometimes meant that persons of lesser status in the household, particularly women, children, and slaves, were not given sufficient or equal portions compared to persons of higher status in the household.[81] Such an injustice in the *oikonomia* would have been best understood by those whom it affected. This petition then becomes an appeal to the Deity for justice, to insure the equitable distribution of material goods necessary for survival in the household. As an expansion of this understanding, yet also within the household model, this petition for bread becomes an appeal to the individual occupying the highest status in the cosmic *oikonomia* to insure the benevolent distribution of food to those occupying the lowest strata in society. The idea is similar to the imperial grain dole in the city of Rome. As David Potter says of sacrifice, "Public sacrifice in celebration of these cults was intended to bind the community together; the distribution of food and other gifts on the occasion of these celebrations were meant to reflect the order of the state."[82] To the individual of higher status, this petition contained an implicit ethical admonition to practice generosity in the distribution of resources.[83] In fact, this admonition calls to mind Cicero's dictum concerning generosity: *Nihil est enim liberale, quo non idem iustum* (*Off.* 1.14.43). In short, the just distribution of food is a matter of *pietas*. Such a social understanding of the petition for bread would have been natural for a Greco-Roman living within the worldview of the Roman Empire in the first century CE.

As discussed earlier, the petition for forgiveness, like the petition for bread, has played an important liturgical role in the life of the church. What is distinctive about the fifth petition in its Matthean version, although it also appears in the recension found in the *Didache*, is its designation of sins as debts or *obligations*: καὶ ἄφες ἡμῖν τὰ ὀφειλήματα ἡμῶν, ὡς καὶ ἡμεῖς ἀφήκαμεν τοῖς ὀφειλέταις ἡμῶν (6:12).[84] This language comes from the social realms of law and commerce.[85] To be sure, Greco-Romans were well acquainted with the problem of debt. The comedic writer, Plautus, commented on how the situation could appear to a higher-status Roman: "You owe them money and they want it. 'Now,' you think, 'I've paid them all.' But into your atrium come more dyers (these use saffron color!) and any other wretched gallow-bird who wants some money" (*Aul.* 522 [Shelton]).[86] As this passage indicates, debt was not confined to persons of lower status. The wealthy, as well as paying for routine expenses and trying to increase their prestige, would often borrow to finance "public works" projects.[87] These would be the same persons who held most positions of compulsory service, including the unenviable position of tax collectors, in the provinces of the empire.[88] Moreover, the government would often assign unproductive public land to the wealthy as a means of generating some revenue in rents (e.g., *P.Oxy.* VI 899, where a woman complains that she has been brought to poverty through the assignment of public land to her).[89] Generally, because of the class system imposed by the empire, the wealthy were able to borrow at reasonable rates and with rather generous provisions regarding repayment. This is because they tended to borrow from one another (e.g., Cicero, *Rab. Post.* 2.4–3.5; Pliny, *Ep.* 3.19). By contrast, the poor were often subjected to borrowing from the wealthy at much higher rates of interest. This was the case regardless of whether repayment was made in cash or commodities. They borrowed from either individuals or money-lending companies (e.g., Plutarch, *Cat. Maj.* 21.1, 3, 5–7),[90] although at times they used the (everpresent) pawnbrokers (see, e.g., *P.Oxy.* I 114 [*BL* I 316; II.2 93; IX 176]).[91]

Greco-Romans found themselves indebted for various reasons. The range of economic activities in antiquity was quite extensive, even though the economy was firmly agricultural in orientation. We have contracts for sales (e.g., *M.Chr.* 260), loans (e.g., *P.Mich.* III 182), deposits (something similar to a loan; e.g., *P.Ryl.* IV 662), and labor (e.g., *Pap.Lugd.Bat.* XIX 3). In addition, we have lease contracts as well as evidence of rent collection (e.g., *P.Charite* 8; *P.Oxy* XXXIII 2680). Sending a person a demand for payment was not uncommon (e.g., *P.Oxy* XLVIII 3403). Still, the type of debt the ancients complained about most vociferously were taxes, although compared to modern economies, the system of taxation in antiquity was rigid but low.[92] It was common for persons charged with the responsibility of tax collection to borrow the money in advance, then use his collections to pay back the amount borrowed.[93] In short, indebtedness was a common occurrence in antiquity.

Sometimes lenders were forced to foreclose on loans, although this was often something they were loathe to do (see, e.g., *Pap.Lugd.Bat.* XIX 6 [*BL* VIII 202]). More often, the indebted person would work off the debt to the lender (see Columella, *Rust.* 1.17.2, 3). Yet, the problem of indebtedness (the possible legal ramifications for not repaying a debt) more severely effected women and the young than it did men. They were considered less productive members of the social order, and so their imprisonment was not considered as vital to a family's economy as that of a man. Government officials regarded men, if left free, as more capable of repaying a debt than women. For example, Kleopatra writes to "family" members saying, "Do all you can to measure out to Moros the builder five artabas of barley, since I am being pressed by the *dekaprōtos* [tax collector]; for I am about to be imprisoned" (*P.Oxy.* XXXVI 2789 [Rowlandson]).[94] The same was true of children (see e.g., *P.Lond.* VI 1915). We even have one agreement selling a child into service in lieu of paying interest on a loan (*SB* IV 7358).[95] At times, the problem of indebtedness could reach the boiling point. Cicero encountered such a problem when he assumed governorship of Cilicia: "I have heard nothing except complaints: people cannot pay the mandatory poll tax; communities have become bankrupt. I have listened to groans and laments from these communities. I have heard about monstrous deeds, deeds of some savage beast, not of a man [i.e., Appius Claudius Pulcher, who was governor before Cicero]" (*Att.* 5.16.2 [Shelton]).[96]

Whenever indebtedness reached a crisis point (either with respect to borrowers or lenders), people appealed to governmental and business officials for relief.[97] One notable example from antiquity concerns a woman, Flavia Christodote, who petitions an Alexandrian banker to follow through on a refinance agreement and pay her the money owed to her by her brother. At one point she comments on her credit situation:

The fact that I am wrestling with debts and am hourly harassed by my creditors is known to all; but in addition, the real property left behind for me in the (province) of Arcadians, from which I derive my essential nourishment, is under the circumstances about to be handed over to my creditors, so that the consequent damage focuses on Your Brilliancy which till now has not furnished me with what is owed to me by It, so that I might be able to free myself from my creditors (*PSI* I 76 [Rowlandson]).[98]

Another example concerns a case involving the murder of a prostitute. The mother of the slain woman petitions that the murderer, a wealthy man, should provide for the woman's continued sustenance, given that her daughter was her only means of support. A high official in Hermopolis decided, on the basis of clemency, that the mother of the slain prostitute receive one-tenth of the land owned by the convicted murderer (*BGU* IV 1024 col. VI [*BL* I 88–89, VII 17, IX 25]). More often, landowners and other wealthy individuals tried to instill some justice into the system, realizing that pushing the poor further into debt would not solve the problem (see, e.g., Columella, *Rust.* 1.7.1–3, 6–7; Pliny, *Ep.* 9.37). Rarely did the highest levels of government become involved in the question of economic inequities, primarily, it seems, because correcting such inequities were often considered to be against their own class interests (e.g., the effort at land reform discussed in Appian, *Bell. civ.* 1.1.7, 9–11). In sum, debt was a pervasive aspect of Greco-Roman life, effecting both rich and poor. Hence, this petition regarding sin as indebtedness would have resonated with people in antiquity, especially those of lower status, who often found themselves on the losing end of the fight to free themselves from its grip.

Indebtedness as an economic reality, however, does not fully explain its use in this petition. The concept of debt has been expanded into a metaphor regarding human social relations. This petition relies on a social paradigm that envisions all human affairs as consisting of mutual obligations. Such an idea would have been well known to the Greco-Roman auditors of the prayer. The everyday occurrences of life were viewed as manifestations of debts incurred and repaid (see, e.g., Cicero, *Mur.* 70–71; Seneca, *Ep.* 19.4; Juvenal, *Sat.* 5.12–22). Within the system of patronage, persons continually felt as if they were either accumulating or discharging some sort of social debt. Such an attitude arose from the context of mutual interlocking obligations, within which most persons lived. Thus, debt, whether real or social, was an omnipresent entity in ancient life and one that never appeared to be satisfied. This may explain why the equating of debt with sin might have been a powerful metaphor for the composer of the LP.

Given the equation presented, the petition posits that these mutual obligations remain to a greater or lesser degree unfulfilled. According to the construction of the petition, it is doubtful that one could ever repay these debts. The magnanimity and continual recurrence of human indebtedness is such that it would be impossible to even keep track of one's debts, much less to fulfill all of them. As a consequence, they are left unfulfilled. Such unfulfilled obligations amount to and constitute human sinfulness. Polycarp, most likely quoting some earlier source, demonstrates how appealing such a notion was to Greco-Roman Christianity (see Pol. *Phil.* 6.1). Such sinfulness could never be *fully* corrected through human action.[99] Thus, the fifth petition is an appeal to divine mercy. Such an appeal again recalls the activity of persons in the legal sphere. An appeal for mercy is only considered legally appropriate when no other recourse is available. For example, Pliny says, "[Mercy] is never more worthy of praise than when there is the justest cause for anger" (*Ep.* 9.21 [Melmoth]).[100] If this appeal is granted, it would restore the individual to her initial legal status. It is a granting of freedom to the individual—a redemption from obligation to another.[101]

Such a relief from obligation does not, by necessity, change the social status of the individual. For example, scholars have pointed out that there is a connection between this petition in the LP and the parable of the unforgiving slave in Matt 18:23–35.[102] What is noteworthy about the parable is that the slave remains a slave. In other words, the freedom granted in the petition is with respect to social obligations and not status. According to the ancients, such a situation was just because equality—or the radical equalization of status—was not an ideal social vision (see Cicero, *Resp.* 1.34.52–53). Mercy was always granted within the confines of hierarchy. In fact, the concept of obligation only reinforced hierarchy in the ancient world. Thus, what the petition for forgiveness seeks to do is loosen the bonds of obligation between persons in a hierarchical system. This appeal for divine remission is a request to reenter the social system in an unencumbered manner. God, as head of the cosmic household, is in a distinctive position to grant mercy to the subordinate members. Such an action restores the individual to his primordial state. Yet, the request is paradoxical in that the orant asking for forgiveness, by reentering the social system, will be forced to ask for forgiveness again and again. At once, this petition is an acknowledgement of the overwhelming benevolence of God as well as an admission of the profound social debt human beings accumulate with respect to each other. For example, Hierocles calls parents "our greatest benefactors," and goes on to say that parents "are lenders of the most valuable things, and take back only things which will benefit us when we repay them" (Malherbe).[103] Release from this heavy social obligation allows for the freedom to reobligate one's self in other ways. However, this appeal can only be enacted if 6:12b is also enacted, that is, the cancellation of all debts owed to the individual. Release from one's own debts, at least according to the parable in Matt 18, requires the releasing of others. It is a socially obligatory generosity that must be shared throughout the social system. Otherwise, a true balancing of the social scales is not possible.

The prospect of being free with respect to what you owe others is not equitable unless one releases others from their requisite social obligations to you. That is, when such an appeal for mercy is proffered, one must be willing to acknowledge that the balance of debts I owe is much greater than the balance of debts owed to me. Otherwise, a new situation of injustice is created.[104] Since this appeal to divine mercy is only possible when one acknowledges that one owes more than one can repay, the only proper and just thing an individual can do is to release others from their indebtedness to himself. Thus, 6:12a is not to be considered just without 6:12b in the LP.

Although all of the petitions in the LP have dealt with the matter of evil tangentially, the last petition, καὶ μὴ εἰσενέγκῃς ἡμᾶς εἰς πειρασμόν, ἀλλὰ ῥῦσαι ἡμᾶς ἀπὸ τοῦ πονηροῦ (6:13), squarely confronts this relation.[105] One of the interesting things about the construction of this petition is its use of πονηρός, rather than the more abstract πονηρία, to describe the "thing" from which humans need rescue. It appears that in older Greek usage, πονηρός could designate, among other things, a person who is morally reprehensible in conduct toward gods and human beings. By the Hellenistic period, this evolved into the idea of the evil *daimon* (πονηρὸς δαίμων).[106] Thus, it is understandable that the masculine form of the term could be used as a shorthand designation for an evil supernatural power, the devil. On the contrary, the neuter form of the word is used to designate evil in an abstract sense.[107] Günther Harder argues that πονηρός generally in Matthew is used in its masculine sense to refer to the devil. Yet, he says that when used in prayers it is meant to be taken in its abstract sense.[108] The ambiguity of the term may actually be intentional in this case. Πονηρός may be referring to both an evil entity and evil as an abstract entity. Nevertheless, a resolution of this problem is not pivotal to an interpretation of this petition.

Equally interesting is the use of πειρασμός (testing) in this petition. It is equally ambiguous as to whether the source of the testing is internal or external.[109] For example, as it is used in the Pauline letters, it is impossible to determine the author of πειρασμός.[110] The Greco-Roman world held a strong sensibility that placed responsibility for human trials on human beings rather than the gods. A good example of this idea can be found in the words of Zeus: "Oh for shame, how the mortals put the blame upon us gods, for they say evils come from us, but it is they, rather, who by their own recklessness win sorrow beyond what is given" (Homer, *Od.* 1.32–34 [Lattimore]).[111] Greco-Romans often understood suffering as an opportunity for education in virtue (see, e.g., Seneca, *De providentia* 2.2, 6; Epictetus, frg. 112). Furthermore, most educated Greco-Romans did not attribute the cause of evil or testing to a deity (see Plutarch, *Mor.* 1102F). The petition, however, does appear to indicate that God is the source of human testing.[112] This may explain why later Christian commentators attempted to distance God from human suffering (see, e.g., John Chrysostom, *Hom. Matt.* 19.6; Cyprian, *Dom. or.* 27; Augustine, *Serm. Dom.* 2.10.36–37). Nevertheless, this petition brings God and testing in close proximity.

As implicitly defined by the LP, evil is the absence of justice, which includes the profanation of God's name, the absence of God's kingdom, the lack of adherence to God's will, and the unjust subordination of God's subjects.[113] Such an absence, by itself, does not translate into evil human deeds. Rather, it is the continued existence of this evil that lures human beings into evil deeds. Such is the very definition of temptation. In essence, God leads humanity into temptation by allowing evil to exist. Such an assertion may appear inappropriate in light of a philosophical understanding of deity, especially to educated Greco-Romans. However, given the analysis conducted above, this is the inescapable conclusion. As *paterfamilias* of the cosmic household, it is God's duty to preserve and promote *pietas*. In its absence, the proper social relations in the hierarchy are undermined, which allows for the present state of injustice. The creation of this unjust state may be the responsibility of human beings, but it finds its stimulus in the freedom allowed humanity by God. Freedom entails risk, and risk involves the possibility for evil deeds. In short, evil is present in the human condition, and is partly the result of unfulfilled human obligations and partly the result of God's not having completed the work of salvation. As envisioned by the LP, the correction of the above-mentioned injustices would result in the reestablishment of *pietas*, at least to the Greco-Roman auditor. The lifting of obligations would free people to be the proper and just individuals they can be in the household of God. Yet, the LP makes it clear that human beings alone cannot establish such a situation. Only God can do what those to whom we are indebted cannot or will not do.[114] Thus, this petition is a request that God abolish temptation and evil simultaneously by rectifying the injustice that exists within and outside the human social order.

To summarize our discussion in this chapter, we have conducted an overview of the LP. We have discussed how the LP has served as a form of cultic *didachē*, pointing out, in particular, its ritual importance. We examined briefly how the LP was used in the liturgy of the early church. Then we quickly examined the petitions of the Matthean version of the LP. We found a prayer with a fundamentally social orientation, at least from the perspective of our theoretical Greco-Roman auditor. We saw how the model of the *familia* could function as an interpretive tool for the prayer's explication. Likewise, we saw how each member of the *familia* had a relationship, an interlocking web of obligations, with other members of the unit. This meant that all members of the household had both responsibilities and needs. In the case of God, we discussed how God's needs (the first three petitions) were related to God's overall responsibilities as the cosmic *paterfamilias*. In addition, as members of the *familia Dei*, human beings have responsibilities and needs, both with respect to God and to each other, that must be fulfilled for the proper functioning of the household. Finally, we discussed how evil could be envisioned as the absence of justice in the relationships of the household's members. This analysis has furnished us with an interpretative touchstone upon which to build our understandings of later actual interpreters of the LP, specifically Clement of Alexandria and Tertullian of Carthage. By looking at the LP within the social context of an imagined Greco-Roman auditor, we can better understand the culturally grounded interpretive strategies employed by these two actual auditors.

Notes

1. For a discussion of this topic, see Roger Beckwith, "The Daily and Weekly Worship of the Primitive Church in Relation to Its Jewish Antecedents," *EvQ* 56 (1984): 65–80; Sharon Burns, "The Roots of Christian Prayer and Spirituality in Judaism," in *The Journey of Western Spirituality* (ed. A. W. Sakler; Chico: Scholars Press, 1980); James Charlesworth, "A Prolegomenon to a New Study of the Jewish Background of the Hymns and Prayers in the New Testament," *JJS* 33 (1982): 265–85; G. J. Cuming, "The New Testament Foundation for Common Prayer," *Studia liturgica* 10 (1974): 88–101; B. Fischer, "The Common Prayer of Congregation and Family in the Ancient Church," *Studia liturgica* 10 (1974): 106–24; G. Glazov, "The Invocation of Ps. 51:17 in Jewish and Christian Morning Prayer," *JJS* 46 (1995): 167–82; G. Sloyan, "Jewish Ritual of the First Century C.E. and Chris-

tian Sacramental Behavior," *BTB* 15 (1985): 98–102; S. Zeitlin, "Prayer in the Apocrypha and Pseudepigrapha," *JQR* 40 (1949–50): 201–3.

2. E.g., F. J. van Beeck, "The Worship of Christians in Pliny's Letter," *Studia liturgica* 18 (1988): 121–29; H. Conn, "Luke's Theology of Prayer," *Christianity Today* 17 (1972): 6–8; G. J. Cuming, "Egyptian Elements in the Jerusalem Liturgy," *JTS* 25 (1975): 117–23; J. W. Holleran, "Christ's Prayer and Christian Prayer," *Worship* 48 (1974): 171–82; C. Kraemer, "Pliny and the Early Church Service: Fresh Light from an Old Source," *CP* 29 (1934): 293–300; J. Lebreton, "La prière dans l'eglise primitive," *RSR* 14 (1924): 105–33; R. Martin, "Aspects of Worship in the New Testament Church," *VE* 2 (1963): 6–27

3. For a bibliography see James Charlesworth et al., eds., *The Lord's Prayer and Other Prayer Texts from the Greco-Roman Era* (Valley Forge, PA: Trinity, 1994), 103–258.

4. See note 2 above.

5. Bernhard Lang, *Sacred Games: A History of Christian Worship* (New Haven: Yale University Press, 1997), 96–98.

6. W. Rordorf, "The Lord's Prayer in the Light of Its Liturgical Use in the Early Church," *Studia liturgica* 14 (1980–81): 1–19.

7. See, for example, Jerome, *Comm. Matt.* 6.11; *Tract. Ps.* 135; Tertullian, *Or.* 6; Cyprian, *Dom. or.* 18–19; Origen, *Or.* 27; Ignatius, *Ign. Eph.* 20.2; *Apostolic Tradition* 21; and Ambrose, *Sacr.*

8. For example, *Did.* 14.1–2; Tertullian, *Or.* 7, 11; Origen, *Or.* 9 and 28.6ff.; Cyprian, *Dom. or.* 23–24; and Irenaeus, *Haer.* 4.18.

9. Lang, *Sacred Games*, 97.

10. Timothy Fry, ed., *The Rule of St. Benedict in English* (Collegeville, MN: Liturgical Press, 1982), 42–43.

11. Lang, *Sacred Games*, 100.

12. For a discussion of the meaning of *invocatio*, see H. S. Versnel, ed., *Faith, Hope and Worship: Aspects of Religious Mentality in the Ancient World* (Studies in Greek and Roman Religion 2; Leiden: Brill, 1981), 2.

13. Hans Dieter Betz, *The Sermon on the Mount: A Commentary on the Sermon on the Mount, Including the Sermon on the Plain (Matthew 5:3–7:27 and Luke 6:20–49)* (ed. Adela Yarbro Collins; Hermeneia—A Critical and Historical Commentary on the Bible; Minneapolis: Fortress, 1995), 375–76 and nn. 346–48; P. B. Harner, *Understanding the Lord's Prayer* (Philadelphia: Fortress, 1975), 25–28; Vernon K. Robbins, "Divine Dialogue and the Lord's Prayer: Socio-Rhetorical Interpretation of Sacred Texts," *Dialogue* 28 (1995): 134.

14. Mark Kiley, ed., *Prayer from Alexander to Constantine: A Critical Anthology* (New York: Routledge, 1997), 150.

15. Betz, *Sermon on the Mount*, 381–82; R. J. Dillon, "On the Christian Obedience of Prayer (Matthew 6:5–13)," *Worship* 59 (1985): 420; cf. Oscar Cullmann, *Prayer in the New Testament* (Overtures to Biblical Theology; Minneapolis: Fortress, 1995), 42.

16. Betz, *Sermon on the Mount*, 382; Harner, *Understanding the Lord's Prayer*, 25–28, 35–46.

17. Suzanne Dixon, *The Roman Family* (Ancient Society and History; Baltimore: John Hopkins University Press, 1992), 1–35.

18. Jo-Ann Shelton, ed., *As the Romans Did: A Sourcebook in Roman Social History* (New York: Oxford University Press, 1998), 31.

19. For more discussion on the balancing of the two sides of Roman familial feelings, see Suzanne Dixon, "Continuity and Change in Roman Social History: Retrieving 'Family Feeling(s)' from Roman Law and Literature," in *Inventing Ancient Culture: Historicism, Periodization, and the Ancient World* (ed. Mark Golden and Peter Toohey; London: Routledge, 1992), 79–90.

20. In a prayer to Augustus, he is invoked as *pater patriae* (*CIL* 12: no. 433).

21. M. Hammond, *The Augustan Principate in Theory and Practice during the Julio-Claudian Period* (Cambridge: Harvard University Press, 1933), 110–13, esp. 112.

22. Shelton, *As the Romans Did*, 229.

23. Ibid., 228.

24. Ibid., 235.

25. *Il.* 1.503; 2.371; 3.276, 320, 365; 4.288; 5.421, 457, 757, 762, 872; 7.132, 179, 202, 446; 8.31, 236; 12.164; 13.631; 16.97, 372; 17.19, 645; 19.121, 270; 21.273, 512; 22.178; 24.308; *Od.* 1.45, 81; 4.341; 5.7; 7.311, 331; 8.306; 9.529; 12.371, 377; 13.128; 17.132; 18.235; 20.98, 112, 201; 21.200; 24.351, 376, 473.

26. Kiley, *Prayer from Alexander to Constantine*, 147.

27. A. A. Long and D. N. Sedley, eds., *The Hellenistic Philosophers* (2 vols.; Cambridge: Cambridge University Press, 1987), 1:323.

28. In one Hellenistic text, a priest is called a god's father (*P.Duk.inv.* 648 R[b]).

29. Kiley, *Prayer from Alexander to Constantine*, 192–93.

30. Betz, *Sermon on the Mount*, 388.

31. Ibid., 382, 389.

32. E.g., Joachim Jeremias, *New Testament Theology: The Proclamation of Jesus* (New York: Scribner, 1971), 61–78.

33. For different perspectives on this issue, see James Barr, "Abba Isn't Daddy," *JTS* 39 (1988): 28–47; Betz, *Sermon on the Mount*, 322–89; Charlesworth, *The Lord's Prayer and Other Prayer Texts*, 1–27; Cullmann, *Prayer in the New Testament*, 41–43; Dillon, "On the Christian Obedience of Prayer," 414–20; K. Gatzweiler, "Jesus in Prayer: Texts of the Our Father," *Lum* 39 (1984): 148–54; M. D. Goulder, "Composition of the Lord's Prayer," *JTS* 14 (1963): 32–45; Harner, *Understanding the Lord's Prayer*, 23–56; Joachim Jeremias, "The Lord's Prayer in Modern Research," *ExpTim* 71 (1960): 141–46; T. W. Manson, "The Lord's Prayer," *BJRL* 38 (1955): 104–5.

34. Charles Hartshorne, *The Divine Relativity, a Social Conception of God* (New Haven: Yale University Press, 1948); H. Richard Niebuhr, *Radical Monotheism and Western Civilization* (Montgomery Lectureship on Contemporary Civilization;

Lincoln: University of Nebraska Press, 1960); Schubert M. Ogden, *The Reality of God and Other Essays* (Dallas: Southern Methodist University Press, 1992),

35. Daniel Patte, *The Gospel According to Matthew: A Structural Commentary on Matthew's Faith* (Philadelphia: Fortress, 1987), 60–62, esp. 62.

36. For a discussion of a *pars epica*, see Versnel, *Faith, Hope and Worship*, 2.

37. The phrase ἐν τοῖς οὐρανοῖς is not common in Greco-Roman literature outside of Christianity. In fact, I could find only one instance of its use in Greco-Roman literature (Aristotle, *Part. An.* 662a8). It is used two times in the LXX, both in the Psalms. Contrariwise, it is found eleven times in Matthew, three times in Mark and Luke, once in the Corinthian correspondence, two times in Colossians, and once in Hebrews. It can be found in the Acts of John, the Apocryphon of John, and the Acts of Thomas. In addition, numerous later Christian writers use the phrase, including Justin Martyr, Pseudo-Justin Martyr, Clement of Alexandria, Clement of Rome, Athenagoras, Eusebius, Basilius, Origen, and Athanasius, among others.

38. Robert M. Grant, *Gods and the One God* (ed. Wayne A. Meeks; Library of Early Christianity 1; Philadelphia: Westminster, 1986), 75–83.

39. Plutarch, *Plutarch's Moralia* (trans. Frank Cole Babbitt; 15 vols.; Loeb Classical Library; New York: Putnam, 1927), 5:245.

40. H. Traub, "οὐρανός, οὐράνιος, ἐπουράνιος, οὐρανόθεν," *TDNT* 5:497–543.

41. Ibid., 520.

42. Betz, *Sermon on the Mount*, 389.

43. Mary Beard et al., *Religions of Rome* (2 vols.; New York: Cambridge University Press, 1998), 1:49.

44. Ibid., 2:105.

45. Ibid., 2:353, 355.

46. Cf. Dillon, "On the Christian Obedience of Prayer"; S. V. Tilborg, "Form-Criticism of the Lord's Prayer," *NovT* 14 (1972): 94–105.

47. Karl Schmidt, "βασιλεύς κτλ.," *TDNT* 1:579.

48. See chapter 2 for more on this subject.

49. Betz, *Sermon on the Mount*, 390; cf. Harner, *Understanding the Lord's Prayer*, 67–75.

50. Betz, *Sermon on the Mount*, 391; cf. Harner, *Understanding the Lord's Prayer*, 74.

51. Ramsay MacMullen, *Paganism in the Roman Empire* (New Haven: Yale University Press, 1981), 73–94.

52. Ronald Mellor, ed., *The Historians of Ancient Rome: An Anthology of the Major Writings* (London: Routledge, 1997), 363; also 35, on how the Senate and people of Rome bestowed upon Augustus the title *pater patriae*.

53. Shelton, *As the Romans Did*, 236.

54. Betz, *Sermon on the Mount*, 392; cf. Harner, *Understanding the Lord's Prayer*, 75–80.

55. See, for example, Cicero, *Fin.* 3.62–68; Stobaeus 2.66.14–67; 2.59.4–60.2; 60.9–24; Sextus Empiricus, *Math.* 9.75–76.

56. Epictetus, *The Enchiridion* (trans. Thomas W. Higginson; Library of Liberal Arts; New York: Macmillan, 1948), 22–23.

57. Betz, *Sermon on the Mount*; Goulder, "Composition of the Lord's Prayer"; Tilborg, "Form-Criticism of the Lord's Prayer."

58. J. Behm, "πρόνοια," *TDNT* 4:1013.

59. Homer, *The Odyssey of Homer* (trans. Richard Lattimore; New York: Harper & Row, 1965), 74.

60. Πρόνοια is not a common term in the NT, which never uses the term as a way of indicating divine πρόνοια (Acts 24:2; Rom 13:14). In philosophical circles, πρόνοια can serve as a technical term for the divinity (J. Behm, "πρόνοια," *TDNT* 4:1011–17). Although not common in the NT, it was a popular term used by many Greco-Roman authors (e.g., Thucydides, Diogenes Laertius, Euripides, Plutarch, Athenaeus, Isocrates, Sophocles, Demosthenes, Herodianus, Isaeus, Aristophanes, Xenophon, Lycurgus, Galen, Plato, and many others.).

61. See relevant discussions in Betz, *Sermon on the Mount*, 393–96; subsequent chapters of this work, on Clement and Tertullian; Cullmann, *Prayer in the New Testament*, 47–51, who speaks of the need to subordinate human will to the divine will; and Harner, *Understanding the Lord's Prayer*, 75–82, who suggests—wrongly I believe—that God's will is somehow opposed by supernatural forces on earth and in heaven.

62. E.g., Betz, *Sermon on the Mount*, 378.

63. There will be an extended discussion of *pietas* in chapter 2.

64. Betz, *Sermon on the Mount*, 397.

65. Ekkehard Stegemann and Wolfgang Stegemann, *The Jesus Movement: A Social History of Its First Century* (Minneapolis: Fortress, 1999), 7–20.

66. Peter Garnsey, *Food and Society in Classical Antiquity* (Key Themes in Ancient History; Cambridge: Cambridge University Press, 1999), 43–61.

67. Ibid., 121.

68. Shelton, *As the Romans Did*, 79–80.

69. F. Agnew, "Almsgiving, Prayer, and Fasting," *TBT* 33 (1995): 239–44; Betz, *Sermon on the Mount*; Charlesworth, *The Lord's Prayer and Other Prayer Texts*; Cullmann, *Prayer in the New Testament*; R. F. Cyster, "The Lord's Prayer in the Exodus Tradition," *Theology* 64 (1961): 377–81; Goulder, "Composition of the Lord's Prayer"; Harner, *Understanding the Lord's Prayer*; Jeremias, "The Lord's Prayer in Modern Research"; Manson, "The Lord's Prayer"; Rordorf, "The Lord's Prayer in the Light of Its Liturgical Use"; P. Trudinger, "The 'Our Father' in Matthew as Apocalyptic Eschatology," *DRev* 107 (1989): 49–54.

70. Rordorf, "The Lord's Prayer in the Light of Its Liturgical Use," 6–9.

71. Michael Joseph Brown, "'Panem nostrum': The Problem of Petition and the Lord's Prayer," *JR* (2000): 603–6. More recently, an eschatological interpretation has been advanced (bread for tomorrow), but this too seems to be another sub-

sequent reinterpretation of the text (Harner, *Understanding the Lord's Prayer*, 89; Trudinger, "The 'Our Father' as Apocalyptic Eschatology," 52–53).

72. Betz, *Sermon on the Mount*, 400; Garnsey, *Food and Society in Classical Antiquity*, xi; Brown, "'Panem Nostrum,'" 601 n. 18; cf. Dillon, "On the Christian Obedience of Prayer," 423.

73. Garnsey, *Food and Society in Classical Antiquity*, 113–27. Such an insight does not necessarily say anything substantive about the composer or context of composition.

74. Brown, "'Panem Nostrum,'" 604–6.

75. Betz, *Sermon on the Mount*, 379.

76. Brown, "'Panem Nostrum,'" 605–6.

77. David S. Potter, *Literary Texts and the Roman Historian* (Approaching the Ancient World; London: Routledge, 1999), 2, 42, 152–55.

78. Brown, "'Panem Nostrum,'" 606–10.

79. Garnsey, *Food and Society in Classical Antiquity*, 82–99.

80. For a fuller discussion of the early church's mind-set and its relationship to petition in prayer, see Brown, "'Panem Nostrum.'"

81. Garnsey, *Food and Society in Classical Antiquity*, 100–112.

82. David S. Potter, *Prophets and Emperors: Human and Divine Authority from Augustus to Theodosius* (Revealing Antiquity 7; Cambridge: Harvard University Press, 1994), 7.

83. For a discussion of the practice of generosity in antiquity, see Cicero, *Off.* 1.14.42–1.15.47.

84. Betz, *Sermon on the Mount*, 400 and n. 479; Tilborg, "Form-Criticism of the Lord's Prayer," 145–46.

85. Betz, *Sermon on the Mount*, 402 and n. 488; Harner, *Understanding the Lord's Prayer*, 99; Cullmann, *Prayer in the New Testament*, 55–58.

86. Shelton, *As the Romans Did*, 127.

87. Roger S. Bagnall, *Egypt in Late Antiquity* (Princeton: Princeton University Press, 1993), 154–55; Ramsay MacMullen, *Roman Social Relations, 50 B.C. To A.D. 284* (New Haven: Yale University Press, 1974), 59–64.

88. E.g., Bagnall, *Egypt in Late Antiquity*, 153–60.

89. Jane Rowlandson and Roger S. Bagnall, *Women and Society in Greek and Roman Egypt: A Sourcebook* (Cambridge, UK: Cambridge University Press, 1998), 201–4.

90. *FIRA* 3:481 (*CIL* 3:950, 951, 2215).

91. Bagnall, *Egypt in Late Antiquity*, 73–78, for a further discussion of money-lending in the Roman province of Egypt.

92. Ibid., 153–60.

93. Ibid., 159.

94. Rowlandson and Bagnall, *Women and Society*, 236.

95. Ibid., 263–64.

96. Shelton, *As the Romans Did*, 144.

97. See, for example, *P.Oxy.Hels.* 26 [*BL* VIII 274]; *P.Cair.Isid.* 64; *P.Oxy* I 71 col. 2 lines 1–16 [*BL* I 314].

98. Rowlandson and Bagnall, *Women and Society*, 205–6.

99. Betz, *Sermon on the Mount*, 402–3; Cullmann, *Prayer in the New Testament*, 56; cf. Harner, *Understanding the Lord's Prayer*, 102–6.

100. Quoted in Stanley K. Stowers, *Letter Writing in Greco-Roman Antiquity* (ed. Wayne A. Meeks; Library of Early Christianity 5; Philadelphia: Westminster, 1986), 160.

101. Betz, *Sermon on the Mount*, 403.

102. Ibid., 401–2.

103. Quoted in Abraham J. Malherbe, *Moral Exhortation: A Greco-Roman Sourcebook* (ed. Wayne A. Meeks; Library of Early Christianity 4; Philadelphia: Westminster, 1986), 91.

104. Betz, *Sermon on the Mount*, 404; and Rordorf, "The Lord's Prayer in the Light of Its Liturgical Use," 10.

105. Cf. Cullmann, *Prayer in the New Testament*, 58–66; Cyster, "Lord's Prayer in the Exodus Tradition," 379–80; Goulder, "Composition of the Lord's Prayer," 41–42.

106. Günther Harder, "πονηρός," *TDNT* 6:548.

107. Ibid., 546–66.

108. Ibid., 560–62.

109. Luke Timothy Johnson, *The Letter of James: A New Translation with Introduction and Commentary* (Anchor Bible; New York: Doubleday, 1995), 177, discusses the possibility of both usages.

110. Heinrich Seesemann, "πειρασμός," *TDNT* 6:29.

111. Homer, *Odyssey of Homer*, 28.

112. Johnson comments on how the statement in James 1:13 contradicts the LP, in *Letter of James*, 203.

113. Betz, *Sermon on the Mount*, 405–6 and n. 514.

114. Ibid., 412; cf. P. B. Harner, *Understanding the Lord's Prayer*, 106–13.

2

Greco-Roman Visions of
Religion and Prayer

Do honor to the divine power at all times, but especially on occasions
of public worship; for thus you will have the reputation both
of sacrificing to the gods and of abiding by the laws.
—Pseudo-Isocrates (*Demon.* 11)

Greco-Roman Culture: A Fusion of Horizons

After providing some sense of how the LP might have been interpreted by a Greco-Roman auditor in the last chapter, I now move to a consideration of Greco-Roman religion as it pertains especially to prayer. In the last chapter, I tried to imagine the LP as heard by a large cross section of Greco-Romans. In this chapter I focus mainly on the thought world of the elite, persons of aristocratic background who have leisure time to discuss intellectual matters. Now I move beyond a focus solely on the LP to a much broader, although more class-specific, discussion. My goal is to inquire into the specific worldviews that would have informed the interpretations of prayer advanced by Clement and Tertullian.

This discussion seeks to tease out the differences between Greek philosophical understandings of religion and that espoused by Roman intellectuals. Such differences clearly did not affect all persons equally. For example, there are several places where one might challenge my presentation of Roman religion by appealing to someone writing in Latin who espouses a view more in line with the Greek philosophers. To be sure, the nature of Greco-Roman culture dissolves many clear and abiding distinctions between Greek and Roman religion. Nevertheless, certain central cultural predispositions can be found in Roman religion as opposed to that of the Greek philosophers. Furthermore, I believe that these predispositions play an important role in how intellectuals interpret texts and ritual acts. In short, I believe it is possible to speak of a Greek philosophical orientation that is distinguishable from a Roman orientation. As conquered and conqueror, the relative social positions of the intellectuals in question played a decisive role in guiding interpretation.

The Greek philosophers took advantage of the importance of argumentation and persuasion in classical Athenian democracy. In opposition to the tendency toward cosmological evaluation during the classical period, some philosophers speculated on the importance of the individual and ethics as matters of intellectual concern. This inevitably led to a reevaluation of matters dealing with religion. Their reexamination of cultic practices made philosophers the producers of cultic *didachai*, as when philosophers attacked what they perceived to be egoism in Greek religious practice, or when they sought to modify perceptions of the gods, superstition, and improper understandings of piety. They provided a renewed understanding of piety that functioned as the lens through which Greek religious practice would be reinterpreted.

The Romans, in contrast, reinvented their religious understanding with the advent of Augustus, the main proponent of Roman religious revival. Although advertised as a restoration of traditional religion, Augustus actually instituted new practices, which helped to redefine Roman identity. Although central concepts such as the *pax deorum* remained pivotal to Roman religious thinking, they were augmented and transformed by other concepts. Romans and Greeks took piety with equal seriousness, but their understandings of piety varied. Nevertheless, some Roman understandings of religion, including prayer, created similarities—as well as important differences—with Greek philosophical understandings of religion.

A Greek Philosophical Perspective

The distinctive element in Greek thought is often understood as its insistence that the world make sense in human terms. Greek philosophy promoted critical and realistic inquiry into the cause of events, whether natural or historical, and developed narratives regarding the meaning and import of all occurrences experienced by human beings. This attitude may have been a by-product of democratic government, which stressed the importance of competition and persuasion as a means of determining validity. Such an orientation, coupled with the absence of any institutionally imposed dogma regarding truth, especially in the context of fifth-century-BCE Athens, allowed Greek thought to venture into realms unexplored by tradition.

In the realm of logic, the Greeks developed a number of argumentative strategies to understand the world around them (e.g., the principle of verification, the argument from analogy, and the argument from opposites). Greek speculation must have been stimulated by contact with other cultures, but it owed more to a social system that allowed for a great amount of leisure time on the part of a select, aristocratic few. In many respects, the freedom and critical inquiry of the few was gained at the expense of the labor or enslavement of the many. Nevertheless, the importance of argumentation and persuasion was unquestioned in the world of fifth-century Athens (see, e.g., Plato, *Phaedr.* 266d; Gorgias, *Hel.* 19).

Argumentation was an important component in the Greek quest for understanding, which sometimes sought a mathematical precision.[1] Such precision spurred the Greek interest in philology, precisely because the Greeks thought that there should be a relationship between a word and its meaning (see Plato, *Crat.* 396a). In addition, Greeks were concerned with the predictability of human behavior, a concern found in rhetorical techniques that developed arguments regarding probability and paradigm (see, e.g., Thucydides, *Peloponnesian War* 1.122; 5.105). Eventually the great sophist, Protagoras, introduced the idea of relativity by claiming that there were two sides to every question (see *Dissoi logoi* 1.3). When extended to the realm of morality, this led to his famous dictum: "Man is the measure of all things." And although to many such an assertion was considered dangerous, it represented a logical conclusion to much of the critical inquiry engaged in by the Athenian elite.

In opposition to this trend, Socrates moved the center of Greek thought from cosmology to a consideration of the position of the human being in the cosmos. He was as concerned with clarity and precision as others were. Yet, his focus was clearly ethical (see, e.g., Plato, *Lach.* 191a). According to his students, Socrates was looking for some kind of stable reality and standard behind the confusion of perception and varying standards (see Plato, *Theaet.* 150b). His quest was not dissimilar to the ideas proposed by thinkers such as Hekataius of Miletus and Herodotus of Halicarnassus, who attempted to detect the logical causes behind historical occurrences.

Such a quest for a reasonable, largely androcentric narrative of human activity was often derailed by the intervention of randomness or chance. For example, the historian Thucydides acknowledged that τύχη played an important and unpredictable part in the unfolding of human affairs.[2] Such a recognition marked a step toward one of the developments of Greek thought that characterized the Hellenistic period: the abstraction of the idea of the gods and other intervening forces in the minds of human beings. As a consequence, philosophers increasingly found themselves forced to reinterpret the understanding of the contemporary religious establishment in light of their intellectual achievements, if they were going to participate in these practices in any intellectually credible manner at all.

By way of critique, philosophers such as Heraclitus, Xenophanes, Plato, and Plutarch sought to interpret (actually, reinterpret) the practice of religion and especially prayer.[3] Philosophers did not seek to destroy the cult, nor did they, for the most part, question the existence of the deities. Still, they felt compelled by conscience to reinterpret theology and cultic practice in light of their new understanding of the cosmos.[4] Friedrich Heiler maintained that the philosophers tried to transform empiric religion into ideal religion. Furthermore, he argued that this philosophic religion was oriented toward the realization of certain moral values.[5] Heiler exaggerated the desire of the philosophers to replace traditional worship with some sort of sanitized and wholly moralized religion. Yet, the philosophers did seek to reinterpret cultic practice. We cannot fully determine the degree to which actual changes in the social and political structures influenced philosophy, or the philosophical schools influenced the development of sociopolitical structures. They, undoubtedly, influenced each other. For example, part of the cultic teaching of the philosophers was based on a growing and sometimes contentious idea of divine monarchy.[6] The growth of this idea naturally developed with the growth of multinational kingdoms, beginning in the Hellenistic period. With the advent of the Roman imperial period, the idea that the cosmos should resemble the prevailing political structure gained increasing currency. The philosophers were instrumental in this process—even the ones who preceded the Hellenistic period—by supplying the intellectual foundation upon which the concept of divine monarchy could be built. In addition to this concept of monarchy, other ideas prevalent in Greek religion changed in light of the new philosophical cosmology.

Traditional Greek religion valued the concept of reciprocity as a way of understanding the human being's relationship to the gods (νομίζειν τοὺς θεούς).[7] Such an idea accorded well with the Greek desire to define relationships and their attendant responsibilities.[8] Most Greeks believed that they had an obligation to the gods, but they were not as certain that the gods had an obligation to them. As a means of creating a reciprocal relationship, they offered sacrifices to the gods. In some ways, sacrifice can be viewed as the creation of a partnership.[9] Yet, according to the philosophical critique, one of the central problems with this understanding of religion was its potential misperception as an ordinary business transaction, or worse as a transaction in which the human being fares better than the god (cf. Plato, *Euthyphr.* 14ce). The philosopher Theophrastus identified such an "economic" understanding of religion in his discussion of sacrifice. He contended that what human beings like about sacrifice is the edible part, which they reserve for themselves. According to Theophrastus, the norm for piety was the principle of profit (frg. 6.1.15 [Pötscher]).[10]

Along with the principle of profit, philosophers criticized what they perceived to be a misdirection of prayer. For example, Heraclitus believed that the average person prayed to the image as if the idol were the actual god (frg. 5). In his mind, this turned the orant into nothing but a braggart whose words do not reach the ears of the god. Moreover, he felt that the language of prayer was not as "exalted" as it should be. He used the verb λεσχηνεύω as a description of the current *mis*practice of prayer.[11] Likewise, Xenophon believed that too many unseemly thoughts were communicated in prayer, and that it was too self-interested.[12] Some philosophers found prayer to be too materialistically oriented and improperly based on the assumption that the gods somehow need the sacrifices of human beings. In short, the problem with prayer was its egocentricity—what some scholars have labeled *Gebetsegoismus*.[13]

According to some philosophers, the problems with the performance of cult could be categorized and overcome with the guidance of reason. There were at least three possible responses to the theology of traditional Greek religion. Plutarch, like some other philosophers, intellectually places these options into a neat formula: ἀθεότης-εὐσέβεια-δεισιδαιμονία, and uses the two extremes ἀθεότης and δεισιδαιμονία as a starting point for his work, *Peri deisidaimonias* (= *Superst*). The first option, atheism, was not popular among philosophers. Usually atheism was defined as θεούς μὴ νομίζειν (not following the traditional cultic practices or disbelieving in the existence of the gods).[14] Plutarch describes the atheist's attitude as a sorry judgment leading to utter indifference. The ultimate outcome of this mind-set is this: "[And] the end which it achieves in not believing in the existence of gods is not to fear them" (*Superst.* 165b2 [Babbitt]).[15] Atheism was reputed to have been a problem in intellectual circles in classical Greece, especially among younger men. This is evidenced in Socrates's speech in the *Apologia*: "Is that, by Zeus, what you think of me, . . . that I do not believe that there are any gods?" (26e3–4 [Grube]).[16]

Some philosophers developed more elaborate definitions of atheism. These advanced definitions generally reflected the basic understanding of atheism with embellishments provided by the particular concerns of the philosophical school. For example, in his definition Plato describes the atheist as one who: (1) denies the existence of the gods, or (2) does not deny the existence of the gods but denies that the gods care about human beings (the πρόνοια of the gods), or (3) does not deny the existence of the gods, nor does she deny the gods' care for humanity, but she believes that the gods can be "bribed" with sacrifices and prayers. The latter attitude was considered ἀσέβεια (*Leg.* 885b–910d). Acknowledging the existence of the gods was not sufficient. One also had to acknowledge certain divine characteristics. Such characteristics protected the gods from the unseemly presentation generally given them by the poets.

Although charged and convicted of atheism, Socrates was no atheist, at least to Plato. His mission was not to disprove or undermine the existence and importance of the gods. Rather, Socrates sought to place the gods within the proper perspective based on the insights of the philosophical critique. On the contrary, it appears that persons like Protagoras the Sophist were atheists, at least in light of the definition advanced above. The Pyrrhonist Timon of Phlius says this of him:

> [Foremost of all early] and later sophists, not lacking in clarity of speech or vision or versatility, Protagoras. They wanted to make a bonfire of his writings, because he wrote down that he did not know and could not observe what any of the gods are like and whether any of them exist, completely safeguarding his honesty. (Sextus Empiricus, *Math.* 9.57 [Timon frg. 779; Long and Sedley])[17]

Despite the bad reputation given them by other philosophers, atheists tended to be intellectuals who could not reconcile the traditional cult with the new cosmological data being uncovered in the philosophical revolution. Plutarch even admits that atheists are actually people of some intellectual substance (*Superst.* 170f11–171b12). They deny the existence of the deities and fend for themselves. Even in Plutarch's critique, their intellectual integrity makes them more admirable than the persons who opt for the other extreme response, *deisidaimonia*.

Superstition, as it has come to be understood, is not exactly the best way to describe the religious feelings and practices of those who felt the constant intervention of the gods in their lives. As Plutarch defined the term, the *deisidaimon* is the one who believes that the gods are determined to spite her and who can only protect herself with the utmost caution:

You see what kind of thoughts the superstitious have about the gods; they assume that the gods are rash, faithless, fickle, vengeful, cruel, and easily offended; and, as a result, the superstitious man is bound to hate and fear the gods. . . . [Though] he dreads them, he worships them and sacrifices to them and besieges their shrines; and this is nothing surprising; for it is equally true that men give welcome to despots, and pay court to them, and erect golden statues in their honour, but in their hearts they hate them and "shake their head." (*Superst.* 170e11 [Babbitt])[18]

Plato criticizes the way in which superstitious people react to things like dreams and other trivial occurrences (*Leg.* 909e–910a). In short, the superstitious person is not irreligious but *overly* religious. He practices religion without the assistance of reason. Superstition involves an unhealthy fear based on a fundamental misunderstanding of the nature and function of deity. The superstitious person is a "throwback" of sorts to the "unenlightened" days.

Prior to the intellectual changes in the classical period, the ordinary Greek appears to have participated in rites of supplication and petition along with rites of placation, purgation, and aversion. In the classical period, supplication and petition gradually overshadowed the others, but to say that the average Greek viewed the gods as benevolent would be an overstatement. In conjunction with the advent of Athenian democracy, a certain degree of responsibility and freedom were introduced into the theological anthropology of the day.[19] Still, it appears that the gods were viewed as a problematic "unknown" in the affairs of the world (see, e.g., Herodotus, *Hist.* 1.32ff.). The philosophers sought to overthrow such a view of the gods. Yet, the *deisidaimon* demonstrated that the older theological convictions did not disappear. Some simply did not accept the philosophic reinterpretation of the cult.

Theophrastus refers to δεισιδαιμονία as a δειλία or cowardice in cultic practice (*Char.* 5.2). "In Theophrastus δειλός is . . . the man who sees danger everywhere, who spots a pirate behind every headland and who asks, when the sea is rough, whether there is anyone who is not initiated."[20] It does not appear that the *deisidaimon* believes in things that are different from anyone else, but that she experiences everything in a distorted manner. This warped perspective translates into an incorrect attitude toward the cult. The *deisidaimon* participates in exorbitant sacrifices and wantonness (τρυφή). He believes that the gods can somehow be bribed with sacrifices, which would make him an atheist according to Plato's definition.

However, this negative connotation of the term did not really arise until Theophrastus's time. As P. A. Meijer intimates,

> The word "deisidaimon" only obtained its unfavorable meaning in a rather later period. For a pious man like Xenophon it is naturally favorable, just as it is for Aristotle who points out, in his *Politica* (5.1315a.1), when discussing the stability of tyranny, that it is as well for the tyrant to show himself to be extremely scrupulous in religious matters: here too the term *deisidaimon* is used. . . . Theophrastus may have been the first person to give a neurotic twist to *deisidaimonia* in his *Characteres*.[21]

Although such a judgment regarding the development of the term may be true, once the philosophers give it its negative connotation, it became normative from then on. Plutarch says that the superstitious person believes that the gods do not help humans but harm them (*Superst.* 165b2). They are confused in thought, weak in character, and paralyzed from constructive activity by fear. According to the critics, this is not truly pious behavior but a reprehensible form of impiety.

A reinterpreted εὐσέβεια was the third and preferable option for the philosophers. Generally, to be pious meant to be "acceptable to the gods."[22] Acceptability entailed understanding the nature of the gods (theology), but it also had implications for cultic performance.[23] One Aristotelian intimates this perspective quite well when he says, "[The] first elements of just behavior are those concerning the gods, the daimons, the fatherland and parents, and the dead. Of these piety consists." "Impiety," he says, "is error concerning the gods and daimons, or concerning the dead, or concerning parents and the fatherland" ([*Virt. vit.*] 1250b2, 1251a2 [Mikalson]).[24] In short, εὐσέβεια was preeminently the proper performance of cultic practices.

As commonly understood, tradition was the primary determinant of εὐσέβεια. Isocrates makes this point when he says, "Our ancestors thought that piety consisted not in great expenditures, but rather in not changing any of those things which their ancestors had handed down to them" (*Areop.* 7.29–30 [Mikalson]).[25] The proper performance of τὰ πάτρια (ancestral practices), τὰ εἰθότα (customary practices), and τὰ νομιζόμενα (traditional rites) was seen as the continuation of the practices of the ancestors.

The rhetoric of the intellectuals notwithstanding, to argue for the *actual* maintenance of ancestral practices is futile. As has been demonstrated, ideas about the meaning and purpose of cultic practices did change in Greek religion.[26] The real issue at stake in the discussion of εὐσέβεια was the correspondence of the present practices with the intention of the ancestors. Betz points out this central concern in his discussion of ritual.[27] In short, the philosophers reinterpreted cultic practice in terms of what they conceived to be the real intention of he cult. They were producing cultic *didachē*.

This reinvented εὐσέβεια of the philosophers consisted in a righteousness directed toward one's neighbor and the larger community. In other words, "a righteous man observes the customs of the laws prescribed by the community so that he be just and good."[28] Εὐσέβεια was true veneration of the gods in the offering of τιμή.[29] Such an idea is clearly evident in Plato's *Euthyphro*. Still, εὐσέβεια was not seen as *total* dedication to the divine, but as a department or complement of righteousness. Εὐσέβεια "regulates our behavior towards those to whom we owe something, although righteousness sometimes also displays the tendency to become synonymous with virtue in so far as the righteous man must satisfy the law established by society."[30] Εὐσέβεια was only a complement of a righteous life.

Theophrastus sketched out such a renewed εὐσέβεια in his discussion of sacrifice. He maintained that what was important in any sacrifice was intention: the one sacrificing must have a νοῦς καθαρός and a ψυχὴ ἀπαθής (frg. 8.1.18). In this respect the ideal state is called συνεχὴς εὐσέβεια by Theophrastus (see, e.g., frg. 8). Apart from creating a relationship of reciprocity, a sacrifice was an instance of the individual's deepest veneration for the benevolent character and activity of the gods.[31] Sacrifice was, first and foremost, an expression of respect and thanks. Only secondarily was it a supplication for something good. Such an attitude was a result of the theological claims that prompted the philosopher's critique of the cult. No longer would the gods desire reverence based on the exchange of material goods. Now the gods demanded a more refined understanding of cult based on the preeminence of noetic qualities in the worshipper. What concerned the gods was the ἦθος of the sacrificer, with the greatest sacrifice being ἡ ὀρθὴ διάληψις. This perspective undercut the pre-classical idea of reciprocity in Greek theology and placed the practice of prayer in a new framework.

Prayer from a Philosophical Perspective

When placed into this context, the purpose and meaning of prayer was altered according to what was deemed appropriate in cultic practice. For example, the *invocatio* and *pars epica* of most philosophical prayers were limited.[32] Plato generally only invoked the name of the god. In addition, the *preces* (request) of the philosopher was different: the philosopher did not pray for unnecessary material things but for τὰ δίκαια δύνασθαι πρήσσειν.[33] Such a change toward material things is evidenced in Solon's prayer:

> Muses of Pieria, glorious children of memory and of Olympian Zeus, hear my prayer. Grant me wealth from the blessed gods, and from all men fair fame to enjoy forever. So let me be sweet to my friends and bitter to my enemies, reverenced by the one and feared by the other. Though I long for wealth, I would not possess it unjustly, wealth that the gods give abides with a man as a tree stands firm from root to top; but wealth that men seek by presumptuous outrage comes not in due course, but follows reluctantly the lure of unjust deeds. (Stobaeus, *Ecl.* 3.9, 23 [Stovaios])

In this prayer one can see the continuation of particular Greek concerns: wealth, fame, clear relationships accompanied by appropriate actions. Yet, under the critique of the philosophers, even these entrenched cultural values were subject to reinterpretation.

The philosophical desire to exalt petition is found in various thinkers. For example, Xenophanes was concerned about the content of petitionary prayers. He wanted to move prayer from egocentricity to concern for neighbor and community. To accomplish this he hypothesized a "supergod" of sorts who could not be reached through the current prayers (frgs. 23–26). This god could not be bombarded with unseemly thoughts.[34] Philosophy called for a revolution in contemporary attitudes toward prayer, attempting to move such attitudes away from narrow selfishness to a kind of altruism.

If one focuses on a particular philosopher, the question of cult, particularly with respect to prayer, becomes even more interesting. For example, the relationship of Socrates to prayer is quite ambiguous. Xenophon maintained that Socrates believed in the efficacy of religion and, as a consequence, prayed a great deal (see *Mem.* 1.3.1–4; *Oec.* 5.19–20). This view, however, is not supported by much evidence from other sources. For instance, few prayers are said in Plato's early Socratic dialogues. In addition, Meijer believes that Socrates's devotional doctrine made the need for frequent prayer superfluous.[35] It may be that the frequency of prayer in the life of the historical Socrates was not high.

However, what is reported of Socrates's devotional doctrine is quite instructive in terms of the philosophical critique of prayer. From what we are told, Socrates participated in the cultic practices of his contemporaries. Still, Socrates's understanding of the *perfectio respectu finis* (the perfection with respect to the end) of prayer is clearly different from that of his average contemporary. He believed it to be dangerous to pray for something concrete because that could lead to disaster. The concrete realization of the good should be left up to the deity, because only the deity knows what is truly good.[36] As Xenophon relates,

> And again, when he prayed he asked simply for good gifts, "for the gods know best what things are good." To pray for gold or silver or sovereignty or any other such thing, was just like praying for a gamble or a fight or anything of which the result is obviously uncertain. (*Mem.* 1.3.2 [Marchant])[37]

Plato does, however, attribute a number of prayers to Socrates. One of the most fascinating is that found in *Phaedo* 117c, where Socrates faces his imminent demise: "I understand, Socrates said, but one is allowed, indeed one must, utter a prayer to the gods that the journey from here to yonder may be fortunate. This is my prayer and may it be so" (Grube).[38] Yet, the most famous prayer attributed to Socrates is the prayer to Pan at the end of *Phaedrus*:

> Beloved Pan and all other gods living here, will you please grant that I become "beautiful" within and that all that I have without be in accordance with what I have within. And may I consider the wise man rich and let the mass of my gold be only what the wise man, and no other, can bear! (279bc [Clayton])[39]

Here Plato has provided us with an example of an ideal prayer, appropriate to its context. It is addressed to Pan because the dialogue is about rhetoric, and Pan—the son of Hermes, who invented rhetoric—through rhetoric reveals all (πᾶν).[40] Moreover, the phrase ἔξωθεν δὲ ὅσα ἔχω, which likely refers to possessions, commodities, or money, is to be interpreted as referring to the beauty of moderation. According to this view, the wise man (σόφος σώφρων) is truly rich because true wealth is wisdom. Thus, Plato's Socrates teaches Phaedrus that what is desirable is not concrete wealth (money or possessions) or even rhetorical skill but inner wealth, wisdom.

For some time scholars have recognized that Plato often uses prayer in his dialogues as a way of supporting a discussion or presenting a difficult idea (e.g., *Tim.* 27bd, 48de). The Pan prayer outlines the threefold ideal of Platonic doctrine: (1) inner beauty, (2) outer beauty (good physical development), and (3) the possession of a reasonable amount of money.[41] Such a rethinking of prayer practice is an excellent example of cultic *didachē* among the philosophers.

One could argue that Plato's cultic *didachē* has more of a social than purely theological import. Plato refers to the importance of the parent-child relationship in prayer in his *Laws* (e.g., 687ce and passim). His idea is that in prayer the parent practices a form of cultic *didachē*. The parent teaches the child the proper cultic performances, which translate into proper social performances. Again, prayer is moved from a form of egoism to a concern for the other.

Along with the teaching of altruism, Plato's reformation of the cult is further enhanced by the impersonal character of prayer in his thought. Such a view laid the groundwork for the abstraction of the concept of deity in the Hellenistic period. Prayers, though directly addressed to the gods, are in reality indirectly addressed to others. Heiler highlights this view in Platonic thought.[42] Given Plato's reinterpreted understanding of the cult, his theology of prayer maintains that the gods do not accept anything (either sacrifice or prayer) from anyone unrighteous, nor can cultic acts assist the guilty person in overcoming the due penalty of her deeds (see *Leg.* 716e–717a). In other words, prayer cannot influence the activity or state of being of the gods.

A Closer Look

As has become evident in this analysis, there is sometimes a close relationship between cultic practice and theology. In many respects prayer is theology verbalized. As a consequence, it is necessary for the historian to focus intently on the theology underlying prayer in order to understand why the philosophers advocated their positions on the subject. Classical Greek religion maintained a theology that saw a god as a being that far surpassed a human. A god was immortal, living a life of comfort and joy. A god had knowledge of what takes place behind the scenes of life and had power over nature and human life. Nevertheless, this classical Greek conception of the divine held the gods in relatively low esteem. Xenophanes well highlights the philosophical critique of this theology:

> Homer and Hesiod laid at the gods' door all that men count shameful and blameworthy, theft, adultery and mutual deceit. . . . So

mortals imagine that the gods go through birth, wear human clothing, with a human voice and form. . . . The Africans give their
gods snub noses and black skins, the Thracians give theirs blue eyes
and red hair. . . . If cattle or horses or lions had hands or could
draw with their hands or make statues as men do, they would draw
the shapes of gods and form their bodies respectively just like their
own (frgs. 11, 14, 16, 15).[43]

In contradistinction to the classical view, the philosophers developed,
among other things, ideas about the unity of God. Such a notion of unity
did not mean the rejection of some gods in favor of others, rather, it consisted of an insistence in the reality of one god present in the world in
diverse forms: "One god is the greatest among gods and men; in neither
form nor thought is he like mortals" (Xenophanes, frg. 10 [Grant]; see also
Seneca, *Nat.* 2.45).[44] This great god was said to act mentally, not physically
like the classical Greek gods: "[Effortlessly] he sets all things astir by the
power of his mind alone."[45]

Xenophanes criticized the classical gods through what Meijer calls a
"decency criterion."[46] He further developed a "projection theory" regarding classical Greek anthropomorphism.[47] Xenophanes' god is pure νόος:
οὖλος δὲ νοεῖ, οὖλος δὲ τ᾽ ἀκούει (frg. 24). In short, God was omniscient.
Furthermore, there is also an unbridgeable gap between Xenophanes' god
and everything else. God is transcendent. Finally, this god possesses
immense power, ruling everything through the force of divine spirit. God
is omnipotent. Such a view was elaborated by Euripides, who outlines a
similar theology in *Troades*:

Sustainer of earth, throned on the earth, whoever you are, hard to
discern, Zeus, whether natural law or human intellect, I call on
you; for moving on a noiseless path you guide all things human
along ways of justice. (884–888 [Biehl])

The Socratic critique of classical polytheism and support for a reformed
concept of deity is found in this citation by Xenophon:

Do you not think then that he who created man from the beginning had some useful end in view when he endowed him with his
several senses, giving eyes to see visible objects, ears to hear
sounds? Would odours again be of any use to us had we not been
endowed with nostrils? What perception should we have of sweet

and bitter and all things pleasant to the palate had we no tongue in our mouth to discriminate between them? Besides these, are there not other contrivances that look like the result of forethought? Thus the eyeballs, being weak, are set behind eyelids, that open like doors when we want to see, and close when we sleep: on the lids grow lashes through which the very winds filter harmlessly: above the eyes is a coping of brows that lets no drop of sweat from the head hurt them. The ears catch all sounds, but are never choked with them. Again, the incisors of all creatures are adapted for cutting, the molars for receiving food from them and grinding it. And again, the mouth, through which the food they want goes in, is set near the eyes and nostrils; but since what goes out is unpleasant, the ducts through which it passes are turned away and removed as far as possible from the organs of sense. With such signs of forethought in these arrangements, can you doubt whether they are the works of chance or design? (*Mem.* 1.4.5–6 [Marchant])[48]

The philosophers argued for a conception of deity that emphasized the benevolent and providential character of divine activity. Instead of being unpredictable and intrusive, the gods were now viewed as acting on behalf of justice.

In Plato's *Respublica* Socrates offers another criticism of classical Greek theology:

[The] shapes of the tales of the gods—what would they be? Something like this: The character of the god that must always be described, no doubt, whether the poetry be epic or lyric or tragic. Yes, that is true. And is not a god good in reality, and the fable must agree with that?. . . . It follows then . . . that God, since he is good, would not be cause of all things, as most say, but cause of a few things to mankind, and of many no cause; for the goods are much fewer for us than the evils; and of the good things God and no other must be described as the cause, but of the evil things we must look for many different causes, only not God. . . . Then . . . we must not accept from Homer or any other poet an error like this about the gods. . . . They must find out some such explanation as we are looking for now—they must declare that God did a just and good work, and they gained benefit by being chastised. But do describe those who were punished and miserable, and to say that God made them so, is what the poet must not be suffered to do. . . . However, to call God a cause of evil to anyone, being good himself, is a falsehood to be fought tooth and nail; no one must allow that to be said in his own city if it is to be well governed, no one must hear it, whether younger or older, no one must fable it whether in verse or in prose; such things if spoken are impious, dangerous for us and discordant in themselves. . . . God is the cause of the good things, not of all things. (2.379a–308c [Rouse])[49]

This effort to limit divine activity to the good was seen by philosophers like Plato as an endeavor to thwart ἀσέβεια. In addition, Socrates builds upon this renewed concept of deity by positing a perfection in the divine nature. He outlines his theory of divine perfection in a subsequent section:

Then everything which is in a good state, either by nature or by art or both, least admits change by something else. . . . [Yet,] God and what is God's is everywhere in a perfect state. . . . [Then] God would be least likely to take on many transformations. . . . Then it is impossible . . . that God should wish to alter himself. No, as it seems, each of [the gods], being the best and most beautiful possible, abides forever simply in his own form. . . . Well then, . . . the gods themselves cannot change. (2.380a–381d [Rouse])[50]

The presupposition here is that any change must be for the worse (degeneration). Plato maintains this view later in the *Laws*, book 10. In this work the argument is that God controls everything and is the measure of all things. The constant companion of the divine is justice. God moves the cosmos as a final cause by being the object of desire (893c–897b). This god of Platonic theology operates in strict conformity to rational laws. Moreover, God arranges everything with a view to the preservation and good of the whole.[51] In Plato one finds the rationale for later Hellenistic theology (the doctrine of divine perfection and the idea of divine benevolence).

The Hellenistic philosopher Cleanthes moved this type of theology to its logical conclusion in his *Hymn to Zeus*:

> Most glorious of immortals, honoured under many
>   names, all powerful forever,
> O Zeus, first cause of Nature, guiding all things through
>   law [νόμος],
> Hail! For it is just for all mortals to address you,

Since we were born of you, and we alone share in the
    likeness
Of deity, of all things that live and creep upon the earth.
So I will hymn you and sing always of your strength.
For all the cosmos, as it whirls around earth,
Obeys you, wherever you lead, and it is willingly ruled
    by you.
For such is the power you hold in your unconquerable
    hands:
The two-forked, fiery, ever-living thunderbolt.
For all the works of nature are accomplished through its
    blows,
By which you set right the common reason, which flows
Through everything, mixing divine light through things
    great and small.
Nothing is accomplished in this world save through you,
    O Spirit,
Neither in the divine, heavenly, ethereal sphere, nor
    upon the sea,
Save as much as the evil accomplish on their own
    ignorance.
But you are yet able to make the odd even,
And to order the disorderly, and to love the unloved.
For thus you have fit together into one all good things
    with the bad
So that they become one single, eternal harmony [λόγος].
They flee it, those among morals who are evil—
The ill-starred, they who always yearn for the possession
    of beautiful things
But never behold the divine universal law. Nor do they
    hear it,
Though if they harkened to it, using intelligence, they
    would have a fortunate life.
But in their ignorance they rush headlong into this or
    that evil:
Some pressing on in an aggressive search for popularity
    and renown,
Others in reckless pursuit of wealth, Others yet in
    laziness or in sensual pleasure. . . .
They are borne hither and thither,

All hastening to become the opposite of what they are.
Zeus the all-giver, wielder of the bright lightning in the
    dark clouds,
Deliver mankind from its miserable incompetence.
Father, disperse this from our soul; give us
Good judgment, trusting in you to guide all things in
    justice,
So that, in gaining honour we may repay you with
    honour,
Praising your works unceasingly, as is always fitting
For mortals. For there is no greater honour among men,
Nor among gods, than to sing forever in justice your
    universal law [νόμος]. (Cassidy)[52]

This hymnic prayer typifies the philosophical view of religion in a number of ways. First, the idea of divine monarchy is presented through the designation of Zeus as the one god "honoured under many names" (line 1). Second, the association of νόμος with Zeus reflects not only the archaic Greek understanding of Zeus as the guarantor of justice, but also the Stoic view that νόμος is at once the law of nature and pattern by which human lives should be governed. Since the universe is united in Zeus (lines 19–20), the νόμος is also the λόγος "which flows through everything" (lines 12–13). Thus, it is imperative that humans, who are in the likeness of Zeus (line 4), follow that νόμος and live in honor according to this divine and rational law of nature which is Zeus (lines 23–24, 34–35). Third, Zeus's thunderbolt, the symbol of his power, is seen as the creative force, the λόγος, which he uses to overcome heterogeneity and contradiction so "that they become one single, eternal harmony [λόγος]" (line 20). Fourth, evil is not the result of Zeus's activity; rather, it is the result of human ignorance (lines 16, 20–30). Fifth, knowledge is understood as the means of deliverance from evil (line 32). Finally, the *preces* of the prayer (line 32) is a request for no specific material thing, but it is a request for a knowledge that enables the human being to develop an ἦθος of honor that results in the offering of the proper gift desired by the deity, τιμή.

In conclusion, the philosophical critique of Greek cultic practice involved a number of theological changes that affected the Greek practice and understanding of prayer. Prayer still remained fundamental to Greek religion. However, philosophy sought to alter the understanding of the practice of prayer. The philosophers developed an idea of divine monarchy. Such a doctrine resulted in the Platonic idea of perfection. This perfection rested on two assumptions: (1) that it is possible to conceive of a meaning for "perfect" that excludes change in any and every respect, and (2) that one must conceive of the divine as perfect in just this sense. These assumptions became the building blocks of Hellenistic theology.

This concept of divinity set up the following course of reasoning about the deity: the god of Platonic philosophy, being defined as perfect in all respects, must be perfect in power (omnipotence). Thus, whatever happens—excluding evil—is divinely ordained to happen. Moreover, since God is unchangeably perfect, whatever happens must be eternally known to God (omniscience). God could not be "ignorant" (imperfect in knowledge). Human decisions and activities could not in any respect alter the divine life, because the divine is beyond change and, therefore, passion. Thus, the concern of the divinity for humanity—πρόνοια—cannot mean that God sympathizes with human plights. This would denote passion. Rather, God's concern for humanity is like the sun's way of doing good, which benefits the myriad forms of life on earth but receives no benefits from the good it produces (omnibenevolence). All of these changes put the question of the proper performance and function of prayer front and center.

The philosophical critique of classical Greek religion made the subject of petitionary prayer the attainment of moral or philosophical goods rather than material ones. The gods granted good "things" through their omnibenevolence, but one's request should not be for some concrete good. Reciprocity, as it was commonly understood, was no longer an operative principle.[53] The gods could not be propitiated through prayer and sacrifice. The intention behind the cultic act and its conformability to tradition became the primary criterion by which to judge its acceptability. This began a further discourse regarding the general righteousness of prayer and the nature of petition. To the disdain of the philosophers, however, the old religious ideas did not just melt away. H. S. Versnel lays out the problem created by the philosophical revolution well because he recognizes that δεισιδαιμονία survived and continued to challenge the increasing hegemony of the philosophical ideal:

> When all is said and done praying looks more difficult than one might have thought. It was not only the wise man who knew this, but also the simple believer who, as Artemidorus V,9 tells us, vows to Asclepius that, if he remains in health for a year, he will sacrifice a cock, and who makes another vow the next day that he will sacrifice another cock if he does not go blind. When Asclepius appears in a dream at night and says: εἷς μοι ἀλεκτρυὼν ἀρκεῖ he

is applying a criticism of prayer (and with the most horrible effect) which was normally reserved for philosophers. . . . We learn from the philosophers that we must pray to the gods for τά καλά τοῖς ἀγαθοῖς and leave it up to them to decide what that is and, negatively, that every other sort of prayer disregards divine providence and undermines morality. Epicurus puts it as follows: "If God were to grant all wishes and prayers, mankind would soon disappear from the face of the earth, so much evil are men for ever wishing on one another." A glance at *defixio* [enchantment] magic and prayers of revenge confirms the accuracy of this statement.[54]

A Roman Perspective

Roman religion was, by nature, conservative. Attempts have been made to make distinctions between Roman and Greek religion. Versnel tried to posit such a distinction when he said, "Greek gods 'live,' Roman gods 'work.'"[55] Yet, he admits he finds it difficult to distinguish between Greek and Roman prayer mentalities.[56] Heiler, using prayer as an example, made a distinction between Greek religion, which he understood as vital, and Roman religion, which he characterized as punctilious.[57] Finally, Georges Dumézil argued that Roman religion was more abstract than that of the Greeks.[58] It matters a great deal which form of Greek religion one compares to that of the Romans. If one compares the popular form of Greek piety with that of the Romans, little distinction can be made. However, if one compares popular Roman religion to that posited by the Greek philosophers, distinct theological differences become more obvious. Yet, such a distinction cannot be pushed too far. Ideas underwent change in Roman religion, as they did in Greek religion. This is especially true in the imperial period. Still, one finds a tendency in Roman religion to espouse ideas that reinforce identity formation through ancient practice (conceptions that reinforce Romanness). The apparent difference between Greek and Roman religion may be one of empiricism versus imagination, at least if one were to accept the general academic discourse on the matter.[59] Roman religion often appears more practical in its aim than its Greek counterpart.

The present discussion focuses on the time period beginning with the age of Augustus, regarded as a golden age for Roman civilization.[60] After a series of wars and other social uncertainties, Rome was reestablished with the advent of Gaius Julius Caesar Octavianus. After 27 BCE, this "Caesar

the Younger" was simply known as Augustus, the chief proponent of a
Roman religious revival. Such a feat led R. M. Ogilvie to assert that the "triumph of Rome is the triumph of religion."[61]

Prior to the Augustan Age, Roman writers say religion had declined
perceptibly. Romans neglected their religious duties. Priesthoods were left
unfulfilled. Temples were in disrepair. Ceremonies were omitted and
neglected. Horace drives home this point: "You will expiate the sins of
your ancestors, though you do not deserve to, citizen of Rome, until you
have rebuilt the temples and the ruined shrines of the gods and the images
fouled with black smoke" (*Carm.* 3.6.1–4 [Beard et al.]).[62] There is more
than enough evidence, however to be suspicious of such a view. As Mary
Beard and others make clear in their assessment of religion in the late
republic, the claim that religion fell apart is a gross exaggeration.[63] Rome
was not in a state of religious collapse but of social revolution:

> The nature of the Roman population changed dramatically in the
> course of this period, so that it becomes progressively more diffi-
> cult to define what it meant to be Roman, or to assess what the reli-
> gious traditions of Rome meant to the inhabitants of the city and
> of Roman Italy.[64]

Such disarray was the result of the rapid expansion of Rome, and the incor-
poration of non-Romans into the Roman social order. As Roman society
diversified, questions about Roman self-definition arose. Since religion was
a central component of that definition, it is not surprising that intellectuals
focused on it as a central concern of the period.[65] Rome was in need of a
savior who could renew its connection to its ancient gods, who could
reestablish the meaning of the term "Roman." But more than that, Rome
needed a leader who could impose order; and in the Roman mind, order
was intimately connected to religion. As Cicero makes quite clear: "Gods
are necessary to prevent chaos in society" (*Nat. d.* 1.3 [Rackham]).[66]

Augustus was instrumental in transforming the definition and understanding of Roman religion. "His success is to be measured by the fact that
Roman religion survived as a more or less vital force for another four hundred years and that Romans did recover their self-confidence."[67] This was
done in a number of steps. First, Augustus reconstructed the physical environment of Roman religion. As he says, "I rebuilt in my sixth consulship,
on the authority of the Senate, eighty-two temples and overlooked none
that needed repair" (*Res gest. divi Aug.* 20.4 [Beard]).[68] It is known that
Augustus made the surviving sons or descendants of original dedicators of

temples responsible for their upkeep and restoration. Livy credited Augustus for the "rebuilding of Rome in marble" and called him "the founder and restorer of every temple" (*Ab urbe condita libri* 4.20.7 [Beard]). Second, he again filled the chief priesthoods and "oiled" the rest of the Roman religious machinery. Third, he singled out Apollo and, to a lesser extent, Mars as objects of worship for the Roman people. Apollo became the figurehead of the new Augustan religious system: "Apollo epitomised everything that was new and young—and successful."[69] In the Augustan revival, Apollo and Mars represented gentle peace and just war.[70] Finally, Augustus focused attention on a figure, himself, in addition to a place, Rome, as a locus for religious attention.[71]

Roman religion was more concerned with what worked than it was with the speculative theology behind religious activities. Yet, this does not mean that there was no such thing as Roman theology. There was. Still, Roman religion was not as highly developed (in the sense of mythology and intellectual speculation) as that of the Greeks. Since this is true of Roman religion in general, it is most certainly true of efficacious and modified or discarded forms that were not as developed.[72] Some might hypothesize that Roman religion, because of its adherence to ancient formulary, would be intolerant of innovative religious practices. This was not entirely the case, as Dumézil makes clear.[73] In addition, some might want to call the Roman religious understanding "economic," in the sense that its basic significance is only practical. This does not, I believe, accurately describe Roman religion. While Roman religion was geared toward the practical, its so-called practicality was part of the overall structure of the Roman worldview. In reality, Roman religion was no more *practical* than Roman political and legal theory. All three were interrelated in the Roman mind, and religion cannot be adequately understood unless it is seen in relationship to political philosophy and legal theory.[74]

Prayer was much more than just a conversation with the deity in Roman religion. It was a technical matter. There had to be persons skilled in the composition, recitation, and performance of such prayers (religious professionals). The overall idea was the maintenance of the *pax deorum*.[75] As a consequence, religious professionals were an extremely important part of the religious machinery.

The religious professionals, the priests, were separated into four colleges: (1) the pontifical college, (2) the college of augurs, (3) the college of *quindecemviri sacris faciendis*, and (4) the college of *epulones*.[76] These persons were representatives of the most established Roman families.[77] At certain times, during certain cultic celebrations, the priests of individual deities (the *flamines*) offered appropriate prayers. At other times, especially when the ritual had to do with the entire state, a magistrate would speak the words of the prayer as dictated to him by a *pontifex*.[78] This need for religious professionals was undoubtedly due to the complex nature of Roman spirituality. The proper wordings of prayers used in the cult were preserved in *breviarii*, read on appropriate occasions. Some of these prayers were so archaic that the speakers themselves no longer understood them.[79] Prayers that had been collected by successive groups of priests were compiled into a manual called the *Commentaries of the Pontifices*. The *breviarii* were used especially when the question of proper procedure was in dispute.[80] At this point one begins to detect the relationship between Roman religion and Roman legal philosophy.[81] The importance of having the words of the ritual spoken in the correct order and at the correct time can be seen in this statement from Pliny the Elder:

> In fact a sacrifice without a prayer is thought to have no effect, or not to constitute a proper consultation of the gods. Besides, one kind of formula is used in seeking omens, another in averting evil, another for praise. We see too that senior magistrates make their prayers using a precise form of words: someone dictates the formula from a written text to ensure that no word is omitted or spoken in the wrong order; someone else is assigned as an overseer to check [what is spoken]; yet another man is given the task of ensuring silence; and a piper plays to prevent anything else but the prayer being audible. There are records of remarkable cases of both types of fault—when the actual sound of ill omens has spoilt the prayer, or when the prayer has been spoken wrongly. Then suddenly, as the victim stood there, its head [that is, a part of the liver] or heart has disappeared from the entrails, or alternatively a second head or heart has been produced. (Pliny the Elder, *Nat.* 28.2(3).10–11 [Beard])[82]

In short, Roman prayer was closely regulated by religious professionals whose duty was to make sure that *certa verba*, or at least *concepta verba*, were used in the performance of a ritual. Otherwise, a prayer lost its efficacy.[83] Philosophical Greek religion was concerned with such matters as language, also, but with a different aim in mind. Greek religion was concerned with the ἦθος of the orant, while Roman religion was interested in the *efficacy* of the linguistic and liturgical construction of the prayer. In other words, while both religions followed particular prayer forms, the emphasis in philosophical Greek religion fell primarily on the *performer* and in Roman religion on the *performance*.[84]

Roman religion was not focused on ethics. The ethical dimension of Roman life was found in the concept of *pietas*, which did have a connection to religion, although it was not seen as a virtue that religious dedication could cultivate. *Pietas* denoted, above all, conformity to normal, traditional, indisputable relationships.[85] For example, *pietas* was possessed by the Roman hero Aeneas and is exemplified in his abandoning Dido.[86] The *pius* (English: pious) person felt a commitment or sense of duty toward much more than just the gods.[87] For a good Roman, one's attitude toward the gods was inseparable from one's attitude toward the rest of life. In short, *pietas* denoted the scrupulous and conscientious attention to maintaining a proper relationship with others, whether human or divine.[88] The importance of *pietas* in Roman self-understanding should not be underestimated, at least on the part of the elites. It was the foundation of Roman civil order. "In all probability," wrote Cicero, "disappearance of piety towards the gods will entail the disappearance of loyalty and social union among men as well, and of justice itself, the queen of all virtues" (*Nat. d.* 1.4 [Rackham]).[89] One of the best and most interesting examples of *pietas* is told in the eulogy of a Roman woman. One of her acts of *pietas* was avenging the murder of her parents:

> The day before our wedding you were suddenly left an orphan when both your parents were murdered. Although I had gone to Macedonia and your sister's husband, Gaius Cluvius, had gone to the province of Africa, the murder of your parents did not remain unavenged. You carried out this act of piety with such great diligence—asking questions, making inquiries, demanding punishment—that if we had been there, we could not have done better. You and that very pious woman, your sister, share the credit for success. (*CIL* 6.1527, 31670 [*ILS* 8393] [Shelton])[90]

The Romans did not look to the gods to make them morally better. As Ogilvie says, "Roman religion was concerned with success not with sin."[91] The Roman psychological paradigm dictated that character was something fixed, given to one at birth. Nothing could ever *fundamentally* alter that character or the actions that flowed from it. At best, one could be shamed or coerced into acting contrary to one's *suum ingenium*, but it would never constitute a radical change of character. As Ogilvie makes clear, "Religion might make a man more humble, by showing up human weakness in comparison with the great powers of nature, but it would not convert him to a new way of life."[92] Thus, *pietas* was conceived somewhat differently in Roman religion as opposed to philosophical Greek religion. Whereas Greek religion was concerned with the ἦθος of the worshipper, Roman religion did not pursue such speculative notions regarding the character of the one performing the cultic act.[93]

Roman religion did differentiate between acceptable and unacceptable forms of religious practice.[94] On one hand, it did accept alternative forms of religious practice if they proved efficacious. On the other hand, the Romans had a term they used to designate religious practices considered unacceptable, *superstitio*. Of course, the application of the term did vary according to the person applying it.[95] This is evident in Cicero's *De natura deorum*, where he bases his distinction between religion and *superstitio* on etymology:

> Those who used to pray for whole days, and used to sacrifice, so that their children might be survivors of them [*superstites*], were called superstitious, which name afterwards extended more widely. But those who carefully reconsidered all things which belonged to the worship of the gods, and, as it were, re-read them, were said to be religious, from re-reading [*relegendo*]. . . . So it was brought about that, of the words "superstitious" and "religious," that one was the name of a defect and one of a merit. (2.72 [Rackham])[96]

It is not to be completely doubted that *superstitio* was connected to the idea of survival. However, it may be the case, as with Cicero, that it refers to an outmoded belief that survives among the ignorant. Some scholars believe that it may have meant "that which survives, or which causes to survive, by reason of its superiority in magic or in divination."[97] It appears that what Cicero is intimating here through *relegendo* is cultic *didachē*. In other words, being religious is a matter of carefully reconsidering the practices related to the cult. And so, Roman religion was not just a matter of mindlessly following ancient tradition, but of carefully considering cultic acts and their appropriateness with respect to divine worship.

The Ciceronian view of religion appears to have held that the natural order proves the existence of the divine. The historical gods of the Romans and others have been derived from a misunderstanding of what order really is. In *De natura deorum*, just before the passage quoted above, he says:

Do you see, therefore, how from natural things, well and usefully discovered, the reason has been drawn to fabricated and invented gods? And this has begotten false opinions, confused errors, and superstitions that are almost old wives tales. (2.70 [Rackham])[98]

During the imperial period, the most common and familiar understanding of *superstitio* was in reference to beliefs and practices that were foreign and strange to the Romans.[99] Of course, as with Cicero, what was "foreign" and "strange" depended on who was making the judgment. The Roman ruling class seemed to define as superstitious the kinds of religious practices and beliefs associated with the cults that had penetrated Roman culture from the outside. For example, the Roman leadership considered the religion of the Celts, the Germans, and the Egyptians to be superstitious. Judaism, although a *religio licita*, was also considered a *superstitio* by many pious Romans. For the Romans to say that a cult was a *superstitio* was not a matter of simple bias or ignorance.[100] To them, it was a matter of preserving efficacious religion from the possible infection of useless religious practices. The Romans had a strong religious sensibility, which entailed a number of social and cultic obligations and was connected to the idea of *pietas*. It meant loyalty to, among other things, the state, which encompassed not only military service and civic affairs, but also participation in religious processions and public banquets. There was no sharp separation in Roman thinking between the sacred and the secular. One's entire existence, along with the overall existence of the empire, was tied intimately to the proper performance of obligations.[101] *Superstitio* was not a matter of being *overly* religious (as with δεισιδαιμονία) but of not being properly religious.[102] It appears that in the mind of the imperialistic Roman, the cultic practices of the conquered could often be nothing more than *superstitio*. Not only were they foreign, they were also useless. That is, if the religion of the conquered were useful at all, they would not be the conquered. Such a view places the conqueror's religion at the forefront and diminishes the perceived validity of the religion of the conquered. As a consequence, one would expect Roman religion to be very ethnocentric or egoistic. In reality, Roman religion was ethnocentric, but the extent of its egoism is a matter of debate.

Egoism in prayer is difficult to determine with respect to Roman religiosity. Versnel points out what appear to be egoistic understandings and orientations in Roman prayer.[103] In fact, one could be led to believe that in prayer the Romans were concerned solely with themselves and their benefit—something severely criticized in philosophical Greek understandings of prayer. Yet, Versnel's claim can be challenged. Recalling that Roman prayers followed precise ancient formulae, the Romans were apt to preserve ancient formulary regardless of the actual theological intent behind the prayer. Phrases such as "me, my house, and my household" were considered obligatory language for prayer discourse. This muddles the idea of egoism, because one cannot be certain as to whether the orant intends to be as egoistic as the prayer sounds.[104] Second, Roman prayer was not *necessarily* concerned with the propitiation of the gods for good things as much as it was concerned with the request for favorable conditions.[105] In some cases, a Roman would pray for the avoidance of evil, but this more often was aimed at circumstances.[106] In a feat of cultic ingenuity, the Romans were able to pray for favorable conditions for themselves, unfavorable conditions for their enemies, and evoke the enemy's god at the same time (see Livy, *Ab urbe condita libri* 5.18.22). The Romans seemed to trust in their own ability to acquire good things as long as the powers of heaven were willing to keep the circumstances favorable. Thus, Roman prayer does not appear to succumb easily to the problem of egoism as long as one views it in the general context of Roman religion, which was definitely ethnocentric but not egoistic.[107]

Along with *pietas* and *superstitio*, another important religiopolitical technical term to be discussed is *auctoritas*. It is a quality associated with an *auctor*, "one who brings about the existence of any object, or promotes the increase or prosperity of it, whether he first originates it, or by his efforts gives greater permanence or continuance to it."[108] As such, it is an ontological concept, and it to be distinguished from two other important terms, *potestas* and *imperium*, both of which are phenomenal concepts related to the exercise of power.[109] *Auctoritas* was a quality of being that enabled its bearer to exercise decisive influence over others. In contrast to *potestas* and *imperium*, *auctoritas* did not need to be exercised for it to be real.[110] In Roman thought *auctoritas* was one of the means to determine the truth. It was often used in conjunction with *ratio*, at times one taking preeminence over the other.[111] Yet, *auctoritas* was a foundational and ubiquitous feature of the Roman cultural mind-set.

It was as a political concept that *auctoritas* gained its greatest significance. During the republic, the main bearer of *auctoritas* was the Senate.[112] As the Romans constructed their worldview during the Hannibalic war, the Senate acquired no new *imperium* or *potestas*; instead, its *auctoritas* grew. The historian Polybius addressed the extent of senatorial *auctoritas* in his discussion of the Roman republican machinery. He ended by saying, "[If] someone resided in Rome at a time when the consuls were absent, to him the constitution appears entirely aristocratic. And many Greeks and many kings are convinced of this, because the Senate handles almost all matters having to do with them" (*Historiae* 6.13 [Shelton]).[113]

One of the cultural notions that gave the Senate its *auctoritas* was the *mos maiorum*. The *maiores* (*majores*) were the founders and builders of the city. The prevailing belief was that if Rome were to prosper, it would do so through the guidance of the customs, rules, laws, ideas, and so on established by the *maiores*. The Senate provided the ideological link between the *maiores* and the present government of the city. The Senate assured the prolongation of the *traditio* of the founders. Stanley Kelley points out the real difference between philosophical Greeks and Romans with respect to this central notion of governance:

> Plato in establishing legitimacy for his state looked to the world of ideas while the Romans looked backwards to the historical act of the foundation of the city for the paradigm by which the city ought to be governed. . . . Unlike Plato, who placed his confidence in the power of reason which could be trusted to guide the state aright since reason and virtue are synonymous, the Romans put their trust in those who founded the city and the *patres* who guided it from the beginning.[114]

The *auctoritas* of the Senate was not based on a constitutional ability to compel obedience to its decrees (*potestas*), but on the cumulative influence of a number of public servants—coming from the most respectable families—whose judgments were seen as carrying greater weight than those of others. In fact, the ideology surrounding *auctoritas* made it an advantageous component in Roman social and political interactions.[115]

Auctoritas as Viewed through the Lens of Augustus

Augustus brought peace back to a city and empire that desperately sought an end to conflict. Some argue that what Augustus really did was to bring an end to Roman freedom. However, no "one wanted freedom if it only meant freedom to indulge in faction, misgovernment, and perhaps civil war."[116] Augustus stabilized the empire, and increased his own *auctoritas*, through an elaborate program of conferred and assumed powers.

As master of the Mediterranean world and "second founder" of the city of Rome, Augustus drew upon and elaborated distinct cultural ideas at his disposal, not all of them entirely traditional or Roman. Yet, he did this through an explicit ideological message of "restoration"—drawing distinctly upon the notion of *mos maiorum*. In 27 BCE he "restored" the old constitution of the republic, but only in outward appearance. In *Res gestae* he claimed that he transferred the state from his own control to the *arbitrium* of the Senate and the people of Rome.[117] In response, the Senate conferred upon him the designation Imperator Caesar Augustus.[118]

Being *imperator* was not, however, the public image Augustus (or several of the following emperors for that matter) tried to portray. Rather, he cast himself in the role of *princeps*. The title *augustus*, a term of vague religious dignity, was chosen by Octavian because it did not challenge the ancient aristocratic names of Rome. It was on a different, even higher, plane.[119] This cultivation of imperial image allowed Augustus to portray himself and his family as the quintessential Romans, which gave them an almost sacred air. Such an appearance was further enhanced by the erection of a golden shield inscribed with the four cardinal virtues attributed to Augustus—valor, clemency, justice, and piety.

In the mundane matter of the exercise of governmental power, Augustus was given a proconsular *imperium* greater than that given to those who governed the provinces left in the care of the Senate (see Dio Cassius, *Historiae Romanae* 53.12.1–3). Such *imperium* meant that in the imperial provinces Augustus' power was his at all times and in all matters. In the other provinces his will would prevail when and where he cared to assert it. In short, he had the first word in his provinces and the last word in all others. He controlled domestic policy through his position in the Senate. In fact, he was called *princeps senatus* and had the right of first speech in all matters. He had the ability to commend men for election as magistrates, an act that made their election a foregone conclusion. His Praetorian Guard functioned as an urban police force. He had the powers of a tribune, but he was not an equal of the annually elected tribunes; and they could not challenge him as an equal. He could prevent any tribune or group of tribunes from doing anything he did not wish them to do. It was an impressive and unprecedented array of powers. Yet, Augustus claimed that he only exceeded others in his *auctoritas*. In the Augustan Principate, the Senate functioned as the junior partner in the governance of the empire, and its *auctoritas* passed to Augustus.[120]

The cultivation of the *auctoritas* of Augustus was also translated into the introduction of the ruler cult. It was Augustus' way of "cementing" and Romanizing the empire.[121] In the eastern part of the empire it was a rather common practice to acknowledge monarchs as benefactors and saviors. For example, Alexander the Great was valorized in such a manner after his eastern conquests. Augustus was viewed as a savior, and he definitely promoted himself as such. Yet, the first indication we have of the apotheosis of a Roman leader was the deification of Julius Caesar (*Divus Iulius*) by proclamation of the Senate.[122] The ruler cult was beneficial to imperial governance and helped garner the loyalty of the provincials. In addition, the Augustan acquisition of the major priestly offices firmly established him as the head and focus of Roman religion.[123] People paid homage to Augustus not necessarily because of his ontic status; rather, they worshipped what Augustus did (past, present, and possible future beneficence); and so it was with all the emperors. In sum, the *auctoritas* of Augustus derived from his role as restorer of the Roman order, as savior and benefactor of the empire. The valorization of the individual with the power to effect order and peace, exemplified most eminently in the cultivation of the image of Augustus, coincided well with the ideas regarding divine monarchy being developed in philosophical circles. The emperor became the earthly exemplar of the divine monarchy. Augustus and later emperors developed this idea of the "divine" individual as a means of further enhancing imperial *auctoritas*. One finds manifestations of various components of this Augustan revolution in thought in a number of religious contexts in antiquity, including Christianity. This will become most manifest in our discussion of Tertullian. In sum, *auctoritas* was an important component in the Roman worldview, and as such it became a fundamental aspect of Roman religious development.

A Roman Perspective on Prayer

As mentioned earlier, Roman prayer appears to be similar to legal diction. This was because prayer was seen as a technical matter. It had to be precise in order to be effective. Thus, the various components of prayer were carefully constructed. First, one had to know how to invoke the god. In other words, "Gods, like dogs, will only answer to their names."[124] If one knew the name of the god, one could compel the god to listen. Also, one had to know which god to invoke. Calling upon the wrong deity could result in failure. Varro makes this evident in a statement quoted by Augustine: "We will be able to know what god we should invoke in every circumstance so that we don't behave like comedians who pray for water from Bacchus and for wine from the Nymphs" (*Civ.* 4.22 [Dods]).[125]

It was the duty of the pontifical college to compile *indigitamenta* or invocations for use on any and every occasion.[126] It is reputed that some gods had names that were never spoken. These divinities were called *nefandi*, unmentionable. In addition, the use of a *cognomen* was popular in Roman religion.[127] For example, in his prayer to Diana, Catullus invokes her by calling her Latona's daughter.[128] In Roman theology, the invocation of a divinity was intimately related to the activity of the god in a particular area, and the *cognomen* served as a way of alluding to that activity.[129] A good example of Roman prayer is the one attributed to Scipio Africanus:

> You gods and goddesses, who inhabit the seas and lands, I pray and beseech you that those deeds, which under my command have been accomplished, are being accomplished and will afterwards be accomplished, may turn out favourably and that you may prosper them all and cause them to succeed for myself, for the Roman nation, for the allies, and for the Latin peoples who follow the lead, command and authority of the Roman people and of myself on land, sea and rivers. I pray that you may preserve us safe and unharmed by the conquered enemy and that as conquerors together with me these soldiers may return home in triumph adorned with spoils and laden with loot. Grant us the opportunity to avenge our enemies, personal and public. And whatever the Carthaginian people have attempted to do to our state, grant me and the Roman people the ability to do to the Carthaginian state as an example. (Livy, *Ab urbe condita libri* 29.27.2–4 [Hickson-Hahn])[130]

The invocation here is vague, addressed simply to gods and goddesses. Yet, this prayer is appropriate because it is addressed to all the deities who control the land and seas. In the Roman mind, such an invocation is fitting because some of the deities who control the land and sea are known, but others may exist who are unknown. It was the unknown component in invocation that concerned the Romans. Consequently, they sought to employ language that diminished the possibility of the god not hearing or responding to the request.

In order to guarantee the god's response and to avoid possible misidentification, the Romans often employed two techniques. First, they listed all the known *cognomina* and epithets of the god. For example, Catullus invokes the aid of Diana by saying, "You are called Juno Lucina by women in childbirth, you are called nightly Trivia, and Luna whose light is not your own."[131] Second, the Romans added at the end of the invocation a blanket expression such as "or whatever name you care to be called." The *pontifices* had a rule always to invoke all the gods after individual invocations.[132] This technique is also visible in the famous phrase *sive deus sive dea.*[133] Catullus's invocation of Diana further drives home this point. He adds the words "by whatever name you please, be hallowed."

The *pars epica* of the prayer sought to convince the god that the request was a reasonable one. The rationale behind this seems to have been that, if done properly, the god would find the request acceptable based on established norms of behavior. The two most common rationales used were that (1) the god had granted such a request in the past, or (2) it was clearly in the competence of this particular deity to grant this request. In the prayer attributed to Scipio Africanus, the rationale was that the gods being invoked had the ability to provide favorable conditions for the Romans. In the prayer to Diana, she is identified as being in control of such things as childbirth and agricultural production. The operative principle seems to have been precedent. Such is evident in the prayer of Augustus at the Secular Games:

> At is has been written in these books for you, for those reasons, and it may be better for the Roman people, the Quirites, so may the rite be performed for you [with specified victims and offerings]. I ask and pray you that, as you have increased the sovereignty and majesty of the Roman people of Quirites, at war and at home, and as the Latin has always been submissive, you may grant to the Roman people, the Quirites, eternal safety, victory, and health, and that you may favor the Roman people of Quirites and the legions of the Roman people of Quirites, and may keep safe the common wealth of the Roman people of Quirites, and may willingly be propitious to the Roman people of Quirites, to the college of the Fifteen, and to me, my house, and my family, and that you may be acceptors of this sacrifice. (Pinsent)[134]

This prayer, performed during the celebration of the gods' benevolence, asks for the continuance of benevolence—a benevolence that had been long-standing since these rites were contained in the *breviarii.*

After the *pars epica*, the prayer naturally moved to the *preces*. Some scholars have argued that Roman prayer was fundamentally petitionary.[135] The validity of that assertion, however, depends on the definition of petition. If one looks at the issue philologically, then Augustus' prayer is fundamentally petitionary. Likewise, if one defines it simply as asking for something, then Roman prayer most likely qualifies as petitionary. However, if one understands petition as requesting something particular for oneself (or others), then Roman prayer rarely qualifies. Further, if the definition involves asking for something material, then Roman prayer is almost never petitionary. Definition and interpretation are key elements in such an analysis. For example, Scipio Africanus asked for benevolence from the gods. The prayers of Augustus and Catullus asked for a continuance of benevolence—a benevolence that had been granted by the gods for a long time. As mentioned earlier, the Romans were not as concerned with the accumulation of good things as they were with the maintenance of favorable conditions. At times an orant might ask the god to deflect an evil and send it to someone else. For example, on one occasion Catullus prays, "May your frenzy never come near my house, goddess; excite others, make others mad."[136] However, this is not the general spirit of prayer in the imperial period.[137] In general, Roman prayers of this period sought out favorable circumstances rather than specific favorable acts. Still, even favorable conditions can lead to interesting outcomes, and the Romans knew that.

The Romans sought to word their petitions as to cover every conceivable possibility. For instance, in the following prayer from the Spanish province, the orant is not absolutely sure whether his clothing was stolen or borrowed. Also, his request is vague—revenge the theft and punish with a terrible death—because precisely what "revenge" and "terrible death" entail are not explicit. He says:

> Goddess Proserpine Ataecina who inhabit the town of Turobriga, I beg, pray and beseech you by your majesty to revenge the theft that has been committed against me and to [punish with a terrible death] whoever has borrowed, stolen or made away with the articles listed below: six tunics, two cloaks. (*AE* 1975, 497 [Faraone and Obbink])[138]

In sum, traditional Roman prayer was founded on a different conceptual basis than philosophical Greek prayer. Although both traditions used prayer in their rituals, the Romans were concerned with issues other than those pursued by the Greek philosophers. The Romans petitioned the gods for conditions favorable for their advancement, while the Greek philosophers believed that petition should be concerned with the acquisition of the good. To the philosophers, this meant petitioning for τὰ δίκαια δύνασθαι πρήσσειν. However, Roman theological anthropology did not allow for such a conception of character. Prayer had to do with addressing the proper deity, in the proper verbiage, at the appropriate time. Nevertheless, they end up being quite congruent in the ends they pursued.

Εὐσέβεια was important in Greek philosophy and its understanding of the proper conditions for prayer. Again, this had to do with the ἦθος of the orant. Εὐσέβεια made the prayer acceptable to the god. This was not the case with Roman prayer. *Pietas* to the Romans had more to do with the modern concept of duty than it did with the ἦθος of the individual. The efficacy of a prayer had little to do with one's morality, nor did determining the actual *intention* of the ancestors greatly effect the discussion. That is, determining what the ancestors had in mind when establishing the cultic *traditio* was important. Following the practices of the ancestors was more important because their actions set the course for Roman imperialism. Yet, determining what they exactly had in mind at the institution of certain cultic practices was not a concern one finds at the center of Roman discourse. The same was true of the concept of *auctoritas*. Although it was an idea that surely had connections to the preservation of Roman ritual, one's *auctoritas* was not the basis upon which one's prayers became efficacious. Moreover, what the Romans would call *superstitio* was not the same as what the Greek philosophers would deem δεισιδαιμονία. It appears that the Greeks would have seen Roman religion as δεισιδαιμονία, while the Romans would have seen the Greek philosophers as somewhat *superstitiosus*. This being said, Roman religion adhered to the scrupulous observance of efficacious ritual.

Roman religion was rooted in ritual and language. Its theology was expressed in its rituals. Therefore, the speculative element of Roman spirituality was much less developed than that of philosophical Greek religion, where theological speculation was the heart of the matter. This is why, although they do appear to exist, cultic *didachai* are rare in Roman religion. As conquerors of the Mediterranean world, the Romans had found the most efficacious form of religious practice. It was in line with the *traditio* of the ancestors and guaranteed them their preeminent position among the nations. Both religious traditions maintained some notion of reciprocity. To the Romans, the *venia* (favor) of the gods was solicited by the worshipper, and the *pax deorum* was considered a benefit surpassing anything that might be specified in any contract for a particular act. It was, at base, *do ut des*. Still, the Roman maintained a dignified and trusting relationship with the gods. Prayer was couched in precise and exact language so that the gods could not fail to know what was requested. Prayer was part of a partnership between humanity and the gods. In order for such a partnership to be effective, both sides needed to be clear as to their abilities and obligations.

This is why precision was important for Roman prayer. It insured clarity. As Beard and others state quite succinctly: "[The gods] were bound only in one sense, that is that they would accept as sufficient exactly what they were offered—no more, no less."[139]

Notes

1. Joint Association of Classical Teachers, ed., *The World of Athens: An Introduction to Classical Athenian Culture* (Cambridge: Cambridge University Press, 1984), 288–90.

2. Ibid., 299.

3. Mark Kiley, ed., *Prayer from Alexander to Constantine: A Critical Anthology* (New York: Routledge, 1997), 2.

4. Cf. Bonnie Bowman Thurston, *Spiritual Life in the Early Church: The Witness of Acts and Ephesians* (Minneapolis: Fortress, 1993), 10–12.

5. Friedrich Heiler, *Prayer: A Study in the History and Psychology of Religion* (2d ed.; ed. Samuel McComb; New York: Oxford University Press, 1933), 87–88. The English edition is only a partial translation of the German: *Das Gebet: Eine religionsgeschichtliche und religionspsychologische Untersuchung* (2d ed.; Munich: Reinhardt, 1920; 5th ed.; 1923).

6. Robert M. Grant, *Gods and the One God* (ed. Wayne A. Meeks; Library of Early Christianity 1; Philadelphia: Westminster, 1986), 75.

7. Teachers, *World of Athens*, 89–90, 107.

8. Ibid., 142–44.

9. Ibid., 107.

10. Theophrastus, *Peri eusebeias: Griechischer Text* (ed. and trans. W. Pötscher; Leiden: Brill, 1964).

11. H. S. Versnel, ed., *Faith, Hope and Worship: Aspects of Religious Mentality in the Ancient World* (Studies in Greek and Roman Religion 2; Leiden: Brill, 1981), 223–24.

12. Ibid., 234.

13. Ibid., 233.

14. Teachers, *World of Athens*, 89–90.

15. Plutarch, *Plutarch's Moralia* (trans. Frank Cole Babbitt; 15 vols.; Loeb Classical Library; New York: Putnam, 1927), 2:457.

16. Plato, *Five Dialogues: Euthyphro, Apology, Crito, Meno, Phaedo* (trans. G. M. A. Grube; Indianapolis: Hackett, 1981), 32.

17. A. A. Long and D. N. Sedley, eds., *The Hellenistic Philosophers* (2 vols.; Cambridge: Cambridge University Press, 1987), 1:22c.

18. Plutarch, *Plutarch's Moralia*, 2:489.

19. E.g., Teachers, *World of Athens*, 282–96.

20. Versnel, *Faith, Hope and Worship*, 259.

21. Ibid., 259–60, 61.

22. Jon D. Mikalson, *Athenian Popular Religion* (Chapel Hill: University of North Carolina Press, 1983), 45; Versnel, *Faith, Hope and Worship*, 246.

23. Mikalson, *Athenian Popular Religion*, 101.

24. Ibid., 103.

25. Ibid.

26. How the Greeks may have understood the issue of fidelity to the practices of their ancestors is not the object of the discussion here. The idea of change and development is endemic to the historiographical process. The issue is whether they *believed* themselves to be faithful to those practices. On the process of history writing in this regard, see Edward Hallett Carr, *What Is History?* (The George Macaulay Trevelyan Lectures Delivered at the University of Cambridge, January–March, 1961; New York: Knopf, 1972), 144–76.

27. Hans Dieter Betz, *The Sermon on the Mount : A Commentary on the Sermon on the Mount, Including the Sermon on the Plain (Matthew 5:3–7:27 and Luke 6:20–49)* (ed. Adela Yarbro Collins; Hermeneia—A Critical and Historical Commentary on the Bible; Minneapolis: Fortress, 1995), 332.

28. Versnel, *Faith, Hope and Worship*, 233; cf. Thurston, *Spiritual Life*, 14.

29. Versnel, *Faith, Hope and Worship*, 246.

30. Ibid.

31. Ibid., 253.

32. Ibid., 233–35. Cleanthes's hymnic prayer to Zeus is an exception to this rule. For a definition of *invocatio* and *pars epica*, see Versnel, *Faith, Hope and Worship*, 2.

33. For a definition of *preces*, see Versnel, *Faith, Hope and Worship*, 2.

34. Versnel, *Faith, Hope and Worship*, 234.

35. Ibid., 235.

36. For more information on this issue, see Terence Irwin, *Plato's Moral Theory: The Early and Middle Dialogues* (Oxford: Oxford University Press, 1977), 53, 224–26.

37. Xenophon, *Xenophon in Seven Volumes* (ed. G. P. Goold; trans. E. C. Marchant; vol. 4; Loeb Classical Library; Cambridge: Harvard University Press, 1929), 45.

38. Plato, *Five Dialogues*, 154.

39. For more information, see D. Clay, "Socrates' Prayer to Pan," in *Arktouros: Hellenic Studies Presented to Bernard M. W. Knox on the Occasion of His 65th Birthday* (ed. B. M. W. Knox; Berlin: W. de Gruyter, 1979), 345–53.

40. E.g., Lucius Annaeus Cornutus, *Theologiae Graecae compendium* 16: "Hermes is rational speech (*logos*), which the gods sent to us out of heaven, Man alone of all living beings that they made on the earth being endowed with reason—the thing which they themselves possessed in transcendent degree" (via Edwin R. Bevan, *Later Greek Religion* [New York: E. P. Dunn & Co., 1927], 103).

41. Clay, "Socrates' Prayer to Pan."

42. Heiler, *Prayer*, 89.

43. Translation from Teachers, *World of Athens*, 282; cf. Grant, *Gods and the One God*, 76–77.

44. Grant, *Gods and the One God*, 76.

45. Ibid.

46. Versnel, *Faith, Hope and Worship*, 221.

47. Ibid.

48. Xenophon, *Xenophon in Seven Volumes*, 4:55, 57.

49. Plato, *Great Dialogues of Plato* (ed. Eric H. Warmington and Philip G. Rouse; trans. W. H. D. Rouse; New York: Penguin, 1956), 176–78.

50. Ibid., 179–80.

51. For more information, see R. F. Stalley, *An Introduction to Plato's Laws* (Indianapolis: Hackett, 1983), 166–78.

52. Kiley, *Prayer from Alexander to Constantine*, 135–36.

53. Cf. Versnel, who says that reciprocity was the operative principle in Roman religion (*Faith, Hope and Worship*, 41–42).

54. Ibid., 25.

55. Ibid., 16.

56. Ibid., 10.

57. Heiler, *Prayer*, 78.

58. Georges Dumézil, *Archaic Roman Religion, with an Appendix on the Religion of the Etruscans* (trans. Philip Krapp; 2 vols.; Chicago: University of Chicago Press, 1970), 1:32.

59. E.g., John Pinsent, "Roman Spirituality," in *Classical Mediterranean Spirituality: Egyptian, Greek, Roman* (ed. A. H. Armstrong; World Spirituality: An Encyclopedic History of the Religious Quest; New York: Crossroad, 1986).

60. Charles Norris Cochrane, *Christianity and Classical Culture: A Study of Thought and Action from Augustus to Augustine* (New York: Oxford University Press, 1957), 1–26; Chester G. Starr, *The Ancient Romans* (New York: Oxford University Press, 1971), 86–114.

61. R. M. Ogilvie, *The Romans and Their Gods in the Age of Augustus* (ed., M. I. Finley; Ancient Culture and Society; London: Chatto & Windus, 1969), 113; Alan Watson, *The State, Law, and Religion: Pagan Rome* (Athens, Ga.: University of Georgia Press, 1992), 4–13.

62. Mary Beard et al., *Religions of Rome* (2 vols.; Cambridge: Cambridge University Press, 1998), 1:118.

63. Ibid., 1:124.

64. Ibid., 1:75.

65. Ibid., 1:120, 166.

66. Marcus Tullius Cicero, *De natura deorum; Academica* (trans. H. Rackham; New York: G. P. Putnam's Sons, 1933).

67. Ogilvie, *Romans and Their Gods*, 113; Pinsent, "Roman Spirituality," 187.

68. Beard, *Religions of Rome*.

69. Ogilvie, *Romans*, 115; Beard, *Religions of Rome*, 1:198–201.

70. Ogilvie, *Romans and Their Gods*, 116.

71. Beard, *Religions of Rome*, 1:186.

72. Pinsent, "Roman Spirituality," 155–64, gives a fuller understanding of the idea; cf. Heiler, *Prayer*, 66; Watson, *State, Law, and Religion*, 30–38.

73. Dumézil, *Archaic Roman Religion*, 14; Pinsent, "Roman Spirituality," 171; Thurston, *Spiritual Life*, 17–18.

74. Alan Wardman, *Religion and Statecraft among the Romans* (Baltimore: John Hopkins University Press, 1982), 1–21, 63–107; cf. Watson, *State, Law, and Religion*, 32–38.

75. Frances V. Hickson, *Roman Prayer Language: Livy and the Aneid of Vergil* (Stuttgart: Teubner, 1993), 1; cf. Pinsent, "Roman Spirituality," 157.

76. Beard, *Religions of Rome*, 1:18; Ogilvie, *Romans and Their Gods*, 106–11.

77. Beard, *Religions of Rome*, 103–4.

78. This procedure was called *praeireverba*, "to anticipate the words" (Ogilvie, *Romans and Their Gods*, 35); cf. Heiler, *Prayer*, 66–67; Wardman, *Religion and Statecraft*, 13, 16–21; Watson, *State, Law, and Religion*, 51–54, 63–72.

79. Heiler, *Prayer*, 67; Pinsent, "Roman Spirituality," 156–57.

80. Hickson, *Roman Prayer Language*, 7–8; Ogilvie, *Romans and Their Gods*, 107.

81. Heiler, *Prayer*, 10 n. 5, 72; Hickson, *Roman Prayer Language*, 7–8; Ogilvie, *Romans and Their Gods*, 35.

82. Beard, *Religions of Rome*, 2:129.

83. Heiler, *Prayer*, 67; Hickson, *Roman Prayer Language*, 7–8.

84. Ogilvie, *Romans and Their Gods*, 36; Jo-Ann Shelton, ed., *As the Romans Did: A Sourcebook in Roman Social History* (New York: Oxford University Press, 1998), 372–73. For a negative view of such rites, see Heiler, *Prayer*, 69.

85. Dumézil, *Archaic Roman Religion*, 133; Pinsent, "Roman Spirituality," 168; Wardman, *Religion and Statecraft*, 83; Robert L. Wilkin, *The Christians as the Romans Saw Them* (New Haven: Yale University Press, 1984), 56.

86. Pinsent, "Roman Spirituality," 170–71.

87. Dumézil, *Archaic Roman Religion*, 132; Wardman, *Religion and Statecraft*, 110.

88. Cochrane, *Christianity and Classical Culture*, 46–47, 51–52.

89. Cicero, *De natura deorum; Academica*.

90. The entire eulogy can be found in Shelton, *As the Romans Did*, 293–96; cf. F. E. Adcock, *Roman Political Ideas and Practice* (Ann Arbor: University of Michigan Press, 1959), 15–17.

91. Ogilvie, *Romans and Their Gods*, 17; Cochrane, *Christianity and Classical Culture*, 35; Wardman, *Religion and Statecraft*, 62.

92. Ogilvie, *Romans and Their Gods*, 18.

93. Ogilvie says, "[There] is practically no evidence from the Augustan period or earlier to suggest that your chances of conciliating the gods depended upon your moral character. There were prescribed methods of treating with the gods which had been proved efficacious by experience, but, provided that you followed them scrupulously, it did not matter whether you were yourself good or bad or whether your prayers were for worthy ends. Prayers will be heard if they are correctly formulated rather than if they come from a penitent and unselfish heart" (ibid., 19).

94. Wardman, *Religion and Statecraft*, 62–63; Watson, *State, Law, and Religion*, 58–62.

95. Pinsent, "Roman Spirituality," 167.

96. Cicero, *De natura deorum; Academica*.

97. Pinsent, "Roman Spirituality," 162.

98. Cicero, *De natura deorum; Academica*.

99. Wardman, *Religion and Statecraft*, 162–68.

100. Wilkin, *Christians as the Romans Saw Them*, 51, with more discussion on 48–54.

101. Cochrane, *Christianity and Classical Culture*, 40–42, 44–45; Pinsent, "Roman Spirituality," 155, 91.

102. Pinsent, "Roman Spirituality," 157.

103. Versnel, *Faith, Hope and Worship*, 18.

104. Cf. Cochrane, *Christianity and Classical Culture*, 46, 55.

105. Hickson, *Roman Prayer Language*, 62–63.

106. Ogilvie, *Romans and Their Gods*, 32–33.

107. Cf. Cochrane, *Christianity and Classical Culture*, 31.

108. Stanley H. Kelley, "*Auctoritas* in Tertullian: The Nature and Order of Authority in His Thought" (Ph.D. diss., Emory University, 1974), 25.

109. For example, "*Potestas* is related to the office or position one holds and says nothing about the nature or character of the holder" (ibid., 50).

110. Richard Heinze, "*Auctoritas*," in *Vom Geist des Römertums: Ausgewählte Aufsätze* (ed. E. Burck; 3d ed.; Stuttgart: Teubner, 1960), 48.

111. Kelley, "*Auctoritas* in Tertullian," 40.

112. Adcock, *Roman Political Ideas and Practice*, 36–37.

113. Shelton, *As the Romans Did*, 226–27.

114. Kelley, "*Auctoritas* in Tertullian," 46–47. While the Roman concept of authority was ontological in that it inhered in the character or being of those who possessed it, nevertheless it was historical in that the Romans looked to their ancestors and to the city's course of development for the *auctoritas* necessary to insure the well-being of the city. What we have with the Romans is an ontological history that should be contrasted with the pure ontology of Plato's theory. *Auctoritas* inheres in the Senate but only as delegated through history from its original source. In this distinction one can begin to detect the ideological differences that crop up between Tertullian and Clement.

115. Ibid., 50.

116. Adcock, *Roman Political Ideas and Practice*, 75.

117. Ibid., 74.

118. Dio Cassius says in *Historiae Romanae* 17.1–11: "The name Augustus was bestowed upon him by the Senate and the people. They wanted to address him by some special name, and while they were proposing one name or another, and deciding on it, Caesar was extremely eager to be called Romulus. When he perceived, however, that people therefore suspected him of yearning for a position as king, he no longer sought this title, but instead accepted the title Augustus, as if he were somewhat more than human; for everything that is most valuable and most sacred is called augustus" (Shelton, *As the Romans Did*, 232–33); cf. the discussion in Beard, *Religions of Rome*, 1:182–83.

119. Dumézil defines *augustus* as "the person or thing endowed with the 'fullness of mystical power'" (*Archaic Roman Religion*, 1:130).

120. Adcock, *Roman Political Ideas and Practice*, 80.

121. Ibid., 86–87; Cochrane, *Christianity And Classical Culture*, 25–26; Ogilvie, *Romans And Their Gods*, 116–23; Pinsent, "Roman Spirituality," 157, 88; Paul Zanker, *The Power Of Images In The Age Of Augustus* (ed. Alan Shapiro; Jerome Lectures 16; Ann Arbor: University Of Michigan Press, 1988), 33–77.

122. From Egypt we have an idea of how this deification was proclaimed. This particular decree was given on the occasion of Trajan's death and the accession of Hadrian: "In white-horsed chariot I have mounted with Trajan to the heavens, whence come I now again to you, O my people, I, not unknown to you, the god Phoebus Apollo, and proclaim unto you the new lord Hadrian. To him be all things happily subject, alike by reason of his virtue and for the blessed fortune of his divine father. Wherefore sacrificing let us light the hearths, refreshing our souls with laughter, intoxicating drinks from the fountain, and ointments of the gymnasium, the whole whereof is furnished to you by the governor's piety toward his master and by his own love for you besides" (Ramsay MacMullen, *Roman Social Relations, 50 B.C. to A.D. 284* [New Haven: Yale University Press, 1974], 77–78); John Ferguson, ed., *Greek and Roman Religion: A Sourcebook* (Noyes Classical Studies; Park Ridge, NJ: Noyes, 1980), 67–73.

123. Beard, *Religions of Rome*, 1:186–92, esp. 92; Adcock, *Roman Political Ideas and Practice*, 87.

124. Ogilvie, *Romans and Their Gods*, 24.

125. Augustine, *The City of God* (trans. Marcus Dods; New York: Modern Library, 1950).

126. Pinsent, "Roman Spirituality," 179, 81.

127. Iiro Kajanto, *The Latin Cognomina* (Commentationes humanarum litterarum; Rome: G. Bretschneider Editore, 1982), esp. 57–62.

128. Kiley, *Prayer from Alexander to Constantine*, 140.

129. Dumézil, *Archaic Roman Religion*, 45.

130. Kiley, *Prayer from Alexander to Constantine*, 152–53.

131. Quoted in Ogilvie, *Romans and Their Gods*, 26.

132. Ibid., 28–29.

133. Dumézil, *Archaic Roman Religion*, 39–48; Hickson, *Roman Prayer Language*, 8–10, 33–34; Ogilvie, *Romans and Their Gods*, 26–28.

134. Quoted in Pinsent, "Roman Spirituality," 160. Cf. Ogilvie, *Romans and Their Gods*, 31–32.

135. E.g., Hickson, *Roman Prayer Language*, 4.

136. Quoted in Ogilvie, *Romans and Their Gods*, 33.

137. Ibid.

138. Christopher A. Faraone and Dirk Obbink, eds., *Magika Hiera: Ancient Greek Magic and Religion* (New York: Oxford University Press, 1991).

139. Beard, *Religions of Rome*, 1:34.

3

The Tableau of Roman Alexandria

Aegyptum imperio populi Romani adieci.
—Augustus (*Res gest. divi Aug.* 27)

Peering through a Stained-Glass Window

The first two chapters served as an overview of early Christian and Greco-Roman understandings of religion and prayer. The lens through which we examined the LP was that of an imagined Greco-Roman auditor. The purpose was to provide a context within which to discuss Clement of Alexandria and Tertullian of Carthage. As in any brief overview, there was much that was left out. Of course, more could have been said regarding other aspects of the religious context of the Roman imperial period (such as the mystery religions or the *collegia*). Still, the purpose of the overview was to focus on the fundamental religious perspectives found among certain types of Greeks and Romans. Since the rest of the book focuses on the particular religious orientations of two distinct Christian writers, the limitation of the discussion serves to highlight ideas that are particularly relevant to Clement and Tertullian.

The early Christian movement is difficult to categorize in terms of institutional development. In fact, Christians themselves were at pains to clarify the contours of the organization. Christian authors proposed various images, and some even proposed multiple images, for conceiving of the communal entity called the ἐκκλησία—this word itself functioning as a technical term for the organization of persons worshiping Christ. Unfortunately, there was no uniform understanding of the ἐκκλησία among early Christians, nor does one find such an understanding among their critics.[1] Orthodox understandings of the church and its practices, although emerging and developing in this period, did not become fixed until much later. Thus, sensitivity to the particular context of each emerging community must be exercised so that their distinctive voices and theological models can be appreciated fully. What may have been deemed heterodox in one context was simply Christianity in another.

As it currently stands, Clement of Alexandria provides scholars with the first postbiblical Christian analysis of prayer.[2] Clement's relationship to the LP is important because it demonstrates how one Christian writer understood and applied his theology of prayer within a particular ethnoreligious context. To understand this key Greco-Christian understanding of prayer, it is important to examine several key areas. Foremost, Clement must be placed in his historical context, and this is the primary purpose of this chapter. It will examine Greco-Roman Egypt and the origins of the Alexandrian church. The goal behind this examination is to obtain an elementary understanding of the Alexandrian context prior to and during the second century CE. A key part of this analysis will involve looking at the interactions of various ethnoreligious groups throughout the period and across the province that give us potential insight into how Alexandrian Christians related to their world. Greco-Roman Egyptian society was complex. Individuals frequently had multiple loyalties cutting across various social categories. Appreciating the complexity of these relationships is paramount to any adequate analysis of the development of Christianity in Alexandria. Appreciation of this matter is also important because part of the rationale behind Clement's writing program is to uphold Christian orthodoxy, as he perceives it, against others who also defined themselves as "Christian."

A lack of appreciation for the complexity of the church's development had led some to conclude that it was started among gnostics. Such a thesis lacks grounding in the historical context. The positing of a gnostic origin for Alexandrian Christianity only serves to distance it from the significant Jewish population that occupied Alexandria before 115 CE. As in other places evangelized by Christian missionaries, the Alexandrian Jewish community serves as the most likely context from which Christianity emerged in the city. Our sources on the matter indicate that among privileged Jews a distinctive understanding of Judaism emerged. In contrast to other diasporic Jewish communities, Alexandrian Jews appear to have been constructively engaged and conversant with the intellectual context of the larger Greco-Roman environment in which they lived. This dialogue is best illustrated in the writings that emerged from this community itself. Alexandrian Christians were the ones to preserve these writings. Thus, Clement's reception and use of this Hellenistic understanding of Judaism makes much more sense if the Alexandrian church had historic ties to the

Jewish community. This chapter will end by doing a partial reconstruction of the Alexandrian Christians as a distinct ethnoreligious group.

Egyptian Glass, Greek Coloring, and a Roman Stain

Alexander the Great died in 323 BCE. Soon after his death, his generals divided up the provinces of his empire. Egypt, which contained the only city Alexander founded west of the Tigris, was given to Ptolemy.

> Ptolemy the son of Lagus was appointed to govern Egypt and Libya and those of the lands of the Arabs that were contiguous to Egypt; and Cleomenes, who had been made governor of this satrapy by Alexander, was subordinated to Ptolemy. (Arrian, *Events after Alexander, FGH*, 156F1, 5)[3]

Ptolemy quickly eliminated Cleomenes. At that point he inaugurated one of the most important dynasties of the Hellenistic period (305–30 BCE) and one of the most productive areas ever known in the ancient Near East. This was a fact that remained true some three hundred years later when Antony took control of the eastern half of the Roman Empire, the half by far richer in persons and treasure (see Virgil, *Aen.* 8.687–688). Interestingly, the Romans often saw Egypt as a troublesome province: "difficult of access, so productive of corn, ever distracted, excitable, and restless through the superstition and licentiousness of its inhabitants, knowing nothing of laws, and unused to civil rule" (Tacitus, *Hist.* 1.11 [Mellor]).[4]

The Political Fragment

Establishing a kingdom meant setting up an infrastructure that could manage the country.[5] So the Ptolemies encouraged Greeks and Macedonians to immigrate to this new "land of opportunity."[6] This situation is highlighted in Herondas's *Mimes* (c. 270 BCE.) when a young woman is confronted with the reality that her lover, Mandris, has left for Egypt and has, presumably, forgotten all about her:

> It's ten months since Mandris went off to Egypt, and you haven't heard a single word from him. He's drunk from a new cup of love,

and he's forgotten you. Aphrodite's headquarters are down there. In Egypt they have everything that exists or is made anywhere in the wide world: wealth, sports, power, excellent climate, fame, sights, philosophers, gold, young men, a shrine of the sibling gods, an enlightened king, the Museum, wine—in short, every good thing he might desire. And women! More women, by Hades' Persephone, than the sky boasts stars. And looks! Like the goddesses who once incited Paris to judge their beauty. (1.23–26)[7]

As the quotation indicates, many saw Egypt as an exotic paradise where a person could find all one's heart desired. The Ptolemies appear to have encouraged such a view. They needed the immigrants and thus established an open-door policy for any and all Greeks willing to make their way to the Greco-Egyptian kingdom.[8] And they came. The first fifty years of Ptolemaic rule saw a large influx of Greeks and Macedonians from all over the Greek-speaking world.

Immigrants found a number of opportunities available to them in Ptolemaic Egypt. First, there were governmental positions available to the new Greco-Macedonian immigrants. This group would become known as the king's "friends."[9] They were persons of various backgrounds who had given up their former lives for the promise of upward social mobility in the emerging Hellenistic kingdom. Over time, this informal situation became institutionalized. A good example of this can be found in the person of a certain Glaukias, a reservist or *cleruch* of Macedonian ancestry, who died in 164 BCE. During the course of his military service, he attained the title "king's cousin."[10] Second, there were military opportunities available to these new immigrants. Whether as mercenaries or reservists, men from all over the Greek-speaking world found that there was money to be made in Egypt. Finally, there were investment opportunities available in Egypt for those who had the resources on hand. They could be found in such lucrative activities as money lending, shipping, tax farming, and land leasing.

Either out of necessity or a concessionary spirit, the Ptolemies adopted the administrative structure of their Persian and Pharaonic predecessors. These administrative districts, called *nomoi* (nomes), were the primary governmental structure linking the monarchy and the people.[11] Each nome was headed by a *strategos* appointed by the king. Literally, a *strategos* was a leader of an armed force. When Alexander overran the Persians, whose governors were called satraps, he installed his military commanders as governors. Thereafter, governors of districts in Ptolemaic Egypt were known as *strategoi*.[12] It appears that their main function was to promote domestic tranquility.[13] The *strategos* headed the civil government of the nome and exercised command over the military forces, including the reservists (*cleruchs*) stationed there. As would be expected, *strategoi* were more often than not persons of Greek descent. It would not be until the middle of the second century BCE that a native Egyptian would occupy the office of *strategos*.

The Romans kept the division of the country into nomes governed by a *strategos*. However, even though the framework remained unchanged, Augustus effected a radical change in the *strategos*'s power. Under the Ptolemies the *strategoi* had both military and civil authority. The Romans reduced the *strategoi* to being purely civil officials. Military commanders now controlled military matters. Similar changes were effected in the responsibilities of many other local governmental officials. The Romans also replaced the top governmental officials with Latin speakers from the Roman equestrian class. Lesser officials generally came from the local population.[14]

The government of the local populace often required the use of bilingual Egyptians or persons of mixed ancestry. Greeks were reluctant to learn Egyptian. Since it was the level of government closest to the people, local officials needed to be able to converse with both groups.[15] Whether as a police chief or village clerk, local administration offered the upwardly mobile Egyptian an opportunity for wealth and status. Take, for example, the case of a certain Menkhes, village clerk of Kerkeosiris, who was designated a "Greek born in this land." He was a native of Egyptian stock who numbered among his male ancestors at least one who had immigrated to Egypt from somewhere else in the Greek world.[16] As village clerk, Menkhes's prime function was to compile information related to land, crops, population, rents, and taxes.[17] Such a position made Menkhes privy to information and opportunities unavailable to other members of the village. As Naphtali Lewis relates,

> What is more, by virtue of his office, the repository of all the village records, [Menkhes] was in a better position than anyone else to know where to find the necessary manpower among the villagers [to work his land] (and no doubt to pressure them to work for him if they could not be persuaded by inducements). And there is every reason to suppose that a man who had held the office of village clerk for so many years as Menkhes had done, was canny enough to involve himself in such enterprises only when he saw the reasonable certainty of a tidy profit.[18]

In short, individuals of pure Greek descent found positions in the upper echelons of government available to them in Ptolemaic Egypt, at least in the early years. By contrast, Greek-speaking Egyptians or persons of mixed ancestry could obtain lucrative positions in local government.

The social standing of the Egyptian populace only became more complex as the Roman class system was superimposed upon the already-existing Ptolemaic structure. Roman citizens now occupied the highest level of the social hierarchy. They were followed by citizens of certain Egyptian cities. Beyond that, everyone else was classified as Egyptian. People who were citizens (or had status) under the Ptolemies instantly lost it. Those of Greek descent resisted this classification, however. They continued to shape their lives and their physical surroundings on the model of the four Greek cities in Roman Egypt.[19] Native Egyptians continued to be confined to the lowest status in the social pecking order. In fact, the word Egyptian came to signify all that was considered rustic and non-Greek.

A division in opportunity—as well as a division of language—also meant a division in the administration of justice. Ptolemaic Greeks had their own court system (*chrematistai*), which concerned itself with contracts transacted either among Greeks or in the Greek language, and the Egyptians had theirs (*laokritai*), which concerned itself with contracts transacted either among Egyptians or in Demotic, the Egyptian language (*P. Tebt.* I 5). Certain people, like the second century BCE soldier Dionysius (Egyptian: Plenis), were able to use this division of justice to their own benefit. According to the evidence at our disposal, Dionysius belonged to a family with both Egyptian and Greek antecedents. This is reflected in the dual names of his family members. Among his papers we find contracts in Greek and Demotic. Two of the loan contracts are of interest to this discussion. On December 16, 108 BCE, Dionysius signed a loan for fifty artabs of wheat (about fifty-eight bushels). This contract was executed in Greek. On the same day, Dionysius' wife and mother signed a loan contract for the same amount to the same lender. This loan was executed in Demotic. It is difficult to understand what these two contracts represent. Did Dionysius borrow one hundred artabs or only fifty? One would assume the former, but there is still some ambiguity in this matter. Why not just execute one contract? Why execute one contract in Greek and the other in Demotic? It is not the case that the women could only handle the Egyptian language, since their names also appear on contracts executed in Greek. The answer may lie in the need to execute contracts according to the ethnicity of the parties, or it may have to do with the contractual differences found in Greek and Egyptian law.[20] At any rate, Dionysius, being bilingual and having a dual status, was able to choose the legal system under which he would enact his contractual obligations.

The judicial structure was maintained for only a short time under Rome. By the middle of the first century CE, it was replaced by a structure more resembling the Roman system. By then Egyptians had become accustomed to conducting their business in Greek. As a consequence, Demotic became extinct as a written language.[21] Under the Roman system, "the laws of the Egyptians" applied to everyone except Roman citizens, urban Greeks, and Jews. They were an amalgam of operative law and custom, some of it Egyptian but most of it Greek in origin.[22]

The Ptolemies operated a closed economic system. They controlled the production and use of currency within their realm.[23] Upon arrival in Egypt, a trader, pilgrim, or immigrant would be required to exchange his currency for Ptolemaic coins.[24] In addition, it was illegal to export Ptolemaic currency.[25] "[At Alexandria, all] persons arriving in Egypt from abroad had . . . to exchange their foreign currency for the Ptolemaic before they could even buy their next meal, let alone conduct any business in the country."[26] In a country like Egypt, fundamentally a barter economy, the introduction of currency was not only novel, but also at times bewildering to the native population.[27]

As a consequence of establishing currency, the Ptolemies introduced a banking system. Banks fell into one of two classifications: they were either "royal" or "concessionary." Royal banks were established in each nome capital with branches in all of the villages, called "tax offices."[28] Midlevel governmental employees operated them, although they often served in other capacities as well. The activities of these banks did not go far beyond simple transactions. They received tax payments and paid out sums due to the government, its employees, religious authorities, and contractors. In addition, they received and paid out money for private accounts, exchanged currency, and at times loaned money on the security of land or precious items.[29] Concessionary banks were introduced in the reign of Ptolemy II (c. 260 BCE).[30] They were limited in number and appear to have been leased out to the highest bidder in the same way as the collection of taxes was farmed out: the successful bidder obtained a government contract allowing him to operate a bank in the locality or region concerned.[31] As Lewis describes them, "The concessionary banks resemble[d] pawnshops more than a present-day bank."[32]

The Romans retained much of the banking system. The "public" banks (as they were now called) functioned primarily as the repository of tax revenues, while the privately owned banks handled all other transactions.

These included such transactions as payments to third parties, transfers of funds to both individuals and other banks, and loans. Very few native Egyptians ever became wealthy enough to function as bankers. The majority of bankers encountered in our sources for the period are Greek, with a few Romans also engaging in the enterprise.[33]

Overall, the Ptolemaic administrative structure garnered considerable economic rewards for the monarchy. According to Jerome, Egypt provided Ptolemy II Philadelphus with annual revenue of 14,800 talents in cash and 1.5 million artabs of wheat (*Expl. Dan.* 11.5). Under Ptolemy XII Neos Dionysius, the annual revenue was estimated to be 12,500 talents (Strabo, *Geogr.* 17.1.13). Even in the first century CE, the revenue of Egypt contributed to the empire an annual amount equal to Caesar's Gallic conquests and more than twelve times the revenue garnered from the province of Judea (see Velleius Paterculus 2.39; Josephus, *B.J.* 2.386–388).[34]

The Ptolemies reaped these benefits by exercising considerable control over the economy. As with banking, they established monopolies over most forms of commerce. For example, the government had complete control over the oil industry. Governmental officials determined when oil-producing crops would be sown, when they were reaped, how and where they were manufactured, and the prices for which they would be sold.[35] Such control demanded an elaborate bureaucracy to make it effective. So the Ptolemies had a chief finance minister (*dioiketes*), a chief accountant, and a chancery of ministers in charge of records, letters, decrees, and so forth. In addition, each nome had its own finance minister (*oikonomos*), who oversaw economic activities within his district. These financial officials were to let no source of revenue escape their attention. For example, according to Frank Walbank, "[The *oikonomos* was] to use the period of the Nile floods, when cattle were perforce concentrated on high ground, to carry out a registration of their numbers for taxation."[36] Interestingly, the finance ministers were not only to collect taxes, they were also charged with boosting morale whenever possible, as this directive from the chief finance minister's office indicates:

> During your tour of inspection try, as you go about, to encourage everybody and make them feel happier; not only should you do this by words but also, should any of them have a complaint against the village-scribes or the village-chiefs about anything to do with agriculture, you should investigate the matter as far as possible to put an end to such incidents.[37]

Such police actions must have been common among nome officials, since we have a petition from Menkhes, the village clerk we met above, attesting to something similar having happened to him (see *P. Tebt.* 43).[38]

Ptolemaic revenue was extracted primarily in taxes and rent. Taxation took various forms. There was a 5 percent tax on house rents and a 10 percent sales tax. There was a 33 percent tax on the sale of pigeons, and a similar tax on vineyards, orchards, and gardens, with the requirement that one-sixth of the produce of vineyards be paid in kind. There was a tax on cattle and slaves, as well as a poll tax and a local customs tax. The all-important grain tax was paid in kind, and persons cultivating what was called crown land often paid over 50 percent of their harvest in tax and rent.[39] The collections were handled by the appropriate governmental officials (or private contractors), and revenue was deposited in the royal banks.

At times people were unable or unwilling to pay their taxes. This presented a difficulty to the *oikonomoi*, who on occasion were deluged with petitions. They were charged with getting the money in, but at the same time they were to make sure that people did not "run away" from their responsibilities. This meant offering some sort of relief. It was in the interest of the taxpayer, especially if he were Egyptian, to emphasize his economic distress and his subsequent inability to pay his taxes, as one letter from the mid-third century BCE highlights:

> I give the amount due on 35 *artabae* (sc. of roasted lentils) a month and I do my best to pay the tax monthly so that you have no complaint against me. Now the people in the town are roasting pumpkins. For that reason then nobody buys lentils from me at the present time. I beg and beseech you then, if you think fit, that I be granted more time, just as has been done in Crocodilopolis, for paying the tax to the king. For in the morning they straightway sit down beside the lentils selling their pumpkins and give me no chance to sell my lentils. (*PSI* 402)[40]

We do not know whether the lentil-cook, Harentotes, ever received some relief from his tax burden or not. What is clear is that the Ptolemaic system of taxation was often seen as burdensome.

People initially saw taxation under the Romans as worse. They felt overwhelmed not by an increase in the number of taxes but by the increased efficiency of their collection. It was such an efficient system that many people fled rather than paid, and the manner of collection made the whole matter worse. The Roman system of tax farming (through publicans, tax collectors) was such that it invited corruption. Soldiers or armed guards often accompanied publicans. They regularly used the soldiers to intimidate citizens. The abuses perpetuated by this system were so widespread that they are even alluded to in the New Testament (see, e.g., Matt 9:10; Mark 2:16; Luke 5:30; 7:34). Governmental officials tried to curb such abuses and periodically offered amnesty. From its perspective, such efficiency only exacerbated problems. As the emperor Tiberius reportedly said to the prefect of Egypt, "I want my sheep shorn, not skinned alive."[41] The emperor Trajan finally addressed the problem and practically eliminated the need for publicans by assigning tax collection as a liturgy (see below).

Along with taxation, the Ptolemies garnered revenue through rents paid on land owned by the crown. At the beginning of their reign the Ptolemies governed as if the entire land of Egypt was their own personal possession. In reality, they were unable to exercise complete control over two important landholding groups: the temples and the reservists. They eventually abandoned their attempts to directly control the temple lands, although they made every effort to control their cultivation and revenues. As an essential part of the economy, land and its ownership provided social status, especially since the Ptolemies modeled their kingdom's operations along the lines of a Greek city-state.[42] The land owned by the temples gave them considerable power. It was a power eventually broken by the Romans.

Royal tenants were mainly native Egyptians, who rented the land at comparatively high cost. As I indicated earlier, a royal tenant could pay over 50 percent of his harvest in tax and rent. Nonpayment could result in direct governmental action (as a possible example, see *P.Petrie* 104). Plots were held on relatively short leases. The seed for planting was provided by the crown, but its equivalent had to be returned after the harvest. The central government controlled what the tenants planted, and this was recorded in the government's schedule of sowing. In 164 BCE, the Ptolemies instituted a practice of compulsory land leases. This land was assigned to citizens and governmental officials. It appears to have been a response to problems encountered during and after the Sixth Syrian War. A native Egyptian revolt erupted during this period, and extensive areas of farmland were devastated or abandoned. Once introduced, the leases quickly became institutionalized and later hereditary.[43]

Land allotted to military reservists—cleruchic land—was carved out of the king's own land. On occasion it came from temple lands or from the large estates previously granted by the king to courtiers and others. This allotment was given in lieu of cash for military services. Such a situation saved the Ptolemies a great deal of valuable currency, which otherwise would have been paid to mercenaries. Cleruchic land was taxed at a lower rate than other lands, and the ownership of land granted status to the soldier.

Military rank played a role in the size of the allotment. Members of the royal guard and cavalry were given between 50 and 100 arouras, while members of the infantry were given between 20 and 40 arouras.[44] Since agricultural production was such an important part of Ptolemaic economic policy, many a cleruchic land allotment also included a sizeable portion of uncultivated land.[45] Cleruchs were expected to put it quickly into production.

Since some allotments were better than others, influential friends and relatives often attempted to secure better allotments for reservists than they might otherwise deserve (see *P. Lond.* 2027). At any rate, in some locales the percentage of land owned by military reservists could be quite high, as indicated by one village in the Arsinoite nome (c. 118 BCE). In this village, fully a third of the 4,700 arouras (i.e., 1,551 arouras or 1,055 acres) in the village were owned by cleruchs as compared to the mere 6 percent owned by the temples (*P. Tebt.* I 60–62).[46] Reservists often leased their land out to tenants, frequently living away from the land in a city or nome capital. In the figures just cited above, only six of the thirty-three cleruchs with Greek names owning land in the village cultivated the land themselves. The rest leased their land to Egyptians. Egyptian cleruchs, who were admitted into the army after 217 BCE and received between five and thirty arouras, frequently cultivated their land themselves. Only two of the thirty-seven Egyptian cleruchs holding land in this (cited) Arsinoite village leased their holdings to others.[47] As the Ptolemaic monarchy declined, cleruchic land ownership went from lifetime tenancy to something approaching outright ownership. In sum, Ptolemaic land policy altered radically the cultural and political situation throughout the Egyptian countryside. Greeks and Egyptians lived in close proximity, although their social statuses were vastly different. Greek influence could be found throughout the country, whether Greeks lived among their Egyptian neighbors or functioned as absentee landlords. Cleruchic landholding created a new class of persons who often styled themselves as a sort of local aristocracy. And as their ownership claims were strengthened, governmental control over the cleruchs weakened.

The Romans abandoned the cleruchic system. They did, however, continue the practice of setting aside land as belonging to the monarchy, the emperor's estates. These were rented out to local farmers and usually required that the farmers pay between five and eight artabs per aroura in tax. This figure was much higher than the tax generally charged on both privately owned land and other public land, usually one artab per aroura and three and a half artabs respectively.[48] The Romans also continued the practice of compulsory land leases. They assigned them in a simplistic fashion. If the land was not already under lease, the government would just assign the land either to an adjacent property or as an "additional assessment" upon a village.[49] In a like manner, if a potential taxpayer fled rather than meet his obligation, the Romans simply divided the tax burden among the remainder of the citizens in that particular locale.[50]

In addition to the armed forces, the Ptolemies maintained power through a complex patronage system. From the outset, the Ptolemies, like all the other new Hellenistic monarchies, sought to legitimize their rule through religious means.[51] The Seleucids adopted Apollo as their patron god. The Ptolemies adopted Dionysius. Of course, they felt the need to control the sometimes "outlandish" activities that could occur in the Dionysiac cult (see, e.g., *BGU* 1211).[52] The worship of evidently Greek deities notwithstanding, the Ptolemies also patronized the native Egyptian deities. They made a special effort to publicly observe the more important Egyptian religious ceremonies. They also promoted and maintained a close relationship with the family in which the Memphite high priesthood was hereditary. Beginning with the reign of Ptolemy V, each new ruler was crowned by the high priest of Ptah in Memphis.[53] The famous Rosetta Stone attests to this relationship between the monarchy and the priesthood. It was issued by a council of priests at Memphis on the first anniversary of Ptolemy's coronation (March 27, 196 BCE).

Ptolemy I also inaugurated a new deity, Sarapis. The Ptolemies rebuilt and renovated the temple at Memphis to demonstrate their patronage of this deity. The Great Serapeum at Memphis was to function as a symbol of the new cultural fusion that was to characterize the Ptolemaic kingdom. (Outside of Memphis, the Serapeum at Alexandria was the most well-known shrine to the deity in Egypt.) According to Lewis, Sarapis was meant to symbolize the equal status of Greeks and Egyptians in the kingdom.[54] He admits, however, that this never came about: "For [the Egyptians] that symbol remained no more than an ideal in a hoped-for future, never becoming a present reality."[55] In fact, there were two forms of cult practiced for Sarapis, one Greek and the other Egyptian. Scholars may disagree as to the extent of Sarapis's popularity in Egypt, but it is clear that this deity became wildly popular throughout the Greco-Roman world.[56]

Alexandria was the focus of a great deal of Ptolemaic patronage. In their new capital they built a Museum and a Library that would become famous throughout the ancient world. Strabo, who saw the Museum in the early Roman period, described it as thus:

> It has a covered walk, an arcade with recesses and seats and a large house, in which is the dining-hall of the learned members of the Museum. This association of men shares common property and has a priest of the Muses who used to be appointed by the kings but is now appointed by Caesar.[57]

The Ptolemies spent vast sums of money buying books and attracting scholars to the city. At its peak, the Library contained some half a million scrolls. In fact, the Ptolemaic appetite for book acquisitions was so great that it spawned a daughter library in the Serapeum.[58] The Museum was a research institute dedicated primarily to the systematic study of philology. It hosted intellectuals such as Euclid, Archimedes, Ctesibius, and Eratosthenes. The intellectual productivity of the Museum was so great that its effects lasted far beyond antiquity. Ptolemaic patronage also brought many poets to Alexandria, and both the study of medicine and biology flourished there.[59] Walbank comments on the accomplishments of Alexandrian intellectuals in this way: "By their commentaries and their studies of the text and the language, these men laid the foundations of Renaissance and modern scholarship."[60]

The Ptolemies recruited a large number of *cleruchs* to assist in their military campaigns and to preserve peace within the country. In addition, they recruited a fair number of mercenaries. These were recruited from all over the Greek and non-Greek-speaking world.[61] They recruited Idoumaians (Edomites), Cretans, Syrians, Arabians, and Jews into their armed forces, especially after 167 BCE, when the Maccabean revolt liberated Judea from the rule of the Seleucids. And it was only a matter of time before the Ptolemies began to recruit Egyptians themselves into the army. They organized these recruits into *politeumata* according to ethnic origin (e.g., the *politeuma* of the Cretans). The diversity of these ethnoreligious groups, along with their connection to the government, was bound to create conflict. All that was needed was a flash point.

Soldiers received both pay and lodging from the authorities. As it has throughout the history of the practice, the billeting of soldiers among the local populace created a great deal of resentment. Making matters worse, soldiers were not always patient enough to wait to be assigned a billet, and from time to time they exercised force to secure their "rights." Take, for example, this letter from Ptolemy II to one of his officers:

> King Ptolemy to Antiochos, greeting. About the billeting of sol-
> diers we hear that some instances of undue violence have occurred
> when, instead of waiting to be assigned lodgings by the finance
> officer [of the nome], they simply march into houses, eject the peo-
> ple and occupy the premises by force. Give orders, therefore, that
> this may not occur again: if they erect their own shelters, well and
> good, but if they need to be assigned billets the finance officers are
> to give them what is necessary. And when they give up their bil-
> lets, they are to restore and release them, and are not to reserve
> them till they come back, as we hear they now do, renting them
> out to others or locking the rooms before they go off. (*P.Hal.*
> 1.166–179).[62]

As this letter demonstrates, the government had to find a way to preserve domestic tranquility while also fulfilling its obligations to its soldiers. From 276 to 261 BCE at least six royal edicts were issued attempting to control the soldiers.[63] One, for example, ordered that a soldier could not occupy more than half of the structure in which he was housed. The other half had to remain in the hands of the owner. If a soldier violated this rule, a heavy fine was imposed (see *P.Petrie* III 20 = *W.Chr.* 450 = *C.Ord.Ptol.* 5–10). Unfortunately, the abuses continued.

Native Egyptians in the armed forces were able to take advantage of some of the perks available to their Greco-Macedonian colleagues. Soldiery gave them status, leisure, and the financial resources to engage in entrepreneurship (see, e.g., *P.Strassb.Dem.* 43).[64] Although they were excluded from some positions in the army and the *politeumata*, Egyptian soldiers frequently found themselves part of the local gentry. Thus, a simplified orientation toward the political structure—Greeks win, Egyptians lose—would not adequately account for the social complexity created by Ptolemaic policy.

The Romans abandoned the cleruchic system. In its place they included army maintenance in their allocation of tax revenue. However, these funds only provided for the basic needs of the army. As a supplement, the army was allowed to requisition supplies and services as needed. As might be expected, this power was often abused. The most common abuses involved billets and transportation. As under the Ptolemies, soldiers frequently misused their power to secure housing. And, as under the

Ptolemies, the government repeatedly tried to stop the practice without success. The army would also forcibly seize means of transportation as they deemed it necessary. Again, the government attempted to curb the practice. Take, for example, the edict issued by Germanicus in Egypt in 19 CE: "The forcible seizure of beasts of burden as they are encountered traversing the city is hereby forbidden, for that is nothing but an act of self-evident robbery."[65] Animals belonging to the imperial estates were exempt from requisitioning; tags tied around their necks identified them as the emperor's. As in the case of housing, however, it was impossible for the government to stop the abuses completely.[66]

As a means of social advancement, the army continued as an attractive option. Augustus had transformed the Roman army into a volunteer professional force. He laid down a period of service for men entering the armed forces, and upon completion of their service they were given a fixed sum of money (12,000 drachmas for a legionary, something less for an auxiliary)—something vaguely similar to our modern retirement system.[67] During most of their rule the Romans kept two legions stationed in Egypt. Auxiliary units comprised of provincials supported the legions. This was the most likely entry point for a man seeking to advance himself. After twenty-six years of service, auxiliary troops were rewarded with Roman citizenship. Initially provincial soldiers were by policy from other parts of the empire. But the Emperor Hadrian initiated a shift toward local recruitment of soldiers, and from the middle of the second century CE veterans settling in Egypt tended to be men from the country towns. And yet, military service was not permitted for native Egyptians. They were barred from almost all recognized routes to privileged status. Lewis sums up well the Roman attitude when he says, "Roman policy toward Egyptians conveys to us a quality of repression suggestive of vindictiveness."[68] This system of military recruitment lasted until the third century CE when the empire underwent a severe financial crisis. Then the system collapsed, and it was followed by a half century of military anarchy.

The Romans also transformed the mechanisms of local government. Instead of paid governmental officials, they instituted a liturgical system. A liturgy (λειτουργία) was a public service performed by a wealthy individual on behalf of the people as a whole. The Romans already had a concept of *munera*, public duties, but in Egypt they infused their understanding of public service with the Greek tradition and created a system of liturgies unparalleled in the ancient world. There were hundreds of separate liturgical offices. These were unpaid positions that often required the designee to pay an entrance fee on taking up his title and duties. In addition, the liturgist defrayed the expenses of the office out of his own pocket. (In the case of tax collection, the liturgists were individually and collectively responsible for turning in the entire amount assessed upon their districts.) Most terms of office were between one and three years, and because of the financial burdens carried by the liturgists, they were to meet certain minimum property qualifications. As Lewis indicates, the system was widespread and involved even the smallest of governmental responsibilities:

> The village elders, village and town clerks and police, collectors of taxes in grain and money, transporters to move the grain from the granary to the river port and from the river port to Alexandria or to an army camp, inspectors of the Nile flood and of the fields reached or not reached by it, inspectors of sowings, of harvests, of dike work, supervisors of public works, of tax collections, of provisions for visiting dignitaries, bankers to handle public moneys, guardians of minors, and the whole roster of metropolitan councilmen and magistrates—all these and more were liturgists in the fully developed system of the second and third centuries.[69]

The Romans enjoyed the benefits of an elaborate governmental system without the expense of paid governmental employees.[70] And yet, the changes in the political structure from Ptolemaic to Roman rule exacerbated tensions between ethnoreligious groups. Routes to advancement were suddenly altered. Existing citizenship structures were changed. Greater burdens were placed upon the poor and the wealthy. In short, the political structure imposed upon Egypt by the Romans did little or nothing to create opportunities in the governmental realm for the majority of the populace.

The Social Fragment

The great Latin poet and satirist Horace once wrote, "People change their skies, not their feelings, when they rush overseas" (*Ep.* 1.11.27). This statement carries with it a certain weight of truth, and yet, as with most statements, one can point to the exceptions. We can find both in Ptolemaic Egypt. Greco-Roman fascination and disdain for Egypt seems to have started early. Homer, Greeks, and (later) Romans saw Egypt as a place of great wisdom (see, e.g., *Il.* 9.382; *Od.* 3.300–302; 4.126–127, 228–232; 14.285–286; 17.425–444). Hellenic deference to Egypt suffused all types of literature from the classical through the Greco-Roman periods (see, e.g.,

Plato, *Phaedr.* 274c–275b; *Leg.* 2.656d–657a).[71] By contrast, Greco-Romans also saw Egypt as an exotic land of magic and mystery—what David Frankfurter classifies as "Egyptomania."[72] As he goes on to say, "By the seventh century and the advent of Islam, Egypt had gained the reputation as a veritable culture of magicians, far beyond the biblical portrait of Pharaoh's indomitable court wizards."[73] This ambivalence regarding Egypt did not stop people from traveling to the country. Actually, it may have encouraged it. Pilgrims, seekers of wealth and fame, ambassadors, soldiers, philosophers, musicians, poets, and others all found passage to Egypt.[74]

It was not an easy journey. Although the sea routes had been used for centuries, there was nothing in antiquity resembling modern commercial travel. To get to Egypt one had to start at the nearest harbor. If lucky, one could find a ship headed to Alexandria. If not, one took a ship going in the desired general direction. Then a traveler made arrangements with the ship's captain for passage. In the summer, a direct trip from Athens's Piraeus to Alexandria would take only six days. Unfortunately, most travelers did not experience such luck. Many ships made multiple stops along the way to Alexandria, and it appears that it was more common for the trip to take at least two weeks. There were no cabins, and passengers had to provide for their own comfort and entertainment. "Occasional travelers, as well as immigrants, would take along not only clothing, but also the household equipment needed for eating and sleeping—food, pots and pans, and bedding."[75]

Travel within Egypt was much easier. According to our sources, travel along the Nile from the Fayyum to Alexandria could take as little as four days (*Sel. Pap.* 1.134). Travel between Alexandria and Upper Egypt appears to have been steady, allowing people to visit the capital for business, pleasure, or study.[76] Of course, as I indicated, travel beyond the country was a more difficult matter. One trip from Egypt in 257 BCE took two months (see *P.Mich.Zenon* 10). Basically, government officials and the powerful found the possibility of travel outside the country within their reach (e.g., Apollonius, the finance minister of Ptolemy II). For those of humbler means, travel outside Egypt involved a great deal of bureaucracy (see, e.g., Strabo, *Geogr.* 2.3.5). In sum, although travel to Egypt was not an easy matter, many risked the dangers for the possibility of economic, religious, or social compensation. This fascination with Egypt may be summarized in the following third-century-CE statement: "Greeks find all Egyptian lore and legend irresistibly attractive" (Heliodorus, *Aeth.* 2.27 [Morgan]).[77]

Jews also found Egypt to be a land of opportunity. They certainly lived in Egypt prior to the Ptolemies, but Jewish immigration grew during their reign. The first Jews to settle in Ptolemaic Egypt appear to have been mercenaries.[78] Soon after, Jews could be found all over Egypt in all sorts of occupations. Although the majority chose to live in Alexandria and its hinterland, there was a Jewish stronghold in Elephantine. And after the Maccabean revolt, a Jewish temple was built in Leontopolis. It was the brainchild of Onias IV, a descendant of the Zadokite priests who fled Judea during the revolt. This temple was meant to replace the defiled one in Jerusalem. It was modeled on the Jerusalem temple, although more modest in its dimensions (see Josephus, *A.J.* 13.3.3).

Because of their close ties to the monarchy, Egyptian Jews were looked upon by native Egyptians with disgust. As Joseph Modrzejewski makes clear,

> As a military representative of an oppressive foreign power—Persian or Greek, it mattered little—the Jew could appear detestable in Egyptian eyes. At the same time, his "separatism" could easily arouse the reprobation of his Greek comrade-in-arms, whose lifestyle he shared but whose table he shunned. Among the Egyptians and the Greeks, negative reactions toward the Jews made their appearance; the image of the Jew in ancient literature was to be profoundly altered.[79]

Despite the problems, Jews were in Egypt to stay. They came from Judea and the areas of the Diaspora. The Ptolemies granted them special privileges, including a *politeuma* of their own. In response, Egyptian Jews became more and more hellenized. In a short time they would lose their facility to read Hebrew and required a Greek translation of their sacred text.

Any discussion of the social setting of Greco-Roman Egypt would be incomplete without some mention of slavery. Slaves were never numerous in Egypt. They tended to work more in the domestic sphere than in agriculture, and many served as business representatives (*pragmateutai*) for their masters. Slaves could be found in Alexandria and the larger towns and villages, but they never formed the backbone of the economy or society as they did in other areas of the ancient world.[80] The labor supply was too large and the time between harvests was too great for the institution to flourish.

Once they arrived in Egypt, immigrants found themselves in a virtual melting pot. Greeks, Macedonians, Jews, Egyptians, and others lived throughout the country—although a good number settled in the area of the delta.[81] It was a society of "haves" and "have-nots"—"us" and "them." Lewis characterizes Ptolemaic Egypt as follows:

> When people of two cultures, speaking different languages, live in close proximity, something of each is bound to rub off on the other. But what has now become clear, and becomes clearer with each new study, is that in Hellenistic Egypt such mutual influences were minimal. From top to bottom, as we now see, the dominant socio-political characteristic of the country was not coalescence, but rather the coexistence of two discrete entities: "we" and "they," the conquerors and the conquered. The king himself had two distinct aspects reflecting the cleavage: in one he was the incarnation of the ideal of kingship formulated by Greek philosophers (as, for example, in Aristotle's *Politics*), while in the other, he retained for the Egyptians the role of successor and continuator of their line of Pharaohs.[82]

Of course, others would disagree with Lewis's statement.[83] Still, the social stratification one finds in Ptolemaic Egypt made it difficult for persons from different ethnoreligious backgrounds to interact on an equal basis. Take, for example, the camel driver (scholars think an Arab) who complains that he has not been paid regularly because he is not of Greek extraction and "I do not know how to behave like a Greek" (*P. Col. Zen.* 66.2.21).[84] Walbank may have said it best: "For Greeks . . . it was one world, easy to move in and one which offered high status and wealth if one was prepared to take a chance. But it was no longer one world once one moved outside the Greco-Macedonian ruling class."[85] The situation was ripe for conflict.

At the beginning of Ptolemaic rule there appears to have been little discontent expressed by the Egyptian populace. However, as time passed the resentment grew.[86] Social inequality meant economic inequality, and in Egypt this took on a nationalistic expression.[87] Central to much of the conflict were cleruchic settlements.[88] As the following indicates, cleruchs were charged regularly with abusing their social privileges:

> To King Ptolemy greeting from Pasis, a[n Egyptian] farmer of Polydeukia. I am wronged by Geroros, a [Greek] holder of seventy arouras. I own a house in the village, and I have been thrown out by him by force together with my cattle, which are [wandering loose] in the open air, even though he has a place in the village that was given to him as his lodgings. I therefore, beg you, O king, if it

please you, to instruct Diophanes the strategos to write to Sosibios the police chief to order the man sent up to him, and, if what I say here is true, not to allow him to throw me out of my own house, so that I may be able to attend to my farming and through you, O king, the common savior of all, I may obtain justice. Farewell. (*P.Ent.* 11)[89]

Likewise, Greeks found themselves assaulted by Egyptians. The following may be illustrative of this type of social conflict:

To King Ptolemy greeting from Herakleides, originating from Alexandros' Isle, now residing in Krokodilopolis in the Arsinoite nome. I am wronged by Psenobastis, who lives in Pysa, in the aforesaid nome. On Phamenoth 21 of year 5 in the fiscal calendar, I went to Pysa in the said nome on a personal matter. As I was passing by [her house] an Egyptian woman, whose name is said to be Psenobastis leaned out [of a window] and emptied a chamber pot of urine over my clothes, so that I was completely drenched. When I angrily reproached her, she hurled abuse at me. When I responded in kind, Psenobastis with her own right hand pulled the fold of my cloak in which I was wrapped, tore it and ripped it off me, so that my chest was laid quite bare. She also spat in my face, in the presence of several people whom I called to witness. The acts that I charge her with committing are: resorting to violence against me and being the one to start [the fracas] by laying hands on me unlawfully. When some of the bystanders reproached her for what she had done, she simply left me and went back into the house from which she had poured the urine down on me. I therefore beg you, O king, if it please you, not to ignore my being thus, for no reason, manhandled by an Egyptian woman, whereas I am a Greek and a visitor, but to order Diophanes the strategos . . . to write to Sogenes the police chief to send Psenobastis to him to be questioned on my complaint and to suffer, if what I say here is true, the punishment that the strategos decrees. Farewell. (*P.Ent.* 79)[90]

Outside of physical assaults, theft and property damage were common complaints. Unlike physical assaults, however, the complaints were mainly Greek against Greek and Egyptian against Egyptian. Power and its displays appear to be behind a great deal of the social conflicts. Egypt under the Ptolemies was a society in which suspicion and antipathy were common.[91]

It would be unfair, however, to characterize Ptolemaic society as one of strong social divisions and just leave it at that. As with most things, the reality is more complicated. Greeks and Egyptians had no choice but to interact, especially in the small villages. In fact, Christopher Haas argues that there is a bias in scholarship against focusing on the interaction between the groups in favor of the conflicts.[92] Greeks, Jews, Egyptians, and others interacted on a daily basis. They contracted for goods and services. They served in the armed forces together, and they interacted in the governmental bureaucracy. For an ambitious Egyptian, social mobility meant interacting with Greeks in their native tongue. It was necessary partly because the Greco-Macedonians sought to understand the Egyptians (and others) through the lens of their own cultural experience. As Walbank says, "Their attitude was clearly open and friendly but what they were hoping to do was not to understand these people in their own environment but to prove that they were really some sort of Greeks."[93]

Change, when it did come, started in the villages. The close proximity of Greeks and Egyptians in the villages, especially the more remote ones, meant that they had no choice but to cooperate. In short order, they began to intermarry. It probably began among the lower classes of both populations and then gradually spread. It appears safe to say that the farther the village was from the great urban centers, like Alexandria, the more quickly and more readily Greeks interacted with Egyptian culture. An excellent example of this type of sociocultural interplay is a second century BCE cavalry officer named Dryton. A citizen of Ptolemais, Dryton was stationed in the remote village of Pathyris in approximately 152 BCE.

Pathyris was a town inhabited almost entirely by Egyptians. The spoken language was Egyptian, and it appears that the residents felt no need to master Greek. About two years after his arrival, Dryton married an Egyptian woman. It was, in fact, his second marriage. His first wife presumably died before he was stationed in the remote village. The marriage immediately raised the status of Apollonia (Egyptian: Senmonthis), Dryton's new wife, and her family. Her new husband was not in the infantry (which is where most Egyptians served) but in the cavalry. In addition, he was not just a member of an elite part of the armed forces, Dryton was an officer. This rise in status did not mean, however, that Apollonia's family abandoned their Egyptian roots. In fact, it was Dryton who changed. As Lewis relates, "From the time he was posted to Pathyris, Dryton's lifestyle became less and less Greek, more and more Egyptian."[94]

Their children were given both Greek and Egyptian names. They had five daughters, which demonstrates Dryton conformed to another Egyptian cultural practice. Greeks did not hesitate to expose neonates, especially girls, to the elements to die. As one letter from a husband to his wife indicates: "If by good fortune you bear a child, if it is male, let it be, if it is female, throw it out" (*Sel. Pap.* 1.105). However, Egyptians, like Jews, kept all their children who were not otherwise snatched away by disease. Dryton appears to have accepted this practice in this Egyptianizing phase of his life.[95] His daughters, although they had Greek names, used their Egyptian ones more often. For them the principal survival of their father's culture was their need to use the Greek language in dealings with governmental officials. In short, interaction and even assimilation could be found in Ptolemaic Egypt.

Sometimes these interactions had devastating results on preexisting family units. For example, there is the case of the twins Thaues and Taous from the mid-second century BCE. They were thrown out of their childhood home when their "mother left [their] father and moved in with Philippos son of Sogenes, a [Greek] soldier" (*UPZ* 18).[96] Not soon after their mother, Nephoris, left, their father died. Their mother took control of the family estate. As the twins describe it, "She threw us out [of our house] and, starving, we fled up to the Serapeion, to Ptolemais, one of the recluses there. Ptolemais, who was a friend of our father's, received us and feeds us." Doubtless, this was an ugly situation. Nephoris abandoned her family apparently for the higher status afforded to those married to Greeks. This change in status may also account for the poor treatment the twins received from their mother. At any rate, it cannot be denied that interactions went both ways and that the results were mixed.

Greco-Macedonians moving to Egypt found a great deal of the physical setting to be familiar. If not, they wasted no time in making it familiar. Take, for instance, the village of Philadelphia, founded by Ptolemy II. It was laid out on the rectangular "grid" characteristic of Greek cities. It had three streets that crossed at right angles dividing the village into blocks, each containing twenty houses, separated at times by alleys.[97]

In addition to the Greek-style cities like Philadelphia, Greeks lived in several Egyptian population centers, such as Memphis and the nome capitals, and there they quickly associated with the resident Greek-speaking community. Within all of these communities one would find familiar Greek-style buildings. In a large town like Oxyrhynchus, the temple of Sarapis would have stood out among other public buildings. Not just a cultic site, it included a cluster of small buildings consisting of workshops, living units, a banking center, and a public market.[98] Since the majority of their lives were spent in the public realm, it is not surprising to find that a great deal of a community's land was set aside for such activities.

At the heart of any Greek-speaking community was the gymnasium. It provided educational facilities, including lecture halls, classrooms, ball courts, a gymnasium (in the modern sense), and baths. It was an exclusive club for the Greek male citizenry. Gymnasia could be found not only in the Greek-style cities and nome capitals, but also in many small villages.[99] They were privately funded, and their alumni frequently formed organizations dedicated to their support. These alumni clubs sought to provide a forum of association for those who had received a Greek education and to promote the Greek way of life.[100] The two higher officials in the gymnasium's organization were the *paidonomoi*, who looked after the classes of boys, and the *gymnasiarch*, who provided funds for sacrifices, to endow and support contests, and when necessary to repair or extend the school buildings (see, e.g., *SIG* 691).[101] Walbank summarizes the importance and role of this institution:

> Brought up in this atmosphere of literature, music and physical exercise, the middle- and upper-class Greek boy, whether he lived in Athens, in Pergamum or on the Oxus, inherited the culture of Greece and with it the traditional feelings of inherent superiority over all other races.[102]

Connected with the gymnasium were the games. These were usually held in a theater and were very popular. To give one example, the theater at Oxyrhynchus had a capacity of about eleven thousand and was the scene of regular gymnastic displays, musical and dramatic performances, mass public meetings, and religious celebrations.[103] In other words, the gymnasium had not only an educational purpose for Greek speakers in Ptolemaic Egypt; it also played an important civic role by providing a form of public entertainment.

In the Roman period entertainment became an empire-wide phenomenon. Performers became professionals. Runners, boxers, wrestlers, gladiators, actors, and others now traveled from place to place and competed year after year. As in the modern world, the most successful achieved empire-wide acclaim, substantial amounts of money, tax exemptions, and other honors.[104] An account from the third century CE shows payment to an actor of 496 drachmas for a single performance—448 drachmas to a reciter of Homer—during a time when skilled laborers might expect to earn only four drachmas a day (see *P. Oxy.* 2548 and 529).[105] One document from the second century CE records the pension of an athlete—a pancratiast (a sport somewhat similar to ultimate fighting)—at 180 drachmas a month. By contrast, a century later—even after a 50 percent pay increase—a legionary soldier could only expect to make about 60 drachmas a month.[106] These renowned entertainers even had their own guilds (e.g., The Sacred Society of World-wide Traveling Victorious-in-Sacred-Games Gold-Crowned Artists Dedicated to Dionysius and Our Lord [name of ruling emperor]).[107]

Although no longer a primary medium for public entertainment, the gymnasia continued to operate. Most scholars classify them as "public" institutions, although membership was still limited to a Greek-speaking cultural group, and so they were not "public" in the sense of being in service to the entire community. Parents registered their sons with elaborate ancestral declarations because they understood the advantages a gymnasial education could bring.[108] The curriculum was still very traditional in the Roman period. They also functioned as cultural centers, and "many probably had libraries."[109] Although their social function was considerable, they nevertheless promoted the interests of a particular ethnoreligious group.

A gymnasium was a characteristic feature of urban life in Roman Egypt. As part of the built environment, gymnasia as well as baths and other civic buildings were prominent throughout the province. Cities like Hermopolis and Ptolemais were typical of many Greek-style cities to be found throughout the empire.[110] They had colonnade-lined streets, tetrastylons, temples, central marketplaces, theaters, gymnasia, baths, and prisons.[111] As with most places in this period, the public facade of these Egyptian cities was quite ostentatious. And ostentation was expensive. For example, Hermopolis allotted 15.5 talents in 266–67 CE to repair the gymnasium porticoes, the equivalent of a year's pay for 65 skilled workers.[112]

It would be misleading, however, to emphasize the Greek character of these cities without acknowledging how their Egyptian environment influenced them. Roger Bagnall points out, "[These cities] can hardly have been recognizable as Greek cities, of the sort the Romans knew in Greece, Asia Minor, and other parts of the East."[113] These cities were Greco-Egyptian. For example, Egyptian temples dominated the nome capitals. Again, Bagnall highlights this well:

> The Egyptian temples were not only large; they were also uncompromisingly Egyptian in style, even those finished by the Romans. A Greek living in a nome metropolis was reminded daily by these temples that the gods of the place were Egyptian, not Greek, even if they were referred to by Greek names—Hermes, Apollo, Aphrodite, and the like—in some cases.[114]

In addition, residential architecture in Egypt was very different from other places were Greeks and Romans lived. Houses were constructed of mud brick rather than timber or stone.[115] Urban dwellers also apparently kept large numbers of animals with them. We hear of cattle, pigs, donkeys, goats, pigeons, and camels being kept in residential quarters. Yet, because of the high concentration of the population, trees appear to have been a rare site (see *P.Oxy.* XLI 2969). The waste from all these people and animals had to be deposited somewhere, and it appears that large areas of most cities were unoccupied at various times. As in modern Egypt, large garbage heaps could be found within cities. In short, the physical setting mirrored the social reality: cities had a Roman facade overlaid on a complex Greco-Egyptian foundation.[116]

Indications of the complexity of the social situation can also be seen in the institution of marriage. Greek fathers had considerable power over their female children in Greece. This power eroded in the Egyptian milieu for two reasons. First, because it ran contrary to the Egyptian legal and moral tradition. An Egyptian woman's consent was necessary for a marriage to be initiated. Early Greek settlers tried to enforce the customary power relations men exercised over women, but over time they began to assimilate their behavior to those prevalent among the Egyptian populace. "Greek marriage contracts increasingly resembled Egyptian ones in tone and content."[117] Second, Roman law and custom saw Greek practices as inhumane. Governmental officials increasingly intervened in marriage disputes enacted according to Greek law and custom. For example, in 128 CE the prefect of Egypt decided: "It matters with whom the married woman wishes to live."[118]

Intermarriage, which had become increasingly common during the Ptolemaic period, was strongly discouraged by Rome. The government imposed severe fines for violations of the class structure. For example, the regulations of the Privy Purse maintained:

39. If a Roman man or woman is joined in marriage with an urban Greek or an Egyptian, their children follow the inferior status.
43. If Egyptians after a father's death record their father as a Roman, a fourth [of his or her property] is confiscated.
52. Marriage between Romans and Egyptians is [not] allowed.
53. Egyptians who, when married to discharged soldiers, style themselves Romans are subject to the provision on violation of status. (*BGU* V 1210).[119]

These and other rules sought to keep people "in their place."[120]

Such impediments to social mobility, imposed upon both Egyptians and Greeks, appear to have encouraged resentment against Rome and at times outright rebellion. Citizens of Alexandria "often mounted public demonstrations, in the streets and in the theater, against the governor of the province and even against a visiting emperor."[121] Insurrections occurred. Take, for example, the rebellion in 152 CE that took the life of the prefect of Egypt and seriously endangered Rome's ability to supply food to its citizens. Greeks and Egyptians also put their resentment down on paper. Greeks had the *Acts of the Pagan Martyrs*. Egyptians had the *Prophecy* (or *Oracle*) *of the Potter*. Characteristically, Rome responded with violence and dispatched legions to put down revolts. In 215 CE the emperor Caracalla slaughtered an untold number of Alexandrian citizens over the course of several days as a response to their criticism of his reign. Oddly enough, it was also Caracalla who attempted to deal with the social impediments by granting citizenship to almost everyone living in the empire.

A great deal of resentment was also directed at Jews living in Egypt. Already seen as collaborators with the imperial authorities, Jews were allowed by the Romans to retain the privileges they had enjoyed under the Ptolemies, including their own council of elders. Augustus granted them this privilege while he stripped the Greek citizenry of Alexandria of its right to a *boulē* (council). Resentment grew between the ethno-religious groups, and violence erupted in Alexandria in 38 CE. A few years later, the temple in Jerusalem was demolished after an unsuccessful revolt. And although the Jews of Egypt remained loyal to the emperor, their temple at Leontopolis was stripped of its treasures and destroyed. Furthermore, a reparations tax of eight drachmas was imposed upon every male in a Jewish household (including slaves), an amount four times larger than the half-shekel tax a Jewish male was required to pay before the temple's destruction. Yet, Jews in Egypt were allowed to retain their special privileges.[122]

The situation changed radically in 115 CE. At the beginning of Trajan's Parthian campaign, Jews in Cyrenaica rallied around a messianic king named Lucuas (Eusebius, *Hist. eccl.* 4.2.3–4). Troop strength had been reduced in Egypt and elsewhere because of the campaign. Within a year, the revolt had spread to Egypt. Egyptian Jews, possibly because of the pogrom of 38 and the destruction it unleashed on their community, joined the campaign, destroying roads and buildings, desecrating temples, and disrupting shipping along the Nile. Eventually, the revolt would spread to Cyprus, Mesopotamia, and even Judea.

Characteristically, Rome responded with violence. It regained Alexandria rather quickly, but for almost three years the up-country of Egypt was wracked by conflict. The great synagogue of Alexandria was demolished (Eusebius, *Chron.* 2.223). The prefect forced some Alexandrian Jews to move outside the city walls. Others were deported to Palestine. Egyptian Jews were stripped of their privileges. Modrzejewski summarizes the aftermath: "In the turmoil of the general disaster, the Hellenized Jews of Egypt perished, with all their worldly possessions."[123] We will not find a Jewish presence in Egypt again in our sources until the fourth century CE.

It would be overly simplistic to conclude that Rome's management of the social situation in Egypt was a disaster. Of course, the reality was more complex. Roman propaganda had painted Egypt as "a land grown dissolute in fabulous wealth, a land ruled by fat and gluttonous kings who capped their debauched existence with incestuous brother-sister marriage."[124] It was the basis for war against Antony and Cleopatra as well as Augustus' special treatment of the province afterwards. This view did not simply fade away. Yet, Rome needed Egypt. In Augustus' imperial design, Egypt was assigned the task of providing one-third of the annual supply of grain needed to feed the capital.[125] The harshness of Roman policy toward Egypt put additional pressure on an already taut social structure.

The presence of Roman citizens in Egypt further complicated the pre-existing hierarchy of ethnoreligious groups in the province. And Rome's social policy exacerbated hostilities between the groups. Urban Greeks and Jews (before the 115 revolt) enjoyed privileges that were summarily taken away from many who had enjoyed status privileges under the Ptolemies. The group to lose the most was the cleruchs. Their privileges were gone, and their ancestry meant nothing to the Roman government. To the government they were Egyptians, nothing more.[126]

By contrast, Egypt's economy grew under Roman rule. There were more people who could be counted as "modestly well-off" under Rome than under its predecessor.[127] The Ptolemies had operated under a closed economic system, and the Romans kept Egypt under a separate economic system until the third century. Still, state ownership of land was reduced, government supervision of private enterprise was relaxed, and paid governmental bureaucracy was abridged severely. This greatly increased opportunities of private enrichment for some.

The government made distinctions between Romans and non-Romans, citizens and noncitizens, urban Greeks and Egyptians. The purpose was to keep people in their places. It does not mean, however, that people stayed in their places. Take, for example, the case of Gaius Longinus Kastor, a veteran of the Roman army. His will, written in Latin, leaves the bulk of his estate to two slave women, Marcella and Kleopatra. According to Jane Rowlandson, "It is reasonable to speculate that Marcella and Kleopatra, or both, were Kastor's common-law wives."[128] This document demonstrates that some people found ways to subvert the social regulations imposed by the government. Roman law prohibited bigamy and strongly discouraged intermarriage. Kastor found a way around those provisions. There was a penalty imposed on Kastor, however. His heirs had to pay a 5 percent inheritance tax.[129] Alan Bowman argues that "the restrictive measures in the law codes do not truly represent the reality on the ground."[130] I believe him to be correct. In short, Roman rule was beneficial to some but devastating to others. And for the majority it was *plus ça change, plus ça reste la même chose.*

Alexandria as a Prism

Roman Alexandria was a cosmopolitan city within the boundaries of the Egyptian province. Yet, it was distinctive. In many ways it typified the syncretistic tendencies inherent in the Roman Empire. And yet, this syncretism existed within a framework that was thoroughly informed by its Egyptian context. Like the rest of the province, it may be conceived as a sphere containing three concentric circles. The outer covering, or form of governance, was Roman. In the inner circle, day-to-day cultural activities were predominantly Greek, but the inner core was steadfastly Egyptian.[131]

Alexandria was founded near the Egyptian village of Rhakotis, which is where the majority of native Egyptians continued to live. The traditional date for its foundation is April 7, 331 BCE. According to Plutarch, the city's founding was associated with omens predicting its future importance in the Mediterranean world:

Since there was no chalk available, they used barley meal to describe a rounded area on the dark soil, to whose inner arc straight lines succeeded, starting from what might be called the skirts of the area and narrowing to the breadth uniformly, so as to produce the figure of a military cloak. The king was delighted with the plan, when suddenly a vast multitude of birds of every kind and size flew from the river and the lagoon on to the site like clouds; nothing was left of the barley meal and even Alexander was much troubled by the omen. But his seers advised him that there was nothing to fear (in their view the city he was founding would abound in resources and would sustain men from every nation); he therefore instructed his overseers to press on with the work. (*Alex.* 26.5).[132]

Its planning and layout are associated with famed architect Dinocrates of Rhodes.[133] As a planned city, it followed a regular grid pattern that gave it a certain aesthetic flow. By 320 BCE it had replaced Memphis as the capital of Ptolemaic Egypt, and it continued to function as the capital of the province under Rome.

One key to Alexandria's importance in the Mediterranean may be found in its relationship to the natural resources of Egypt. As one anonymous second-century poet said of the city,

> Seat of the immortal gods, august and wealthy, foundation of Alexander! The gentle climate and fertile soil of Egypt provide you with all good things, happy land! There is abundant grain, infinite flax; from your harbours sail ships with rolls of papyrus and brilliant glass.[134]

Alexandria used the interior to its benefit. During the Roman period, the most famous goods produced at Alexandria were papyrus, glass, and linen.[135] Yet, it also produced spices, perfumes, candies, medicines, precious stones, and wines. It exported barley, dates, fish, waterfowl, and above all grain. During Rome's height, it received 83,000 tons of grain per year from Egypt by way of Alexandria. This meant that over 32 fully loaded grain ships departed from Alexandria's harbors on a weekly basis over four and a half months (see *P. Turner* 45, which indicates that grain began arriving in Alexandria in mid-April).[136]

Alexandria also owed a great deal to its remarkable geographical setting. It is built on a kilometer-wide limestone ridge, which also allows much of the city to be built on an elevation that catches the favorable sea breeze. It lies at the intersection of two continents and provides access to lands surrounding the Mediterranean. In antiquity it was linked to the Nile by a network of canals, which permitted river traffic to sail directly into the city. Furthermore, its southern boundary was defined by Lake Mareotis, a large freshwater lake. [137]

The crowning glory of Alexandrian topography was its twin harbors, the Eastern or Great Harbor and the Western or Eunostos Harbor.[138] They were divided by a causeway seven stadia long, which linked the mainland with the island of Pharos. On the island was the temple of Isis Pharia, protector of sailors. Alexandria's legendary lighthouse dominated the island. Haas thus describes the lighthouse:

> This immense structure, rising just above the height of the Statue of Liberty, acted as a beacon to sailors still some dozen of miles out to sea, and guided their course among the treacherous reefs that lay just beyond the city's harbors. This was accomplished by means of a fire which blazed at the summit during the night and a mirror which reflected the sun's rays by day.[139]

Along the harbors were various dockyards and warehouses, and toward the western end of the Great Harbor stood the Emporion, where duties on imports and exports were collected. Nearby sat the Caesareum, or Temple to the Divine Augustus, adorned with two huge obelisks Augustus had plundered from Heliopolis. Just east of this location was the former quarter of the Ptolemaic rulers, the Bruchion. The area was adorned with palaces, parks, the royal docks, and the pyramidal tomb of Alexander the Great. It also included the famous Museum.

Near the eastern sector of the city was the great theater, which provided spectators with a view of the Great Harbor and Pharos. In the southwestern corner of the city was the Serapeum. Built to take advantage of the limestone ridge, it gave citizens a wide view of the entire city, particularly the Eunostos Harbor. It was sometimes called Alexandria's acropolis. As a large complex of buildings and the sanctuary for the god Asclepius-Imhotep, the Serapeum was a hub of activity. It included a library, lecture halls, and shrines to Isis and Anubis. Rufinus describes the sanctuary as an impressive sight:

> The whole edifice is built of arches with enormous windows above each arch. The hidden inner chambers are separate from one another and provide for the enactment of various rituals acts and secret observances. Sitting courts and small chapels with images of the gods occupy the edge of the highest level. Lofty houses rise up there in which the priests, or those which they call *agneuontas*, that is, those who purify themselves, are accustomed to live. Behind these buildings, a freestanding portico raised on columns and facing inward runs around the periphery. In the middle stands the temple, built on a large and magnificent scale with an exterior of marble and precious columns. Inside there was a

statue of Serapis so vast that the right hand touched one wall and the left the other.[140]

The avenue leading to the temple was lined with shops and booths serving food, selling souvenirs, and other goods and services to the visitors and pilgrims, including a captive audience of invalids and their family members. Of course, these locations were rented to vendors by the temple authorities. It was one source of temple income. The other major source of temple income was the fees suppliants paid: an entrance fee, ritual purification fee, and a fee to spend the night in the presence of Asclepius-Imhotep. And if the deity responded to the suppliant's concern, there was a fee to interpret the dream the god gave the pilgrim.[141]

The Via Canopica bisected the city on its east-west axis. On the eastern side of the city was the Gate of the Sun. The eastern gate area was known for its visitors' hostels. It also appears to have been Alexandria's red-light district. On the western end of the city was the Gate of the Moon. The Via Canopica was bounded by double rows of columns, which opened up at the Alexandrian agora. Most city streets intersected with this grand boulevard. The length of the Via was so impressive that one pilgrim said it took nearly nine hours to traverse it from end to end.[142]

At the center was the agora. Porticoes surrounded it, and there was a four-sided monumental arch at one end. It was the ceremonial heart of the city and bustled with all types of activity including shoppers haggling with merchants, beggars seeking a few coins, and the imprecations of philosophers and teachers. In the same area one would find numerous public buildings, including one of the city's gymnasia.

The area outside the city, called the hinterland, can be subdivided into two regions: Mareotis (south and west of the lake) and the *chōra* (land east of the lake to the Nile). The eastern region contained the extensive landholdings of Alexandrian citizens and furnished the city with meat and vegetables. Also in the east were the hippodrome and the garrison camp at Nicopolis. The *chōra* contained quarries and mines, which supplied building materials for the city. It included a district known as *Boukolia* (pasturage), which herdsmen and their flocks sparsely inhabited. Mareotis included the lake itself, which contained fish, waterfowl, and extensive papyrus marshes. It also included a number of villas for the wealthy. Viticulture appears to have been the main economic engine for this region, although it also boasted a number of pottery factories during antiquity.

Alexandria's population was far greater than that of any other Egyptian city and even of most other cities in the empire. Estimates of the population in this period are in the range of 500,000 to 600,000.[143] The united population of Alexandria and its hinterland would have comprised a significant portion of the overall Egyptian populace, possibly as much as a third. In a population of four to five million, this means that nearly 1.7 million people lived in and around the metropolis. In fact, the degree of urbanization in Roman Egypt was so high that it would not be rivaled again until modern times.[144] In this and other ways Alexandria was as different from the rest of Egypt as New York City is from the majority of the United States.

Alexandria was an assortment of ethnicities and social groups. Romans, Greeks, Jews, philosophers, sailors, indigenous Egyptians, transplanted Egyptians, pilgrims, military personnel, and governmental officials all interacted within its urban space. Despite the various ethnoreligious groups present in the city, it can be conceived as a two-tiered social organism: a small group of upper-class individuals and a large number of lower-class persons. The relationship between rich and poor in this urban environment was fundamentally symbiotic. The patronage system in the Roman Empire was such that the wealthy needed the support of the lower classes to maintain control, and sources indicate that Alexandria was a particularly difficult city to govern.[145] According to the author of the *Expositio totius mundi* 37.1–5, the governing authorities were often reluctant to enter the city without arms.[146] This was most likely an overstatement. Still, a city with the size and diversity of Alexandria would pose a challenge to any ancient governmental body. The heterogeneity of the urban population called for a particular vigilance on the part of the imperial authorities. In addition, these ethnoreligious groups often aligned themselves according to particular and sometimes overlapping allegiances.

According to our sources, the city was divided into districts called *grammata*. These quarters were named for the first five letters of the Greek alphabet, and these were further divided into smaller subdistricts. These divisions were first implemented in the third century BCE and were in use up through the fourth century CE. In addition, each citizen was a member of a tribe and dēmē, a system of social organization borrowed from the Greek homeland. However, by the time of Diocletian this form of division had all but disappeared.[147] All these forms of social organization were imposed upon the city by the governing authorities. These "primary communities," as they are sometimes called, tended to focus on a particular trade, distinguishing topographical feature, or the ethnoreligious identity of its residents. For example, Rhakotis, in the southwest corner of the city, functioned as a primary community for native Egyptians. Such communities could elicit intense loyalty from their members. Whether their loyalties were religious or ethnic or class based, residents of Alexandria aligned themselves with particular communities that sought to advance their group agendas. This explains why Egyptians, Romans, Greeks, Jews, and others shared this civic space in an often-uneasy relationship.[148]

For the first three centuries of Roman rule, the dominant ethnoreligious group was a rather heterogeneous amalgam we designate as the pagans. According to some scholars, paganism and Alexandrian identity were intimately intertwined in the ancient mind. This may not be saying much since there were few challengers to pagan hegemony. As the majority, Alexandrian pagans would have found it difficult to distinguish between religious life and the general practices that defined the culture.[149] The nature of paganism, allowing the worshipper to participate in several cults at the same time, undoubtedly contributed to the widespread religious tolerance that characterized Alexandrian life. Yet, the large Jewish presence in the city up to 115 challenges any overly simplistic conception.[150] Greek deities, Roman divinities, and Near Eastern gods all found an audience in the city. At the foundation of this religious structure were the gods of the Egyptians. Distinctive Egyptian ideas regarding the divine exercised considerable influence over these imported deities. Add to this structure the ideas of the gnostics, Hermeticists, and others, and the complex nature of the social situation becomes evident.[151]

The Church as a Refraction

The advent of the Christian movement in Egypt added yet another dimension to the ethnoreligious groupings present in Roman Alexandria. According to Eusebius, Christianity arrived in Egypt through Mark the evangelist:

> Mark is said to have been the first man to set out for Egypt and preach there the gospel which he had himself written down, and the first to establish churches in Alexandria itself. (*Hist. eccl.* 2.16.1 [Williamson])[152]

Mark was a Jewish-Christian missionary who is said to have assisted in various evangelization enterprises.[153] It is believed that his evangelization of Egypt would have occurred during the reign of the emperor Claudius (41–54 CE). Today, Coptic Christians continue to revere St. Mark, who they believe brought the gospel to Egypt.

According to the Acts of the Apostles, Apollos was the first Alexandrian follower of Jesus:

> Now a Jew named Apollos, a native of Alexandria, came to Ephesus. He was an eloquent man, well versed in the scriptures. He had been instructed in the way of the Lord; and being fervent in spirit, he spoke and taught accurately the things concerning Jesus, though he knew only the baptism of John. (18:24–25)

In addition to the preceding, the text of Codex Bezae (D) adds the following: "He had been instructed in his homeland."[154] Scholars disagree as to whether this statement means that Christianity had become established in Alexandria by 50 CE.[155] Nevertheless, Luke appears to have believed that Christianity reached Alexandria at an early date.[156] And both traditions point to an understanding among early Christians that Alexandrian Christianity was initially Jewish in orientation, and that the earliest Alexandrian Christians were from the Jewish community.

The composition of the Alexandrian church changed after the Jewish Revolt of 115. Jewish residents of the city were slaughtered, deported, or banished. The government would not have made any distinction between Jewish Christians and other Jews. In other words, as in the case of the church at Rome, the leadership and basic constituency of the Alexandrian church was decimated overnight.[157] And although the basic sources for its theology remained accessible, the people interpreting those sources changed. They became predominantly Gentile, and the church's Hellenistic Jewish past was subjugated to the concerns of its new leaders. This change in the composition of the Alexandrian church may explain why we do not hear from it until the middle of the second century. Furthermore, the type of Christianity being developed in Alexandria may account for the lack of information concerning the church before the episcopacy of Demetrius.[158]

Some scholars have characterized the type of Christianity that arrived and developed in Egypt prior to Demetrius as an "undifferentiated Christianity." What they mean by this is that the concepts and practices of the Christian faith as they took root in Egypt could not be deemed orthodox or heterodox. Orthodoxy is a theological category that was actually developed later than many of these concepts. What one finds in Egypt is a mix of "orthodox" and "heretical" practices and beliefs. For example, Colin Roberts pointed out that among the earliest Christian texts found in Egypt (dated between 100 and 199 CE) there was a mixture of both canonical and noncanonical works.[159] Of the canonical works, many came from the HB (e.g., Genesis, Exodus, Deuteronomy, Psalms). This appears consistent with the historical scenario described above: a Hellenized Jewish group was transformed into a Gentile group overnight. And although the basis for its theology remained, the new leaders of the Alexandrian church did not feel confined to either a predetermined list of texts or a predetermined method of interpretation. As it had in so many other ways, Alexandria developed its own direction. For example, C. Wilfred Griggs argues,

> The archaeological evidence rather seems to point toward an undifferentiated Christianity based on a literary tradition encompassing both canonical and non-canonical works (both categories being named as such here in light of their *later* status as defined by the Catholic tradition). The forces which caused the narrow geographical and literary outlook of the Western Church . . . do not appear to have been felt strongly in Egypt during the first two centuries of the Christian era. Bauer may be correct in asserting that what later heresiologists attacked as "gnosticism" in Egypt at first may have been simply "Christianity" to Egyptian Christians, but he does not pay sufficient heed to the evidence of so-called "orthodox Christianity" existing alongside it.[160]

I believe Griggs to be correct in his assessment. As in the case of Apollos, the type of Christianity taught at Alexandria was somewhat different from that taught by other Christian missionaries, such as Paul. Indeed, various understandings of the gospel circulated during the early phase of Christian missions. Paul did not agree with the apostles in Jerusalem (as shown in Galatians). Other Christian missionaries did not agree with Paul (see, e.g., 2 Corinthians). As the Acts account demonstrates, persons within the Pauline orbit thought Apollos's understanding of the gospel was incorrect on some matters. According to Acts 18, Apollos taught accurately the things concerning Jesus, but in the following verses we are told that Priscilla and Aquila take him aside to teach him more accurately. Indeed, in Acts 19 Paul rebaptizes some believers who had been baptized by Apollos because they were not taught correctly. It would be unfair to say that Apollos taught a heretical form of Christianity. Rather, it would be fair to say that the patterns and practices of normative Christian theology were developing at the time. Some representatives of the Jerusalem church did not consider the gospel preached by Paul as normative, but over time (and through writings such as the Acts of the Apostles) it was incorporated into a pattern of thinking and practice that Christians considered normative. Something similar should be kept in mind when evaluating early Alexandrian Christianity.

One of the major industries in Alexandria was education. Shortly after the Ptolemies established the Museum, Alexandria began to play host to many of the ancient world's leading intellectuals. Not all were associated with the Museum. In fact, by the end of the Ptolemaic period, there were various institutions throughout the city offering instruction to students. These were essentially private enterprises, although many flourished due to the patronage of wealthy Alexandrians. An exciting intellectual center, the city allowed for a great deal of cross-fertilization that probably could not have happened anywhere else. And yet beneath the surface of this intellectual cosmopolitanism, the business of education in Alexandria also promoted class-consciousness and communal differentiation.[161] Jews had their synagogues (see Philo, *Spec.* 2.15.62). Pagans had their gymnasia and lecture halls, and Christians had the Catechetical School as well as others. According to Haas, the Alexandrian educational enterprise promoted the ideals and traditions of particular ethnoreligious communities.[162] Thus, it makes sense that a school would be at the center of the emerging Alexandrian Christian community. As a vehicle for promoting and galvanizing a distinctive Christian communal orientation, the School and its leaders played a pivotal role in the church's development. In other words, the development of the Catechetical School tells us something distinctive regarding the development of Alexandrian Christianity in general.

Although one of the earliest and best known of the school's leaders, the background of Clement of Alexandria is shrouded in obscurity. Even his name presents something of an enigma. Although names do not give scholars enough information concerning individuals, they nonetheless can be revealing. They can provide essential information to which additional details can be added. Clement's name is no different. He has a Latin name. This basic fact tells us that he was a Roman citizen, although it says nothing about his ethnicity or place of birth. What it may indicate is social standing. For example, John Ferguson says his name "suggests that an ancestor was a freedman of T. Flavius Clemens, a relative of emperors and himself perhaps a Christian convert."[163] Likewise, Dimitris Kyrtatas says,

[Clement's name] is exactly the same as that of emperor Domitian's cousin, once a consul and later put to death on a charge of atheism. (It is believed by some that the ex-consul may have also been a Christian and that the Church Father was a member of the imperial *familia*).[164]

In short, Clement's name tells us that he was a Roman citizen, and some believe he was a member of the *familia Caesaris*. Undoubtedly, Clement was a member of the Alexandrian bouleutic (counselor) class, and an elite member at that. His level of education and prolific writing program could only have been accomplished by a person of considerable financial means. If indeed Clement was a member of the imperial household, it may indicate a certain inconsistency between his actual social position and how others perceived him. Freeborn aristocrats were generally unaccepting of freed persons and their descendants. Commonly, members of the *familia* were financially well-off, but because of their slave backgrounds, even after manumission they were denied many of the privileges normally given to the wealthy (cf. *Cena Trimalchionis*).[165]

Clement would have been a member of that group within Alexandria that held civic magistracies. For the Alexandrian elite, status and its indicators were extremely important. Interestingly, "a particular cultural or religious allegiance does not seem to have been a determining factor in [elite] class identity."[166] Many were urban landlords, holding property both within Alexandria and throughout the province, and more than a few engaged in business activities through personal agents (or *pragmateutai*). Alexandrian elites believed they had a lot to lose, and so they frequently avoided political positions that might be considered offensive to the government. As Haas says, "The political realities of the day called for 'easy natured men' (*eukoloi*)."[167] In the case of someone like Clement, the reality of the political situation might suggest that he was not your typical Alexandrian elite. But then, maybe he was. We possess little information regarding the Christianization of the Alexandrian elite.[168] Although Christians for the most part were not singled out for persecution by the authorities, they did face the possibility. The sporadic nature of these persecutions may have led many to believe they were relatively secure. When persecutions did arise, we hear of aristocrats as well as commoners being persecuted for their faith.[169] In fact, Clement was forced to leave Alexandria during the Severan persecution of 202 CE. He died, according to Quasten, "without having seen Egypt again."[170]

There is some question as to whether Clement was born in Alexandria or Athens. Epiphanius records two traditions regarding Clement: "And Clement, who some say is an Alexandrian, but others say is an Athenian" (*Pan.* 32.6).[171] According to Annewies van den Hoek, the tradition advocating Athenian origin "has long been accepted [by scholars] as the most probable."[172] It appears to me that the argument on behalf of Athenian birth contains an implicit bias against the ramification of Alexandrian birth for Clement. That is, if Clement were born in Alexandria, would that not make him Egyptian? On the one hand, one is inclined to make this connection. On the other hand, the concept of ethnicity in the ancient world is not comparable to that concept today. Furthermore, the indicators for determining ethnicity in antiquity are slippery. Things like nomenclature can be misleading. For example, Koen Goudriaan in his study on the issue of ethnicity in Egypt writes, "Nomenclature proved to be a wholly unreliable guide for establishing the ethnic identity of the persons mentioned in our sources, and this conclusion is valid from the end of the third century BC onwards."[173] One is forced to find other types of evidence to establish ethnicity, and this too can often be unreliable. In short, it would be impossible to determine the exact ethnic origin of someone like Clement. Yet, this does not mean that the bias of scholarship should be taken as the final word.

What is also disturbing and implicit in the argument against Clement as a true Alexandrian is the notion that somehow he could not have acquired such a classical education in the Egyptian metropolis. Scholars point out that Clement traveled widely to acquire his education. Clement himself acknowledges this:

> But my memoranda are treasured up for my old age as a remedy against forgetfulness, simply an image and a scene-painting of those clear and animated speeches which I was honored to hear, and of blessed and truly noteworthy men. Of these, one was in Greece, the Ionian, and others were in Magna Graccia (southern Italy); another one was from Coele-Syria, one was from Egypt, and others were in the East; one was from the land of the Assyrians, and another was a Hebrew by origin in Palestine. But when I met the last one (though in power this one was the first), having hunted him out from his concealment in Egypt, I rested. The Sicilian, in reality the bee, having plucked for himself the flowers from the prophetic and apostolic meadow, engendered in the souls of those who listened an undefiled measure of knowledge. (*Strom.* 1.1.31–38)

These travels, however, do not entirely exclude the possibility that Clement was an Alexandrian. In fact, I find it interesting that two of Clement's teachers were connected to Egypt. The last teacher, almost certainly Pantaenus, was the most influential in Clement's education, and he resided in Alexandria, although Clement says he was of Sicilian ethnicity. As a center of scholarship in the ancient world, Alexandria would be the perfect place for such an education. Scholarship's bias against Alexandria is based, I believe, on a latent idea of Egyptian exoticism—one that has prevailed in Western minds since antiquity.[174]

Clement's actual ethnic background notwithstanding, he does appear to know quite a bit about the community in which he lives. As Haas points out, Clement knows very well the various ethnoreligious communities that inhabit second-century Alexandria.[175] For example, Clement comments on various Egyptian religious practices (see *Strom.* 5.7; 6.4.35.3–37.3; *Paed.* 3.2.4; *Protr.* 2.3.9). Although he comments on them as an outsider, this is plausibly due to his "status" as a Christian, and is not a firm indication of Clement's ethnic background. Also, we do not have any information regarding Clement's religious practices before his conversion. What these comments do indicate is that Clement was informed about the world around him. Alexandria undoubtedly had a direct impact on his scholarship. As Haas says, "It is hardly conceivable that Alexandria's bustling urban milieu failed to influence profoundly the development of [Clement's thought]."[176]

In the end, given the material presently available, there is almost no conclusive way to determine Clement's origin or ethnicity. What can be determined is that Clement was a wealthy Alexandrian of the bouleutic class, possibly a descendant of the *familia Caesaris*, and a leading intellectual in the growing Alexandrian Christian community. He was a Roman citizen, which placed him at the head of the Alexandrian elite. According to our sources, he was ordained a presbyter in the Alexandrian church after he began his association with the Catechetical School (Jerome, *Vir. ill.* 38; Photius, *Lex.* 111). Pantaenus headed the School at that time.

Eusebius's comments regarding the Catechetical School seem to indicate that Christian scholarship in Alexandria was established some time before Pantaenus (*Hist. eccl.* 5.10). The exact curriculum of the School is unknown, as is the content of the teaching of Pantaenus. What we do know is that his influence on Clement was great. Eusebius credits Clement's great erudition to his tutelage under Pantaenus: "In his time Clement was noted at Alexandria for his patient study of Holy Scripture [with Pantaenus]" (*Hist. eccl.* 5.11.1 [Williamson]). Given Clement's writings, we may deduce that Greek philosophy was a prominent part of the School's curriculum, and that the writings of Alexandrian Jews like Philo also played an important part in the School's teaching.

With Clement the social location of the early Alexandrian church becomes clearer. It was a Greek-speaking body consisting primarily of persons who were literate and financially stable.[177] Its leaders were drawn from the bouleutic class, and many appear to have come from the province. This appears to be true throughout the Roman period. One need only look at the various thinkers (both orthodox and heretical) who occupied positions of leadership in this emerging organization (loosely defined). For example, Basilides, according to Hippolytus, lived in Egypt and learned his philosophy there.[178] Epiphanius says that he successfully spread his understanding of Christianity throughout the province (*Pan.* 24.1). Carpocrates, according to Clement, was an Alexandrian (*Strom.* 3.2). Epiphanius says that Valentinus was an Egyptian educated in Alexandria. He was most likely the first individual after Apollos to spread Egyptian-style Christianity outside the province. The popularity of Valentinus's understanding of the gospel appears to have lasted in Egypt well into the fourth century (*Pan.* 31.7–12).

Origen may have been the first true Egyptian to head the Catechetical School. Although his date and place of birth are uncertain, scholars believe him to have been born in Alexandria around 185 CE. His family was left destitute after the martyrdom of his father, Leonides. After Clement's departure during the same persecution, Origen succeeded him as head of the Catechetical School. According to our sources, an Alexandrian woman of means cared for Origen's family.[179] Her patronage of Origen allowed for the considerable growth of the Catechetical School. Then again, this patronage made Origen somewhat independent of the control of Demetrius, bishop of Alexandria. His independence of Demetrius may have been the basis for their famous discord. This conflicted relationship eventually drove Origen from Alexandria in approximately 231. He was succeeded by one of his students, Heraclas.

Heraclas had one distinct advantage over his teacher in terms of his relationship with the patriarch of Alexandria: he was ordained a presbyter by Demetrius (Eusebius, *Hist. eccl.* 6.19.13). Demetrius now had greater control over the Catechetical School. The truth of this assessment can be illustrated by the fact that when Demetrius died after 43 years as prelate, Heraclas succeeded him as bishop of the city. This began a system of succession that lasted well into the fourth century.[180] Dionysius, a man of great wealth, succeeded Heraclas. He is reputed to have donated a church that was (later) named after him.[181] Add to this list such wealthy notables as Athanasius, and it becomes clear that Christianity in Alexandria relied considerably upon the participation and financial support of the upper class.[182]

This support by the wealthy translated into a system of patronage that secured the allegiance of many of lesser means in the city. Although benefactions to the poor validated the patriarch's holiness and compassion, it also allowed him to carve out significant areas of support among the populace. In addition to the poor, the sick, widows, orphans, refugees, prisoners, and cripples, the patriarch also supported and garnered support from merchants, maritime workers, and others.[183] The Alexandrian church distributed cash and food to the poor, cared for the diseased, and provided shelter to the homeless. As its wealth grew, the church was able to establish itself as the city's central philanthropic institution. For example, when John the Almsgiver ascended the episcopal throne in 609/610, he found 8,000 pounds of gold in the church's treasury, along with great quantities of wealth in kind. In addition, he possessed a fleet of ships that could be used for trading ventures throughout the empire.[184] Out of these funds, the patriarch was able to support over 7,500 of the city's poor and needy.[185] In sum, the support of the wealthy allowed the church to make inroads into the larger population. This, in turn, established the Christians as a formidable ethnoreligious group within Alexandrian society.

To sum up our discussion in this chapter, we have conducted an analysis of Roman Alexandria by looking at the context of Greco-Roman Egypt. We found it to be a complex and multifaceted society that fostered both cooperative and antagonistic interactions between ethnoreligious groups. The power differential between these groups was played out within the distinctive Egyptian context. As a setting for the lives of people in this period, the land of Egypt exercised the most influence over their souls, including their constructions of reality. Alexandria is just the most shining example of a society consciously both Egyptian and Greco-Roman. It was a society holding things that appear to be contradictory to a modern as a single whole. And this almost peculiarly Egyptian trait is also found in the Alexandrian church.

Alexandrian Christianity began among Jews in the city. It developed its theological outlook by reliance on texts from the HB (in Greek translation) and Hellenistic Jewish interpretations of those texts. It spoke the philosophical language of Hellenism through thinkers such as Philo. And yet, its voice was silenced after the revolt of 115. Gentile Christians now developed the voice of the community. They took the sources left to them by their Jewish predecessors and added texts that advanced their own theological predispositions. In true Alexandrian fashion, the school became the medium through which they forged their sense of communal understanding. It was where Alexandrian followers of Jesus attempted to define ἐκκλησία for themselves. In so doing, they created their own powerful eth-noreligious identity, one that was not always in agreement with the canons of the emerging orthodoxy.

Notes

1. E.g., Hans von Campenhausen, *Ecclesiastical Authority and Spiritual Power* (Stanford: Stanford University Press, 1969); Elaine H. Pagels, *The Gnostic Gospels* (1989 Vintage Books ed.; New York: Vintage Books, 1989), 33–56; Robert L. Wilkin, *The Christians as the Romans Saw Them* (New Haven: Yale University Press, 1984), 1–47.

2. Robert L. Simpson, *The Interpretation of the Lord's Prayer in the Early Church* (ed. S. L. Greenslade; Library of History and Doctrine; Philadelphia: Westminster, 1965), 36–38.

3. Quoted in F. W. Walbank, *The Hellenistic World* (rev. ed.; Cambridge: Harvard University Press, 1992), 100.

4. Ronald Mellor, ed., *The Historians of Ancient Rome: An Anthology of the Major Writings* (London: Routledge, 1997), 483.

5. Alan K. Bowman, *Egypt after the Pharaohs: 332 BC–AD 642 from Alexander to the Arab Conquest* (Los Angeles: University of California Press, 1986), 56.

6. Walbank, *Hellenistic World*, 108.

7. Quoted in Naphtali Lewis, *Greeks in Ptolemaic Egypt: Case Studies in the Social History of the Hellenistic World* (New York: Oxford University Press, 1986), 10.

8. Ibid., 14.

9. Walbank, *Hellenistic World*, 75–78.

10. Lewis, *Greeks in Ptolemaic Egypt*, 74.

11. Ibid., 57.

12. Ibid., 56–57; Walbank, *Hellenistic World*, 105.

13. Lewis, *Greeks in Ptolemaic Egypt*, 58.

14. Naphtali Lewis, *Life in Egypt under Roman Rule* (Oxford: Oxford University Press, 1983), 15–17.

15. Lewis, *Greeks in Ptolemaic Egypt*, 106.

16. Ibid.

17. Ibid., 111.

18. Ibid., 110–11.

19. Lewis, *Life in Egypt*, 39.

20. Lewis, *Greeks in Ptolemaic Egypt*, 124–39.

21. Roger S. Bagnall, *Egypt in Late Antiquity* (Princeton: Princeton University Press, 1993), 235–40.

22. Lewis, *Life in Egypt*, 186–87.

23. Bowman, *Egypt after the Pharaohs*, 40.

24. Lewis, *Greeks in Ptolemaic Egypt*, 15.

25. M. M. Austin, ed., *The Hellenistic World from Alexander to the Roman Conquest: A Selection of Ancient Sources in Translation* (Cambridge: Cambridge University Press, 1981), no. 238; quoted in Bowman, *Egypt after the Pharaohs*, 92.

26. Lewis, *Greeks in Ptolemaic Egypt*, 48.

27. Ibid., 47; Walbank, *Hellenistic World*, 160–61.

28. Lewis, *Greeks in Ptolemaic Egypt*, 49.

29. Ibid., 46–47.

30. Ibid., 49.

31. Ibid., 48.

32. Ibid., 49.

33. Lewis, *Life in Egypt*, 147–48.

34. Bowman, *Egypt after the Pharaohs*, 93.

35. Walbank, *Hellenistic World*, 110–12.

36. Ibid., 107.

37. Austin, *Hellenistic World*, no. 256; quoted in Bowman, *Egypt after the Pharaohs*, 59.

38. Quoted in Lewis, *Greeks in Ptolemaic Egypt*, 116–17.

39. Walbank, *Hellenistic World*, 110.

40. Quoted in ibid., 112.

41. Quoted in Lewis, *Life in Egypt*, 160.

42. Walbank, *Hellenistic World*, 159.

43. Lewis, *Greeks in Ptolemaic Egypt*, 110.

44. Ibid., 24.

45. Ibid., 25.

46. Ibid., 25–26.

47. Ibid., 32.

48. Lewis, *Life in Egypt*, 165–66.

49. Ibid., 166.

50. Ibid., 172.

51. Walbank, *Hellenistic World*, 210.

52. Quoted in ibid., 211–12.

53. Lewis, *Greeks in Ptolemaic Egypt*, 80.

54. Ibid., 70.

55. Ibid.

56. Walbank, *Hellenistic World*, 121; Bowman, *Egypt after the Pharaohs*, 175–79.

57. Bowman, *Egypt after the Pharaohs*, 224.

58. Ibid., 225.

59. Walbank, *Hellenistic World*, 188–89.

60. Ibid., 177.

61. Ibid., 67–68.

62. Quoted in Lewis, *Greeks in Ptolemaic Egypt*, 22–23.

63. Ibid., 20–24.

64. Ibid., 141.

65. Quoted in Lewis, *Life in Egypt*, 173.

66. Ibid., 172–76.

67. Ibid., 21.

68. Ibid., 33–34.

69. Ibid., 178.

70. Ibid., 177–84.

71. David Frankfurter, *Religion in Roman Egypt* (Princeton: Princeton University Press, 1998), 218.

72. Ibid., 217–18.

73. Ibid., 216.

74. Walbank, *Hellenistic World*, 63, 67, 72–73; Lewis, *Greeks in Ptolemaic Egypt*, 15–20.

75. Lewis, *Greeks in Ptolemaic Egypt*, 13. For a general description of travel to Egypt, see 12–14.

76. Bowman, *Egypt after the Pharaohs*, 155.

77. Quoted in Frankfurter, *Religion in Roman Egypt*, 217.

78. Joseph Modrzejewski, *The Jews of Egypt: From Ramses II to Emperor Hadrian* (trans. Robert Cornman; Princeton: Princeton University Press, 1997), 136.

79. Ibid.

80. Walbank, *Hellenistic World*, 116, and Bowman, *Egypt after the Pharaohs*, 138.

81. Bowman, *Egypt after the Pharaohs*, 19, 141.

82. Lewis, *Greeks in Ptolemaic Egypt*, 4.

83. E.g., Bowman, *Egypt after the Pharaohs*, 122–24.

84. Quoted in Walbank, *Hellenistic World*, 115.

85. Ibid., 78.

86. Ibid., 114.

87. Ibid., 167.

88. Lewis, *Greeks in Ptolemaic Egypt*, 68; Walbank, *Hellenistic World*, 110.

89. Quoted in Lewis, *Greeks in Ptolemaic Egypt*, 60.

90. Quoted in ibid., 61.

91. Bowman, *Egypt after the Pharaohs*, 64.

92. Christopher Haas, *Alexandria in Late Antiquity: Topography and Social Conflict* (Ancient Society and History; Baltimore: John Hopkins University Press, 1997), 12.

93. Walbank, *Hellenistic World*, 63.

94. Lewis, *Greeks in Ptolemaic Egypt*, 92.

95. Ibid., 92–94.

96. Quoted in ibid., 81.

97. Ibid., 26.

98. Bowman, *Egypt after the Pharaohs*, 143.

99. Lewis, *Greeks in Ptolemaic Egypt*, 27.

100. Walbank, *Hellenistic World*, 117–18.

101. Ibid., 182–83.

102. Ibid., 184.

103. Bowman, *Egypt after the Pharaohs*, 144–45.

104. Lewis, *Life in Egypt*, 103.

105. Ibid., 61.

106. Ibid., 150.

107. Ibid., 148–49.

108. Haas, *Alexandria in Late Antiquity*, 100.

109. Ibid.

110. Ibid., 45.

111. Ibid., 45–46.

112. Ibid., 47.

113. Ibid., 55.

114. Ibid., 48.

115. Lewis, *Life in Egypt*, 51.

116. Haas, *Alexandria in Late Antiquity*, 54.

117. Ibid., 189.

118. Lewis, *Life in Egypt*, 56.

119. Quoted in ibid., 32–33; and Jane Rowlandson and Roger S. Bagnall, *Women and Society in Greek and Roman Egypt: A Sourcebook* (Cambridge, UK: Cambridge University Press, 1998), 175–77.

120. Lewis, *Life in Egypt*, 33–35.

121. Ibid., 201.

122. Ibid., 30.

123. Modrzejewski, *Jews of Egypt*, 198.

124. Lewis, *Life in Egypt*, 34.

125. Ibid., 15.

126. Ibid., 27–28.

127. Bowman, *Egypt after the Pharaohs*, 101.

128. Rowlandson and Bagnall, *Women and Society*, 188.

129. Ibid., 188–89.

130. Bowman, *Egypt after the Pharaohs*, 129.

131. Haas, *Alexandria in Late Antiquity*, 139.

132. Quoted in Bowman, *Egypt after the Pharaohs*, 204.

133. Ibid., 205.

134. Quoted in Haas, *Alexandria in Late Antiquity*, 33.

135. Ibid.

136. Ibid., 41–42.

137. Ibid., 21–22.

138. Ibid., 24–25.

139. Ibid., 25–26.

140. Rufinus of Aquileia, *Hist.* 2.23; quoted in ibid., 148.

141. This description of the Serapeum is dependent upon the description given by Lewis, *Greeks in Ptolemaic Egypt*, 71–72.

142. Haas, *Alexandria in Late Antiquity*, 30.

143. Roger S. Bagnall and Bruce W. Frier, *The Demography of Roman Egypt* (Cambridge Studies in Population, Economy, and Society in Past Time 23; New York: Cambridge University Press, 1994), 54.

144. Ibid., 56; Haas, *Alexandria in Late Antiquity*, 312.

145. Haas, *Alexandria in Late Antiquity*, 57.

146. Ibid., 69.

147. Ibid., 48.

148. Ibid., 47–50.

149. Ibid., 132.

150. Ibid., 10, 13.

151. Ibid., 139.

152. Eusebius, *The History of the Church* (trans. G. A. Williamson; New York: Penguin, 1965), 89

153. Clayton Jefford, "Mark, John," *ABD* 4:557–558.

154. Bruce M. Metzger, *A Textual Commentary on the Greek New Testament* (New York: United Bible Societies, 1971), 466; J. Finegan, *Encountering New Testament Manuscripts* (Grand Rapids: Eerdmans, 1974), 64, for a brief statement on the nature of the text.

155. L. D. Hurst, "Apollos," *ABD* 1:301; Ernst Haenchen, *The Acts of the Apostles: A Commentary* (trans. Robert McL. Wilson; Philadelphia: Westminster, 1965), 549–51.

156. Gerd Lüdemann, *Early Christianity according to the Traditions in Acts: A Commentary* (trans. John Bowden; Minneapolis: Fortress, 1987), 207–9.

157. H. Dixon Slingerland, *Claudian Policymaking and the Early Imperial Repression of Judaism* (ed. Jacob Neusner; South Florida Studies in the History of Judaism 160; Atlanta: Scholars Press, 1997).

158. C. Wilfred Griggs, *Early Egyptian Christianity: From Its Origins to 451 CE* (rev. ed.; Brill's Scholars' List; Leiden: Brill, 2000), 33–34.

159. Colin Roberts, *Manuscript, Society, and Belief in Early Christian Egypt* (The Schweich Lectures of the British Academy; London: Oxford University Press, 1979).

160. Griggs, *Early Egyptian Christianity*, 32–33.

161. Haas, *Alexandria in Late Antiquity*, 62.

162. Ibid.

163. Titus Flavius Clemens, *Stromateis: Books 1 to 3* (ed. Thomas P. Halton; trans. John Ferguson; The Fathers of the Church; Washington, DC: The Catholic University of America Press, 1991), 3.

164. Dimitris Kyrtatas, *The Social Structure of the Early Christian Communities* (London: Verso, 1988), 78.

165. Wayne A. Meeks, *The First Urban Christians: The Social World of the Apostle Paul* (New Haven: Yale University Press, 1983).

166. Haas, *Alexandria in Late Antiquity*, 53.

167. Ibid., 54.

168. Ibid., 232.

169. Ibid.

170. Quoted in Griggs, *Early Egyptian Christianity*, 58.

171. Quoted in ibid., 56.

172. Annewies van den Hoek, "How Alexandrian Was Clement of Alexandria? Reflections on Clement and His Alexandrian Background," *HeyJ* 31 (1990): 179.

173. Koen Goudriaan, *Ethnicity in Ptolemaic Egypt* (Dutch Monographs on Ancient History and Archaeology 5; Amsterdam: J. C. Gieben, 1988), 117.

174. On ideas of Egyptian exoticism, see Frankfurter, *Religion in Roman Egypt*, 217–21 and passim.

175. Haas, *Alexandria in Late Antiquity*, 8.

176. Ibid.

177. For a possible criticism of this view, see ibid., 181.

178. Griggs, *Early Egyptian Christianity*, 50.

179. Haas, *Alexandria in Late Antiquity*, 257.

180. Ibid., 217.

181. Ibid., 208.

182. Ibid., 235.

183. Ibid., 252–58.

184. Ibid., 249.

185. Ibid., 253.

4

Clement of Alexandria's
Vision of Prayer

Righteousness is a combination of community and equity.
—Clement (*Strom.* 3.8.1)

Seeing the Cosmos through Clement's Eyes

In our last chapter I discussed the context in which the Alexandrian Christian community developed. As I indicated, Christianity in Egypt did not fit into the narrowly construed theological categories that would later be deemed orthodox by its adherents. The complex social and political structures that prevailed in the Roman province undoubtedly influenced the development of the Christian faith in this context. Egypt under Roman rule was a mottled and interesting amalgam of Roman, Greek, Egyptian, and other cultural influences. Its history under the Ptolemies had forged a society divided into distinctive and often competing ethnoreligious groups. The ways these cultures interacted was further problematized by the advent of Roman rule. Under Rome, life in the once-proud kingdom was structured according to the political philosophy and social practices of the imperial provinces. This complication culminated in a society where people had various allegiances based on ethnoreligious and sociopolitical identifications. As a matter of course, this arrangement fostered social conflict. Defined as "the perceived divergence of interest, or a belief that the parties' current aspirations cannot be achieved simultaneously," this conflict played itself out between Jews and Greeks, Egyptians and Romans, citizens and noncitizens, rich and poor, males and females.[1] Psychologists who study social conflict would categorize many of these as "struggle groups."[2]

In the second century CE, Christianity constituted such a struggle group. As such, it manifested both the positive and negative aspects of

121

social conflict. On the positive side, it fostered group unity, nourished social change, and facilitated the reconciliation of people's legitimate interests.[3] On the negative side, it promoted social instability, moved rapidly from local to global concerns, moved from self-preservation to the annihilation of the other, and increased the number of parties to the conflict.[4] Clement of Alexandria embodied the entirety of this social context. His struggle against his pagan and gnostic contemporaries can be identified clearly through his writing.

This chapter focuses on one aspect of Clement's apologetic program and theological vision in *Stromata 7*, his treatise on prayer. Although the discussion in this chapter is primarily intellectual, I ask the reader to remember that Clement's theological vision is informed and influenced by his social context. In order to accomplish the chapter's primary aim, I will examine the Alexandrian Jewish contribution to Alexandrian Christian thought. Then I will look at the diffusion of quotations of the LP in Clement's writings. After this, I will sketch out Clement's theological vision by discussing major themes in his three greatest works. Next, I will use Clement's theological vision as a prism through which to tease out his theology of prayer. Finally, this cultic understanding will serve as the instrument through which we will attempt to hear the LP through Clement's ears.

Clement and the Alexandrian Jewish Lens

Alexandrian Christianity owed a great debt to Hellenistic Jewish thought, especially the type of Judaism manifested in the writings of Philo of Alexandria.[5] It thus is not surprising to find Clement using many concepts developed by Philo. It is well known that Clement borrowed Philo's allegorical method and some of his more elaborate allegories.[6] Furthermore, Clement co-opted Philo's doctrine of the Logos as the central concept in his presentation of Christianity.[7] Linking the Hebrew phrase "the word of the Lord" with the Stoic doctrine of the *spermatikos Logos* and Plato's doctrine of ideas, Philo constructed a conception of "a divine, rational, and spiritual principle immanent in man and in the universe. He also found a divine personality, or quasi-personality, to come between the Absolute and the world."[8] Philo's Logos mediates between humanity and God.[9] Clement alters this doctrine by equating Philo's Logos with the historic Jesus.[10]

Some scholars have argued that Philo's ideas have some affinities to Gnosticism, although this is by no means conclusive.[11] Clement shares the following ideas with Philo: (1) an emphasis on the transcendence of God, (2) an emanationist conception of God, and (3) a general disparagement of the sense-perceptible world. Philo's doctrine of divine transcendence is a combination of Platonic philosophy and the HB. He tends toward a *theologia negativa*. Although he believes one cannot *know* God, he does maintain that God communicates with humanity. By contrast, in Clement there "is a silence concerning God that not even the initiated can penetrate."[12] God's transcendence is such that it takes the Logos to establish any sort of relationship between humanity and the divine. Clement's Logos reveals a needed and higher knowledge of God. He believes this knowledge to be inseparable from faith. Clement's God is immutable, impassible, and anonymous. These characteristics place God beyond all human capacity to conceive and relate in linguistic terms.[13] It is the Logos who overcomes this chasm between God and the world.

Another Philonic idea shared by Clement is the repudiation of radical dualism. In their shared view, all creation derives from God. This includes all beings above humanity on the hierarchy of powers. And so, the divine spark operates on various levels of being. This spark resides in humanity, and it must be recognized and cultivated for a true relationship with God to occur. Beings occupying the higher levels of the hierarchy are closer to God in terms of being, but their intentions at times can be malevolent. And yet, Philo's intermediaries are not the wicked and rebellious archons of gnostic myth.

Although he disparages the sense-perceptible world, Philo's ideas are far removed from the gnostic myth of a premundane fall (see *Opif.* 15–17, 24). Philo's ideas seem to be governed by models presented in the HB, and this almost requires the dismissal of certain gnostic ideas like the rejection of materiality, which could mean the rejection of procreation. Clement appears to hold the same view. For example, in his argument against the Marcionites, he says, "They stand in opposition to their creator and make haste towards the one they call god, who is not (they say) god in another sense. . . . So they are abstinent not by an act of will but through hatred of the creator and the refusal to use any of his productions" (*Strom.* 3.3.12.2 [Ferguson]).[14] He goes on to say that the purpose for bodily existence is to be led and to lead others to salvation (see 3.9.65.3). In short, as an inheritor of Alexandrian Jewish thought Clement and the Alexandrian Christian community used these ideas as a basis for their own theology. Of course, the second-century Alexandrian ἐκκλησία developed their own ideas, but these ideas have their basis in thinkers such as Philo.

The Diffusion of the Lord's Prayer in the Writings of Clement

Clement never quotes the LP in its totality. This may raise the question as to whether he actually knew it. Based on the evidence, I believe, three arguments demonstrate that Clement knew the LP and developed his theology of prayer in relationship to it. First, the presence of manuscripts like Luke and Matthew in Egypt demonstrate that Clement would likely have had access to these works, including their presentations of the LP.[15] In fact, scholars have concluded that there are over 150 direct and indirect quotations from Matthew alone in Clement's writings. Of these quotations, at least 59 come from the SM. Moreover, it would seem odd that he would not have known the prayers presented in these Gospels, particularly since the Alexandrian Christian community developed out of the Alexandrian Jewish community. As far as we can tell, prayer was a fundamental part of the developing liturgy of the synagogue, and presumably it would have been important to the ἐκκλησία also. In addition, since the LP is presented as a form of ritual instruction in the Gospels, it is perplexing that Clement would not have used it in his discussion of prayer, unless he specifically discounts its validity.

Second, Clement knows at least parts of the LP. He quotes it on several occasions. In *Paedagogus* 1.8 he says, "And the Lord says in his prayer, 'Our Father, who art in heaven'" (*ANF* 2:228).[16] In *Fragments from Cassiodorus* 1.1 he says, "For so you have in the Lord's Prayer, 'Hallowed be Thy Name'" (*ANF* 2:572). In *Stromata* 4.8 he maintains, "The earthly Church is the image of the heavenly, as we pray also 'that the will of God may be done upon earth as in heaven'" (*ANF* 2:421). Finally, in *Quis dives salvetur* he says, "[The] Lord commands us each day to forgive the repenting brethren" (*ANF* 2:602). Not only does Clement quote from the LP, he also attributes the words of the prayer to the Lord himself. Since Jesus is the Logos of God, any exposition of prayer Clement undertakes would presumably be in line with the teachings of the Logos. *Stromata* 7, however, does not appear to follow this reasoning. It makes the inquiring person question why Clement would knowingly neglect the ritual instruction of the Lord on such an important issue.

Finally, one could argue that Origen's commentary on the LP serves as proof that Alexandrian Christian scholarship was concerned not only with prayer in general, but the LP in particular. Robert Casey argues that it was precisely Origen's task to interpret and explain Clement's theology to others. However, Origen's *De oratione* appears strikingly different from *Stromata* 7. As Casey explains,

What is not to be found in Clement is anything corresponding to Origen's long disquisition on the meaning of εὐχή and προσευχή, his careful exegesis of the Lord's Prayer, his long discussion of the times for prayer and the postures appropriate to it, and his classification of prayers into four types based on 1 Tim. 2.1.[17]

Origen justifies the use of the LP in the personal and corporate worship of Christians in Alexandria. We cannot be certain as to Origen's exact apologetic aim in composing his treatise on prayer. However, it is clear from his work that this great thinker considered any discussion of prayer without reference to the LP as theologically invalid. It further indicates that the LP was known and used in the Alexandrian ἐκκλησία during the second century CE. Again, the question arises as to why these two theologians, one presumably the teacher of the other, would hold very different convictions about the validity and utility of the LP. As a member of the Alexandrian Christian community, we would expect Clement's comments to somehow reflect his social context. Generally, we understand this reflection to be positive. Yet, this may be an instance in which an interpreter actually rejected the dominant understanding advanced by his interpretive community. The rationale for Clement's negligence of the LP must lie in his overall theological vision.

Clement's Theological and Literary Vision

Clement's theological writings are extensive, but his apologetic aim is singular. He seeks to define what he believes to be orthodox Christianity against those who attempt to disassociate it from its Jewish roots, particularly gnostic groups operating in Egypt. He attempts to accomplish this feat through his trilogy: *The Exhortation to the Greeks* (*Protrepticus*), *The Instructor* (*Paedagogus*), and the *Stromata*. These works form the core of Clement's theological endeavor. In order to understand his exposition on prayer in *Stromata* 7, it is important that more than Clement's debt to Philonic philosophy be outlined. The philosophical relationship between these three works needs to be outlined in order to place Clement's ideas regarding prayer in the proper perspective. So this section will address Clement's relation to Greco-Roman philosophical movements, and then the character of the works indicated above will be analyzed.

Eusebius tells us that Clement learned Stoic philosophy from Pantaenus.[18] Stoicism was an intellectual movement in the Roman world that upheld strong moral ideals. Clement adopted the Stoic formula of "life according to nature" and modified it in relation to the Aristotelian idea of *metron*.[19] Stoicism's doctrine of "life according to nature" represented an allegiance to an idyllic "state of nature" in which the corruptions of civilization were unknown. In such a state, God and humans formed one polity, one order. The apparent division between humanity and God could be erased in this ideal state. When the Stoic achieved this state of nature, he became one with the cosmos. The Stoic considered himself a "citizen of the world" and a "son of God" (see Epictetus, *Diatr.* 2.8).

Stoic philosophy, which strove to maintain the dignity and freedom of the individual, argued that human beings come into the world with some innate idea of good and evil, as if taught by nature (see Plutarch, *Stoic. abs.* 1041e). It is through the comparison of these innate ideas with those of others that philosophy develops. This concept of innate ideas lays the groundwork for Clement's argument regarding truth. He maintains that truth exists in all cultures, and that the Logos places it there.[20]

The Stoics also developed the doctrine of the *spermatikos Logos* as a means of discussing the development of these ideas into philosophy (see Zeno, frg. 102). The rational faculty of the individual (*logos*) was the most important component of this philosophy: "The Stoics say that the commanding-faculty is the soul's highest part, which produces impressions, assents, perceptions, and impulses. They also call it the reasoning faculty" (Aetius 4.21.1 [*SVF* 2.836, part; Long and Sedley]).[21] What this rational faculty could attain was *gnōsis,* and it was this knowledge that placed the human being in contact with the divine mind. In that sense, the attainment of knowledge became an *imitatio Dei*.[22] By the second century CE, Stoicism ceased to be an effective force in the popular philosophical and religious thought of the Greco-Roman world, although it still influenced thinkers. Clement was a thinker.

Thinkers were also attracted to the philosophical system called Gnosticism. It was somewhat popular in Egyptian intellectual circles. Thinkers such as Basilides, Carpocrates, and Valentinus embraced it. Clement was no exception. However, the definition of Gnosticism presents us with a problem. In the famous Messina Colloquium on the Origins of Gnosticism, scholars distinguished between *gnōsis* as "knowledge of the divine mysteries reserved for an elite," and the "Gnosticism of the Second Century sects."[23]

Most so-called gnostic groups used titles like the "spiritual ones," the "perfect," the "elect," and the "free" (with regard to this world) as a means of self-designation. Each of these titles can be found, in some measure, in Stoicism, Platonism, and Clement's own writings. Among the Christian gnostics like the Valentinians, terms like "disciples of Christ" and concepts like the ἐκκλησία were also used to express their self-understanding.[24]

Each person in the community had a certain "level" or "measure" of *gnōsis*.[25] The person recognized as the "leader" held the highest level of *gnōsis*. These groups did not have a community system based on a hierarchical administration, nor could they ever, so long as they proclaimed salvation based on the charismatic concept of *gnōsis*. These communities, like those of Valentinus and Basilides, had a lot of the character of philosophical schools. Such schools looked to their leader or teacher to enlighten them on the divine mysteries (see Chrysippus, *Etymologicum magnum*). Unlike other Christian schools, the gnostic schools did not congeal around a *regula fidei*.[26] This core doctrinal statement served as the basic point of agreement and departure for emerging orthodox thinkers. It enabled them to point to something objective in their endeavor to cultivate a unified community. This lack of a "center" among gnostics created problems based on the same charismatic quality that the community espoused, namely, *gnōsis*. As Kurt Rudolph points out, "When the founder or leader died leadership evidently passed to disciples, a process which often led to divisions in the originally unified community, as we can see very clearly in the school of Valentinus which split into several branches (two in particular)."[27]

Christians in Alexandria shared a distinctive understanding of the faith that makes it difficult to distinguish easily between the orthodox and the heterodox. Outside of their own claims and agendas, many Alexandrian Christian intellectuals agreed on various theological concepts. At times, Clement quotes Valentinus and the Valentinians approvingly (see, e.g., *Strom.* 3.1.4, 7; 6.6).[28] Clement and the Valentinians shared a number of ideas, for example, (1) an emanationist doctrine of God, (2) the doctrine of salvation as *gnōsis*, (3) an ethic for ideal life characterized as moderate asceticism, and (4) a doctrine of eschatological ascent, just to name a few. In short, Clement shared many doctrinal positions with other Egyptian gnostics, but he viewed himself as a defender of orthodoxy over against the philosophical perils of these other systems. His self-understanding was grounded in his commitment to what he considered true Christianity, one centered on the *regula fidei* as a basis for the construction of his theological claims. This style of Christianity was not identical to Philonic Platonism, Stoicism, or heterodox Christian Gnosticism, although it shares concepts in common with all three. This philosophical matrix serves as the basis for the construction of Clement's theological categories and interpretive principles.

At the beginning of *Stromata* 7, Clement makes an interesting statement that reveals a great deal about his overall theological and hermeneutical vision:

> And if our words seem to some of the uninstructed to be different from the Lord's Scriptures, let them know that it is from the Scriptures that they draw their life and breath, and that it is their object, taking these as their starting point, to set forth, not their phraseology, but their meaning only. (7.1.1)

In other words, Clement has more at stake in his hermeneutical endeavors than just the mere paraphrasing of texts. As this hermeneutical principle illustrates, he is more concerned with the rationality of his argument than he is with whether his argument agrees with the *literal* words of the scriptural text. According to Clement, the test of a Christian theological claim is not its agreement with the Lord's scriptures but its agreement with the Logos, the de facto authority standing behind these texts. He understands the Lord's scriptures to be often confusing and contradictory. This necessitates some sort of hermeneutical principle that can be used to organize and explicate these texts in an edifying manner. Clement accomplishes this feat by appealing to the authority of the Logos. The Logos is that extra-textual authority that guides the proper interpretation of texts.

Clement of Alexandria uses his distinctive concept of the Logos as a hermeneutical device.[29] As a consequence, he follows a two-pronged approach to the interpretation of scriptural texts that places primary authority on theological categories somewhat independent of the texts they are used to interpret. First, he adheres to a body of knowledge he calls the "tradition of the elders," the *regula fidei*. This knowledge consisted of teachings passed down from Jesus to certain teachers who then transmitted them to their students, and so on. Second, he adopts an understanding of the Logos that maintains it to be the original divine voice found throughout creation.[30] Both prongs find their origin in the Logos. This hermeneutical tool gives him the ability to incorporate large amounts of Greco-Roman and Jewish philosophical literature into his works without discounting their ability to transmit truth effectively. Since truth can be found in all cultures, the astute exegete will be able to discern that truth whether it be found in specifically Christian writings or not. David Dawson comments on this method: "Clement's mode of reading consequently relativizes all texts—whether classical literature, the Septuagint, or the New Testament—by subordinating them to an underlying divine discourse."[31]

In effect, Clement's sources for the construction of theological claims are subject to the authority of the Logos as manifested through the divine voice and embodied in the *regula fidei*.

The *Protrepticus*

Thus, the Logos is at the center of Clement's three great works. In the *Protrepticus* he presents a refutation of Greco-Roman religion and a proof of the superiority of Christianity over all other religious practices and philosophies. Clement's doctrine of God (and by implication the Logos) forms the center of the discussion in the text.[32] Piety (εὐσέβεια) in this treatise is defined as a "godliness [that] makes man as far as can be like God" (*Protrept.* 9.86.2).[33] Since εὐσέβεια involves the proper performance of religious rituals and ethical acts, this godliness is an outgrowth of the reception of *gnōsis*. Εὐσέβεια means acting in accordance with the will of God in one's daily affairs. It is an imitation of the Logos as manifested in the ministry of Christ. It is a complement to the noetic comprehension of the deity. By necessity this involves the interpretation of texts in a manner that reveals their dependency on the authority of the Logos. And so, the NT does not serve as a de jure authority for Clement. It has a de facto authority in that it in some way gives voice to the Logos. The same is true of the HB and the Greco-Roman philosophers (*Protrept.* 8.77.1; *Paed.* 1.3.9). Thus, Clement does not feel bound to the *words* of the text, but he is bound by the *voice* of the Logos behind the text.

The *Paedagogus*

Clement meant for the *Paedagogus* to serve as a manual of Christian morals and ethics.[34] As he understands it, the Christian life (εὐσέβεια) is properly the fulfillment of the purpose of the Logos. The treatise begins with a discourse on the functions of the Logos. "In fact, it is constructed on an elaborate pun on the word *logos*."[35] Clement maintains that exhortation (προτρεπτικὸς λόγος) deals with habits and customs (τὰ ἤθη), and that similarly it is the duty of the Logos to lead persons from their old habits and customs to the new and better ones found in the Christian philosophy. Persuasive rhetoric (ὑποθετικὸς λόγος) is concerned with a human being's conscious acts, those acts attributable to deliberate choice (αἱ πράξεις), and it is the office of the Logos to preside over the voluntary acts of Christians.

Instruction (διδασκαλικὸς λόγος) also has its counterpart in the revelation of doctrine made by the Logos. The title for the work itself comes from the world of elementary education. It can also be found in Gal 3:24–25 where Paul calls the law the *paidagōgos* of believers. Clement expands on Paul's idea by equating the law with the Logos. The Logos became our *paedagogus* (companion-teacher) because we were sinners and the remedy for sin is education (cf. Plutarch, *Mor.* 439c–f; Plato, *Lysis* 208c, 223a). Christopher Stead highlights Clement's program well:

> Clement of Alexandria has a well-conceived educational program which coheres with his metaphysics and theology, and aims at leading the mind away from material things to the study of transcendent realities.[36]

Clement appears to draw his ideas concerning the necessity of education from Plato's *Laws*. Plato believed that the lawgiver should supervise all the activities of his citizens and instruct them as to right and wrong. In other words, the legislator has an educational role. In Clement's theology, the lawgiver is the Logos.

The Logos works through the ἐκκλησία and serves an educational role in the life of the believers (*Strom.* 7.2.6). This educational role is carried out through the application of moral norms to the believer. These norms involve both persuasion and coercion.[37] As in the *Laws*, it is the role of the Logos to instruct and educate the unenlightened in the ἐκκλησία (cf. *Leg.* 857c–e). Education is accomplished by means of preambles that use persuasion as well as threats to induce the proper behavior (*Leg.* 722c–723d). Part of this training in proper behavior involves the "correct training of the emotions."[38] Plato believed "that only a limited number of citizens can come to a fully rational understanding."[39] This idea of Logos as *paedagogus* corresponds well with Clement's idea of the role of the Logos in the life of the ἐκκλησία (see *Strom.* 7.1.3).

According to Plato, the human soul and its virtue are to be preferred above all other human goods (see *Leg.* 631b–c, 697b, 726–728c). Within the soul it is the immortal element of reason (*logos*) that is divine, not the mortal elements, passions, and desires (see *Leg.* 644c–645c, 713e; cf. *Tim.* 42c–44d, 69d–e). All subordinate goods properly look to reason (*logos*) as their leader (631c–d). The soul is honored by resisting the blandishments of pleasure and enduring both pain and fear (727c). And so, the goal of life (εὐσέβεια) is to struggle against pleasure in order to subordinate oneself to the dictates of reason.[40]

According to Clement, everything that is contrary to sound reason is sin (*Strom.* 7.11.66). Virtue is a disposition of the soul in agreement with reason throughout the whole of life (*Paed.* 1.13). Thus, the Christian life (εὐσέβεια) fulfills the purposes of the Logos by the application of a system of rational behavior (*Paed.* 1.13.102.3; see also *Strom.* 7.7.47). Casey comments on this understanding:

> "Reason" in this connection is ambiguous, since it may refer either to the mind of man or to the divine Logos, but it is probable that both are intended and the Logos is conceived as guiding men by the natural processes of their thought and by the commandments he has issued in Scripture for them to obey.[41]

The argument in the *Paedagogus* provides further explanation to passages found in *Stromata* 7: Clement demonstrates that God uses various means to educate: some listen to persuasion, but others must be threatened.[42] This disciplinary action on the part of the Logos is not to be seen as dysphoric. Clement argues that God disciplines out of love.[43] God's anger is really a sign of divine love, and God's so-called wrathful acts are all designed to cure humanity of sin. They are not signs of ill will but of good will (*Paed.* 1.8.70.1).

The *Stromata*

One scholar has described Clement's third work, *Stromata*, as "a prolegomenon to the study of systematic theology."[44] Casey comments further on the work: "From the literary point of view the Stromateis is the weakest of all Clement's works, but in its thought it is the most important one."[45] On the one hand, many have argued that the *Stromata* is structureless. For example, T. B. Glover says, "Such works imply some want of the creative instinct, or originality, and they are an index to the thinking of the age, impressed with its great ancestry."[46] On the other hand, Louise Roberts argues that "all such works display extreme care in joining the material together."[47] She goes on to say,

> The literary form of the *Stromateis* has to be understood by grasping the relation among the *kephalaia* constituting a systematic development which produces a work of reciprocal relations. Clement's method of presenting his doctrine is through a concate-

nation of texts or propositions that are related to another by a kind of logic forming a system (σύστημα).[48]

Clement intends the *Stromata* to unveil the truth gradually. This is a truth that has been previously announced and grasped through knowledge of the underlying meaning. Thus, Roberts concludes that the *Stromata* belongs to a class of *hypomnematic* literature. As a form of rhetoric it is concise and reliant on the process of implication.[49]

Stromata 7

Stromata 7 begins with Clement's assertion that he will prove that the Christian gnostic alone is truly pious (7.1.1). That is, the Christian gnostic is the only true worshiper of God, "worshipping the true God as befits him, . . . the worship which befits God including both loving God and being loved by him" (7.1.2). Since this is a treatise on prayer, it involves the issue of εὐσέβεια. As mentioned earlier, εὐσέβεια involves the proper performance of ritual activities in accordance with reason (see 2.9). Thus, this exposition on εὐσέβεια, which deals specifically with the ritual activity of prayer, is a form of ritual instruction and reflection (cultic *didachē*) aimed at those earnestly desiring to worship God properly. This is why it is astounding that Clement totally neglects the LP. It would seem to contradict the premise of his hermeneutical strategy: adherence to the tradition and teaching of the Logos. The meaning behind this exclusion will now be pursued.

Clement says that *gnōsis* comes through the Logos, and is given in measure to a person's ability to understand (7.1.2). The Logos plays a much larger role in Clement's theology than does the Father.[50] His theology moves more toward the Logos because of his acceptance of an emanationist doctrine of God. Clement's Logos is invested with a degree of personality (see 7.2.6). Through the ministry of Jesus the Logos became the great high priest. By taking on human form, the Logos became an agent and model for human salvation.[51] In itself the Logos is the source of providence and the agent of creation. As such it is "never divided, never dissevered, never passing from place to place" (7.2.5). As the source and guiding force for creation, the Logos serves as the logical focal point of contemplation that brings disparate humanity into harmony. As Clement says,

> Let us who are many hasten to be gathered unto one love according to the unity of the monadic essence. Since we do good, let us in like manner pursue unity by seeking the good Monad. But the unity of many arising out of a multitude of separate voices takes on

a divine harmony and becomes one concordant sound, following one director and teacher, the Logos, and coming to rest at the Truth itself saying, "Abba, Father." (*Protrept.* 9.88.2–3)

The governance of Christ provides an interesting insight into how Clement employed both Philonic and Stoic notions of the Logos as a means of formulating a Christian understanding of the relationship between the Father and the Son. As he says, "[All] activity of the Lord is referred to the Almighty, the Son being, so to speak, a certain activity of the Father" (*Strom.* 7.2.7). As the bridge between creation and God, the Logos plays a pivotal role in Clement's understanding of revelation and soteriology. The Logos is the active agent of human salvation.

God has a plan for the cosmos: to bring humans into a state of salvation through *gnōsis*. God is intimately involved in this process through the agency of the Logos. In this regard Clement quotes an old Pythagorean dictum:

God is one and is not, as some suppose, outside creating but in it, existing wholly in the whole cycle, cause and guardian of all, the blending of the universe and fashioner of his own power of all his works, the giver of light in heaven, and father of the universe, mind and animating principle of the whole cycle, mover of all. (*Protrept.* 6.72.4–5)

Since the providential purpose of God is that humans receive salvation, one could be led to believe that God compels persons to be saved. Clement rejects such a view of providence. Drawing upon Plato's *Respublica* (617e), he says, "The conditions laid down by God are equal for all, and no blame can attach to him; but he who is able will choose, and he who wills prevails" (*Strom.* 7.3.20). Instead, God's power persuasively draws people into a state of salvation (7.2.10). Clement believes that it is God's constant purpose to save humanity, and if human beings would only believe, they can be saved (*Protrept.* 11.116.1). It is a sign of God's benevolence. As Casey says, "This fixed intention on God's part is the sure proof of his friendly concern for man, his φιλανθρωπία."[52] Again, Clement shares a lot with Platonic philosophy. His idea of contemplation as leading to salvation appears quite similar to a corollary idea found in Plato's writings. For example, in the *Respublica* Plato discusses the idea of the diversion of the soul toward contemplation and concludes: "So the study of the 'one' would be one of the studies which lead and divert the soul toward the contemplation of real being" (525; see also 620e).

Clement's God is apathetic, without passion (*Strom.* 7.2.6). He sees this as proof of divine perfection.[53] Thus, any notion, even in the Scriptures, that God or Jesus is passionate becomes a mistaken idea about God. He says, "It seems that we continually think of the Scriptures in worldly terms in such respects, making analogies from our own passions, wrongly accepting our understanding of the will of God (who is impassible) by the analogy of stirrings within us" (2.16.72.2 [Ferguson]).[54] This passionless portrayal of God seems to contradict the biblical portrait of the divine.[55] However, Clement is steadfast in his rejection of anthropomorphism even in its more refined forms, like ascribing to God not the *physical* characteristics of human beings but their emotions and passions (see 2.16.72.1–4; 4.23.151.1–2; 6.8.64.1).

Out of Clement's argument regarding divine apathy springs his novel contribution to theology: God is immaterial.[56] Clement was aware that the common definition of God as spirit (πνεῦμα) meant that God possessed some sort of substantive existence.[57] Contrary to the philosophical doctrines of the day, Clement argued that spirit was immaterial (ἀσώματος; see 1.11.51.1; cf. *Protrept.* 5.66.3; *Strom.* 7.7.37.1–2).[58] He constructs this doctrine of divine immateriality upon the Platonic doctrine of the world of ideas. According to contemporary Platonism, immateriality meant belonging to the world of intellectual things.[59] Clement argued that the nature of God is synonymous with the world of ideas, the world of pure mind (νοῦς).[60] He equated πνεῦμα to νοῦς. In this endeavor he found some help in the writings of Paul who, in some cases, interpreted πνεῦμα as an intellectual reality (see Rom 1:9; 8:16; cf. Rom 12:2; 14:5; 1 Cor 2:11).[61] He augmented these Pauline ideas of πνεῦμα with Platonic epistemology and metaphysics to construct a revolutionary view of the divine being.[62] To believe that God is noetic is to believe that God is immaterial, because the nature of the intellect and of its objects is immaterial (*Strom.* 3.171.103.3; 5.28.4–5; 5.11.67.1–3; 5.14.109.1; 5.11.71.1–5).[63] This leads to even more statements that can be made about the divine nature and action. For example, God acts mentally and not physically. As pure νοῦς God is omniscient. Being immaterial, God is also transcendent, far beyond human understanding. This leads to even more statements claiming, for example, that God is inexpressible and uncircumscribable. Clement's God is the wholly other. Without the agency of the Logos, God would be completely unknown.[64] As Deirdre Carabine makes clear,

> It is important to note that although Clement comes very close to the idea that God's transcendence is such that He is essentially

unknowable, he never makes his concept actually explicit. He follows *Timaeus* 28c: the father is difficult to know [*Strom.* 5.11]. He does mention the altar to the Unknown God (Acts 17:22–23), but says that the Unknown can be known both through divine grace and through the *Logos* [5.12]. Another idea which is derived from this Platonic text is that the knowledge of God cannot be divulged to the multitude and here Clement uses two very interesting texts to make this point: Exod. 20:21 and 2 Cor. 12:2–4 [5.12]. According to Clement the cloud represents the fact that God is invisible and ineffable, although the darkness refers to the unbelief and ignorance of the multitude.[65]

In addition to his doctrine of God, Clement puts forward a doctrine of the human situation that does not define the central human problem as sin in the sense of acts committed against God or the corruption of human nature by means of the fall, but as ignorance or entanglement in passion. He bases this doctrine on the Platonic idea that God is the author of good and not evil. As Plato says,

> It follows then, said I, that God, since he is good, would not be cause of all things, as most say, but cause of a few things to mankind, and of many no cause; for the good are much fewer for us than the evils; and of the good things God and no other must be described as the cause, but of the evil things we must look for many different causes, not only God. (*Rep.* 379b)

This idea can also be found in Stoicism. As Plutarch says,

> And yet [Chrysippus] himself says in his book *Concerning the Judicial Function* and again in his work *Concerning the Gods*, Book II, that "It is not reasonable to suppose that the Divine Being has any share in the causation of foul things. Just as Law can have no share in the causation of impiety, so it is reasonable to hold that they cannot have any share in the causation of what is foul." Yes indeed, someone may say, as he commends Euripides for saying: "If they do foolishness, then gods are no gods," and again: "The easiest way, to hold the gods in fault!"[66]

Thus, God cannot be held responsible for evil or for the outcome of a person's life. As Plato says, "No Destiny shall cast lots for you, but you shall

all choose your own Destiny. . . . The blame is for the chooser, God is blameless" (*Resp.* 617e; cf. *Ep.* 2.312e). Clement makes this explicit in *Stromata* 7.12.72: "[He] who refuses to eradicate the passion of his soul causes his own death." Human beings are responsible for sin. It is the by-product of ignorance, and an indication of the distance between creature and Creator.

In *Stromata* 7.4.26 Clement says, "[The] true God regards nothing as holy but the character (ἦθος) of the just man, nothing as polluted but what is unjust and wicked." In Clement's anthropology those who have overcome ignorance are capable of proper religious performance: "worshipping the true God as befits him" (7.1.2). He believes this performance to be characterized by a certain reciprocity, namely, loving God and being loved by God (7.1.2). Justo Gonzalez has pointed out that Clement's anthropology is similar in many respects to that of Irenaeus.[67] Humanity was created with a childlike innocence. This innocence, however, is not equivalent to perfection (see 7.1.4.86). Rather, humanity was created to grow toward perfection. Thus, perfection is always a possibility. As Clement says, "It is essential that the person who hopes to find God's approval should be so far as possible like God" (2.22.132.4 [Ferguson]).[68] Alienation from God took place because humans made use of their sexual capabilities before God had intended it, and humanity, thus, became subject to sin and death (3.17.103.1–4). Clement differs from Irenaeus in that for him Adam is not the head of humanity, but rather a symbol for that which happens in each person individually.[69] This does not mean, as it does in some other theological visions, that human freedom and individual accountability are destroyed. God, through the agency of the Logos, offers faith. A human being must decide whether to accept it or not, which means exercising her freedom (see 7.2.6, 9, 12). And yet, this faith is only the beginning of the new life (see 7.7.45). It must be followed by fear and hope, which lead to love and finally to true *gnōsis*.

The ἐκκλησία has an extremely important role to play in this process of salvation. It functions as the "Mother of Believers" (*Paed.* 1.5). It is within the ἐκκλησία that the process of divinization takes place, which leads ultimately to the life of the true gnostic. One enters the ἐκκλησία through baptism, and is nourished within it through the Eucharist. Baptism is fundamental to Clement because it is the ritual through which the act of illumination takes place. Yet, it is only the first step in the process. As he says, "Being baptized, we are illuminated; illuminated, we become sons; being made sons, we are made perfect; being made perfect, we are made immortal" (1.6). Baptism brings one into the church, but it is not the end of the process. It is rather the starting point for further growth that leads to perfection (see *Strom.* 7.14.88). A key component of this growth is the proper performance of religious acts.

Service to God, called θεραπεία θεοῦ by Clement, is defined as a process of self-discipline (7.1). It appears to be analogous to an obedience to the commandments of God (7.3.16). And yet, it is not some authority completely external to the believer. Rather, self-discipline is "the habit of mind which preserves the fitting attitude toward God" (7.1.3). It is the knowledge of both the theory and practice of right living. Godliness is fundamentally a matter of the intellect.[70] Out of his intellectual disposition the believer acts in ways that conform to εὐσέβεια and the commandments of God.

The role of the ἐκκλησία is important because it effectively counteracts individualist tendencies that can be deduced from Clement's soteriology. This appears to have been developed in conversation with groups such as the Valentinians, who split on the idea of whether gnostics and nongnostics could all be considered part of the ἐκκλησία. The so-called Eastern Valentinians argued that only gnostics were part of the true ἐκκλησία. This is exemplified in the teaching of Theodotus. He defined the ἐκκλησία as the "chosen race, . . . chosen before the foundation of the world" (*Exc.* 4.1; 41.2). As he conceived it, the ἐκκλησία was a purely spiritual entity composed exclusively of spiritual people. By contrast, Ptolemy and Heracleon, both teachers in the so-called Western Valentinian school, claimed that the ἐκκλησία consisted of the spiritual *and* the unspiritual, "*both* gnostic and non-gnostic Christians stood within the same church."[71] They based this claim on their interpretation of Jesus' statement that "many are called, but few are chosen" (Matt 22:14). Nongnostic Christians are the "many who are called," which then explains why they constitute the majority in the ἐκκλησία. The gnostics are "the few [who] are chosen." As Elaine Pagels explains, "Heracleon taught that God had given [gnostics] spiritual understanding for the sake of the rest—so that they would be able to teach 'the many' and bring them to *gnosis*."[72] Thus, the two groups have a somewhat symbiotic relationship. Nongnostics need gnostics to fulfill their ultimate destiny in Christ. Gnostics, likewise, need nongnostics to bring their ministries to completion.

The author of the *Interpretation of the Knowledge* amplifies this theological viewpoint well in speaking to those who are nongnostics: "Do not accuse your Head [Christ] because it has not appointed you as an eye but rather as a finger; and do not [be] jealous of that which has been put in the class of an eye or a hand or a foot, but be thankful that you do not exist outside the body" (18.28–34 *NHL*). Likewise, the author addresses those who are gnostics:

> [The gnostic] ought to rejoice [and] be glad and partake of grace and bounty. Does someone have a prophetic gift? Share it without hesitation. Neither approach your brother jealously. . . . How do you know that someone is ignorant? . . . Your brother [also has his] grace: [Do not] belittle yourself, but [rejoice and give] thanks spiritually [and] pray for that [one in order that] you might share the grace [that dwells] within him. So do not consider [him foreign] to you." (15.34–16.25)

Although there is a clear distinction in Valentinian theology between gnostics and nongnostics, there appears to be a clear consensus that both were part of the ἐκκλησία, at least among certain Valentinian groups.[73] And so, it is fair to say that Valentinians had differing views on the makeup of the ἐκκλησία. In the end, however, their conceptions of the ἐκκλησία only perpetuated the biases and distinctions prevalent in the larger society. By contrast, Casey says, "Clement avoids the defects of Valentinian theology, that God might be considered a respecter of persons, and leaves no room for favoritism in the plan of salvation."[74]

Clement argues that all Christians are in reality equal and perfected in the sight of God. The basis for his argument resides in the sacrament of baptism: all Christians are made perfect in baptism. He appeals to Christ's baptism as the model: "But is [Christ] perfected by the washing—of baptism—alone, and is [he] sanctified by the descent of the Spirit? Such is the case. The same also takes place in our case, whose exemplar Christ became" (*Paed.* 1.6). Jesus became perfect at his baptism. "The notion of this perfection is one of Clement's subtlest thoughts, for in spite of the assertion that Christians share in the perfection of Christ, the meaning is not that Christ and Christians are exactly alike."[75] Perfection (τελείωσις) is understood by Clement in a relative, not an absolute, sense. His soteriology does not exclude important differences between Christ and the believers, nor does it obscure important differences among believers themselves. Τελείωσις and equality are posited solely in terms of God's providential purpose, which may vary from case to case. Christians are perfect, not because they all have the same measure of faith or gifts, but because in knowing God they have equally realized the divine will and can fulfill with equal acceptability God's purpose for their lives.

This notion of Christian equality does not mean that all Christians possess an equal measure of abilities. On the contrary, Clement recognized that all people, especially those within the ἐκκλησία, had differing talents and functions. In the case of the gnostic, Clement realized that the *gnosis* that his faith called for was of a different variety from that deemed adequate to most Christians. The gnostic was part of a divine aristocracy, which represented the maximum degree of divinity that a human being was capable of absorbing.[76] From one perspective it is inappropriate to say that one Christian's *gnosis* is better or greater than that of another. All the faithful have the *gnosis* of God given to them at baptism. And it appears as if there are at least two ways of knowing God.[77] The nongnostic knows God through the will. The gnostic knows God through the intellect.[78] The ultimate goal for all believers can be understood as the νόησις τοῦ θεοῦ, in which comprehension is so perfect that the distinction between subject and object becomes unreal.[79]

In *Stromata* 7 Clement defines the gnostic as one who has come into the knowledge of her true nature, a somewhat common definition (see, e.g., *Gos. Thom.* 38.4–10; 45.30–33; *Dial. Sav.* 134.1–22; *Gos. Truth* 21.22–22.15). He interprets the Delphic maxim, "Know thyself," to mean, "Know for what purpose we are made," another common definition of the idea. It is a "kind of perfection of man as man" (*Strom.* 7.10.55). This recognition begins the process of becoming divine. And only those persons who have had this recognition are suitable for relationship with God. The gnostic has the type of ἦθος deemed appropriate by God. Whenever she acts, her actions lead toward the good. On the other hand, when the individual totally devoid of *gnosis* acts, even if it is on principle, her actions do not lead to the good, because her actions are without basis in *gnosis*.

Clement designates the nongnostics in the ἐκκλησία as "children" (7.11.67). He says that they are "blessed," but he maintains that they are not mature like the gnostics. They may act out of desire for the "crowns" of the ἐκκλησία—or out of fear—but not on the basis of *gnosis* itself. These are those for whom government is a necessity. As Clement makes clear in *Stromata* 7.3.19, God has placed certain persons in governance over others for the sake of education. The gnostic is a citizen of this government, but he is also a citizen of a higher world. And when it comes to ecclesiastical governance, Clement says that the true gnostic is one "according to the rule of the church" (7.7.41). Unfortunately, one gathers the distinct impression that Clement does not posit more than an *essential* and *tenuous* equality among nongnostics and gnostics in the ἐκκλησία. And gnostics are "archetypal" members. So despite Clement's "equality of salvation" argument, in practice nongnostics are denigrated whenever they are compared to their gnostic counterparts.

Clement's Theology of Prayer

The question of the relationship between nongnostics and gnostics in the ἐκκλησία is brought into greater focus when one turns to Clement's exposition on prayer in *Stromata* 7. The key questions he addresses are, *What is prayer? What does it accomplish?*[80] First and foremost, Clement says that the true gnostic must be a member of the ἐκκλησία. Only the gnostic in the ἐκκλησία "has his petition [in prayer] . . . granted according to the will of God" (7.7.41). This is because true faith and love only belong to the ἐκκλησία (7.10.55).[81] Near the end of *Stromata* 7 he states plainly why true prayer only happens within the confines of the ἐκκλησία. In his attack upon the other gnostics, he maintains that it is only within the ἐκκλησία that the entirety of Christian philosophy is taught. The gnostics, by contrast, have what are better labeled as schools than churches (7.15.90, 92). He goes on to attack their use of Scripture by saying that they are "incapable of apprehending the grandeur of the truth," and that their readings are, at best, superficial (7.16.97). He concludes that "the heretics are empty of the divine purposes and of the traditions of Christ" (7.16.99). In fact, they postdate and are derivative of the ἐκκλησία (7.17.106). Their divisiveness, a demonstration of their lack of faith and love, undermines the very principle of unity on which the church is built. This is because unity derives from the doctrine of monotheism:

> I think it has been made plain that unity is a characteristic of the true, the really ancient Church, into which those that are righteous according to the divine purpose are enrolled. For God being one and the Lord being one, that also which is supremely honored is the object of praise, because it stands alone, being a copy of the one First Principle: at any rate the one Church, which they strive to break up into many sects, is bound up with the principle of Unity. We say then, that the ancient and Catholic Church stands alone in essence and idea and principle and pre-eminence, gathering together, by the will of one God through the one Lord, into the unity of the one faith, built upon the fitting covenants (or rather the one covenant given at different times) all those who are already enlisted in it, whom God foreordained having known before the foundation of the world they would be righteous. (7.17.107)

Clement's gnostic must remain in the ἐκκλησία. In his mind there is a unity between gnostics and nongnostics that can only be found in the catholic ἐκκλησία. According to Clement, it is the catholic ἐκκλησία that guards the true tradition of the Logos. This, in turn, guarantees a true understanding of how to interpret the Scriptures (see 7.16.94–96). In other words, Clement provides a variation on the Ignatian dictum that there is no truth outside the established ἐκκλησία.

Speaking of those outside the ἐκκλησία, Clement addresses others among them as well. He places all those outside the ἐκκλησία among the atheists and the *deisidaimons*. Clement advances common philosophical definitions of both (7.1.4). They question the πρόνοια of God (7.2.6–7). In fact, they may believe that God can be swayed by sacrifices and offerings (7.3.15). Clement sums up their position:

> [Their] incontinence in pleasure, being involved both in cross accidents and pains out of common course, and losing heart at their calamities, say that there is no God, or that, if he exists, he is not the overseer of all. (7.3.15)

Against such claims, Clement draws upon his understanding of divine perfection. He says God "has regard for us all" (7.2.6). As an attribute of divine perfection, πρόνοια means that God is "unchangeably the same in his just beneficence" (7.3.15; cf. Plato, *Leg.* 885b, 907a, 908bc). Evil in its various manifestations cannot be attributed to God because God, by his very nature, only wills the good for all creation (see 7.3.16).

Such ill-informed theology is attacked directly in *Stromata* 7.4.23, where Clement uses the term "atheists" for those who adhere to the popular cult:

> Those are atheists who liken the divinity to the worst of men. For either they make the gods injured by men, which would show them to be inferior to man as being capable of receiving injury from him; or, if this is not so, how is it that they are embittered at what is no injury.[82]

Like his philosophical counterparts, Clement criticizes popular religious expression as impious (ἀσέβεια). In this case, ἀσέβεια has to do with an improper conception of the deity. However, the εὐσέβεια that Clement advocates is one that can only be carried out in the ἐκκλησία. As a consequence, those individuals outside the ἐκκλησία, unless presumably they are *deisidaimons*, are atheists.

Clement does give attention to the issue of δεισιδαιμονία. He defines the *deisidaimon* as one "who fears the demons and who deifies everything down to stocks and stones, having brought into slavery the spirit and the inner man which lives in accordance with reason" (7.1.4). It is characteristic of the *deisidaimon* to "think that whatever happens is a sign and cause of evil" (7.4.24). Such a view causes the *deisidaimon* to act out of ignorance rather than *gnōsis* (7.4.25). The *deisidaimon* performs τὰ νομιζόμενα, but in a distorted manner. In Clement's terms, it cannot be anything other than distorted since the *deisidaimon* is ignorant of the true nature of the deity; his religious practices can be nothing other than erroneous and inappropriate. And so, it is impossible for the *deisidaimon* to practice εὐσέβεια as defined by Clement: νομίζειν τὸν θεόν. As in the case of the person who practices popular religion, the *deisidaimon* is misinformed theologically. This makes the *deisidaimon* analogous to the atheist. In this way, Clement has effectively altered the Platonic definition of atheism to include those who would have been previously considered improperly pious. In other words, Clement limits the range of religious personalities to the proper theist and the atheist.[83]

Thus Clement places the non-ἐκκλησία-affiliated gnostics, the *deisidaimon*, and practitioners of popular religion (including philosophers!) under the category of atheists. Then he addresses an issue that consistently undermines any theological vision that places importance on the suppliant's εὐσέβεια: "sinners [who] sometimes succeed in their prayers" (7.12.73). Clement gives two answers. First, "this occurs but rarely" (7.12.73). Second, the apparent granting of a sinner's petition is not due to the sinner's prayer *as such*, but to the prayer's conformity to providence (7.12.73). As he explains,

> [The] gift is not bestowed for the sake of the petitioner, but the divine ordering has a foresight of the person who will be saved by his means, and thus reasserts the character of justice in the benefit imparted. (7.12.73)

In sum, Clement denies the possibility of true prayer to all those who hold an improper view of God. This includes other gnostics, practitioners of popular religion, and the *deisidaimons*. As persons outside the ἐκκλησία, they are not only ignorant of the divine nature, but they are also incapable of honoring God properly. This makes them atheists by definition: θεὸν μὴ τὸν νομίζειν. And so, he argues that if it appears that the prayers of the impious are answered, it is by the chance of their prayers having accorded with providence, not because of the ἦθος of the individual.

Clement further addresses a number of the issues discussed in chapter 2 regarding the Greek philosophical critique. For instance, he agrees with

his philosophical counterparts that the problem with popular prayer is egoism. A large part of *Stromata* 7 is concerned with egoism in prayer. The
true gnostic is the functional example of one who overcomes the problem
of egoism through the proper practice of εὐσέβεια. This is the point of the
statement Clement makes in *Stromata* 7.1.3:

> The gnostic . . . pays service to God by his constant self-discipline
> and by cherishing that which is divine in himself in the way of
> unremitting charity. . . . For he alone is truly devout who minis-
> ters to God rightly and unblameably in respect to human affairs.

Drawing upon his philosophical forebears, Clement says this ministry
involves caring for oneself and for others (7.3.16). Caring for oneself does
not mean that the gnostic seeks to acquire material possessions. Quite the
contrary, the gnostic is one who has discovered that material goods are not
of ultimate importance. In fact, the gnostic must stand "ready to impart to
others of all that he possesses" (7.3.19). In short, Clement defines proper
service to God as service to others. As he says, "The Master and Savior
accepts as a favor (χάριν) and honor (τιμήν) to himself all that is done for the
help and improvement of men" (7.3.21). He makes this point even more
forcefully: "[The] gnostic who regards good done to his neighbors as his
own salvation, might well be called a living image of the Lord" (7.9.52). This
means that the gnostic practices justice in all of his interpersonal interactions (7.12.69). This may include impoverishing herself for the sake of others (7.12.77). This becomes an *imitatio Christi* in that the gnostic must take
on another's sins as his own (7.13.82; see also 7.14; 7.3.17; 7.7.48; 7.12.80).

As in the case of the Greek philosophers, Clement bases his theological anthropology on his larger metaphysical vision. A gnostic cannot be
considered truly pious unless he understands correctly the purpose of the
universe and the providential order:

> [The divine science's] function in regard to the divine things is to
> investigate what is the First Cause and what that through which all
> things were made and without which nothing has been made, what
> are the things that hold the universe together partly as pervading
> it and partly as encompassing it, some in combination and some
> apart, and what is the position of each of these, and the capacity
> and the service contributed by each; and again in things concern-
> ing man, to investigate what he himself is, and what is in accor-
> dance with, or is opposed to his nature; how it becomes him to act

and be acted on, and what are his virtues and vices, and about things good and evil and the intermediates, and all that has to do with manhood and prudence and temperance, and the supreme all-perfect virtue, justice. Prudence and justice he employs for the acquisition of wisdom, and manhood not only in enduring misfortunes, but also in controlling pleasure and desire and pain and anger, and generally in withstanding all that sways the soul either by force or guile. (7.3.17)

Clement is following in the footsteps of his Greek predecessors by linking proper conduct to a correct cosmology. Here Clement says that a proper metaphysics includes (1) a correct conception of God and the Logos, (2) a correct understanding of the nature of humanity, and (3) a correct understanding of how to enact justice in one's interpersonal relationships. This metaphysics is similar to that of his contemporaries, particularly the Platonists, in that in its emphasis upon apathy, altruism, rationality, and incorporeality it becomes an *imitatio Dei*.[84] Through this cosmology the gnostic is enabled to act in accordance with the Logos, a key characteristic of εὐσέβεια.

This understanding of εὐσέβεια comes into sharper focus when Clement discusses the issues surrounding the proper worship of God.[85] He defines the proper worship as "loving God and being loved by him" (7.1.2). He later expands upon this definition by giving examples of what he conceives to be proper worship by redefining the concept of sacrifice. Clement maintains that an acceptable sacrifice is the joining of an unboastful heart to right understanding (7.3.14). This is achieved through proper education in the divine mysteries (7.4.27; see also *Strom.* 2.19.97; cf. *Protrept.* 4.59.2–3; *Paed.* 1.3.9.1–2). As a matter of course, this education involves holding the proper metaphysical outlook: the theological conviction that God is not affected by the human activity of sacrifice. As he says, "[It] is useless to offer meat to that which is in no need of sustenance" (*Strom.* 7.6.30). Hence, the "economic" view of sacrifice represents an improper conception of the deity, one that leads to ἀσέβεια:

Where then there is an unworthy conception of god, passing into base and unseemly thoughts and significations, it is impossible to preserve any sort of devoutness, either in hymns or discourses or even in writings or doctrines. (7.7.38)

According to Clement, what constitutes εὐσέβεια is a sacrifice of thanksgiving (7.12.79). This appears to be in accordance with the Greek philosophical critique that defines εὐσέβεια in terms of one's actions toward one's neighbors and the offering of honor to the deity. Εὐσέβεια also flows into proper prayer language, just as ἀσέβεια flows into improper prayer language. Clement makes it clear that the gnostic will only use proper and fitting language in his prayers: "[He] has acquired freedom of speech, not the power of a mere random fluency, but the power of straight-forward utterance, keeping back nothing that may be spoken in fitting time before a right audience, either from favor or fear of influential persons" (7.7.44).

With regard to the content of one's sacrifice to God, Clement substitutes prayer for the flesh of animals. This view is clearly stated in *Stromata* 7.6.30–7.7.35. Clement begins by opposing the proper view of the deity to an improper one. An improper understanding of the deity results in an economic view of sacrifice—a perspective that seeks to benefit human beings while at the same time offending God. Clement agrees with his philosophical ancestors that the purpose of popular sacrifice is to benefit human beings and not to give true honor to God: "assigning to us gods nothing but the dog's portion" (7.6.30; see also 7.6.31, 32). By contrast, the proper view of God would involve the offering of honor through prayers rather than animal flesh. As he says,

> But if the deity, being by nature exempt from all need, rejoices to be honored, we have good reason for honoring God by prayers and for sending up most rightly this sacrifice, the best and holiest of sacrifices when joined with righteousness, venerating him through whom we receive our knowledge, and through him glorifying him (i.e., the Father) whom we have learnt to know. . . . Our altar here on earth is the congregation of those devoted to the prayers, having . . . one common voice and one mind. (7.6.31; see also 7.7.49)

Here Clement lays out a number of fundamental ideas. He argues that prayer is the only proper sacrifice, and it must be made in accordance with εὐσέβεια. In addition, Clement maintains that the worship of an uncircumscribable God cannot be circumscribed to a particular sacred site or edifice (see 7.5.28–29; 7.7.49). Proper worship is conducted within the ἐκκλησία united under the *regula fidei* that shares "one common voice and one mind." In other words, the immaterial God is only honored through the immaterial sacrifice of an immaterial institution (7.6.32).

Clement draws upon the Greek philosophical critique of sacrifice and weaves together Greco-Roman and Jewish understandings of sacrifice to restate his theology of prayer as sacrifice (7.6.34). Yet, Clement does not stop here. He calls upon the idea of an uncircumscribable God to dismiss the idea that religious rituals, particularly prayer, should be conducted at certain times and places.[86] This claim is in definite opposition to the idea of fixed hours of prayer presented in such documents as the *Didache*: "Thus you shall pray three times a day" (8.3). The entire life of the gnostic is a religious festival.[87] And so, the practice of worshipping God at designated times is unnecessary. In contrast to the popular religious understanding, the gnostic worships god in the proper fashion, "doing this not on special days, as some others do, but continuously all our life through and in all possible ways" (7.7.35). Here Clement's understanding of gnostic devotion appears analogous to Theophrastus' doctrine of συνεχὴς εὐσέβεια, an idea that also developed out of a reinterpretation of sacrifice.[88]

Beginning at *Stromata* 7.7.38, Clement faces the issue of petition directly. He starts with the claim that most petitions are base in nature. The objects of our impulses, he says, form the content of our prayers. He then proceeds from the content of petition to the issue of its intention: "We pray therefore for the same things that we request, and we request the same things that we desire; and praying and longing are on the same footing as regards the possession of good things and the benefits attached to their acquisition." In short, prayer reflects the basic desires of the individual.[89] And so, an appropriate prayer to God would consist of a request for things pertaining to the soul. This is why the gnostic does not pray for material things but for the ability to be good.[90] What separates an appropriate prayer from an inappropriate one is the content of the petition. And yet, the petition's content is entirely dependent upon the ἦθος of the orant (see 7.7.39; 7.12.73). Danger arises whenever a suppliant petitions for something that is out of line with the providential order. Such requests represent only folly: "[It] is the height of folly . . . to ask what is inexpedient, under the impression that it is good" (7.7.39). It is the request for the truly good that separates the gnostic from others and joins the gnostic to the angels.

Clement understands prayer and its attendant rituals to be a practical theological statement on how one is to approach God. As a practice that highlights the orant's εὐσέβεια, prayer gives one insight into the ἦθος of the orant. Having outlined the theological framework in which prayer operates, I will move to Clement's definition of prayer as such. Clement offers his own definition of prayer in *Stromata* 7. It is found in 7.7.39: ἔστιν οὖν, ὡς εἰπεῖν τολμηρότερον, ὁμιλία πρὸς τὸν θεὸν ἡ εὐχή ("So prayer, to speak somewhat boldly, is converse with God").[91] Conversation implies relationship. And relationship implies a certain degree of reciprocity.

Clement chooses a particular term, θεραπεία, to describe his understanding of divine service. It also referred to the treatment or healing of the sick in the Greco-Roman period.[92] And so, prayer is understood by Clement to have a therapeutic effect. The object of this therapy is undoubtedly the orant. Being entirely noetic and incapable of alteration, such prayer cannot have any sort of effect, therapeutic or otherwise, on God. As a conversation with God, this makes prayer a rather one-sided interaction. Boldly speaking, prayer cannot be a conversation in the ordinary human understanding of the term. Instead of dialogue, prayer is more like a monologue. Clement appears to understand this reality because he says that prayer is "a return back on itself of Providence and a responsive feeling of loyalty on the part of the friend of God" (7.7.42). To put it another way, prayer is the verbalization of the goals of the gnostic life and the rededication of the gnostic to the way of providence.[93]

The absence of reciprocity in the prayer relationship becomes clearer when one examines Clement's understanding of the requests God answers. Although he argues that petition is important, Clement also believes that God acts benevolently whether a petition is made or not. As he says, "God knows generally those that are worthy to receive good things and those that are not; when he gives to each what belongs to him. For this reason if request were made by unworthy persons he would often refuse to give it, but would give unasked provided they were worthy" (7.7.41). Clement agrees with positions on God's activity that are found in texts like Matt 6.8. Thus, in Clement's theological scheme it is unnecessary to ask God for material things (see also 7.11.61, 64–65). In fact, a request for something material would be somewhat inconsistent with the immaterial nature of the divine itself. God's beneficence is not predicated on human petition. Quite the contrary, God acts out of his nature. As he says,

> God . . . does not do good of necessity, but of his own free will he befriends those who turn to him of their own accord. For the providence that comes to us from God is not ministrative, as though it proceeds from inferiors to superiors; but it is from pity of our weakness that the nearer dispensations of providence are set in motion. (7.7.42)

Yet, even though God cannot be petitioned for material things, God can and must be petitioned for something else. What must be petitioned for are the conversion of one's neighbors (see 7.7.41; 7.14.84) and the *gnōsis* necessary to be good (see 7.7.38–39; 7.12.74).

Another understanding of prayer is found in *Stromata* 7.7.43: ἐξε-
τάζεται διὰ τῆς εὐχῆς ὁ τρόπος, πῶς ἔχει πρὸς τὸ προσῆκον ("the test of the
attitude toward what is fitting"). The idea presented here is that through
prayer an individual examines his own character to determine what is fitting for the purpose of the Logos. In prayer one *vocalizes* the good.
Clement understands the good as those things pertaining to the soul that
require the joint effort of the orant and God. It does not give the orant
"good things," but makes the orant good (7.7.38). Like his Greek predecessors, Clement agrees that the ἦθος of the human being determines the efficacy of the prayer and also the content of those prayers. This means the
gnostic would not ask for anything that is unworthy of request: "For when
the Giver of all good meets with readiness on our part, all good things follow at once on the mere conception of the mind" (7.7.43). In fact, it could
be no other way. Providence dictates that God know one's material
requests in advance. And so, material things are determined in advance (see
7.7.45). Neither the gnostic nor anyone else is capable of altering the divine
dispensation in that regard, "since even before the creation [God] knew
that it would come into our mind" (7.7.43). What is open to petition is the
individual's possession and reception of *gnōsis*. This is the only good for
which one must pray. To put it another way, the gnostic does not possess
the good in full actuality, but it is possessed in potentiality (see 7.7.47). The
gnostic must ask that the potential be transformed into the actual. Good
things are only accessories to the gnostic, because the gnostic's chief end is
gnōsis and action in accordance with *gnōsis* (see 7.7.48). In prayer, the gnostic is not to ask for new material things, but for the continuance of things
she already possesses, fitness for what is about to happen, and indifference
for what shall be denied (7.7.44). In short, one's material existence is not a
proper topic of petition, since any adjustment in one's material state is
entirely dependent on providence. Providence even transforms the character of prayer itself. Given that the Logos has foreseen that the gnostic will
ask for *gnōsis*, her prayer is not actually a petition but an expression of
thanksgiving: "And the form of [the gnostic] prayer is thanksgiving for
what is past and what is present and what is future, as being already present
through his faith; and this is preceded by the acquisition of knowledge"
(7.12.79).[94]

To highlight the contrast, Clement then turns his attention to those
who utter inappropriate prayers. He says that the wicked pray for those
things that are hurtful to themselves and others (7.7.44).[95] These things are
hurtful to them because they are ignorant of how to use these "pieces of
good fortune:" "For they pray to obtain what they have not got, and they

ask for apparent, not real good" (7.7.44). This is not the object of the gnostic's prayer. The gnostic "does not even desire anything which he has not" (7.7.44). This lack of interest in material possessions on the part of the gnostic resides in knowing what is truly important and recognizing what is capable of petition (see 7.7.46; 7.12.75–76; 7.13.81, 83). In Clement's view, the gnostic "is not lacking in the good things that are proper to him."[96] Thus, in agreement with his Greek predecessors, Clement believes that proper prayer is directed toward those things that are open to alteration, the reception of *gnōsis* and its connected behaviors, and not toward things that are material in nature.

This immaterial orientation is highlighted further in Clement's understanding of God's reception of prayer. Clement lays out the following chain of reasoning: if God is immaterial, and prayer is an immaterial sacrifice offered by an immaterial institution for immaterial things, then God's reception of such prayers must be immaterial also. In *Stromata* 7.7.36 he says,

> For [the gnostic] is persuaded that God knows all things, and hears not only the *voice* but the *thought*, since even in our own case the hearing, though set in action by means of the passages of the body, causes apprehension, not by the power of the body, but by a certain *mental impression* and by the intelligence which distinguishes between significant sounds. (emphasis added)

In other words, God receives prayer primarily through the orant's thought (ἔννοια). Hearing is only a metaphorical way of describing the (mental) transmission of the orant's request to the mind of God. He says, "Even if we address him in a whisper, without opening our lips, or uttering a sound, still we cry to him in our heart. For God never ceases to listen to the inward converse of the heart" (7.7.39). Or, as he says in *Stromata* 7.7.43, "God has no need to learn various tongues, as human interpreters have, but understands at once the minds of all men." The theological framework that allows Clement to dismiss the need for actual speech in prayer also allows for the practice of silent prayer. Pieter van der Horst makes it clear in his article on silent prayer in antiquity that the motives for silent prayer were closely related to theology: "A completely new motive to say prayers without words evolved in hand with a change in the conception of the nature of deity. It was of course in philosophical circles that this change took its point of departure."[97] Clement seems to follow in this line. The immateriality of silent prayer—mental communication with God—is easily adapted to the immaterial understanding of all other aspects of prayer in Clement. A noetic understanding of God naturally leads Clement to advocate silent prayer. Again, he may be drawing part of his understanding of the need for silent prayer from Matt 6.8. At any rate, Clement argues strongly that the immaterial God receives immaterial prayers, through an immaterial means, only for immaterial things.

Clement's advocacy of the immaterial even influences his disavowal of rituals in prayer. And still, he does describe some prayer rituals in this treatise. First, he outlines a ritual involving the raising of the head, lifting of the hands, standing on tiptoes, and giving an outburst of prayer in *Stromata* 7.7.40.[98] The purpose of this posture in prayer is "to detach the body from the earth by lifting it upwards along with the uttered words, we spurn the fetters of the flesh and [the] constrain[t] [of] the soul . . . to ascend into the holy place" (7.7.40). This ritual is theologically appropriate since the ultimate aim of the gnostic's prayer is union with God (7.7.40, 42).

In another passage, Clement advocates the ritual of praying toward the east. This is because the east "symbolizes the day of birth" (7.7.43) and "the rise of dawn" (7.7.42). In addition, both Jews and Gentiles have always seen praying toward the east as the proper direction, according to Clement, because of its symbolic relationship to light and the banishment of ignorance.[99] So although Clement rejects adherence to ritual generally, he does advocate at least two rituals in *Stromata* 7. Hence, these rituals must have a much deeper significance in the theology of Clement than mere performance. I believe they express Clement's deep theological conviction that release from the flesh and union with God is the ultimate goal of the gnostic. This explains why Clement can dismiss fixed hours of prayer, call for a transcendence of ritual in prayer, and yet advocate for these two rituals in the gnostic practice of prayer (see 7.10.57).

Inclusion and exclusion are important in Clement's thought. This is because the exclusion of the LP is quizzical, especially since its exclusion allows for the inclusion of others. These are both positive and negative. The first prayer is to be found in *Stromata* 7.4.24. Here Clement quotes the prayer of the *deisidaimon*: "Ye very precious gods, send me good luck!" It is inappropriate in that Clement would reject any idea of luck as commonly perceived. As already seen, the superstitious person holds an improper theological view. Belief in fate is a misappropriation of the notion of providence. It is the result of ignorance concerning the divine πρόνοια. It is likening "the divinity to the worst of men" (7.4.23). This is an improper approach to God because it characterizes God as fickle. And so, Clement criticizes this prayer because it is not really prayer at all. It is the expression of an improper theological vision. Its inclusion is meaningful when compared to Clement's silence regarding the LP.

The second prayer quoted by Clement is found in *Stromata* 7.7.48. He quotes it approvingly. It is the prayer of an Olympian athlete. It reads: "If I, O Zeus, have now done all that was fitting on my part in preparation for the contest, do thou make haste to bestow the victory I deserve." This sounds analogous to Epictetus's prayer in *Discourses* 2.15:

> Deal with me hereafter as Thou wilt: I am as one with Thee: I am Thine: I flinch from nothing, so long as Thou thinkest it good. Lead me where Thou wilt. Put on me what raiment Thou wilt. Wouldst Thou have me hold office, or eschew it, stay or fly, be poor or rich? For all this I will defend Thee before men. I will show each thing in its true nature, as it is. (Bevan).[100]

In his *Hymn to Zeus*, Cleanthes expresses a similar attitude.[101] To put it another way, Clement maintains that true prayer is not a matter of petitioning for material things but for the proper ἦθος, one in accord with the Logos. Whatever material things come to the gnostic, come by the will of the Logos, who has predetermined whether they shall be granted or not (see 7.7.41).[102]

The final prayer quoted by Clement is undoubtedly paradigmatic for the gnostic. He says that the gnostic, who has a virginal ἦθος, is the only one capable of saying this prayer:

> We long to receive thee, O Lord, at last: we have lived according to thy commandments, we have transgressed none of thy precepts: wherefore also we claim thy promises; and we pray for what is expedient for us, feeling that it is unfitting for us to ask of thee the highest rewards: even though they may seem to be evil, we will receive as expedient all the trials that meet us, whatever they may be, which thy ordering employs for our training in steadfastness. (7.12.72)

This prayer is appropriate to the gnostic for several reasons. First, what the gnostic desires to receive from the Lord is *gnōsis* communicated by the teachings of the Logos (see 7.14.86). Second, the gnostic acknowledges her allegiance to the Logos, which is demonstrated by past adherence to the commandments and precepts of the Lord. This is another indication of prayer as a rededication of the orant to the way of providence. Third, only the gnostic can truly claim the "promises" of the Lord. Clement says in *Stromata* 7.13.81 that a prayer for the forgiveness of one's tormentors is "the claiming of a promise from the Lord." What one's enemies need is not punishment (in the normal sense of the term) but the *gnōsis* that can only come from the Lord. And so the gnostic is precluded from praying against his enemies (7.14.84). This language recalls the doctrine of God's πρόνοια. Fourth, the gnostic asks only "for what is expedient for us." Clement maintains that if the gnostic asks for what is expedient, "he will receive it at once, but things inexpedient he will never ask for, and therefore will never receive: so he will always have what he desires" (7.12.73). Asking for what is expedient is, essentially, asking for nothing materially particular at all. The gnostic trusts in the benevolence of providence, and thus "he has good reason for not being troubled by anything that happens, nor is he suspicious of any of those things which come to pass for good according to the divine order" (7.13.83). In a more focused passage, Clement says, "[The] gnostic will not ask for a superfluity of wealth for himself to distribute, but will pray that there may be to them a supply of what they need" (7.13.81). In sum, the final prayer cited by Clement is an appropriate prayer for the gnostic in that it fulfills all the necessary criteria for the worship of God.

The results of this analysis of Clement's theology of prayer have yielded considerable information that can be used to explain why Clement ignores the LP as a proper prayer to be uttered by the gnostic. To summarize: Clement argues that only those in the ἐκκλησία possess the true teachings of the Logos and thus are able to utter appropriate prayers. True εὐσέβεια consists in serving others. This can only occur when one has a right understanding, which comes through education in the divine mysteries. True prayer is an immaterial sacrifice offered by an immaterial institution to an immaterial God for immaterial things. Anything else would not be in accordance with providence—and thus demonstrative of an improper conception of the deity.

This brings us back to one of the original questions raised at the beginning of this chapter: What does prayer accomplish? According to the theology laid out here, the efficacy of prayer is found in its ability to influence the individual's reception and maintenance of *gnōsis*. As the highest ideal to which the human being can aspire, a petition for *gnōsis* represents a recognition of that which is needed beyond all other things, and the only thing truly worthy of human striving.[103] Again, Clement may be drawing upon another principle found in the SM: "But strive first for the kingdom [of God] and its righteousness and all these things shall be added to you" (Matt 6.33; translation mine).

Clement's Hearing of the Lord's Prayer

I would like to focus the remainder of the discussion on the implicit and operative issue that drives this analysis in Clement's decision not to evoke it in *Stromata* 7. Clement was acquainted with the prayer. His quoting of the prayer in his other writings indicates that he saw it as authoritative, at least in certain contexts. And so, his silence is deafening in this instance. Is it that Clement is actually making a statement regarding the LP by excluding it? Earlier, I indicated that inclusion and exclusion are important categories to consider in an analysis of Clement's vision. This is especially true in this case, when the available evidence only serves to underscore the fact that it is left out. And since this is not just an oversight, the purpose for its exclusion lies in Clement's hearing of the prayer.

Clement listens for the voice of the Logos whenever he engages a text. In practice, this gives him considerable latitude. He can incorporate material and take theological positions that would appear inconsistent with prevailing Christian understanding and practices. Although the majority of the ἐκκλησία heard the voice of the Logos in the LP, Clement understood the Logos to be silent. Greco-Romans in the ἐκκλησία, for the most part, heard the LP as a theological statement on the proper performance of a cultic act. It outlined the proper way to approach God, and it demonstrated what things were appropriate to request in prayer.[104] By contrast, Clement's theological vision muted any possibility that he would hear the Lord speaking through this text. And so, instead of contradicting the majority in the ἐκκλησία, he simply excludes it from his discourse on the topic.

When one listens closely to the LP, one finds a couple of issues that stand in direct conflict with Clement's theology of prayer. The first appears to be the overall theological orientation of the prayer. The LP is a petitionary prayer. It envisions a socially integrated universe in which the relationship between God and creation involves the expression and fulfillment of needs on both sides. The LP assumes that God is a God with certain needs: to have his name sanctified, his kingdom come, and his will be done.[105] Likewise, human beings have particular needs that must be brought before God. I believe Clement hears such an orientation in the prayer and automatically deems it theologically inappropriate.

The second is the language used in the prayer and what it intends to convey. The language of the *invocatio* may be metaphorical (Πάτερ ἡμῶν ὁ ἐν τοῖς οὐρανοῖς), but it still stands in tension with Clement's theology. He prefers to emphasize the hiddenness of God. He uses the term "father" as a way of addressing the Creator and sustainer of the universe. Likewise, he would not have a problem describing God as if he were a *paterfamilias*, especially since he calls the church the mother of believers. And yet, it is rather clear that from Clement's theological perspective believers have more interaction with the Logos than they do with the Father as such. Being immaterial, God is understood primarily through intellectual means (see *Strom.* 8.8). Any comprehension of God beyond the noetic is in some way a falsification of the being of God. The same is true of the locative indicator used in the prayer (ἐν τοῖς οὐρανοῖς).

The ideas of social hierarchy and egoism evoked in the prayer by the use of the pronoun "our" would be acceptable in Clement's theological vision. Like the Greek philosophers, he would dismiss the idea that prayer should be egotistical in orientation. The hierarchical implications of the prayer would also be compatible with Clement's vision. As a member of the Alexandrian bouleutic class, Clement was undoubtedly well acquainted with the patronage system. In fact, if it is true that Clement was a member of the *familia Caesaris*, then he would have participated in that system both as a patron and a client. The potential benefits of this social arrangement were apparent to someone of his communal standing. Membership in the *familia Dei* would then confer certain benefits, as well as responsibilities, upon an individual. Being a member of the ἐκκλησία initiates one into this divine *familia*. Thus, the notion that God functions as the ideal patron would be in line with Clement's understanding.

Early Christian interpreters used the LP as a vehicle for distinguishing between insiders and outsiders. Since Clement excludes the LP from his treatise on prayer, it would be inappropriate to conclude that he would understand the pronoun "our" to mean Christian. And yet, it is evident from our analysis that Clement's theology privileges some over others in the cosmic household. In *Stromata* 7.2.5 he says that there are three classes of people: friends, faithful servants, and merely servants. The last group is outside the church, and the Logos uses corrective discipline on them. Within the church, gnostics or friends occupy a higher status than do faithful servants. And so, it would be fair to say that although Clement maintains that the entire creation belongs to God, this claim is not indicative of a radical equalization of status among human beings. Clement clearly supports the idea of a hierarchical social structure, even within the ἐκκλησία. Such a stratified social conception may be a by-product of his cultural environment. The complex social arrangements that prevailed in the province of Egypt elicited and intensified tendencies toward differentiation among residents. As a Roman citizen, Clement's theological vision is cast in such a way as to reify the Roman social structure, including its privileges and biases, in his ecclesiology. Thus, certain forms of prayer would be more appropriate to the gnostic, while others would not. It appears that to Clement particular forms of divine address are appropriate based on one's status in relation to God. Hence, without the correct cosmological conception, an individual is incapable of appreciating the import of any form of divine invocation. Distinguishing between insiders and outsiders is a central concern in Clement's theology; consequently, it is manifested in his conception of prayer.

Another sign of Clement's tendency to distinguish between insiders and outsiders can be found in his use of the first petition of the prayer, ἁγιασθήτω τὸ ὄνομά σου (*Fragments from Cassiodorus* 1.1). As part of a commentary on 1 Peter, Clement argues that only the righteous can sanctify God's name. They are able to do this because they have the correct conception of God's nature. Others are incapable of hallowing God or the Logos because they are uninformed or badly informed of the divine nature. As I pointed out in chapter 1, one understanding of this petition might be that an exemplary intervention of God is necessary to eradicate the evil that manifests itself in the profanation of God's name. Such a request is unnecessary, according to Clement's theological vision, because God has already intervened to correct the problem. Since ignorance is the central human problem, Clement believes that God, through the agency of the Logos, has placed truth in all cultures, manifested truth explicitly through the incarnation, and continues to reveal truth as the *paedagogus* of humanity, using both persuasion and coercion. Clement says, "[Every] time and every place is holy in which we entertain the thought of God." And since God's name is sanctified whenever the righteous (probably the gnostics) give thought to God, and he maintains that they think on God continually, God's name is always being sanctified. Of course, this is not presently a universal reality. Still, this petition from the LP would be superfluous because it is tantamount to asking God to do something that the Logos has already done.

A similar problem is encountered in petition 2: ἐλθέτω ἡ βασιλεία σου. It is inappropriate as a theological request, which may explain why Clement never quotes it. The petition could be understood as a request that God manifest God's dignity and worthiness and establish a just and humane social order. In contrast, in every passage of Clement's writings where he makes mention of the kingdom of God, it is always under the assumption that the kingdom is already present. For example, in *Stromata* 4.6 Clement interprets Matt 6:33 by saying, "'But seek first the kingdom of heaven, and its righteousness,' for these are the great things, and the things which are small and appertain to this life, 'shall be added to you.' Does He not plainly then exhort us to follow the gnostic life, and enjoin us to seek the truth in word and deed?" (*ANF* 2:415). From Clement's perspective, God's kingdom came with the advent of creation itself. The Logos has governed the cosmos continuously since its inception. As he says,

> The Son is the highest pre-eminence, which sets in order all things according to the Father's will, and steers the universe aright, performing all things with unwearying energy. . . . To him is subjected the whole army of angels and of gods—to him, the Word of the Father, who has received the holy administration by reason of him who subjected it to him; through whom also all men belong to him but some by way of knowledge. (7.2.5)

It is this last phrase, "but some by way of knowledge," that highlights the theological difference between Clement and our imagined Greco-Roman auditor. To Clement, the problem is not that God's kingdom needs to be established, but that it is not recognized. By means of the Logos, God offers *gnōsis*, which enables one to recognize the presence of God's kingdom. Those who accept *gnōsis* are part of God's kingdom. Again, ignorance is the problem, to which education is the proper response.

The same holds true with petition 3. The request, γενηθήτω τὸ θέλημά σου, ὡς ἐν οὐρανῷ καὶ ἐπὶ γῆς, can be interpreted to mean that the orant should submit to God's πρόνοια. Clement would agree with the petition at this point. In a passage on proper relations in the household, Clement quotes this petition: "And the earthly Church is the image of the heavenly, as we pray also "that the will of God may be done upon the earth as in heaven" (4.8 [*ANF* 2:421]). Members of the household should submit to one another on earth as an imitation of the divine order that prevails in heaven. By contrast, Clement would dispute the idea that God's πρόνοια can be successfully opposed. Individuals oppose Providence out of ignorance. And yet, the will of God, as manifested through the Logos, always prevails. As he concludes, "[Nor] could the Lord of all be hindered by opposition from without" (7.2.6). In other words, this petition is inappropriate because it implies that providence can be thwarted when it cannot.

God's πρόνοια is also at the heart of the petition for daily bread. According to Clement, the divine πρόνοια is an expression of God's power and benevolence. The request found in the LP, τὸν ἄρτον ἡμῶν τὸν ἐπιού-σιον δὸς ἡμῖν σήμερον, could call either power or benevolence, if not both, into question. Discussing the activity of the Logos in *Stromata* 7, he contends, "For either the Lord does not care for all men; and this is the case either because He is unable (which is not to be thought, for it would be a proof of weakness), or because He is unwilling, which is not the attribute of a good being" (7.2 [*ANF* 2:524]). And since God's power and benevolence are beyond scrutiny, this petition is inappropriate. Earlier, I pointed out that Clement's theological framework maintains that God has already decided the parameters of an individual's material possessions (see also 7.7.42, 46, 48; 7.13.81). In short, Clement's theological vision renders such a petition useless.

Another reason for the petition's uselessness may have to do with Clement's social context. I mentioned the possible influence of the Alexandrian context on Clement's tendency to distinguish between insiders and outsiders in my discussion of the *invocatio*. Here it is possible to tease out yet another social influence upon this Christian intellectual. Roman citizens occupied privileged positions within the Egyptian province's social structure. And since travel was difficult and expensive in antiquity, it is unlikely that one would encounter an impoverished Roman in the provinces. Therefore, it would be fair to conclude that, as a Roman citizen, Clement was wealthy. Furthermore, the wealthy were somewhat shielded from the vagaries of food supply and consumption. This would mean that the acquisition of food was not a high priority for the wealthy. In fact, ascetic practices often influenced more philosophically minded elites, especially in Egypt.[106] Clement was an advocate of asceticism. I believe that Clement's theological vision and the influence of his social context converge in a way that makes any material interpretation of this petition useless.

I mentioned in chapter 1 that early Christian interpreters of the LP confronted a similar problem in their readings of the prayer. As a means of preserving the idea of God's benevolence, they spiritualized the idea of bread. Clement may have acted in a similar manner. For example, in *Paedagogus* 1.6 he says, "[The] Word declares himself to be the bread of heaven," and concludes that through his sacrifice the Lord has become "baked bread" (*ANF* 2:221). If this interpretive move were applied to the bread of which the LP speaks, then it is actually a petition for the reception of the Logos. Or, to put it another way, by requesting daily bread the orant is in fact saying, "Give me the *gnōsis* that can come only from the Logos." And herein lies the problem. The gnostic has already received the *gnōsis* that the bread symbolizes. Of course, she could pray this petition on behalf of those who do not possess *gnōsis*, but it would be entirely inappropriate to pray it on her own behalf (see also 7.13.82).

Clement advocates the practice of forgiveness of sins. As he says, "[The] Lord commands us each day to forgive the repenting brethren"

(*Quis div.* 39 [*ANF* 2:602]). Acting in this manner is a demonstration of εὐ-σέβεια and an *imitatio Dei*. In *Stromata* 7.13.81 Clement bases his understanding of the practice of forgiveness on the doctrine of monotheism: since all created beings derive from God and God forgives them, refusing to forgive another is tantamount to a rejection of God's will. The righteous person will act appropriately when faced with such a situation. Or, as Clement says, "[The gnostic] never remembers those who have sinned against him, but forgives them; wherefore also he has a right to pray: 'Forgive us, for we forgive'" (7.13.81). What is missing from Clement's idea of forgiveness is the distinctive representation of sin as indebtedness.[107] According to Clement, sin is the result of human ignorance and the entanglement of the individual in passion. God forgives and overcomes human sinfulness through the bestowal of *gnōsis*. Once one has received *gnōsis*, he no longer needs forgiveness for himself because he is no longer embroiled in ignorance and passion.

In a discussion of sin in *Stromata* 2.14–15, Clement distinguishes between voluntary and involuntary acts. Of involuntary acts he says, "The involuntary does not come under judgment" (2.14.60.1 [Ferguson]).[108] On the other hand, of voluntary acts he says, "Voluntary action corresponds to desire, choice or an intellectual thought" (2.15.62.1 [Ferguson]).[109] According to Clement, these acts constitute the basis of sin. As I mentioned in chapter 1, in the LP the absence of justice by itself does not constitute sin. It is the continued existence of this absence that lures human beings into committing evil deeds. God, as the cosmic *paterfamilias*, is partly responsible for evil because God allows this situation to exist. By contrast, Clement argues that *apparent* evil is in reality part of the divine educational project. Those who lack *gnōsis* do not understand this. God is not responsible for temptation in the sense that God seeks to do harm to human beings, nor does God simply allow evil to persist, but God uses evil as an instrument for education.[110] Thus, Clement could not agree with the petition καὶ μὴ εἰσενέγκῃς ἡμᾶς εἰς πειρασμόν, ἀλλὰ ῥῦσαι ἡμᾶς ἀπὸ τοῦ πονηροῦ.

Hopefully, this analysis has demonstrated the purpose behind Clement's exclusion of the LP in his discourse on prayer in *Stromata* 7. To close this discussion, I would like to point out that Clement does allude to a cultic paradigm that he endorses. This one also carries the mandate of the Logos:

> Thus the Lord also prayed, returning thanks for the accomplishment of his ministry and praying that as many as possible might

share in knowledge, in order that God, who alone is good, alone is savior may be glorified through the Son, in those who are being saved through the salvation which is according to knowledge, and that the knowledge of him may grow from age to age. Howbeit the mere faith that one will receive is itself also a kind of prayer stored up in a gnostic spirit. (7.7.41)

This is an allusion to the prayer uttered by Jesus in John 17. Clement then does endorse a prayer tradition that he attributes to the Lord. The gnostic should pray for the bestowal of *gnōsis* on others. This prayer is appropriate as an expression of εὐσέβεια because it is an *imitatio Christi*. As our analysis has demonstrated, the petition for *gnōsis* is appropriate because it is something within the cosmos that is open to alteration.

To summarize our discussion in this chapter, the results of this analysis indicate clearly why Clement excludes the LP from his discussion of prayer in *Stromata* 7. First, the orientation of the prayer makes it an inappropriate means of approaching God. As a petitionary cultic act, the LP runs counter to Clement's vision of what proper prayer is and does. Second, the language of the LP presents theological difficulties for Clement, especially with respect to God's needs and the problem of evil. As a member of the Alexandrian ἐκκλησία, it would have been difficult for Clement to reject the LP out of hand. It was part of what his interpretive community valued. And so, Clement's discourse on prayer in *Stromata* 7 is constructed in contradistinction to the prevailing cultic practices of his community. This makes *Stromata* 7 even more interesting as a cultic *didachē* since it has a definite apologetic aim. In his battle against the followers of Marcion, Basilides, Carpocrates, and Valentinus, Clement presents a vision of prayer that is incongruous with that espoused by the majority of Christians in Alexandria. And yet, this is the first postbiblical treatise on prayer available to us.

Notes

1. Dean G. Pruitt and Jeffrey Z. Rubin, *Social Conflict: Escalation, Stalemate, and Settlement* (Topics in Social Psychology Series; New York: Random House, 1986), 4.

2. Pruitt and Rubin present the idea of a struggle group as such: "Dahrendorf (1959) has specified three conditions that foster development of a struggle group and hence encourage conflict: (1) continuous communication among the people in question; (2) availability of leadership to help articulate an ideology, organize a

group, and formulate a program for group action; and (3) group legitimacy in the eyes of the broader community—or at least the absence of effective community suppression of the group" (ibid., 16). Their reference is to Ralf Dahrendorf, *Class and Class Conflict in Industrial Society* (London: Routledge & Kegan Paul, 1959).

3. Ibid., 6–7.

4. Ibid., 7–8.

5. Cf. Christopher Haas, *Alexandria in Late Antiquity: Topography and Social Conflict* (Ancient Society and History; Baltimore: John Hopkins University Press, 1997), 120.

6. Robert Casey, "Clement of Alexandria and the Beginnings of Christian Platonism," in *Studies in Early Christianity: A Collection of Scholarly Essays* (ed. Everett Ferguson et al.; The Early Church and Greco-Roman Thought; New York: Garland, 1993), 140.

7. T. B. Glover, *The Conflict of Religions in the Early Roman Empire* (Boston: Beacon Hill, 1960), 271.

8. Ibid., 289.

9. Christopher Stead, *Philosophy in Christian Antiquity* (New York: Cambridge University Press, 1994).

10. Casey, "Clement of Alexandria and Christian Platonism," 107.

11. Robert McL. Wilson, "Philo of Alexandria and Gnosticism," *Kairos* 14 (1972): esp. 215.

12. Raoul A. Mortley, *Connaissance religieuse et herméneutique chez Clément d'Alexandrie* (Leiden: Brill, 1973), 58.

13. Joseph C. McLelland, *God the Anonymous: A Study in Alexandrian Philosophical Theology* (Patristic Monograph Series 4; Cambridge: Philadelphia Patristic Foundation, 1976), 160; A. H. Armstrong, "The Self-Definition of Christianity in Relation to Later Platonism," in *Jewish and Christian Self-Definition: The Shaping of Christianity in the Second and Third Centuries* (ed. E. P. Sanders; Philadelphia: Fortress, 1980), 92–97; and Salvatore Romano Clemente Lilla, *Clement of Alexandria: A Study in Christian Platonism and Gnosticism* (Oxford Theological Monographs; London: Oxford University Press, 1971), 217–26.

14. Titus Flavius Clemens (Clement), *Stromateis: Books 1 to 3* (ed. Thomas P. Halton; trans. John Ferguson; The Fathers of the Church; Washington, DC: The Catholic University of America Press, 1991), 264.

15. Colin Roberts, *Manuscript, Society, and Belief in Early Christian Egypt* (The Schweich Lectures of the British Academy; London: Oxford University Press, 1979), 12–13.

16. Unless otherwise noted, all translations of Clement's work come from the *ANF*, volume 2.

17. Casey, "Clement of Alexandria and Christian Platonism," 143.

18. See the discussion in chapter 3, after note reference no. 176.

19. Eric Osborn, "Clement of Alexandria: A Review of Research, 1958–1982," *SecCent* 3/4 (1983): 226.

20. James E. Davison, "Structural Similarities and Dissimilarities in the Thought of Clement of Alexandria and the Valentinians," *SecCent* 3/4 (1983): 209.

21. A. A. Long and D. N. Sedley, eds., *The Hellenistic Philosophers* (2 vols.; Cambridge: Cambridge University Press, 1987), 1:315.

22. Glover, *Conflict of Religions*, 62.

23. Ugo Bianchi, "Le Colloque International sur les Origines du Gnosticisme," *Numen* 13 (1966): 151–60; Ugo Bianchi, ed., *The Origins of Gnosticism* (SHR 12; Leiden: Brill, 1967), 151–60.

24. Kurt Rudolph, *Gnosis: The Nature and History of Gnosticism* (1st ed.; ed. and trans. R. McL Wilson; San Francisco: Harper & Row, 1984), 205–7.

25. See the discussion in Elaine H. Pagels, *The Gnostic Paul: Gnostic Exegesis of the Pauline Letters* (Philadelphia: Fortress, 1975), 43.

26. See the discussions in Justo L. Gonzalez, *A History of Christian Thought* (rev. ed.; 3 vols.; Nashville: Abingdon, 1970), 1:146; and Elaine H. Pagels, *The Gnostic Gospels* (1989 Vintage Books ed.; New York: Vintage Books, 1989), 133.

27. Rudolph, *Gnosis*, 213.

28. Everett L. Proctor, "The Influence of Basilides, Valentinus, and Their Followers on Clement of Alexandria (Egypt)" (PhD diss., University of California, 1992).

29. David Dawson, "Ancient Alexandrian Interpretation of Scripture" (PhD diss., Yale University, 1988).

30. David Dawson, *Allegorical Readers and Cultural Relativism in Ancient Alexandria* (Los Angeles: University of California Press, 1992), 184.

31. Ibid.

32. Casey, "Clement of Alexandria and Christian Platonism," 95.

33. Ibid., 102.

34. Ibid., 103.

35. Ibid., 104.

36. Stead, *Philosophy in Christian Antiquity*, 84–85.

37. R. F. Stalley, *An Introduction to Plato's Laws* (Indianapolis: Hackett, 1983), 42.

38. Ibid., 43.

39. Ibid.

40. Ibid., 67; cf. Plato, *Tim.* 44c, 87a–b; Bonnie Bowman Thurston, *Spiritual Life in the Early Church: The Witness of Acts and Ephesians* (Minneapolis: Fortress, 1993), 12.

41. Casey, "Clement of Alexandria and Christian Platonism," 105.

42. Ibid., 112.

43. Cf. ibid., 132.

44. Ibid., 90.

45. Ibid., 114.

46. Glover, *Conflict of Religions*, 268; cf. Casey, "Clement of Alexandria and Christian Platonism," 114.

47. Louise Roberts, "The Literary Form of the *Stromateis*," *SecCent* 1 (1981): 212.

48. Ibid., 216.

49. Ibid., 219.

50. Cf. Casey, "Clement of Alexandria and Christian Platonism," 102; Robert L. Simpson, *The Interpretation of the Lord's Prayer in the Early Church* (ed. S. L. Greenslade; The Library of History and Doctrine; Philadelphia: Westminster, 1965), 149.

51. Glover, *Conflict of Religions*, 297.

52. Casey, "Clement of Alexandria and Christian Platonism," 97.

53. Diedre Carabine, "A Dark Cloud: Hellenistic Influences on the Scriptural Exegesis of Clement of Alexandria and Pseudo-Dionysius," in *Scriptural Interpretation in the Fathers: Letter and Spirit* (ed. Thomas Finan and Vincent Twomey; Dublin: Four Courts, 1995), 65; Stead, *Philosophy in Christian Antiquity*, 127–30; W. D. Palmer, "Atheism, Apologetic, and Negative Theology in the Greek Apologists of the Second Century," *VC* 37 (1983): 243.

54. Clement, *Strom.*, 206.

55. Casey, "Clement of Alexandria and Christian Platonism," 101, 32.

56. Ibid., 126; cf. Carabine, "A Dark Cloud," 65 n. 20.

57. Ibid., 125.

58. Ibid., 122.

59. For a discussion of matter and the mistakes moderns make concerning it, see Dale B. Martin, *The Corinthian Body* (New Haven: Yale University Press, 1995), 6–15.

60. Casey, "Clement of Alexandria and Christian Platonism," 121–22.

61. Ibid., 125.

62. Stead, *Philosophy in Christian Antiquity*, 55.

63. Casey, "Clement of Alexandria and Christian Platonism," 124.

64. Carabine, "A Dark Cloud," 67.

65. Ibid.

66. Taken from Edwin R. Bevan, *Later Greek Religion* (New York: E. P. Dunn, 1927), 22.

67. Gonzalez, *A History of Christian Thought*, 1:202.

68. Clement, *Strom.*, 246.

69. John N. D. Kelly, ed., *Early Christian Doctrines* (2d ed.; London: A & C Black, 1960), 179.

70. Casey, "Clement of Alexandria and Christian Platonism," 134.

71. Pagels, *The Gnostic Gospels*, 139.

72. Ibid.

73. Ibid., 142.

74. Casey, "Clement of Alexandria and Christian Platonism," 108–10; cf. John Ferguson, *Clement of Alexandria* (New York: Twayne, 1974), 152.

75. Casey, "Clement of Alexandria and Christian Platonism," 111.

76. Ibid., 116.

77. Ibid., 126.

78. Ibid., 111.

79. Ibid., 120.

80. Cf. Simpson, *Interpretation of the Lord's Prayer*, 115.

81. Ferguson, *Clement of Alexandria*, 151, and Stead, *Philosophy in Christian Antiquity*, 51.

82. Casey, "Clement of Alexandria and Christian Platonism," 141; and H. S. Versnel, ed., *Faith, Hope and Worship: Aspects of Religious Mentality in the Ancient World* (vol. 2; Studies in Greek and Roman Religion; Leiden: Brill, 1981), 224.

83. Clement rejects out of hand those persons following Prodicus, who counseled against prayer (*Strom.* 7.7.41).

84. Casey, "Clement of Alexandria and Christian Platonism," 132ff..

85. Cf. Simpson, *Interpretation of the Lord's Prayer*, 152.

86. Casey, "Clement of Alexandria and Christian Platonism," 135.

87. Stalley, *An Introduction to Plato's Laws*, 130.

88. Cf. Versnel, *Faith, Hope and Worship*, 51–60.

89. Casey, "Clement of Alexandria and Christian Platonism," 137; Versnel, *Faith, Hope and Worship*, 6–8; Friedrich Heiler, *Prayer: A Study in the History and Psychology of Religion* (2d ed.; ed. Samuel McComb; New York: Oxford University Press, 1933), 17, 59; and Simpson, *Interpretation of the Lord's Prayer*, 37–38, 110.

90. Casey, "Clement of Alexandria and Christian Platonism," 137.

91. Clement, *Strom.* 7.7.42.

92. BAGD, s.v. "Θεραπεία."

93. Casey, "Clement of Alexandria and Christian Platonism," 135; and Heiler, *Prayer*, 38, 84–85.

94. Casey, "Clement of Alexandria and Christian Platonism," 136.

95. Heiler, *Prayer*, 89–90.

96. Ferguson, *Clement of Alexandria*, 152.

97. Pieter W. van der Horst, "Silent Prayer in Antiquity," *Numen* 41 (1994): 9. Also, it would serve as no surprise that Clement's philosophical cohorts were inclined to recognize this form of prayer. Seneca in *Ep.* 41.1 says, "We do not need to uplift our hands toward heaven, or to beg the keeper of a temple to let us approach his idol's ear, as if in this way our prayers are most likely to be heard. God is near you, he is with you, he is within you." Porphyry in his *Abst.* 2.34.2 says, "Let us sacrifice in such a manner as is fit, offering different sacrifices to different powers; to the God who is above all things, as a certain wise man said, neither sacrificing nor consecrating anything that belongs to the world of the senses. For there is nothing material which is not immediately impure to an immaterial nature. Hence neither is vocal language nor internal speech adapted to the highest god, when it is defiled by any passion of the soul; but we should venerate him in profound silence with a pure soul and with pure conceptions about him."

98. This sounds similar to Origen's description of prayer in *Or.* 31.2: "Further,

while there are many ways of bodily deportment, there can be no doubt that the position of extending one's hands and elevating the eyes is to be preferred above all others; for the position taken by the body is thus symbolic of the qualities proper to the soul in the act of praying. This we say should be, except under particular circumstances, the normal position taken."

99. Again, this ritual is later reflected in Origen's treatise on prayer, *Or.* 32: "It should be immediately clear that the direction of the rising sun obviously indicates that we ought to pray inclining in that direction, an act which symbolizes the soul looking towards where the true light rises."

100. Bevan, *Later Greek Religion*, 111.

101. Long and Sedley, *Hellenistic Philosophers*, 1:326.

102. This idea is an allusion to the famous *conditio Jacobaea* found in the NT book of Jas 4:15. The phrase, however, is much older than the work and is particularly found in the writings of Plato. For example, in Plato's *Phaedo* 80d one finds the phrase "if god wills." Cf. Hans Dieter Betz, *The Sermon on the Mount: A Commentary on the Sermon on the Mount, Including the Sermon on the Plain (Matthew 5:3–7:27 and Luke 6:20–49)* (ed. Adela Yarbro Collins; Hermeneia—A Critical and Historical Commentary on the Bible; Minneapolis: Fortress, 1995), 394; Martin Dibelius and Heinrich Greeven, *A Commentary on the Epistle of James* (rev. ed.; ed. Helmut Koester; Hermeneia; Philadelphia: Fortress, 1975), 233–34, particularly n. 21.

103. Simpson, *Interpretation of the Lord's Prayer*, 133, 36.

104. Ibid., 111; Betz, *Sermon on the Mount*, 376–78.

105. Betz, *Sermon on the Mount*, 378–80.

106. Peter Garnsey, *Food and Society in Classical Antiquity* (Key Themes in Ancient History; Cambridge: Cambridge University Press, 1999), passim; Teresa M. Shaw, *The Burden of the Flesh: Fasting and Sexuality in Early Christianity* (ed. L. Michael White; Minneapolis: Fortress, 1998), 1–26.

107. Clement only uses ὀφείλημα once in his writings, at *Strom.* 3.18.107.5. The obligation he acknowledges in this passage is the one to produce children in marriage.

108. Clement, *Strom.*, 199.

109. Ibid., 200.

110. The understanding of πειρασμός as an educational tool can be found near the end of chapter 1.

5

A Picture of Roman Carthage

Delenda est Carthago
—Plutarch (*Cat. Maj.* 27)

Refocusing Our Lens

In our last two chapters I discussed the context of the Alexandrian Christian community as well as Clement's hearing and imagined interpretation of the LP. As already recognized, Egyptian Christianity did not conform to what later Christian intellectuals would define as orthodoxy. Likewise, Clement, although he saw himself as a defender of orthodoxy, championed an understanding of prayer that would stand in stark contrast to that espoused even by the members of his own community. His neglect of the LP in his treatise on prayer was understandable, I argued, because he saw it as an inappropriate manner in which to approach the Christian God. I have thus outlined the social location and theology of one of the major figures of our analysis. Now the focus of this investigation will turn to the other context that occupies our discussion, Roman Carthage.

The origins of Latin Christian literature are to be found, not in Rome, but in North Africa. For about two centuries Africa was the center of Latin Christian thought. In Africa the theological vocabulary of the Western church received its basic shape. Of course, Rome would come to dominate the Western church, but at its inception Rome was the pupil rather than the *magister*. According to our sources, the church at Rome was theologically sophisticated and wealthy. No other church could boast its credentials. It had the *cathedra Petri* and the *memoria Petri*. Over time Rome would develop its own voice, but early on it had a strong relationship with its sister church in Africa. The two episcopal sees "stayed in close contact, supporting one another in times of persecution, offering comfort and advice in periods of adversity. . . . [The] two usually espoused similar views."[1] Discipline and ecclesiology were other matters. Here Africans and Romans saw things differently. By contrast to Rome, martyrs and rigorists represented the African church. For the Africans, the church symbolized their protest against the laxity and accommodation that characterized the larger pagan world.[2]

This chapter focuses on the founding and development of the North African city of Carthage in the Roman period. As part of this examination, I will discuss the vision early Roman leaders such as Julius Caesar and Augustus had for the city. I will examine the political and physical vision the early Roman colonists of the city embraced in an effort to promote *Romanitas*, the particular cultural understanding residents of the empire had regarding what it meant to be Roman. In this process, I will also examine the social and cultural development of both Carthage and Africa as its residents forged their own ethnoreligious understanding of what it meant to be Roman as well as African. Looking at their distinctive religious context, I will argue that the citizens of Roman Carthage created their own idiosyncratic cultural environment, one that will influence the thinking and actions of its Christian residents. Finally, I will look at the development of the Carthaginian *ecclesia*, focusing on its dominant representation, to determine as accurately as possible what the vision of these early Christians was. This partial reconstruction of the Carthaginian Christian community will then give us a picture—a snapshot in time—with which to appraise Tertullian's vision of prayer.

The Translucence of Roman Culture

The Vision of a Colonia

"Carthage must be destroyed!" These were the words of Marcus Porcius Cato (the Elder) on the floor of the Senate before the Third Punic War. They represented the culmination of years of competition between the two city-states. Carthage and Rome had vied for control of Sicily and Spain. As a great naval power, Carthage posed a particular threat to any further ideas of Roman expansion. And yet, as with most things, Carthage did not start out as a maritime power and rival to Rome.

Carthage began in roughly 814 BCE near the river Miliana in modern Tunisia.[3] It was a regular port of call for Phoenician traders expanding their activities into the western Mediterranean. They encountered a people in

North Africa whom we may call Libyans. Eventually, the Phoenicians settled permanently in this area. Within a couple centuries, Carthage rose to
prominence over its sister city, Utica. They battled the Greeks for control
of Sicily and explored the western African coast. Carthage acquired and
dominated a considerable amount of territory in the interior. According to
Polybius, Carthage controlled territory at least 93 miles inland (*Historiae*
1.66.6, 10). Estimates say that, at its height, Punic Carthage had a population of almost 400,000 Phoenicians, Libyans, Greeks, and others.[4] As one
scholar has described it, "The cosmopolitan residents of ancient Carthage
lived in attractive multistory stone houses that had courtyards equipped
with even sinks and bathtubs."[5] It was a major maritime power with its
own distinctive culture.

As republican Rome started its expansion, it was only a matter of time
before their interests conflicted. The flashpoint was Sicily. Carthage and
Rome fought for control of the region beginning in 238 BCE, the First
Punic War. Carthage suffered a major defeat. Rome took Corsica and Sar-
dinia. Tensions were revived in 218 BCE, when Hannibal captured Sagun-
tum (Spain) from the Romans. In the Second Punic War, Rome was
surprised by Carthage's military tactics and brought to the verge of extinc-
tion. The tide did turn, however. In 205 BCE Publius Cornelius Scipio
(Africanus) invaded Africa. Three years later the Romans defeated the
Carthaginians at the Battle of Zama. Rome took Spain, parts of Africa, and
decimated the Carthaginian military. The Numidian king Masinissa
goaded Carthage into breaking its subsequent treaty with Rome, and the
Third Punic War had begun. The rivalry ended in 146 BCE, when Scipio
destroyed Carthage and reportedly consecrated the site (see Cicero, *Agr.*
1.5; 2.51; Appian, *Bell. Civ.* 1.24). Polybius records this victorious moment:

> Scipio, beholding this city, which had flourished 700 years from its
> foundation and had ruled over so many lands, islands, and seas, as
> rich in arms and fleets, elephants, and money as the mightiest
> empires, but far surpassing them in hardihood and high spirit, . . .
> now come to its end in total destruction, . . . shed tears and pub-
> licly lamented the fortune of the enemy.[6]

Utica and Hadrumetum, also Punic cities, had sided with Rome against
Carthage. They received the status of independent cities under the new
Roman regime (*civitates liberae et immunes*). The Numidians, who provoked Carthage into this final conflict with Rome, received land as a recompense for their support. The Romans marked out a new boundary (*fossa*

regia) between their new province and their Numidian neighbors. The remainder of the land was offered to Roman investors as *ager publicus*, except for the land already occupied by natives, which was deemed *ager stipendarius*, land subject to taxation.[7]

Rome came into conflict with Numidia within thirty-five years of its defeat of Carthage. The war lasted for six years, but its resolution brought no formal changes between Rome and Jugurtha, the Numidian king.[8] And yet, as civil war later raged in the republic between Caesar and Pompey, Juba I, the current king of Numidia, sided with Cato the Younger and Metellus Scipio against the conqueror of Gaul. Their forces were defeated in 46 BCE at Thapsus. Rome annexed Numidia into its empire, calling this new province Africa Nova. The boundary that had once separated the province of Africa and Numidia now served as the boundary between the two provinces.

Julius Caesar was assassinated in 44 BCE. In the wake of the chaos that followed, a civil war erupted between the governors of Africa Vetus and Africa Nova. As a measure of domination, Lepidus controlled Africa between 40 and 36 BCE. In 35 BCE the two provinces were combined into one, called Africa Proconsularis, a designation that would endure until the time of Diocletian.[9] With the coming of the empire, greater attention would be placed on Carthage and Africa Proconsularis.

Romans lived in Carthage, even before its fall in 146 BCE (see Polybius, *Historiae* 36.7). As a great trading power, Carthage attracted a number of Roman and Italian businessmen. Upon annexing Carthage and its territory, the Romans surveyed the land and divided it into parcels as they had done with Veii in 396 BCE. Formal associations of Roman citizens (*conventus civium Romanorum*) were attracted to the area in the later part of the second century BCE, primarily for investment and trading purposes. The first formal attempt to reinhabit Carthage came in 122 BCE under the tribunate of Gaius Sempronius Gracchus (see Appian, *Hist. rom.* 136). It had 6,000 colonists, each receiving about 132 acres. Gracchus established *Junonia*, a tribute to its Punic past. Unfortunately, upon his return, his enemies murdered Gracchus. His failed colony could not live on, but the colonists would not die. Those who had already arrived in Africa were guaranteed their allotments by the *Lex Agraria* of 111 BCE (*FIRA* 1.102–21).

According to Appian, Caesar, while sleeping near the ancient city, dreamed that he should refound Carthage. The extent of Caesar's *colonia* is uncertain, but Appian says that he assigned land in Carthage (as he had in Corinth) to the poor.[10] Augustus championed Caesar's vision by sending three thousand colonists to the site, and a new Carthage, *Colonia Concordia Iulia Carthago*, was finally reconstituted under his guidance.[11] The Romans resettled Carthage as a *colonia*; Augustus granted it land in the adjacent regions (*territorium*), rebuilt the city, and surrounded it with villas.[12]

Carthage: A Political and Physical Representation of Rome

It was a city of Roman character with Punic heritage. Augustus was determined to make Carthage one of the great cities of the empire.[13] Romans, Numidians, Libyans, Greeks, and remnants of the Phoenicians lived together in a rather tolerant stability. Herodian once said of the city in the second century CE, "[Carthage] is next after Rome in wealth, population and size, though there is rivalry for second place between it and Alexandria in Egypt" (*Ab excessu divi Marci libri octo* 6.6.1 [Whittaker]).[14] Carthage had arrived again.

As a *colonia*, Carthage was reconstituted under roughly the same conditions as other *coloniae*. And so, we can take a cue from the legislation establishing other colonies as a means of determining the political makeup of Carthage.[15] First, legislation was passed in the Senate enabling the emigration of colonists and supplying general administrative conventions for the new municipality. After some modifications, this would later become the colonial charter inscribed on bronze tablets.[16] It was the constitution of the new town. Second, the political officials were appointed for the new settlement. The first magistrates and priests would have been appointed under the colonial charter. The new *colonia* would have had the same basic political organization as republican Rome. The chief officers were the *duoviri*, the two men who served as the chief judicial and presidential officials. Under them were the aediles, who took their name from the *aedes* of Ceres.[17] They served as executive officials, with a particular responsibility for public works, and they could even take the place of the *duoviri*. Beneath the aediles were the quaestors, financial officials. The *duoviri quinquennales*, elected every four years, were responsible for the census and enrolling new members in the local council. The *praefectus iure dicundo* was the judicial representative of the *duoviri* to the Carthaginian *territorium*.

Of course, the higher magistrates had religious as well as political responsibilities, as in Rome (see Tertullian, *Idol.* 17.3). The *duoviri* and aediles had a paid staff for their year in office. This included a *tibicen*, a flute player, and a *haruspex*, an expert in divination through the entrails of a sacrificed animal.[18] Carthage also had pontifices and augurs.[19] There were three in each college; barring any sort of condemnatory action, they served for life. Like the other magistrates, pontifices were required to "possess a domicile within a mile of town."[20] These officials were allowed to wear the *toga praetexta* and have special seating at public events as a visible sign of their prestige.[21] In sum, these officials, along with others, constituted the *ordo decurionem*, the order of decurions that comprised the local council.

Decurions formed the lowest level of the Roman imperial elite, below senators and equestrians. Qualifications for inclusion in the *ordo* were free birth (generally) and a net worth of at least 25,000 denarii. A man had to be at least 25 or 30 years of age to be enrolled in the *ordo*, although the sons of decurions could be admitted earlier as *praetextati*, honorary nonvoting members.[22] Once a member of the *ordo*, one was a member for life. The names of the members of the *ordo* were displayed in a prominent public place (see *Dig.* 50.3.1). As such, the *ordo decurionem* represented the identifiable local elite of Carthage, somewhat analogous to the bouleutic class in Alexandria.

As the chief decision-making body of the *colonia*, the *ordo* had authority over public buildings, public finances, embassies to the emperor, the water supply, public cults, and public business generally. The money to enact the decisions of the *ordo* came from various sources. It realized income, first of all, from members of the *ordo* itself. The assumption of a seat or position on the local council required the payment of an initiation fee, "known variously as the *summa legitima* or *honoraria.*"[23] The one example of a *summa honorarium* we have from Carthage is for a *duovir quinquennales*, who paid 9,500 denarii for the privilege of office, a figure nearly two times as high as any other *honorarium* known from Africa Proconsularis (*ILS* 9406).[24] Carthage also received income from rent, fines, entry fees, and local taxes.[25]

Citizens of the city itself, as citizens also of Rome, were exempt from imperial taxation. As James Rives highlights,

> The evidence thus suggests that Carthage possessed a large *territorium* in which were located a number of native towns. Within this region, the citizens of Carthage could own property free from the normal Roman taxation, while the non-citizen inhabitants had to pay taxes.[26]

Carthage was *immunitas*, a property of the *pertica Carthaginiensium*, a technical term for the land assigned to a *colonia* (cf. *ILS* 6509). Taxes, however, were received from the *castella* (fortresses) in the *territorium*. This is confirmed by an inscription from Uchi Maius: "M. Caelius Phileros had divided the *castellum* and established boundaries between the *colonia* and the Uchitani" (*CIL*² 26274 with *ILTun* 1370).²⁷ M. Caelius Phileros was a freedman who once held the position of *praefectus iure dicundo* and was responsible for contracting out tax collection among the various *castella* (*ILS* 1945).²⁸

Carthage's extensive territory meant prosperity for the burgeoning metropolis. The Romans increased the amount of land under cultivation. Within the course of two centuries, the Carthaginian *territorium* would consist of a couple hundred cities, especially in the farming region. Although small, these cities were prosperous and laid out according to Roman stylistic sensibilities.²⁹ They were places where "the wealthy surrounded themselves with beauty."³⁰ Neighboring the plains were the hills and their villages. It was a place for hunting boar and even lions. In these villages "poor men, with never enough land to go around, had acquired a solid identity against the civilized life of the plain."³¹ Augustine frequently described the mountains that predominate a large part of the province (see, e.g., *Enarrat. Ps.* 25.9).

In the cultivated territory the North Africans grew a tremendous amount of produce. The Punic Carthaginians exploited the region's production of olive oil and wine. The Roman Carthaginians grew corn and olives. Olive groves dotted the countryside adjacent to the fields of corn. Great presses were built throughout the rural areas to extract the precious oil. The cultivators of olives were extremely proud of their work, and they made every effort to demonstrate their share in the obvious prosperity of the region: "Here lies Dion, a pious man; he lived 80 years and planted 4000 trees" (*ILTun* 243).³²

The Romans also planted vineyards and most importantly grain. African wheat was especially prized for its quality. It reported yields of 150 to 1, although this is likely an exaggeration.³³ The huge grain estates of North Africa were well known and purported to supply two-thirds of Rome's grain in the first century CE (see, e.g., Pliny, *Nat.* 18.35).³⁴ One scholar described them in this manner:

> To exploit these productive agricultural resources, the land was organized in large estates cultivated by slaves or peasants who reaped little benefit from the production. The Romano-African owners lived very well, some in manor houses on their estates but more often in houses in town so they could participate in the urban life that so defined the Roman culture.³⁵

In the countryside one could encounter wildlife, birds as well as lizards and other creatures, in addition to the abundance of agriculture. And a vast network of roads built by the Roman army connected it all. However, the commodity that predominated Africa more than agriculture was light. As Augustine intimated, "The African sunlight was the 'Queen of all Colours pouring down over everything.'"[36]

The smaller settlements surrounding Roman Carthage, many of which had been established before the great *colonia* itself, contained various examples of Roman cultural influence. Thugga, for example, had a forum, theater, shrine to Ceres, and Capitol, a definite indication of strong Roman affiliation.[37] Thuburbo Minus, another town settled as a Roman *colonia*, was located in the region known as Rome's breadbasket. It had all the amenities of Roman culture. Thuburbo was about thirty-three miles west of Carthage and was purportedly the hometown of the martyr Vibia Perpetua.[38] Hippo Regius, the second port of Africa, had existed for over six hundred years before the founding of Carthage as a *colonia*. It had a forum, a theater that could seat over five thousand, temples, and a public bath. In addition, it had villas overlooking the harbor. It was prosperous, primarily because it had an abundance of trade and food.[39]

As in Rome, the focus of civic life for Roman Carthage was the forum. It was located on the Byrsa hill, the site of the "acropolis" of Punic Carthage. At the Byrsa the main thoroughfares of the city crossed, the *cardo maximus* and the *decumanus maximus*.[40] Carthage's land was divided into blocks or *insulae* of 480 by 120 Roman feet.[41] Initially, the Byrsa was not large enough to construct a suitable forum, "so [the Romans] increased its size by building large columns over the rubble of the Punic houses to support the ground of the new forum."[42] Upon completion, the new forum of Carthage was more than 98,000 square feet.[43]

At the northern end of the forum were a basilica and a temple at facing ends. To the south was another plaza surrounding another temple. Carthage's forum was designed along the lines of the new imperial forums in Rome. On its eastern end sat a basilica. Likely built in the first quarter of the first century CE, basilicas were great centers for commercial exchange that represented the grandeur of Roman imperialism. On its western end was a Capitol, a temple to the cult of the Capitoline triad of Jupiter Optimus Maximus, Juno Regina, and Minerva (see, e.g., Cyprian, *Laps.* 24).[44] Along with the forum, visitors to Roman Carthage would have seen numerous typically Roman civic structures, such as plazas, arches, and porticos.

Under the emperors Hadrian, Antoninus Pius, and Marcus Aurelius, further structures were added to the Carthaginian forum. Included among these buildings were a library, bookstores, and schools that drew many from throughout the province and the ancient world, including a young Augustine in the fourth century (see Apuleius, *Flor*. 18.8–9).[45] Near these structures, probably next to the governor's residence on the Byrsa hill, was the prison. According to our sources, such prisons were "simply crude holding areas for prisoners until they were moved elsewhere. The most secure area of a temporary prison would likely be an underground storage area, thus in the dark."[46]

In another imitation of its Roman predecessor, Carthage had a circus, likely constructed in the late first century CE. Located on the western edge of the city, it was one of the largest in the empire, only roughly 262 feet shorter than the Circus Maximus in the capital. Carthage's circus was almost 1700 feet long.[47] This entertainment facility drew great crowds in the city. As in other imperial cities, like Alexandria, the "Carthaginians were famous for their passionate devotion to the chariot races."[48] Great crowds also attended the theaters located on the eastern edges of the city.[49] The great amphitheater of Carthage, located in the northwest area of the *colonia*, was second in size only to that in Rome. Built in the early second century CE, and later renovated in the 160s, its external dimensions were roughly 512 by 420 feet, with the arena itself measuring about 212 by 209 feet (slightly shorter than an American football field). It had subterranean corridors that were used to ferry prisoners and animals into the arena. Probably built of Kedel limestone, a hard, rose-tinted stone, the amphitheater of Carthage surely made an impression.[50] One traveler from the twelfth century described it in this manner:

> There is a theater which has no parallel in the entire world. The form of the building is circular and it consists of fifty surviving vaults. Above each vault there are five rows of arches, one rising above the other, all of the same form and size, made out of blocks of stone of the type called *Kaddzan*, of incomparable beauty. Above each row of arches, there is a circuit of panels, on which there are various reliefs and strange figures of persons, animals and ships, made with incredible skill.[51]

Near the sea were located the Antonine Baths, another indication of North African Romanization. They had a magnificent view of the sea and enclosed an area of about 58,500 square feet. They were larger than any in the empire except those built by Nero in Rome.[52] And this raises a central problem the Romans had to face in their urbanization of North Africa, the scarcity of water.

As in Egypt, the ways of Roman agricultural production demanded great quantities of water. In addition, they needed vast amounts of water to supply the baths, latrines, and fountains throughout the city. Water was brought down from springs in the mountains by means of an aqueduct. Also one of the largest in the Roman world, the aqueduct of Carthage was built under the guidance of Hadrian. "It brought water from thirty-five miles south of Carthage, meandering for about seventy-five miles before its water flowed into the city at a remarkable rate of almost eighty gallons a second."[53] In addition, the Romans built dams, reservoirs, and gigantic cisterns to supplement the supply. Although grand in its conception and construction, Roman Carthage was still like many urban areas in the imperial period. As Joyce Salisbury tells us, "[We] should remember that, from a modern perspective, ancient cities were remarkably crowded, filthy, and dangerous because of both crime and disease."[54]

Carthage: A Social and Cultural Representation of Africa

By the second century Carthage was one of the wealthiest and most cosmopolitan cities in the Roman Empire. At Carthage one could see people and goods from all over the Roman world and beyond. Merchants sold their wares in crowded stalls in its forum. The city was a mix of Romans, Jews, Greeks, Numidians, Phoenicians, Libyans, governmental officials, intellectuals, merchants, and others. And its prosperity extended far beyond the city's forum. As the engine for North African prosperity, the economy of Roman Carthage stretched well into the hinterland that supported the city. The results were remarkable. As Peter Brown once said, "Since the first century B.C., an 'economic miracle' had transformed the hinterland of North Africa. Never again would prosperity be extended so effectively over so wide an area."[55] The potential for social mobility that this economic boom created was not forgotten among the residents of the province. As one proudly proclaimed, "I grew up in the country, the son of a poor, uneducated father: in my time, I have come, through my pursuit of literature, to live the life of a nobleman" (Aurelius Victor, *De Caesaribus* 20.5).[56]

The early settlers of the *colonia* were a mix of veterans, the poor, and others. These transplanted Roman citizens were duly enrolled in the *tribus* Arnensis, one of the thirty-five tribes used for the purpose of voting in the Roman popular assembly. Each male citizen belonged to a tribe and included it as part of his formal name, although in the imperial period affiliation in a *tribus* had no practical significance. For our purposes, however, membership in the tribe Arnensis is a good indication of Carthaginian citizenship.[57] In thinking about that early period, Rives is undoubtedly correct: "When the Caesarian and Augustan colonists first arrived in Africa, they constituted an island of Roman culture amidst a sea of Libyan and Punic civilization."[58]

The citizen body in Rome was divided into *curiae*, although by the imperial period the *curia* had lost most of its function.[59] In the *coloniae* outside Rome, the citizen body was also divided into *curiae*. Frequent attestations to this institution in Africa indicate that it had evolved from a mere civic division into an institution resembling other *collegia* throughout the empire. For example, the *curia* of Jupiter in Simitthu appears to have had bylaws similar to those of the *collegium* of Diana and Antinous (see *ILS* 6824).[60] In this and many other ways, the original colonists of Carthage were following the *mos maiorum*, the cultural notion that if Rome were to prosper, it would do so through the guidance of the *maiores*.[61] Another example of cultural continuity was the dress of the colonists. The magistrates of Carthage wore the familiar *toga praetexta*, and it appears that typical Roman dress dominated the province until the fourth century CE.[62]

Although the new colonists were citizens of Rome, the context of the empire created a new and distinct political situation for its inhabitants. As scholars have indicated, the idea of civic identity in the Roman Empire was split for these Roman colonists. Since they were no longer residents of Rome and thus did not participate in Roman civic affairs, their standing as citizens became an abstract political status rather than a concrete local reality.[63] Such a divided identity would have a profound effect upon how Carthaginian citizens understood and represented their civic loyalties. But it appears fair to say that the initial colonists of Carthage had self-understandings more Roman than African.

In other places throughout the empire, the government frequently involved itself in the promotion of Roman culture and its identification. For example, in Britain the imperial government, through its governor, promoted the construction of temples, basilicas, forums, baths, and houses. In fact, Agricola, one of Britain's governors, introduced a Roman form of education as a means of integrating the province into the empire (see Tacitus, *Agr.* 21.1). These and other measures were not necessary in Africa Proconsularis, however. With its long history of urbanization under the domination of the Phoenicians, this senatorial province did not need the same level of encouragement as Britain. And yet, imperial and local authorities alike did encourage the outward identification of the African residents with the Roman *patria*. The constructed environment of Carthage and its surrounding territory (outlined above) is just one indication of how the colonists (and their governmental backers) promoted the Romanization of the new province.[64]

As in Alexandria, Rome, Ephesus, and other imperial cities, daily life was lived predominantly in the public eye. Most of an average Carthaginian's day would have been spent among others in the forum, at the theaters, on the street, in the temples, and even in the baths. Such a situation meant that individuals had to learn to adjust to the inconveniences that undoubtedly occur when one lives in the public sphere. An ability to function well in such a public environment was apparently a highly prized quality among many in North Africa. "I have enjoyed the clear sunlight for most of my days," proclaimed one African; "I was always pleasant to everybody; why should not everyone regret me?" (*ILAlg* 820).[65] Interestingly enough, along with the very public character of ancient existence, as we saw in Alexandria, also went strong ethnoreligious affiliations and loyalties.[66]

Roman Africans were concerned about reputation, both their own and that of their group. Of course, as many scholars have demonstrated, issues of honor and dishonor permeated Roman imperial society generally, from the emperor down to the anonymous peasant in the village of Bulla Regia. And yet, as we shall see, North African culture promoted its own distinctive brand of honor and ethnoreligious affiliation. Brown offers us an insight into this culture: "This was a public life, in which a man was committed, above all, to maintaining his reputation: to 'live forever in the mouths of the people' was the ambition of the successful African."[67] Such African determination was well known throughout the Greco-Roman world. They were known to be rigorous and resolved, although some would call them pigheaded. Plutarch once said that they were "stubborn in adhering to [their] decision."[68] Take, for example, Patricius and Monica, the parents of Augustine. In his *Confessions*, Augustine describes his father as a *tenuis municeps*, a citizen of Roman Thagaste with but slender means (*Conf.* 2.3.5). And yet, Patricius was determined to give his son an education. His family had to go around poorly dressed (see *Serm.* 356.3). They scraped and saved. There was even an interruption in the process when Patricius did not have the money to send Augustine to school for a year, but his determination eventually won out. Likewise, Monica was a relentless figure in Augustine's life. Despite the various twists and turns of his intellectual and social development, she was convinced that "the son of such tears could not be lost," and she too won out; Augustine became a Christian (*Conf.* 3.12.21).[69] The concern for reputation, widespread in the Roman world, and the distinctive North African quality of determination will mark this province as different from the rest. For a moment let us, however, look at the various ethnoreligious groups that comprised Roman Carthage.

Since the founding of Carthage as a *colonia*, the dominant ethnoreligious group was the Romans. Members of the *tribus* Arnensis were greatly outnumbered when they first arrived on the shores of Africa. They quickly decided to remake the physical and political landscape of the province into an image of Rome. This sort of social hegemony, by design, had an impact upon the local populace. It held up Rome and its values as the paradigm of civilization, the necessary avenue for upward social mobility. Along with the political structures and the built environment, another good example of Roman ethnoreligious influence is the building of the temple of Capitoline Triad. Jupiter, Juno, and Minerva had been the great patron deities of the Roman state since the days of Etruscan domination. The Capitol was the scene of some of Rome's most important religious ceremonies. Annually at the Capitol, the new consuls entered office with the sacrifice of a bull to Jupiter in thanks for the god's blessings. The oldest and greatest of the city's games, the *ludi Romani*, were held in commemoration of the Capitol's dedication (see Dionysius of Halicarnassus, *Ant. rom.* 7.72–73).[70] This cult, more than any other, represented Roman religious and civic identity. Its replication in Carthage, which does not seem to have been a requirement, demonstrates the early colonists' desire to differentiate themselves from the locals as well as to flaunt their relationship to imperial power. The message would be clear: We are the conquerors. You are the conquered.[71] The same is likely true with the initial establishment of the cult of Ceres.[72]

Within the community of Roman citizens, status was tightly controlled. There were significant differences between someone like Patricius and a member of the *ordo decurionem*, and these differences had their public representations. In addition to the *toga*, magistrates and other members of the *ordo* held assigned seats of prestige at public ceremonies in the theaters and amphitheater. Such signs of prestige were so important that fines were imposed on anyone violating the status markers. According to our sources, the fine for violating the seating regulations was 5,000 sesterces (or 1,250 denarii), roughly five years' wages for a laborer during the time of Julius Caesar.[73] Even Augustine emphasized the importance of maintaining status indicators, "by which the ranks of men are distinguished" (*Doctr. chr.* 2.25.39).[74]

Roman citizens living outside Carthage were called *pagani*, persons living in a district outside the metropolis. Amid the local populace of Libyans and others, the *pagani* represented a privileged group. Their land was *immunitas* and their citizenship status, as both Roman and Carthaginian citizens, meant they could have municipal careers in the provincial capital. In Thugga, for example, the *pagani* were initially well-to-do colonists who decided to purchase country estates away from the hustle and bustle that characterized Carthaginian life. Although they had no official civic standing in a place like Thugga, the *pagani* constituted an informal *ordo* in such towns.[75] As Rives has pointed out, "[One] of the most pressing needs of the *pagani*, living in the midst of a long-established African community, must have been to assert their status as Romans and as citizens of colonia Concordia Iulia Karthago."[76] One of the earliest examples of such a desire to promote Roman cultural hegemony in Thugga was inscribed on a shrine in 36–37 CE:

> To Imperator Tiberus Caesar Augustus, son of the deified Augustus, pontifex maximus, in the thirty-eighth year of his tribunician power, having been consul five times; L. Manilius Bucco, the son of Lucius, of the *tribus Arnensis, duovir*, performed the dedication; L. Postumius Chius, the son of Gaius, of the *tribus Arnensis*, patron of the pagus, in his own name and that of his sons Firmus and Rufus, paved the forum and the area in front of the temple of Caesar, and caused to be built at his own expense an altar of Augustus, a shrine of Saturn, and an arch. (*ILAfr* 558)[77]

The donor of the altar, shrine, pavement, and arch, L. Postumius Chius, was a citizen of Carthage (*tribus Arnensis*). His name suggests he was the son of a freedman, although Chius himself was a Roman citizen. He does not appear to have held any public office, although he knew at least one influential Carthaginian power broker, L. Manilius Bucco. As a person of obvious wealth, Chius served as a "patron of the pagus" in Thugga. However, as discussed in chapter 3 with Clement, the stain of a slave background could influence the social standing of future generations.[78]

Another point the Thugga inscription helps to illustrate is the importance of patronage to the promotion of Roman culture in a local context. In Carthage as in other imperial cities, the prestige of the elite was often defined by their voluntary benefactions. Of course, *munera* or liturgical service was an important component of the life of a local elite. However, since the law often required *munera*, it did not properly constitute a civic benefaction. To demonstrate his generosity, a member of the *ordo* had to present the city with an additional gift. Such additional gifts were called *pollicitationes*, or promises, and their concrete manifestations were left up to the discretion of the giver. Once a *pollicitatio* was made, however, the donor was legally bound to carry it out (see *Dig.* 50.12.1–2). For example, the *duovir quinquennales* (discussed above) paid an additional 50,000 denarii to sponsor four days of games after he had paid 9,500 denarii as a *summa* for entry into the office (*ILS* 9406). Other games, like the *ludi Romani* (or the version of it celebrated in Carthage), were paid partially with civic funds and the remainder with the funds of a particular magistrate.[79] Such benefactions could be expensive. Take, for example, the construction of a temple. The Capitol at Lambaesis cost 150,000 denarii to build, the equivalent of over sixteen years' wages for a sewer cleaner in the third century (see *CIL* 3).[80] Even in smaller cities like Thagaste, one could find patrons like Romanianus contributing such benefactions to the civic life of his community.[81]

Carthage, and North Africa in general, was known as a "nursery of barristers" (Juvenal, *Sat.* 7.148).[82] If the Greeks had philosophy as an emblem of their intellectual life, for the Romans it was law. Forensic oratory seems to coincide with the general cultural climate that pervaded Africa Proconsularis. Augustine once mentioned the power and prestige that went with such oratory in the African mind: "That's a great thing, to have eloquence wielding great power, to have clients hanging on every word of the well-turned speech of their protector, pinning their hopes on his mouth" (*Enarrat. Ps.* 136.3).[83] Brown is likely correct in saying, "The average African was . . . notorious as a lawyer."[84]

It was the rhetoric that seems to have attracted the North Africans to law. What was said of Augustine could also be said of Tertullian and others in the province:

> The gifted African, for instance, delighted in the sheer play of words, in puns, rhymes and riddles: as a bishop, Augustine will be hugely admired by his congregation, for being superbly able to provide a display of verbal fireworks. Such a man needed controversy. He throve on self-justification. He aimed to impress his fellows by eccentric turns of phrase, by vivid and far-fetched similes.[85]

In such cities as Madaura and Carthage, North Africans cultivated their intellectual lives, and not simply within the schoolhouses. The province was the home of the orator Fronto, the philologist Sulpicius Apollinaris, and the philosopher Lucius Apuleius, whose great work the *Metamorphoses* serves as an invaluable description of the second century. Carthage was known for its intellectual vibrancy.[86] Private conversations were complemented by public orations. The comedies of Plautus could be seen along with tragedies, not to mention pantomimes, jugglers, and dancers. Astrology and magic were studied along with philosophy and law. Novels, such as *Metiochos and Parthenope* and *The Ethiopian Story*, were widely circulated and read. The fact that most novels were written in Greek gives us some insight into the multilingual character of the colony.

According to Apuleius, the residents of Carthage were well versed in both Latin and Greek (see *Flor.* 18.38).[87] Magical texts, for example, were written in Greek and required a fairly high level of literacy to be understood.[88] According to our sources, knowledge of Greek was common among Carthage's elite, but probably not widespread in the province. In fact, outside Carthage the ability to use Greek was noteworthy (see *ILS* 7761).[89] Some who could converse in Latin and Greek could also apparently speak Punic. For example, Salisbury argues that the family of Vibia Perpetua was trilingual.[90] There is a problem with such an assertion, however. As we shall see, it is difficult to determine what is exactly meant by the term Punic. Many in North Africa, like Augustine, will use the term to refer to any language spoken in the province that did not happen to be Latin or Greek.[91]

The inclusion of Punic in this discussion serves to highlight a social shift that occurred among the descendants of the original colonists. Living in an area where many enjoyed their own sense of ethnoreligious allegiance, one that preceded the coming of the Romans, such distinctive characteristics as dress, language, and religion were not easily supplanted.[92] In addition to the Greeks, Syrians, and Egyptians who regularly found residence in the North African port cities, the Roman colonists also had frequent contact with Libyans and Phoenicians.[93] Over time, these interactions would transform the ethnoreligious understanding of Carthage's citizens.[94] By the late second century CE, increasing numbers of indigenous Africans would be added to the Carthaginian *ordo*.[95] As well, the descendants of the original Roman colonists would increasingly come to identify themselves with the land in which they lived. Consequently, it became prestigious for the elite to claim African origin.[96]

The clearest indication of such a shift in ethnoreligious self-understanding can be found in the increasing numbers of Carthaginians with typically African *cognomina* such as Datus, Saturninus, and Fortunatus.[97] No longer simply Romans, but Romano-Africans, the Carthaginians embraced and promoted elements of the Punic ethnoreligious tradition. The most spectacular example of this is most likely the introduction of the cult of Caelestis in the second century.[98] Outside of Carthage the cult of Tanit had survived without a break. When the Carthaginian *ordo* decided to institute the cult in the city, however, they modified its rites in accordance with their Romano-African self-understanding. Gone were the more offensive aspects of the Punic cult. In their place the Carthaginians appear to have introduced more Greco-Roman rites.[99] And yet, the temple of the god itself was constructed according to a Punic architectural model.[100] Writing in the fifth century CE, Quodvultdeus described it as "an excessively large temple, surrounded by the shrines of all deities, the courtyard of which, adorned with a mosaic pavement and costly columns and walls, extended almost 2,000 feet" (*Prom.* 3.44).[101] The promotion of the patron deity of Carthage, also known as the *genius terrae Africae* (the presiding spirit of Africa), marks quite pointedly the ethnoreligious transformation that occurred among the colonists. No longer deriving their identity solely from Rome, the addition of this formerly Punic cult to the *sacra publica* of Carthage is testament to a community that understood itself as simultaneously Roman and African.

Of course, it was not only the descendants of the colonists who were transformed by the social alterations that occurred in Carthage. Numidians, Phoenicians, and Libyans were changed by the advent of the Romans as well. Many participated in a cultural transformation we commonly call Romanization. As in Ptolemaic Egypt, the Roman immigrants that first occupied North Africa, over time, began to intermarry with members of the local populace. The consequences of such intermarriage were evident throughout the province. In cities like Thugga, for example, the Romanization of the local Punic community can be seen as early as 48 CE. In that year an altar was dedicated to Divus Augustus and the emperor Claudius by Julius Venustus, a member of the local elite (*ILS* 6797). His father, Faustus Thinoba, had a name that was half-Latin and half-Libyan. By acquiring a Latin name, Thinoba represents a process of *Romanitas* that continued in his family. He gave all his sons Latin names, and Thinoba himself held the position of flamen of the *civitas*. Julius, one of his four sons, may have even been a Roman citizen. His wife, Gabinia Felicula, was undoubtedly a citizen, increasing the possibility that the same would have been true of her husband.[102]

One of the more interesting features of this altar was that its dedicatory inscription was written in Latin alone, without even a Punic or Libyan translation. Such an inscription must have been provocative in a city like Thugga, with its strong Libyan heritage and Punic governmental structure. Along with the Numidian gods Vihinam and Bonchor, the indigenous residents of Thugga consciously Romanized themselves through such institutions as the imperial cult.[103] They erected bridges between their African heritage and the culture of the *pagani*, which represented the surest route to social advancement. Not only did they adopt Latinized names like Felix and Saturnus, but also they likewise Romanized various elements of their own ethnoreligious tradition (see *CIL*[2] 15325, 15447, 27106, 1532). Such an example of local Romanization would be the family of A. Gabinius Datus. A Roman citizen, enrolled in the *tribus Quirina*, Datus was not a *paganus* in origin. His assimilation to Roman culture is evident in a dedication that was erected near the end of his life. It identifies him as a *conductor praediorum regionis Thuggensis*, a lessee (*conductor*) of the local imperial estates (*praedia*). As Rives indicates, "Such a position would fit with a non-citizen origin, for while requiring wealth and bestowing a certain amount of prestige, it did not necessarily entail high social status."[104] Datus's youngest son, also named A. Gabinius Datus, would complete the family's Romanization by becoming a member of the *tribus* Arnensis and holding the positions of aedile, flamen of Divus Titus, and augur in Carthage (see *ILAfr* 569; *ILTun* 1513). And yet, this family also built a shrine in Thugga that included the gods Frugifer and Liber Pater, demonstrably African deities.[105] In short, locals and colonists worked together to form a cultural environment properly designated Romano-African. Unlike Egypt, with its often-fierce ethnoreligious tensions, Africa Proconsularis appears to have fostered an environment wherein individuals could claim and nurture an identity that was both local and imperial. This may explain the strong local affiliation felt by such notables as Apuleius, Tyconius, Perpetua, and Augustine. In fact, it would be Augustine who would remind others of his self-conscious "Africanity" (see *Ep.* 17.2; 138.4.19).[106]

I end this discussion of ethnoreligious groups in Carthage by exploring the Jewish presence in the *colonia*. Our sources indicate that Jews arrived in North Africa in the first century CE. According to Acts 2:9–11, Jews could be found in Libya, although it specifies that they resided in the parts around Cyrene. Philo also mentions Jews of North Africa, but he never claims that any live in Carthage (see *Legat.* 36.283; *Flacc.* 6.43). Some time within the next century, however, the Jewish population in the Roman Empire expanded to include Carthage and its surrounding territory. Most scholars agree that this most likely occurred as a consequence of the Jewish revolt of 66 CE and the subsequent Bar Kokhba revolt in 132.[107] Titus reportedly settled thousands of Jews in Carthage as slaves after the destruction of the Jerusalem temple. Evidence from a Jewish necropolis near Carthage indicates, however, that the community was probably much smaller, somewhere between 300 and 500 people.[108] In fact, the majority of the Jews buried in the necropolis had names "of the sort that might have been given to slaves or adopted by people of lower status."[109] This community would continue to grow in Carthage, reaching its height in the fourth century. As in other parts of the empire, Carthaginian Jews influenced their neighbors, and yet, they do not appear to have held the same status as the Jewish community of Alexandria before 115 CE (see Tertullian, *Adv. Jud.* 1.1-2; cf. *Nat.* 1.13.3-4).

The Amalgam of Politics and Religion

In their two-volume work *The Religions of Rome*, Mary Beard and others make a point that will apply as equally to Carthage as it does to Rome: "It would have made no sense in Roman terms to have claimed rights to political power without also claiming rights to religious authority and expertise."[110] Although Augustine will later object to it, Romans conceived of their political life as a household of which the emperor was *paterfamilias*.[111] As indicated in chapter 1, the distinction between *pater patriae* and *paterfamilias* in the Roman mind was more a matter of scale than actual concrete differences between the *sacra familia* and the *sacra publica*.[112] As the move from republican to imperial government advanced, religious authority became concentrated in the hands of the emperor. Augustus successfully accumulated the positions of "pontifex maximus, augur, quindecemviri sacris faciendis, septemvir epulonum, frater Arvalis, soldalis Titius et fetialis" (*Res. gest. divi Aug.* 7.3). Combined with his political authority (*imperium*) and senatorial primacy, Augustus and later emperors counteracted the diffusion of religious authority that predominated the republican period. Through his *beneficia*, the emperor permitted games in Ephesus, Thyatira, Carthage, and elsewhere. More direct imperial involvement can be seen in the construction and dedication of the temple of Caelestis by Marcus Aurelius.[113] And yet, the political and religious acts of the emperors fell far short of a positive and coherent policy on such matters—at least until the mid-third century CE.

The general religious policy of the Roman Empire can be described best as one of negation, which activities were licit and illicit, rather than positive promotion. The emperors controlled the religious activities of the various *collegia*, the practice of magic and astrology, as well as celebrations of the Bacchanalia and the religious lives of Jews.[114] Take, for example, Augustus' decision to ban Egyptian religion from being practiced within the *pomerium*, the strip of land that served as the religious boundary of ancient Rome (see Dio Cassius, *Historiae Romanae* 53.2.4).[115] The banning of various religious groups in Rome and the provinces was presumably a matter of maintaining public order and political stability.[116]

After this declarative statement on the general tenor of imperial religious policy, let me nuance the matter a bit by pointing out that the emperors appear to have promoted the imperial cult actively and consistently, as well as other religious practices from time to time.[117] Celebrations for the reigning emperor and his deified predecessors could be found throughout the empire.[118] As a means of uniting the various ethnoreligious groups that comprised the empire, the imperial cult served an important political function that dovetailed with its religious significance. To promote their cult, the emperors sent approved models of portraits as well as vows to the provinces.[119]

Septimius Severus was one such emperor. His official family portrait was the basis for disseminating his image throughout the provinces.[120] Born in 146 CE in Lepcis Magna, Severus would become the first African emperor of Rome. Although provided with a good education, he never lost his Tripolitanian accent. His sister could barely speak Latin at all. Under Marcus Aurelius, Severus served Rome in Spain, Italy, Gaul, and Syria. After the demise of the emperor Pertinax, Severus marched on Rome and deposed Julianus, whom he dubbed a usurper. He ascended to the imperial throne in 193, but it would take another four years before he could defeat his rivals, Albinus and Niger, and claim sole rule of Rome. More of a warrior than a statesman, Severus was also the *paterfamilias* of a household that included four children, two boys and two girls. In typical Roman fashion, his daughters, the progeny of his first marriage, to a North African woman named Marcia, were married to Roman men of standing in an effort to consolidate Severus's position as emperor. His sons, Antoninus (better known as Caracalla) and Gela, were the products of his second marriage, to Julia Domna, the daughter of a prominent Syrian priest. Although he attempted to provide the best for them, even naming Caracalla as Caesar in 197 CE, Severus's sons will forever grace the pages of history as profiles in imperial tragedy.[121]

As promoter of the imperial cult, one of Severus's first deeds was to create a public ceremony to apotheosize his murdered predecessor Pertinax. He arranged for a wax replica of the assassinated emperor to be placed in the Roman forum so that the people and the state could praise and mourn his memory. When Pertinax's effigy was burned, an eagle was released simultaneously, marking his apotheosis. This gesture on behalf of his own political career and the imperial cult demonstrates one of the ways an emperor promoted what could be called a religious program. Patronizing a particular deity was another.

Augustus patronized Apollo, Commodus patronized Hercules, and Severus patronized Sarapis. During a trip to Egypt in the early part of the third century, Severus found himself deeply influenced by the cult of this Greco-Egyptian god. Afterward, Severus was officially portrayed wearing his hair and beard in the style of Sarapis. In fact, on an arch he dedicated in Lepcis, his hometown, Severus portrayed himself as Sarapis and his wife Julia Domna as Isis.[122] In many respects, such an act of association was understandable. As a Greco-Egyptian deity, Sarapis symbolized both localism and universalism. As a manifestation of the ancient Egyptian god, Osiris, the cult of Sarapis had its roots in Severus's native Africa. At the same time, as a deity worshipped according to Greco-Roman rites, Sarapis was a god who could be (and was) worshipped throughout the empire.

I began by claiming that the general policy of the emperors regarding religion was one of negation, of placing limits on acceptable religious practice.[123] My discussion of the religious devotion (*pietas*) of Septimius Severus might lead one to believe that imperial religious policy was more proactive than reactionary. In fact, the edict issued by Severus in 202 CE forbidding conversion to Judaism and Christianity could arguably be seen as an example of imperial promotion of a religious identity. However, while it may be true generally that Severus promoted the worship of Sarapis to the detriment of other cults, in practice the repression fell hardest on Alexandria (see, e.g., Eusebius, *Hist. eccl.* 6.1–2). In other words, Severus's actions did ·not constitute a coherent and proactive religious policy, especially as compared to the acts of Decius and Diocletian years later.

In Africa Proconsularis, the proconsul held the reigns of political power on behalf of the central government. As a move along the *cursus honorum*, Africa was a plum senatorial assignment. Future emperors such as Galba, Vitellius, and Vespasian served as proconsuls of the province.[124] The governor's administrative authority, or *imperium*, was backed by the presence of the Legio III Augusta in Theveste.[125] In Carthage, the proconsul had a staff of heralds, scribes, lectors, and others. He also had a cohort of troops he commanded in the city to maintain domestic tranquility (see *ILS* 2487). Under Augustus, the proconsul had direct command of the troops stationed at Theveste, but this power was subsequently taken away by Gaius and given to a separate legate (see Tacitus, *Hist.* 4.48; Dio Cassius, *Historiae Romanae* 59.20.7). As the intermediary between the provincial populace and officials back in Rome, the proconsul served an important role in the promotion of *Romanitas*.

Provincial administration was supposedly defined by the *lex provin-ciae*, a set of laws determining legal status, boundaries, and internal regulation among other things. In practical terms, however, the proconsuls had few specific duties. They had a general obligation to enforce the *lex* and to maintain order in the province. By appearance, a proconsul's concern could be directed pretty much however he wished (see, e.g., *Dig.* 1.16.9). And yet, much of a governor's time was taken up with judicial and administrative matters.[126] For example, the governor, acting on the emperor's behalf, routinely decided whether towns could build expensive public works projects (see *Dig.* 50.10.3.1). As indicated in chapter 3, a provincial governor, more often than not, would decide certain legal matters that came before him and handle other provincial concerns, such as dam repair and tax collection.[127]

It was routine, it appears, for the governor to administer an oath of allegiance to the soldiers and provincials upon the accession of a new emperor (see, e.g., Pliny, *Ep.* 10.52–53). In other matters, however, the role of the governor appears to have been more fluid. As in the case of Agricola in Britain, a provincial governor might promote the Romanization of the populace. Q. Marcius Barea, proconsul of Africa from 41 to 53 CE, for example, promoted the imperial cult in the province during his tenure (see *CIL*[2] 11002; *IRT* 273). He did not build the shrines and temples, nor does he appear to have supplied the initiative for them, but his interest was apparent nevertheless. What Barea and the other proconsuls provided was patronage by means of prestige. As Rives says, "The religious role of the proconsul, in so far as he had one, derived from his ability to lend prestige and to heighten the identification with Rome rather than from any particular religious authority."[128]

As representative of the emperor, it was the proconsul's duty to enact legislation coming out of Rome. When the emperors set the limits of religious acceptability, it was the proconsul's responsibility to enforce their edicts and determinations. For example, P. Aelius Hilarianus, then proconsul of Africa, carried out Severus's edict discussed above. Outside of such specific decrees, determining the limits of the acceptable was left to the governor's discretion.

In addition to the proconsul and his staff, Africa Proconsularis had another supramunicipal and quasi-political body, the *concilium provinciae Africae* (see, e.g., *ILS* 6813). It was an assembly of delegates sent from towns throughout the province. The *concilium* was preeminently a religious body, based on the eastern model of the *koinōn* or league, which promoted the imperial cult in the province.[129] According to the *Lex Narbonensis*, towns without Roman or Latin status, like Utica and Thugga, were excluded from representation in the *concilium*.

The assembly was led by the *sacerdos provinciae*, the priest of the province, who was elected annually. As with the Carthaginian magistrates, the provincial priest wore the *toga praetexta* and was given a seat of honor at public events. A staff of lectors also accompanied him. It was his responsibility to preside over the sacrifices that commemorated various imperial anniversaries.

Although its main function was religious, the *concilium* maintained its own treasury and heard proposals that went beyond administering the imperial cult. As a body representing the entire province, the assembly frequently communicated its concerns to the emperor (see *Cod. theod.* 11.30.15; cf. 8.4.2; 11.7.4). Such acts made it a de facto component of the provincial administration. This is probably why the emperors regulated the existence of the provincial assemblies. Initiative for a *concilium* originated in the province, but only the emperor could grant it official recognition. Since the provincial assembly's survival was dependent upon imperial goodwill, it would be fair to say that the province's collective identity "was defined by its relationship to the emperor."[130]

Although the *concilium provinciae Africae* was responsible for the promotion of the imperial cult throughout the province, it did not have any apparent authority (*imperium*) in implementing this cult (or any other) in the various towns of Africa.[131] The introduction of cults was the task of the *ordo*. The process appears rather simple. The *duoviri* proposed the introduction of a particular cult, like Caelestis, in the *curia* when a quorum of two thirds of the decurions was present. They voted. Proposals that received a majority then became law and part of the *sacra publica* of Carthage (see, e.g., *Lex Ursonensis* LXIV; Apuleius, *Flor.* 16.36–46).[132] The same was true of monuments, statues, altars, and inscriptions placed on public land.[133] Approval by the *ordo* was indicated by the words *locus datus decreto decurionem*, "space given by decree of the decurions."[134]

If the religious policy of the emperors and their subordinates can be described as one of determining the limits of acceptability, then the religious policy of the *ordo* might best be characterized as "the golden rule." Prestige and financial feasibility were the most important factors considered by the *ordo* in the institution of a cult.[135] Both were golden. And yet, there is another way to understand this golden rule policy that also appears to have influenced the decisions of the ordo: the one who has the gold makes the rules. Most shrines and temples were actually proposed and funded by wealthy and influential citizens. In fact, "in Africa as a whole more temples were built by individuals than by public bodies."[136] Unlike republican Rome, where the *sacra publica* was controlled in order to maintain Roman identity, religion in Carthage and elsewhere appears to have followed no policy other than that set by influential individuals and their religious tastes. And since the construction and maintenance of these cults required significant financial appropriations, it may have made sense to the decurions to relinquish their control of the *sacra publica* in Carthage in favor of a program that amounted to religious anarchy.[137]

The absence of a religious policy at the imperial level before the third century CE finds its basis in the same rationale that placed decisions regarding the *sacra publica* of Carthage in the hands of the *ordo*. This was based on the Roman belief that religion was fundamentally a civic matter.[138] As mentioned earlier, however, the dualistic nature of the Carthaginians' citizenship status meant sometimes competing, but often overlapping, affiliations and loyalties. In the Roman imperial environment, with its various ethnoreligious groups interacting on all social levels, this civic model "was increasingly out of place."[139] Life in North Africa was also typified by the impotence of the *ordo* in Carthaginian political matters and the absence of any real religious policy, other than some sort of broad consensus.[140]

Religion in a Roman Mode

In true Roman fashion Cicero once maintained that "no one shall privately have new or foreign gods unless publicly recognized" (*Leg.* 2.19).[141] Such a view was characteristic of republican Rome with its tightly controlled *sacra publica*. Implicit in this statement is the idea that religion is a component of civic identity. In the context of the empire, however, the idea of an ethnoreligious civic identity became blurred rather quickly. As an abstract legal status, Roman citizenship brought with it identification with the political and religious structures of the capital. Roman citizens enjoyed privileges that were denied Greeks, Egyptians, Jews, Syrians, Numidians, and others (e.g., tax breaks and the right to appeal to the emperor). The practical implications of such privileges could be seen throughout the provinces. What was missing, however, was a unilateral identification of provincial Roman citizens with the traditional gods of Rome. In its place there developed a complex and multivalent form of religious self-understanding that included the gods of Rome as well as local and regional deities and also mystery cults, *collegia*, and other forms of theological speculation.[142] Although the degree of an individual's religious practice may at times have been limited by financial concerns, the sheer variety of religious options available to persons was remarkable.

Just a simple survey of the names of cities and colonies can attest to the variety of religious identifications that permeated the empire. In the early period of Roman colonization, it was customary, it appears, for Rome to decide on the settlement's official name. This was definitely true of Carthage, whom Caesar identified with the god Concordia.[143] Over time, however, local councils rather than officials at Rome determined the religious identifications of their towns. So Hadrumentum would identify itself with the African god Frugifer (*ILS* 6111). Sitifis, a veteran colony, would identify itself with Mars (*CIL*[2] 8438). Aulodes, Thugga, and Thysdrus would likewise identify themselves with Liber (*ILS* 6792, 2911). More often than not, towns throughout the empire chose to identify themselves with deities other than the traditional gods of Rome.[144] The Carthaginian religious calendar attests to the variety of religious observances provincial Africans enjoyed. Local deities, like Caelestis, were worshipped alongside the Capitoline Triad. In other words, the *sacra publica* of Carthage reflected a bilateral ethnoreligious affiliation, being both Roman and African.[145] Outside of the public sphere, residents of Carthage would have even more religious options.[146]

Roman provincials would continue to support traditional Roman deities like Mater Matuta.[147] Roman matrons used this cult to express not only Roman religious identification but also ethnoreligious privilege.[148] At the same time, these citizens of Rome incorporated the rites of Ba'al (now called Saturn), Frugifer, and other pre-Roman deities (often identified as the *genius* of a town or area).[149] Such a process was meant to demonstrate that these African gods were simultaneously great Roman gods.[150]

Local African gods of fertility, like the god called Frugifer, were popular in agricultural towns like Thugga and Mustis. Liber Pater, probably the Latinized name for the Punic deity Shadrapa, who was sometimes associated with the Greek deity Dionysus, was worshipped throughout North Africa (see *ILS* 6796; *IRT* 294; Apuleius, *Apol.* 55.8). The Libyan water god, Maqur, would come forth in Roman times with the name of the Roman god, Neptune. Whether it was the Punic gods Eshmoun or Ba'al, or the Libyan gods Monna and Bacax, Rives is undoubtedly correct in declaring, "The Africans of the Roman period largely abandoned the use of non-Roman divine names and instead employed Latin titles for their traditional deities."[151]

This *interpretatio Romana* would signal the melding of once-distinct ethnoreligious traditions into a unity. Libyan, Numidian, and Punic traditions did not die; they received new life as they were translated and incorporated into the province's growing self-understanding. For example, a third-century hymn to the god Panthea associates a traditional Libyan deity with Greco-Roman literary images and understandings (see *ILS* 4428).[152] Traditional Roman deities would become Africanized as well. As mentioned earlier, the initial cult of Ceres in Carthage was more Roman than Romano-African.

Ceres was traditionally the patron deity of the Roman plebs. Some scholars believe that Caesar used this god as a symbol of his populist image. In fact, after the battle of Thapsus, which was won right before the *ludi Cereales,* Caesar paid his troops with coins that included the image of the god. Since Caesar's colonial program included the resettlement of the poor, it makes sense that this god would be found in the new African *colonia.* Attestations to the cult indicate that it was part of the *sacra publica* of the city (see, e.g., *ILS* 9404; *CIL*[2] 23820). Over time, however, the cult of Ceres and the African cult of the Cereres were identified as the same in the minds of many North Africans. Tertullian mentions the priestesses of Ceres Africana, women who remained chaste out of devotion to the god (*Ux.* 1.6; *Exh. cast.* 13). Female priesthoods were rare in the Roman tradition, and none were associated with Ceres. Likewise, information from Carthage mentions female priests of the god ranked in a hierarchical fashion (*ILS* 4468). These are clear indications of the presence of Punic influence upon the public religion of the city. Rives suggests that these female priests would have been placed under the authority of the officially recognized priest of Ceres. And so, this typical Roman cult was transformed into something more reflective of its Romano-African environment.[153]

Although it did not receive official recognition, the cult of Saturn (Punic: Ba'al) was widespread. It was arguably the most important regional cult in North Africa. Brown describes this Punicized Numidian deity as the "High God of Africa, . . . a 'Supreme Father,' a 'Holy One,' an 'Eternal One,' . . . called, in reverent dread, 'The Old Man.'"[154] Worshipped near Carthage on top of the Djebel bou Kournein, Saturn had at least 18 temples and shrines throughout the province. Indigenous Africans and Roman provincials alike visited them. The Romanization of the cult can be seen in cultic practices, cult statues, and ideas and traditions related to the god. In fact, the formula *Saturno Augusto sacrum,* "sacred to Saturn Augustus," was so common that it was often abbreviated on inscriptions. Likewise, there appears to have been a neighborhood of Saturn in Carthage (*vicus Saturni*), an indication that a shrine to the deity was located there (see

Acta Cypriani 2). Since this manifestation of Saturn was worshipped almost exclusively in Africa, it serves as a good example of the ethnoreligious tradition that arose there under Roman domination.[155]

Closely associated with both agricultural fertility and the underworld, the Punic god Ba'al Addir was worshipped in Africa under the name of Pluto, the Greek deity of the underworld (see *ILS* 4453; *AE* [1982] 932; *CIL*² 26472). In the colony of Zama Regia, the magistrates dedicated two statues to this "great king" as *summa honoraria* (*ILS* 4454). Giufi, another African town, made dedications to Pluto Augustus that were accompanied by feasts, and in Madauros there was a regular priesthood to the god (see *CIL*² 12379–12381; *ILAlg* 2208, 2211, 2224, 2229).[156] In a similar manner, the Greco-Roman deity Aesculapius (Greek: Asclēpius) was worshipped in Carthage and throughout Africa in a manner reminiscent of its Punic predecessor, Eshmoun, including the prohibition on swine as a sacrificial victim and the god's Punic dress (see, e.g., Tertullian, *Pall.* 1.2).[157]

As already mentioned, the cult of Caelestis was introduced in Carthage, and she was the patron deity of the city. Brown describes her relationship to Saturn: "In Carthage, however, this terrifying father was eclipsed by a great, feminine deity, the *Dea Caelestis*, the 'Goddess of Heaven'; an all-absorbing, maternal figure, to whom even Christian parents wisely dedicated their children."[158] According to Augustine, she was worshipped well into the fourth century (*Civ.* 2.4.14).[159] To some Romans, she was identical to the god Diana (see *CIL* 5765).[160] Nevertheless, in the minds of many this African god was as great as Artemis of Ephesus (see, e.g., Tertullian, *Apol.* 24.7; cf. *Nat.* 2.8.5). The institution of her cult at Carthage is representative of the new ethnoreligious environment that permeated the city. As Rives explains, "No longer was Carthage simply a mirror of Rome, whose institutions it copied. It was a glorious city in its own right, ruled by a great deity whose cult extended as far back as that of Jupiter Optimus Maximus."[161]

In addition to the Africanized Greco-Roman gods discussed already, Africans also worshipped impersonalized Roman deities such as Securitas.[162] Other deities for whom worship has been documented in Africa include Bellona (a Roman god), Heros (a Thracian god), Silvanus (an Italian god), and Sarapis (a Greco-Egyptian god).[163] The worship of Sarapis is interesting because it is likely an example of an peculiar ethnoreligious cult. Probably promoted by a group of Alexandrian merchants, Sarapis is a good example of the various religious options available to the average Carthaginian.[164] In addition, Carthaginians would have had access to mystery cults such as Mithras and Magna Mater, and various *collegia*.[165] In short, "a tremendous number of religious options were available in Carthage, not merely to the economic and cultural elite, but to the entire populace."[166]

Latin Church, African Rigor, and Slanderous Images

As Timothy Barnes once wrote, "Knowledge of Christianity in Africa begins with slander and innuendo."[167] The slander to which he was referring had to do with the Scillitan martyrs. The arrest, trial, and execution of these individuals is the first unfortunate image we receive of the presence of Christianity in the African province. As a consequence, the image of martyrdom will function as the dominant form of North African Christian self-definition for the next two centuries. According to W. H. C. Frend, "The North African Church provides the first example of Christianity as a social movement intent on severing earthly fortunes in preparation for the Millennium of the saints."[168]

In the North African *ecclesia* the true Christian was at odds with the world.[169] Allegiance to Christ placed many in opposition to the emperor, at least to the extent that he symbolized the promotion of paganism.[170] As an ethnoreligious movement, African Christians incorporated many of the affiliations already outlined. It was simultaneously Roman and African. Among the values espoused by Christians in the province were allegiance to the church, separation from the world of unbelievers, and the promotion of African identity.[171] Even as late as the fourth century CE, the average African saw the world as a battlefield upon which she must be prepared to fight for survival.[172] Since these were the last days, the *ecclesia* had to concentrate on its own growth as well as the persecution and martyrdom of its members.[173] This view is epitomized in Tertullian's famous statement that the blood of the martyrs is the seed of the church (*Apol.* 50.61).

In contrast to Christianity in other parts of the empire, Christians in Africa believed martyrdom to be part of their cultural heritage.[174] At crucial points in Carthaginian history prominent residents sacrificed themselves for the greater good. According to legend, Queen Dido built her own funeral pyre, climbed on it, and killed herself with her sword. Augustine, in his *Confessions*, recalled hearing this story and crying on her behalf. Likewise, the general Hamilcar Barca, while fighting the Greeks in 485 BCE, threw himself on a sacrificial pyre for the sake of his troops. At the end of the Third Punic War, the wife of Hasdrubal killed her children and threw them into the fires that were destroying the city. She then plunged in after them. According to Appian, Hasdrubal's wife demonstrated the type of courage a good Carthaginian should have in such a situation, "as Hasdrubal should have died himself."[175]

Phoenicians in North Africa practiced human sacrifice before the destruction of Carthage in 146 BCE. They believed the spilling of sacrificial blood to be a powerful agent in securing divine blessings. And although this practice was repressed in the Roman period, the Carthaginians continued to support gladiatorial combat, a peculiar form of human sacrifice. Many in North Africa revered the fearlessness of gladiatorial combat, at least as demonstrated by the mosaics that have been found in their homes. In his novel, the *Metamorphoses*, Apuleius tells of a woman who avenged her husband's killers and subsequently committed suicide at his grave. Even the great aqueduct in Carthage carried with it a legend of self-sacrificial martyrdom. As Salisbury says, "[The] wary Carthaginians could rely on sacrificial blood to ensure the continuation of the water supply to the city." In short, the opportunity to give one's life for a cause was a consummate Carthaginian value.

As the *ecclesia* of Carthage represented its local ethnoreligious affiliation, it was also very Roman in character. This can be seen most clearly in the absence of the Punic language in the African *ecclesia*. Fergus Millar points out that "the extensive works of Tertullian and Cyprian, written entirely in Africa, contain not a single reference to Punic."[176] This piece of information tells us something about the ethnoreligious allegiance of at least the leaders of the Carthaginian *ecclesia*. If Punic was a commonly spoken language in Carthage, then why is there no evidence of its use among those who scholars say comprised the *ecclesia* of Carthage, those of humbler means and lower status?[177] The answer seems to be that as language is a vehicle of culture, the Punic culture of Carthage was considered antithetical to most Christian forms of self-definition. Unlike the Christian movement in provinces like Egypt, where the church used Coptic, Christianity in Africa served to reinforce Roman culture rather than indigenizing itself. As Brown says,

> The Christian culture of Africa . . . was exclusively Latin. . . . This, I would suggest, was the cultural function of the rise of Christianity in Late Roman Africa: far from fostering native tradition, it widened the franchise of the Latin language.[178]

As we have seen, however, not everything Carthaginian was abandoned by the *ecclesia*. Like many good Romans, African Christians held tradition to be an important aspect of culture, particularly with respect to religion.[179] And so, we find Tertullian writing *De pallio* in defense of a native tradition.[180] In it he argues against wearing the Roman *toga* in favor of the traditional Carthaginian *pallium*.[181] In this and other ways, the Christian inhabitants of Carthage demonstrated their Romano-African ethnoreligious allegiance.

Carthaginian Christians may have seen themselves as aliens in this world, but that does not mean they were a people without social standing.[182] This view is confirmed by Thomas Giallanza's study of Latin *cognomina* in the Carthaginian clerical hierarchy. He concluded that the clergy generally appear "to be composed of largely Romanized Africans of humble, though not impoverished, background. Some . . . appear to have belonged to families of middling status. All appear to have been at least partially educated."[183] I argue that Christians could also be found among the Carthaginian elite. For example, Tertullian warns Scapula, then proconsul, that if he were to institute a persecution, he would capture "perhaps also men of your order, and matrons, and all the leading personages, and even the relatives and friends of your own people" (*Scap.* 5.2). In his *De cultu feminarum* he addresses problems that would only be of importance to women of elite status (*Cult. Fem.* 2.9.4). Likewise, in *De idololatria* Tertullian deals with the problem of a Christian serving as a magistrate, something that would have required at least decurion status (*Idol.* 17). In other words, such discourse would have been unnecessary without the presence of persons in the Christian community to whom these and related matters were a concern.[184] The early third-century martyr, Vibia Perpetua, was definitely one of the people Tertullian had in mind. Although the initial arrest was of her household slaves, Perpetua's capture demonstrates that persons of elite status formed part of the *ecclesia*. Her family was surely of decurion status, if not higher; and Perpetua's brother was also a Christian.

If Tertullian's statement that Christians in Carthage were everywhere and of every age, sex, and condition is remotely true, then Christianity was established quite early in the metropolis (*Apol.* 1.7).[185] Estimates are that about 2,000 residents of Carthage were Christians.[186] Although a small fraction of the city's population, the numbers would be large enough to be noticeable, especially among the elite. They were certainly too many to meet in one household, which is why some scholars believe Christians in Carthage must have had a more formal gathering place.[187] And yet, we should see what we can learn from the scandal of the Scillitan martyrs.

The Scillitan martyrs came from small communities near Carthage.[188] There is nothing in their names to indicate that they held important social standing, although several of them have typical African names.[189] They were tried before the proconsul P. Vigellius Raius Plarius Saturninus, who, according to Tertullian, was the first to persecute Christians (*Scap.* 3.4). If Christianity had spread to communities outside Carthage by 180 CE, the Christian community in the city was established well before this time.[190] These twelve individuals were beheaded, the form of execution customary for Roman citizens. What the *Acts of the Scillitan Martyrs* tell us is that Christianity had planted roots among a cross section of North Africans by the close of the second century, roots that probably took at least a generation to grow.[191] And so, most scholars believe that Christianity arrived in Africa in about 150 CE.

As to the origins of Christianity in Carthage, nothing definite is known. There are at least three prominent theories. The first supposes that Christianity came to Carthage with merchants or missionaries from the east.[192] This is supported primarily from liturgical evidence.[193] The second is that Christianity arrived at Carthage by way of the Jewish community.[194] This is supported by evidence of Jewish immigration to the province after the destruction of the Jerusalem temple. The third is that the *ecclesia* in Carthage was a product of the missionary efforts of the Roman church.[195] By contrast, Rives argues that Christianity came by means of various sources.[196] However, as Barnes concedes, "If reliable evidence is wanted, the enquiry cannot penetrate beyond the nature of the African Church in the days of Tertullian and the beliefs concerning its origin which are reflected in the *De praescriptione haereticorum*."[197] He concludes his argument by saying, "Neither Tertullian nor his readers, it must be concluded, possessed any precise knowledge of how Christianity came to Africa."[198] And this is likely true. However Christianity found its way to Africa, this *ecclesia* took on a decidedly more Latin character in the following years and was thoroughly Romanized by the time of the incident of the Scillitan martyrs.

From Montanism to Donatism: The Dominant Image of the Carthaginian Christian Community

Eusebius mentions the diversity of charismatic gifts present in the Christian community. Prophecy, glossolalia, dreams, and trances were all part of the community's worship experience. Eusebius says,

In fact, it is impossible to enumerate the gifts which throughout the world the Church has received from God and in the name of Jesus Christ crucified under Pontius Pilate, and every day put to effectual use for the benefit of the heathen, deceiving no one and making profit out of no one: freely she received from God, and freely she ministers. (*Hist. eccl.* 7 [Williamson])[199]

His statement would most definitely be true in Africa. As described by Brown, it was unexceptional for African Christians to seek out ecstatic experiences. Dreams and trances were common, even in the fourth century.[200] Carthaginians not only read Scripture and preached, baptized and celebrated Eucharist; they also sang and prophesied under the influence of the Spirit. They even preserved the recorded visions of the martyrs and read them during service.[201] Such exuberance and joy was a manifestation of the Spirit, they believed. And what was paramount for the validity of Christian worship in the Carthaginian mind was the presence of the Holy Spirit.[202] Thus, Montanism was easily accepted by the African *ecclesia*.

Montanus was reportedly a pagan priest who converted to Christianity and was baptized around 155 CE, although more recent scholarship would place the beginnings of the movement about a decade later.[203] According to tradition, Montanus fell into a convulsive frenzy and uttered prophetic oracles in the name of the Holy Spirit (see Eusebius, *Hist. eccl.* 5.17). This took place, initially, in the Phrygian village of Mysia. Montanus was soon joined by two women, Priscilla (or Prisca) and Maximilla, who also prophesied.[204] These prophecies claimed that a new dispensation had begun with a fresh revelation given by the Spirit. Although they did not contradict what had been given in the writings that were being collected and designated as the NT, these prophecies surpassed the NT in their rigor and eschatological urgency. In short, Montanism was a millenarian movement.

The rigor of Montanist ethics was likely a protest against the developing penitential system and progressive ecclesial adaptation to the larger culture.[205] The Montanists also opposed the more popular view that martyrdom was to be avoided, if possible. They believed that it was the duty of every true Christian to die for the faith. Furthermore, they rejected the increasingly popular Christian doctrine of sexuality that advocated marriage almost as an obligation.[206] In Montanist circles, widows and widowers were not allowed to remarry.[207] Such controversial stances were based on the expectation of an imminent *eschaton*. According to its leaders, the final period of revelation had been inaugurated, and the end was coming soon. The "New Jerusalem" would be established at Pepuza in Phrygia, and many followers reportedly gathered there to witness this event.[208]

Montanists were not opposed, in general, to the emerging ecclesiastical organization of bishops, presbyters, and deacons. They saw no contradiction between their revelation and such a church structure.[209] Before its official condemnation, Montanism developed its own hierarchical structure, and it rapidly spread throughout Asia Minor, as well as to Rome and North Africa.[210] It was not, as some suppose, a protest movement against a perceived excessively organized church in favor of a purely charismatic structure. The Christians who embraced this prophetic movement did not view it or themselves as subversive or heretical, but they did see themselves as perpetuators of the prophetic tradition proclaimed originally by the Christian faith.

As the movement gained adherents, officials in the more established church increasingly denounced it. The churches of Asia Minor repudiated Montanus and his prophecies, deeming them inspired by the devil, and they quickly excommunicated him and his followers. By contrast, the bishop of Rome was almost won over to the Montanist cause.[211] Eventually, however, the Roman church denounced Montanism. It was in Africa, however, that Montanism achieved its greatest success. The church in and around Carthage was enthusiastic for what they called the new prophecy. In the early third century Montanism was considered part of the established church in Africa. For example, Perpetua's Christian contemporaries accepted her as a catholic martyr, although the *Passio Perpetuae et Felicitatis* indicates she held views congruent with Montanism.[212]

The new prophecy resonated with the Carthaginians because it supported many of their Romano-African values, especially rigor, martyrdom, and prophecy. Evidence indicates that Romans began their interest in prophecy in the second century BCE.[213] Of course, signs or augury had been a traditional part of Roman religion, but the consultation of oracles and other forms of prophecy increased in the imperial period.[214] Since Christianity, like Roman religion, was a process of constant communication with the deity, the Montanist emphasis on prophecy struck a deep ethnoreligious chord in Carthage. The Romans maintained their relationship and communication with the gods through divination and other means; the Christians maintained it through the inspiration of the Holy Spirit and prophecy.

Although Christian communities throughout the empire rejected Montanism, the average African believed, as Tertullian did, that she was more faithful to the tradition of the great church than many of its other members.[215] And even though Barnes argues that the North African *ecclesia* accepted and obeyed the determination of the bishop of Rome, he likewise concedes that adherence to Montanism would have been acceptable in Carthaginian Christian society. As he says, "[How] could one deny that the

Holy Spirit still spoke to men?"[216] In truth, Montanism created an intellectual conflict in the *ecclesia* of Carthage. Two theological traditions appeared to be in mortal combat: either one adhered to the tradition of prophecy or one adhered to the tradition of apostolic succession. Tradition and prophecy were both important ingredients of a leader's *auctoritas*. Prophets and martyrs appealed to prophecy as the source of their authority. Bishops appealed to apostolic tradition for theirs. Although limitations were placed on prophetic authority, and Cyprian would undermine the authority of martyrs, a Carthaginian Christian in the second century would still maintain that the *ecclesia* is not a "conclave of bishops, but the manifestation of the Holy Spirit" (see Tertullian, *Pud.* 21.17).[217] When Augustine later proclaimed, *Voce ecclesia loquor*, "I speak with the voice of the church," he meant his own voice as bishop. Two centuries earlier prophets and martyrs could make the same statement (*Serm.* 129.4).

The Africans saw their *ecclesia* as a strong woman (Augustine, *Serm.* 37.2). As the Christian analogue to Caelestis, the *ecclesia* nurtured her children in the values that permeated the African homeland. By the second century CE, the African Christians had translated their sacred Scriptures into Latin.[218] They were a strong-knit community that sought to care for both their own members and the community at large.[219] They repudiated the ordinary Greco-Roman concern for material possessions and shared of their wealth liberally. They looked after the poor, orphans, elderly, sick, prisoners, and destitute.[220] It constituted an alternative family, and there were many in the Carthaginian Christian community who would see it that way. Although it had survived the martyrdom of twelve of its members, it had to develop its own rationale for the seemingly random nature of persecution.

The arbitrary nature of their executions contributed to the belief that such martyrs were chosen by God. It was, in reality, a gift. Of course, all members of the community did not take martyrdom in such a positive way. These were the Christians who reverted to the old Roman practice of bribery.[221] Others in the *ecclesia*, however, welcomed the possibility of persecution, some even voluntarily offering themselves for the experience. Such is the case of Saturus, one of the martyrs executed with Vibia Perpetua. This incident may shed more light on the Carthaginian *ecclesia*.

Sometime after 201 CE, the African emperor, Septimius Severus, issued an edict forbidding conversion to Judaism and Christianity. The effectiveness of the edict, however, relied heavily on the zealousness of provincial governors. Egypt and particularly Alexandria were affected disproportionately by this decree. Carthage had such a zealous proconsul in the year 203. P. Aelius Hilarianus assumed the governorship of Africa Proconsularis after serving Rome in Asia and Spain. He was a devoutly religious and ambitious man. For reasons unknown to us, Hilarianus decided to celebrate the birthday of the emperor's son Geta. He was apparently looking for victims to offer up in the arena during the celebration, but we have no idea why he settled on the household of the Vibii. At any rate, the narrator's description of the arrest indicates that the first to be arrested were slaves, an act that would not offend the nobility of Carthaginian society. Unfortunately for Hilarianus, the situation did not turn out as expected. Perpetua apparently stepped forward as the slaves were arrested. Embodying the values of her Romano-African context, she voluntarily placed herself on the altar of sacrifice.[222]

As in Rome, the proconsul conducted judicial proceedings in the forum on the Byrsa hill. One morning, as they ate breakfast, Perpetua and her cohorts were suddenly taken to the forum for their hearing. In front of a large crowd, the potential martyrs admitted that they were Christians. Even the pleadings of Perpetua's father and the proconsul could not change her mind. "Have pity on your father's grey head; have pity on your infant son," said Hilarianus.[223] But she resolutely refused. Hilarianus's sentence was particularly harsh. The martyrs of 180 CE had been beheaded; this group would be thrown to the beasts for sport. Although an unusual sentence, Perpetua recalled the event by saying, "We were condemned to the beasts, and we returned to prison in high spirits."[224]

By confessing Christianity and becoming a martyr, Perpetua made herself a de facto leader of the Christian community in Carthage. Prophets, martyrs, and clerics were the triumvirs of the African *ecclesia*. Prophets were prohibited from taking money, and according to the *Didache*, were only allowed to remain in a community for three days. Clerics struggled against the prophets and martyrs for a dominant voice in the community. Martyrs were esteemed by the faithful.[225] In his vision Saturus demonstrates quite clearly that he believes martyrs to be the true leaders of the church.[226] Many believed that they had the power to forgive sins, a problem that Cyprian will later address.[227] The dreams and visions of martyrs were faithfully recorded, and as stated earlier, they were read in worship alongside Scripture.[228] To the members of the *ecclesia*, martyrs embodied the sacred text.[229] They were the signs of the true *ecclesia*.[230] In this incident, however, we also see the leftovers of a continuing conflict that will divide Christians in North Africa.

The virtual veneration of martyrdom among Christians in Carthage, gave a Roman matron a great deal of authority. She was chosen by God and so must have a special relationship to the deity. As with Montanism, such charismatic authority increasingly became an irreconcilable point of contention in the *ecclesia*. Perpetua's vision of the Christian community was one of an egalitarian family, an idea that would have offended many a status-conscious Roman, who would even divide citizens into *honestiores* and *humiliores*.[231] The solution, advanced by Cyprian and his successors, would be to model the *ecclesia* not on the egalitarian family of Perpetua's vision, but on the traditional hierarchical family that she rejected. In other words, to assimilate Christian organizational practice to that of the larger society. And this supposed remedy would bring about the second point of contention to divide the church. One of the core North African Christian values was separation. The adoption of a transparently Roman model of social organization broke down the wall that divided believers from unbelievers.[232] Both conflicts would be addressed in the ministry of Augustine. He placed the power of prophecy in the hands of the one authorized to interpret the dream rather than the visionary.[233] Likewise, Augustine permanently altered the African sense of separation with the phrase *mundus reconciliatus ecclesia*, the reconciled world is the *ecclesia* (*Serm.* 96.6–8). And yet, to understand the importance of Augustine's resolution of these problems and their meaning in the life of the *ecclesia*, we must look at the actors who preceded him.

Some have identified Quintus Septimius Florens Tertullianus with a lawyer of that name who appears in the *Corpus Iuris Civilis*, although making a final determination regarding that identification is not possible.[234] As stated earlier, North Africans were fond of forensic argument, and since many of Tertullian's writings were apologetic, the use of legal language and metaphors would naturally appear appropriate. In any case, the generally accepted history is that Tertullian lived in Rome for several years, and after his conversion, which took place when he was about forty years old, he returned to Carthage, where he had been born around the year 150 CE.[235] According to Lactantius, Tertullian was an expert in every literary genre (*Inst.* 5.1.23). Eusebius wrote that he was learned in Roman law, and well known among the Roman powerbrokers (*Hist. eccl.* 2.2.4). Jerome later identified Tertullian as the son of a proconsular centurion and a Carthaginian presbyter (*Vir. ill.* 53). Although all these statements are debatable, they do point to a singular truth: Tertullian was not a man from a humble background.

Not even a casual reader of Tertullian could ever doubt his erudition.[236] He was a literary powerhouse in an age of general Latin literary decline. Unlike the Persians, Greeks, and later the British, the Romans were never able to make Latin the language of the empire. In fact, the majority of Christians chose to write and relate their theological ideas in Greek rather than Latin. Octavian may have defeated the forces of Hellenism at Actium, but true cultural pride of "place was passing to the once despised Greeks."[237]

Even the Roman emperors, the embodiments of *Romanitas*, began to court Greek culture, something unthinkable in the age of Augustus. The emperor Hadrian is said to have written in fluent Greek, and his fondness for things Greek would create periodic rumblings in the Senate. His second successor, Marcus Aurelius, wrote his famous *Meditations* in Greek and studied Greek philosophy extensively. As one scholar put it, "When Marcus became emperor, Latin literature was already unfashionable."[238] Septimius Severus, whose identification with the Greco-Egyptian Sarapis contributed to the martyrdom of Perpetua, studied in Athens and reportedly passed his days in conversation in both Latin and Greek.[239] Although Latin was the language of the conquerors, Greek rhetoric flourished in a movement that came to be called the Second Sophistic.[240]

The Second Sophistic was a period when Greek rhetoric experienced a renewal. It originated in reflection upon the ideal of the politically active wise person, which first found its roots in the sophists of Athens. The movement was accompanied by a renewal of interest in classical Athens. The leading advocate of this movement was said to be Herodes Atticus, a teacher of Marcus Aurelius. Atticus, a wealthy and politically active man, used his influence to push this Greek revival forward. And Atticus's influence was felt at the very heart of Roman imperial power: his wife, Regilla, was related to Faustina, wife of the emperor Antoninus Pius.[241]

Despite the ascendancy of Greek literature, Latin literature did not simply vanish from the intellectual landscape. It persisted, especially in legal philosophy, an intellectual arena not dominated by traditional Greek thought.[242] This was particularly true in Roman Africa, where "the polite arts were still practiced."[243] Even though Apuleius wrote his famous novel in Greek, he regularly composed orations in both languages. Christians in Carthage, like their Jewish predecessors in Alexandria, made haste to translate their sacred scriptures from Greek to Latin.[244] Likewise, Christians in Africa transformed their liturgy from Greek to Latin.[245] Although presumably not translated in Carthage, one could find many translations of the Greek philosophers in the city. The franchise of the Latin language was so strong in Africa that many, like Augustine, felt no need to learn Greek.[246] This was possible because cosmopolitan Carthage was a major intellectual center of the Western empire.[247] It attracted scholars from inside the province and throughout the Greco-Roman world.[248] As Apuleius aptly proclaimed, "Carthage the venerable teacher of the province, Carthage the heavenly Muse of Africa, Carthage the inspiration of the Roman world" (*Flor.* 20).[249]

Capable of reading and writing in both Latin and Greek, Tertullian's education was beyond what could be obtained generally by somebody of humble means. Many scholars find his Latin prose difficult and eccentric, but as Rives correctly points out, Tertullian's style demonstrates the abilities of someone who both knew the rules and was willing to break them. Tertullian's writings display "an absolute command of rhetorical techniques, which he used to devastating effect in his attacks on pagans, heretics, and eventually orthodox Christians."[250] Some scholars have suggested that Tertullian was of equestrian status, but such a designation is tenuous.[251] What appears undisputable, however, is that Tertullian's level of education betrays someone of relatively high social standing. He must have been at least of decurion status.

Tertullian's ecclesiology confirms his placement among members of the *ordo decurionem*. Like Perpetua and other North Africans, Tertullian conceived of the *ecclesia* as a community of the elect.[252] The purity and virtue of this strong woman had to be maintained apart from the various possible contaminants found in the larger society. Tertullian also agreed with the deacon and martyr Saturus that the clerical hierarchy did not represent primary authority in the *ecclesia*:

> Are we laity not also priests? It is written, "He has made of us a Royal house, to serve as the priests of his God and Father" [Rev 1:6]. The authority and honour of the church, through the assemblies of the clergy (*ordo*) consecrated to God, has established the difference between the clergy and the laity (*plebs*). Where there is no assembly of the clergy of the church, you the laymen offer the Eucharist and baptize, you are for yourself the only priest; in short, where there are three, there is the church, even if those three are laity. (*Exh. cast.* 7.3)[253]

True authority in the Christian community comes from God through the working of the Holy Spirit (see *Virg.* 1.4). Thus, whomever God chooses to exercise authority, whether it is priest, prophet, or martyr, can rightly speak with God's voice. Episcopal authority, although derived from apostolic tradition, does not confer upon its recipient any special power or standing in the community. As he would say to one bishop regarding his assumed authority to forgive sins, "You show yourself neither prophet nor apostle: therefore you lack the power in virtue of which pardon is granted" (*Pud.* 21).[254] Tertullian understood the clerical hierarchy of the *ecclesia* to be analogous to the civil authorities. His use of the terms *ordo* and *plebs* in the above quotation and elsewhere illustrate a mind-set that characterized many of elite status (see, e.g., *Exh. cast.* 7.2; *Marc.* 4.5.2; *Idol.* 7.3; *Mon.* 12.1). As in republican Rome, many elites believed that religious authority had to be shared among members of a properly designated group. During the republic, members of the Senate diffused religious authority in a tightly regulated fashion.[255] It appears that Tertullian saw authority in the *ecclesia* as similar to this ancient republican paradigm. In contrast, he appears to view the authority claimed by Agrippinus, prelate of Carthage, and other bishops as analogous to the concentration of religious authority under the emperors. This may explain Tertullian's use of the term *adlectio* (election) to describe the process of joining the clergy (see, e.g., *Praescr.* 43.5; *Ux.* 1.7.4; *Exh. cast.* 7.6).

Despite Tertullian's obvious intellectual prowess and rhetorical ability, two separate but related acts will serve to undermine his vision of the *ecclesia*. Although Christians claimed to pray *pro salute imperatoris*, the emperor Decius in 250 CE issued an edict ordering all residents of the empire to sacrifice to the gods. Scholars doubt that this edict was directed solely toward Christians, but Decius did secure for himself a place among the worst ten persecutors of the *ecclesia*. At any rate, during the persecution many apostatized, even in stalwart Carthage. As the persecution waned and eventually ceased, the question of the status of those who had apostatized, now called *lapsi*, loomed large. Presbyters acting on their own authority had already readmitted some to the church; others received letters (*libelli pacis*) from martyrs awaiting execution that pardoned them. The bishop of Carthage had been exiled during the persecution, but when he returned he dealt decisively with the authority of the martyrs.

Caecilius Cyprianus Thascius came from a wealthy Carthaginian family. He was apparently well educated. The *Vita Cypriani* (2) mentions his immersion in liberal studies, the sort of education that could not be obtained without a reasonable income. According to Jerome, Lactantius, and Augustine, he was a renowned teacher of rhetoric (Jerome, *Vir. ill.* 67; Lactantius, *Inst.* 5.1.24; Augustine, *Serm.* 312.4). Also according to the *Vita* (15), Cyprian sold his Carthaginian estate after his conversion to support the poor. Such an act did not exhaust his apparent resources: he continued to donate money for the maintenance of good works during the persecution.[256] Even at the time of his martyrdom he was able to present his exe-

cutioner with 25 gold coins (*Acta Cypriani* 5). His status, like that of many
Romans, determined his treatment by civil authorities. Under the Valerian
persecution, he was exiled to a small town on the coast of the province
(*Acta Cypriani* 1). When finally condemned for his refusal to deny the faith,
he was beheaded in the gardens of the governor's palace. By contrast, a
group of bishops in Numidia were sentenced to hard labor in the mines and
subjected to cruel beatings. Such treatment suggests quite strongly that
Cyprian was an *honestior*, a person of at least decurion status, from the
upper levels of the local aristocracy.[257]

Upon his return from exile, he addressed the problem of the *lapsi*. He
convened a council at Carthage in 251 to discuss the issue. It asserted the
authority of the bishops and the council that of the martyrs in the
matter of readmitting the *lapsi* to communion. Only the bishop could
grant absolution, a statement that would have been unacceptable to Tertullian. Two years later he proclaimed a general amnesty of sorts for the
lapsi. This further strengthened his position that the bishop alone had
authority in such matters. If the bishop is the judicial representative of
Christ (*iudex vice Christi*) in the *ecclesia*, and there can be no salvation outside the *ecclesia*, there can be no source of authority opposed to the bishop.
Any other authority, whether clerical or lay, that does not submit to the
authority of the bishop is outside the *ecclesia*. As he says, "If you leave the
Church of Christ you will not come to Christ's rewards, you will be an
alien, an outcast, an enemy" (*Unit. eccl.* 6 [Greenslade]).[258] And so Decius's
edict and the problem of the *lapsi* would converge during the episcopacy of
Cyprian to dismantle the remnants of nonecclesiastical authority in the
Carthaginian Christian community.

Like Tertullian, Cyprian's privileged status would serve to undermine
the other major point of contention in Carthaginian Christianity. He
describes his role as bishop as much like that of a proconsul managing his
province as the representative of God. He even describes the territory cov-
ered by his diocese as his *provincia*.[259] As bishop, Cyprian has a staff almost
as extensive as the governor's, including *corniculari*, *commentarienses, fru-
mentarii*, and *beneficiarii*.[260] He even describes the ranks of the clerical hierarchy as a *cursus*.[261]

To make matters worse for Christians like Perpetua, Cyprian describes
the members of the community as *plebs*, as did his predecessor Tertullian.
They were analogous to the citizenry who exercised their will only during
episcopal elections, which he appropriately describes as *suffragium*. To
Cyprian an episcopal election was the ecclesiastical equivalent of the
clientes' support of a *patronus* in a municipal election. As *iudex vice Christi*,

Cyprian conceived of his station as one in which he acted as governor of his people, dispensing patronage to those whom he deemed worthy. What was implicit in Tertulian's use of *ordo* became full-blown in Cyprian's ecclesiology:

> You can see that there are all these numerous and significant examples from the past in which God upholds with His blessing the authority and power of His bishops. What do you then think of those who make war on those bishops, who rise in rebellion against the catholic Church, who are not deterred by the warnings and threats of the Lord, not even by His vengeance in the judgement to come? In truth, heresies and schisms have their source and origin precisely in circumstances where people fail to obey God's bishop and where they forget the fact that in a church there is but one bishop and judge who acts in Christ's stead for the time being. But if all the brethren gave their bishop their obedience as God's teachings prescribe, no one would make any move against the college of the bishops; after God has made His choice and the people have cast their vote and fellow bishops have expressed their concurrence, no one would set himself up to pass judgement not on the bishops now but on God Himself. No one would tear the Church of Christ apart by the destruction of her unity, no one would have the arrogant self-conceit to establish a new heresy outside and beyond the Church. (*Ep.* 59.5.1–2)[262]

And yet, Cyprian's position would not spell the certain demise of the martyr's authority in North Africa. Although Cyprian tilted the scale in favor of episcopal authority and further assimilation to secular governmental models, Christians in Carthage would continue to venerate those who had given their lives in opposition to the larger pagan society. They incorporated his martyrdom into their collective memory and even incorporated others.

From Numidia would come the *Passio Sanctorum Mariani et Iacobi*, in which one of its main characters, Marian, dreams that Cyprian himself welcomes the martyr into heaven. From Carthage would come the *Passio Sanctorum Montani et Lucii*, the tale of the beheading of Montanus and Lucius conducted during the same persecution that saw the death of Cyprian. From the persecution under Diocletian we receive the *Acta Crispinae* and the *Passio S. Typasii Veterani*. The authority of the martyrs, although officially repressed, was not dead. Now they represented more than ever the separation that characterized North African Christianity. Such an under-standing of the *ecclesia* would be represented most succinctly in the Council of Cirta held in 305 CE. At this conclave of bishops, the central issue was the election of a successor to Bishop Paulus, who had recently died. Separation was such a strong concern for the twelve bishops who attended the council that the revelation that Bishop Purpurius of Limata had murdered two of his nephews was considered inconsequential in relation to his conduct during persecution.

  Matters came to a head, however, as a consequence of the election of Caecilian as bishop of Carthage. There were strong rumors that one of Caecilian's consecrators had been a *traditor*, a bishop who apostatized during the persecutions. Hence, his consecration was invalid. Maureen Tilley is probably correct that the roots of opposition to Caecilian probably go back to his actions against the Abitinian martyrs while he was a deacon under Mensurius, then bishop of Carthage.[263] Unacceptable to the Abitinians and others throughout North Africa, the opposition elected its own candidate to the episcopal throne of Carthage, a man by the name of Marjorinus. After his death, a Numidian cleric named Donatus was declared bishop in his stead, and the movement known as Donatism was born. Although eventually defeated by Augustine and other Catholic bishops, the movement soon became the dominant voice of African Christianity. Among other things it embraced the core African value of separation. While Augustine claimed the world for the *ecclesia*, Donatists saw themselves as the *collecta*, the assembly of Israel on a long pilgrimage amid pagans.[264]

Contrasting Representations of a Universal Church

  To sum up our discussion in this chapter, we conducted an analysis of Roman Carthage by looking at its development as a *colonia* under Augustus and its influence on and relationship with the rest of Africa Proconsularis. We found it to be a cosmopolitan and self-consciously Romano-African society that fostered both cooperative and sometimes antagonistic interactions between ethnoreligious groups. Although from its inception power was held firmly in the hands of the Roman colonists, they soon included Libyans, Numidians, and Phoenicians among their ranks to forge an ethnoreligious identity that was both African and Roman. As in Egypt, the geographical location of its residents exercised considerable influence over the souls of Carthage's citizens. They worshipped Jupiter alongside Caelestis, Africanizing Roman gods and Romanizing African gods in a manner that bespeaks their dual loyalties and complex self-understanding. Others in the Greco-Roman world characterized Carthaginians as fiercely independent and stubborn; yet, much of Carthage's Romano-African character was manifest in its Christian community.

The origin of the Carthaginian church is unknown. Although various possibilities have been offered, none appears to be totally satisfying. If Christianity came to Carthage from the east, this would explain the early eastern character of its liturgy. If it came with Jews deported from Palestine at the end of the Jewish revolt, this would explain the strong relationship between aspects of Carthaginian theology and Judaism. If it came from Rome, this would explain the close relationship between the two churches, a relationship that continued well into the period of the Arab conquest. And yet, even the Carthaginians appear not to have known exactly how their church began. What is certain, however, is that the leaders of this community expressed their most cherished theological convictions in the forensic and political language of Roman oratory. Carthage thus established and gave basic shape to the theological lexicon that influences Western Christianity to this day. At the center of their theological concern was the church, with the *ecclesia* as the conceptual category used almost exclusively in the development of Carthaginian communal understanding. In doing so, they created their own powerful ethnoreligious identity, one that set the parameters for the emerging orthodoxy but that refused to be dominated by it or anything else.

It is evident how different the church of Carthage was from the church of Alexandria. Alexandrian Christian intellectuals used the language and conceptual categories of Greco-Roman philosophy to discuss subjects ranging from the nature of God to the disposition of one's possessions. By contrast, Carthaginian Christian intellectuals used the language and conceptual categories of Roman legal and political philosophy to discuss the same topics. Each would find its voice in the larger Christian world, and both would come into conflict around differences in conceptual outlook and translation. Although both Alexandrian and Carthaginian intellectuals claimed to speak on behalf of the universal church, their understandings of the meaning and purpose of this entity were heavily influenced by their respective ethnoreligious affiliations and contexts. In other words, the grammar of early Christian discourse, while striving for universal acceptance and applicability, was invariably limited by the social locations of its various intellectual proponents. Since this was true with respect to theology in general, it was undoubtedly true when it came to biblical exegesis and application.

Notes

1. Jane E. Merdinger, *Rome and the African Church in the Time of Augustine* (New Haven: Yale University Press, 1997), ix.

2. William Hugh Clifford Frend, *The Rise of Christianity* (Philadelphia: Fortress, 1984), 346–47.

3. J. B. Rives, *Religion and Authority in Roman Carthage: From Augustus to Constantine* (New York: Oxford University Press, 1995), 17.

4. Joyce E. Salisbury, *Perpetua's Passion: The Death and Memory of a Young Roman Woman* (London: Routledge, 1997), 35.

5. Ibid.

6. Quoted in ibid., 38.

7. Peter Jones and Keith Sidwell, eds., *The World of Rome: An Introduction to Roman Culture* (Cambridge: Cambridge University Press, 1997), 12.

8. Rives, *Religion and Authority*, 20.

9. Ibid., 22.

10. Ibid., 21; Salisbury, *Perpetua's Passion*, 39.

11. Salisbury, *Perpetua's Passion*, 39.

12. For information on the founding of *coloniae*, see Helmut Koester, *History, Culture and Religion of the Hellenistic Age* (vol. 1 of *Introduction to the New Testament*; 1st ed.; New York: Walter de Gruyter, 1982), 332–36; and Mary Beard et al., *Religions of Rome* (2 vols.; Cambridge, UK: Cambridge University Press, 1998), 1:315, 328–34.

13. Rives, *Religion and Authority*, 22–23.

14. Translation from Herodian, *Herodian* (trans. C. R. Whittaker; 2 vols.; LCL; London: Heinemann, 1969).

15. This section was based on Rives, *Religion and Authority*, 28–32.

16. Bronze tablets were used in the Flavian period, but that does not mean the structure and content of the charters changed considerably from the Julian to the Flavian period. Also, ibid., 28.

17. Lesley Adkins and Roy A. Adkins, eds., *Dictionary of Roman Religion* (London: Oxford University Press, 1996), 2; N. G. L. Hammond and H. H. Scullard, eds., *The Oxford Classical Dictionary* (Oxford: Oxford University Press, 1970), 11–12.

18. Ibid., 97, 223.

19. Ibid., 23, 181–82.

20. Rives, *Religion and Authority*, 30.

21. Jones and Sidwell, *World of Rome*, 90.

22. Rives, *Religion and Authority*, 32.

23. Ibid., 34.

24. Ibid.

25. M. Corbier, "City, Territory and Taxation," in *City and Country in the Ancient World* (ed. John Rich and Andrew Wallace-Hadrill; Leicester-Nottingham Studies in Ancient Society; London; New York: Routledge, 1991), 211–40.

26. Rives, *Religion and Authority*, 24.

27. Quoted in ibid.

28. Ibid. On the organization of taxation in Africa, see Sigfried J. de Laet, *Portorium: Étude sur l'organisation douanière chez les Romains, surtout à l'époque du Haut-Empire* (Roman History; New York: Arno, 1975), 247–54.

29. See, e.g., Peter Robert Lamont Brown, *Augustine of Hippo: A Biography* (Berkeley: University of California Press, 1967), 20.

30. Salisbury, *Perpetua's Passion*, 42.

31. Brown, *Augustine of Hippo*, 192.

32. Quoted in ibid., 20.

33. Salisbury, *Perpetua's Passion*, 41.

34. Rives, *Religion and Authority*, 26.

35. Salisbury, *Perpetua's Passion*, 42.

36. Brown, *Augustine of Hippo*, 35.

37. Rives, *Religion and Authority*, 105–6, 18–21.

38. Salisbury, *Perpetua's Passion*, 44–45.

39. Brown, *Augustine of Hippo*, 189–91.

40. Rives, *Religion and Authority*, 23.

41. Ibid.

42. Salisbury, *Perpetua's Passion*, 39.

43. Ibid.

44. Adkins and Adkins, *Dictionary of Roman Religion*, 39.

45. Salisbury, *Perpetua's Passion*, 40.

46. Ibid., 85.

47. Rives, *Religion and Authority*, 27.

48. Ibid.

49. Brown, *Augustine of Hippo*, 39; Salisbury, *Perpetua's Passion*, 40.

50. Salisbury, *Perpetua's Passion*, 119–20.

51. Quoted in ibid., 119.

52. Ibid., 40.

53. Ibid., 44.

54. Ibid., 49.

55. Brown, *Augustine of Hippo*, 19.

56. Quoted in ibid, 21–22.

57. Jones and Sidwell, *World of Rome*, 6–7; Rives, *Religion and Authority*, 22.

58. Rives, *Religion and Authority*, 158.

59. Olivia F. Robinson, *The Sources of Roman Law: Problems and Methods for Ancient Historians* (ed. Richard Stoneman; Approaching the Ancient World; New York: Routledge, 197), 3–5.

60. Rives, *Religion and Authority*, 207.

61. See chapter 2, following note reference no. 116.

62. Brown, *Augustine of Hippo*, 26.

63. Rives, *Religion and Authority*, 9–10.

64. Ibid, 82.

65. Quoted in Brown, *Augustine of Hippo*, 32.

66. Ibid.

67. Ibid.

68. Quoted in Salisbury, *Perpetua's Passion*, 37.

69. Quoted in Brown, *Augustine in Hippo*, 31.

70. Adkins and Adkins, *Dictionary of Roman Religion*, 134.

71. See the discussion in Rives, *Religion and Authority*, 39–42.

72. Ibid., 159.

73. Ibid., 31.

74. Quoted in Brown, *Augustine of Hippo*, 193.

75. Rives, *Religion and Authority*, 104–5.

76. Ibid., 110.

77. Quoted in ibid., 106.

78. See chapter 3, between note reference nos. 162 and 165.

79. Rives, *Religion and Authority*, 37.

80. On the cost of the Capitol, see ibid., 34. On the wages of a sewer cleaner, see Jo-Ann Shelton, ed., *As the Romans Did: A Sourcebook in Roman Social History* (New York: Oxford University Press, 1998), 131.

81. Brown, *Augustine of Hippo*, 21.

82. Quoted in G. S. M. Walker, *The Churchmanship of St. Cyprian* (Ecumenical Studies in History 9; London: Lutterworth, 1968), 7.

83. Quoted in Brown, *Augustine of Hippo*, 23.

84. Ibid.

85. Ibid., 22.

86. Salisbury, *Perpetua's Passion*, 45–49.

87. Ibid., 46.

88. Rives, *Religion and Authority*, 198.

89. Ibid., 193.

90. Salisbury, *Perpetua's Passion*, 33, 46.

91. Brown, *Augustine of Hippo*, 22.

92. Maureen A. Tilley, *The Bible in Christian North Africa: The Donatist World* (Minneapolis: Fortress, 1997), 18–19.

93. Brown, *Augustine of Hippo*, 191; Rives, *Religion and Authority*, 14–17.

94. Rives, *Religion and Authority*, 100.

95. Ibid., 161.

96. Ibid., 162.

97. Ibid.; Salisbury, *Perpetua's Passion*, 41.

98. Rives, *Religion and Authority*, 162–69.

99. Ibid., 163–64.

100. Ibid., 165.

101. Quoted in ibid, 164.

102. Ibid., 111.

103. Ibid., 101–3.

104. Ibid., 125.

105. Ibid., 126–29.

106. R. A. Markus, *Saeculum: History and Society in the Theology of St. Augustine* (Cambridge: Cambridge University Press, 1970), 114–15.

107. Rives, *Religion and Authority*, 217; Salisbury, *Perpetua's Passion*, 59–60.

108. Rives, *Religion and Authority*, 214–23, esp. 21.

109. Ibid., 218.

110. Beard, *Religions of Rome*, 1:135.

111. Markus, *Saeculum*, 94.

112. To revisit my discussion of the emperor as *paterfamilias*, see chapter 1, after note reference no. 17.

113. Rives, *Religion and Authority*, 66.

114. Ibid., 234–35.

115. Ibid., 238–39.

116. Ibid.

117. I recognize, however, that there was no such thing as *the* imperial cult. For more information, see Beard, *Religions of Rome*, 1:348.

118. See, e.g., Bruce W. Winter, *After Paul Left Corinth: The Influence of Secular Ethics and Social Change* (Grand Rapids: Eerdmans, 2001), 269–86.

119. Rives, *Religion and Authority*, 62–63.

120. Salisbury, *Perpetua's Passion*, 151, figure 6.1.

121. Ibid., 17–22.

122. Ibid.

123. Beard, *Religions of Rome*, 211–44.

124. Rives, *Religion and Authority*, 27.

125. Ibid., 145.

126. Ibid., 77.

127. See chapter 3, just before note reference no. 118.

128. Rives, *Religion and Authority*, 83.

129. Ibid., 85–96.

130. Ibid., 92.

131. Ibid., 94–95.

132. Ibid., 177.

133. Ibid., 185.

134. Ibid.

135. Ibid., 177–79.

136. Ibid., 178.

137. Ibid., 32–39, 174–93.

138. Ibid., 5, 9–11.

139. Ibid., 9.

140. Ibid., 171–72.

141. Quoted in ibid., 7.

142. Ibid., 191, 247.

143. Ibid., 44.

144. Ibid., 135–36.

145. Ibid., 170.

146. Ibid., 173.

147. Adkins and Adkins, *Dictionary of Roman Religion*, 148.

148. Salisbury, *Perpetua's Passion*, 13.

149. Rives, *Religion and Authority*, 134.

150. Ibid., 153.

151. Ibid., 133; Rives, *Religion and Authority*, 127–53.

152. Rives, *Religion and Authority*, 190.

153. Ibid., 45–51, 157–61.

154. Brown, *Augustine of Hippo*, 33.

155. Rives, *Religion and Authority*, 65–66, 109, 110, 142–50, 154, 209–12.

156. Ibid., 139, 141–42, 153–54.

157. Ibid., 154–56, 181–83.

158. Brown, *Augustine of Hippo*, 33.

159. Ibid., 41.

160. Rives, *Religion and Authority*, 189.

161. Ibid., 168–69; *Religion and Authority*, 65–71, 162–69.

162. Rives, *Religion and Authority*, 191.

163. Ibid., 185–88.

164. Ibid., 185–86, 211, 212–14, 264.

165. Ibid., 72–75, 204, 206, 208–9.

166. Ibid., 247.

167. Timothy David Barnes, *Tertullian: A Historical and Literary Study* (Oxford: Clarendon, 1971), 60.

168. William Hugh Clifford Frend, *Saints and Sinners in the Early Church: Differing and Conflicting Traditions in the First Six Centuries* (Theology and Life Series 11; Wilmington: Michael Glazier, 1985), 95.

169. Markus, *Saeculum*, 167.

170. Frend, *Saints and Sinners*, 95.

171. Ibid., 106–7.

172. Brown, *Augustine of Hippo*, 212–13.

173. Markus, *Saeculum*, 31; Tilley, *Bible in Christian North Africa*, 20.

174. For a further discussion of this idea, see Salisbury, *Perpetua's Passion*, 53–57.

175. Ibid., 54.

176. Fergus Millar, "Local Cultures in the Roman Empire: Libyan, Punic, and Latin in Roman Africa," *JRS* 58 (1968): 134.

177. Peter Robert Lamont Brown, "Christianity and Local Culture in Late Roman Africa," *JRS* 58 (1968): 85.

178. Ibid., 92.

179. Friedrich Heiler, *Prayer: A Study in the History and Psychology of Religion* (ed. Samuel McComb; 2d ed.; New York: Oxford University Press, 1933), 98.

180. For a description of the *pallium* and its continued use in Roman Catholicism, see James-Charles Noonan, *The Church Visible: The Ceremonial Life and Protocol of the Roman Catholic Church* (New York: Viking, 1996), 359–63.

181. See the discussion in Barnes, *Tertullian*, 85.

182. Salisbury, *Perpetua's Passion*, 71–72.

183. Thomas Henry Giallanza, "The Organization and Administration of the Church of Carthage under St. Cyprian: Evidence from the Letters" (MA thesis, University of Virginia, 1988), 48.

184. Rivas, *Religion and Authority*, 271–73.

185. Michael M. Sage, *Cyprian* (Patristic Monograph Series 1; Cambridge: Philadelphia Patristic Foundation, 1975), 8–11.

186. Salisbury, *Perpetua's Passion*, 61.

187. Ibid., 78.

188. Barnes, *Tertullian*, 63.

189. Ibid.; David Rankin, *Tertullian and the Church* (Cambridge: Cambridge University Press, 1995), 11.

190. Barnes, *Tertullian*, 63.

191. Ibid.

192. Ibid., 68; Tilley, *Bible in Christian North Africa*, 19.

193. Rivas, *Religion and Authority*, 226; Tilley, *Bible in Christian North Africa*, 20.

194. Barnes, *Tertullian*, 64; Giallanza, "Organization and Administration of the Church of Carthage," 1–2; Rankin, *Tertullian and the Church*, 16; Salisbury, *Perpetua's Passion*, 59–62; Tilley, *Bible in Christian North Africa*, 19.

195. Merdinger, *Rome and the African Church*, x; Rivas, *Religion and Authority*, 225.

196. Rivas, *Religion and Authority*, 225–26.

197. Barnes, *Tertullian*, 64.

198. Ibid., 67; cf. Rankin, *Tertullian and the Church*, 9.

199. Eusebius, *The History of the Church* (trans. G. A. Williamson; New York: Penguin, 1965), 210.

200. Brown, *Augustine of Hippo*, 33.

201. Salisbury, *Perpetua's Passion*, 92.

202. Rivas, *Religion and Authority*, 232; Salisbury, *Perpetua's Passion*, 63–71, 74–77, 92.

203. Christine Trevett, *Montanism: Gender, Authority and the New Prophecy* (Cambridge: Cambridge University Press, 1996), 41–42.

204. Ibid., 1–15, 159–62; and the review by William Tabbernee in the *Journal of Early Christian Studies* 5/4 (1997): 595–96, which questions some of Trevett's conclusions.

205. Ibid., 77–150.

206. Elaine H. Pagels, *Adam, Eve, and the Serpent* (1st Vintage Books ed.; New York: Vintage Books, 1989), passim.

207. Trevett, *Montanism*, 109–13.

208. Ibid., 15–25.

209. Hans von Campenhausen, *Ecclesiastical Authority and Spiritual Power* (Stanford: Stanford University Press, 1969), 181–92.

210. Trevett, *Montanism*, 46–76.

211. Barnes, *Tertullian*, 82.

212. Ibid., 77; Rankin, *Tertullian and the Church*, 13.

213. Beard, *Religions of Rome*, 1:102.

214. Georges Dumézil, *Archaic Roman Religion, with an Appendix on the Religion of the Etruscans* (trans. Philip Krapp; 2 vols.; Chicago: University of Chicago Press, 1970), 2:498.

215. Barnes, *Tertullian*, 43.

216. Ibid., 83.

217. Ibid., 83–84.

218. Rives, *Religion and Authority*, 224.

219. Salisbury, *Perpetua's Passion*, 73.

220. Ibid.

221. Ibid., 80–81.

222. Ibid., 81–83.

223. Quoted in ibid., 90.

224. Ibid., 91.

225. Ibid., 86.

226. Ibid., 114.

227. Ibid., 104.

228. Ibid., 97–99.

229. Tilley, *Bible in Christian North Africa*, 10.

230. Ibid., 41.

231. Salisbury, *Perpetua's Passion*, 72.

232. Brown, *Augustine of Hippo*, 239.

233. Markus, *Saeculum*, 13–15.

234. Barnes, *Tertullian*, 4, 23–27, 117; Stanley H. Kelley, "*Auctoritas* in Tertullian: The Nature and Order of Authority in His Thought" (PhD diss., Emory University, 1974), 3.

235. William Hugh Clifford Frend, *The Early Church* (Philadelphia: Fortress, 1982), 80; Frend, *Rise of Christianity*, 345, 48–50; Justo Gonzalez, *A History of Christian Thought* (rev. ed.; 3 vols.; Nashville: Abingdon, 1970), 171–73.

236. Kelley, "*Auctoritas* in Tertullian," 186–87; Rankin, *Tertullian and the Church*, 17.

237. Barnes, *Tertullian*, 187.

238. Ibid., 188.

239. Ibid., 187–90.

240. Ibid., 189.

241. For more information on the Second Sophistic, see G. W. Bowersock, *Greek Sophists in the Roman Empire* (Oxford: Clarendon, 1969); E. L. Bowie, "Greeks and Their Past in the Second Sophistic," in *Studies in Ancient Society* (ed. M. I. Finley; London: Routledge, 1974), 166–209; Koester, *History, Culture and Religion of the Hellenistic Age*, 352–53.

242. Barnes, *Tertullian*, 189.

243. Ibid., 192.

244. Rives, *Religion and Authority*, 224 n. 107.

245. Tilley, *Bible in Christian North Africa*, 20.

246. Brown, *Augustine of Hippo*, 22.

247. Barnes, *Tertullian*, 194–210.

248. Ibid., 194–95.

249. Quoted in ibid., 195.

250. Rives, *Religion and Authority*, 274.

251. Ibid., 274 n. 35.

252. Markus, *Saeculum*, 106–7.

253. Quoted in Rives, *Religion and Authority*, 282.

254. Quoted in ibid., 281–82.

255. Beard, *Religions of Rome*, 103–4.

256. Rives, *Religion and Authority*, 286.

257. Ibid., 287.

258. S. L. Greenslade, ed., *Early Latin Theology: Selections from Tertullian, Cyprian, Ambrose, and Jerome* (Library of Christian Classics: Ichthus Edition; Philadelphia: Westminster, 1956), 127.

259. See the discussion in Rives, *Religion and Authority*, 290.

260. Ibid., 291.

261. Ibid.

262. Quoted in ibid., 293.

263. Tilley, *Bible in Christian North Africa*, 9–10.

264. Ibid., 55.

6

Tertullian of Carthage's
Vision of Prayer

[The church is not] a conclave of bishops.
—Tertullian *(Pud.* 21.17)

A Vision Permeated by the Spirit

Chapter 5 discussed the context in which the Carthaginian Christian community developed and recognized that Christianity in North Africa created the vocabulary for later Latin Christian theological discourse. The complex social and political structures that prevailed in the Roman *colonia* undoubtedly influenced the development of the Christian faith in that context. North Africa developed its own distinctive culture, one that was Romano-African and also influenced by Phoenician, Libyan, Egyptian, and other cultures. Once a prosperous Punic mercantile power, colonial Carthage was a robust image of its former Phoenician self. Under Rome life in Carthage was structured according to the political philosophy and social practices of the imperial capital. Roman colonization of North Africa created a society where people learned to combine their various ethnoreligious identifications and allegiances creatively. Although social conflict in North Africa was minimal compared to what we saw in Egypt, it was present nevertheless. Various competing groups existed among the North Africans.

In the second century CE, the Carthaginian ecclesial community also constituted such a group. As outlined in the introduction to chapter 4, struggling groups have the ability to manifest the positive and negative aspects of social conflict. Needless to say, the church of the martyrs developed its primary self-understanding within the crucible of social confrontation. As a spokesperson for this community, Tertullian of Carthage raises and discusses many of the issues involved in various types of social conflict. His struggle against pagans and heretics typifies the kind of rhetoric one finds in such situations.

This chapter focuses on one aspect of Tertullian's theological vision, his understanding and application of the LP in *Prayer* (*De oratione*). Although the discussion in this chapter is primarily intellectual, I point to various forms of thinking and practice that illustrate the influence of Tertullian's Carthaginian and North African context. To accomplish the chapter's primary aim, I examine the Carthaginian's theological and literary vision as embodied in five of his writings, including *Prayer*. Then I look at Tertullian's hermeneutical strategy, an understanding of tradition and Scripture influenced deeply by Tertullian's understanding of the Holy Spirit and its work. Next, I use Tertullian's theological vision as a prism through which to tease out his theology of prayer. Finally, Tertullian's cultic vision will serve as an instrument through which we see the LP as a devotional document used by Christians on the North African coast.

Tertullian's Theological and Literary Vision

Tertullian was the author of a large number of works.[1] A general, even if somewhat unflattering, assessment of his writings is given by Timothy Barnes: "They display flashes of genius in a rambling and ill-organized structure."[2] The first among his literary undertakings was the *Apologeticus adversus gentes pro christianis*, simply called the *Apology*, written in 197 CE. In it he defends Christianity in a manner reminiscent of a lawyer.[3] Although his first known work, the *Apology* set the stage for the construction of Latin Christian theology. Not merely a defense of the faith, it attacked Christianity's accusers and gave a constructive response to both actual and imagined critics.[4] Likely a reaction to an incident in the *colonia*, its size and erudition indicate it was written for a highly literate audience.[5]

A prolific writer, Tertullian penned works that were not only apologetic but also polemical, moral, practical, and doctrinal. Among his more celebrated are *The Prescription against Heretics* (*De praescriptione haereticorum*), *Against Marcion* (*Adversus Marcionem*), *Against Praxeas* (*Adversus Praxean*), and *On Baptism* (*De baptismo*). The source of Tertullian's theological vision can be found in the soil of his native Africa. He was the product of a vibrant and self-consciously Romano-African environment, and in his thought one can detect not only Roman influence but also African idiosyncrasies that defy simple attempts at logical consistency. For example,

Tertullian often criticizes Greco-Roman philosophy, yet one can clearly detect the influence of Stoicism on his thought. In fact, he speaks so highly of Seneca that he seems to contradict his own negative appraisal of the enterprise (see *An.* 20).[6] He calls the gospel a new law and defends Christianity by using forensic oratory, and yet his ecclesiology is dominated by a charismatic doctrine of the Spirit. All such apparent contradictions come across in the vision he projects through his writings.

The *Praescriptio*

Tertullian is a Roman, which typically means he has a penchant for practical and concrete thinking.[7] None of his works appears to have been written for the mere pleasure of writing or speculating, but with a definite and practical purpose in mind. A good example of this is his *Prescription against Heretics*. Written to protect ordinary Christians in Carthage from the influence of the heretics, including those of Hermogenes and Prodicus, the central argument of the book arises out of a statement found in *Apology* 47.9–10. In this passage Tertullian denies any similarity between the competing Christian groups and the established *ecclesia*, and he condemns all those who disagree with the established *ecclesia* as falsifiers.[8]

As a Roman legal maneuver, a *praescriptio* was an argument that a party in a trial presented, not usually referring to a particular aspect of the trial, but to the validity of the proceeding itself. A *praescriptio* is most often an objection affirming that the opposite party is out of order, and that the proceeding should not continue. H. F. Jolowicz's *Historical Introduction to the Study of Roman Law* outlines a *praescriptio* as part of the formulary for judicial proceedings.[9] They were typically of two sorts: *pro actore*, on behalf of the plaintiff, or *pro reo*, on behalf of the defendant. The formula of proper procedure was very important to the Roman judicial process, especially in the Greco-Roman period. Fritz Schulz, another Roman legal scholar, makes this clear:

> The settling of the formula was . . . an extremely technical process, for which professional help was indispensable, since neither the parties nor the magistrate, unless by exception he happened to be a jurist himself, would possess the requisite legal knowledge.[10]

The type of *praescriptio* Tertullian may have imagined when he wrote his treatise can be described as follows:

The most important of these [legal reasonings regarding property], after the decline of mancipation and *in jure cession*, was [*praescriptio*], whereby one becomes the owner of a thing on the ground that he has possessed it for a long time under certain specific conditions. This mode of acquisition was based upon public expediency, and was established, as Gaius says, that the titles of property might not remain uncertain.[11]

In short, in his *Prescription against Heretics*, Tertullian was not trying to discuss the actual doctrines of the heretics; rather, he was attempting to deny them the very right to argue against the so-called orthodox. Although in other works he would deal in detail with the content of their teachings, in the *Prescription* he makes the general statement that heresies spring not from faith but from philosophy:

For philosophy is the material of the world's wisdom, the rash interpreter of the nature and the dispensation of God. Indeed heresies are themselves instigated by philosophy. From this source came the "Aeons," and I know not what infinite "forms," and the "trinity of man" in the system of Valentinus; he was a Platonist. From the same source came Marcion's better god with his Tranquility; he came of the Stoics. Then, again, the opinion that the soul dies is held by the Epicurean; while the denial of the restoration of the body is taken from the uniform teaching of all the philosophers; also, when matter is made equal to God, then you have teaching of Zeno; and when any doctrine is alleged touching a god of fire, then Heracleitus comes in. The same subject-matter is discussed over and over again by heretics and philosophers; the same arguments are reconsidered. Whence comes evil? and why? Whence man? and how? Besides the question which Valentinus has very lately proposed—Whence comes God? No doubt from desire and abortion. . . . Away with all attempts to produce a Stoic, Platonic, and dialectic Christianity! We want no curious disputation after possessing Jesus Christ, no inquisition after receiving the gospel! When we believe, we desire no further belief. For this is our first article of faith, that there is nothing which we ought to believe besides. (*Praescr.* 7 [Stevenson])[12]

The heretics confuse philosophy with revelation. They contaminate faith with Platonism and Stoicism. They mistake the speculations of Heracleitus

and Zeno with the truth of Christ. The confusion of philosophy with revelation results in a corruption of faith, for "what has Athens to do with
Jerusalem?" (7). And yet, it would be a mistake to label Tertullian a blind
irrationalist. Like Augustine, he appears to believe that certain Christian
truths, like the efficacy of baptism, are a part of the *mysteria fidei*. This is
not a general claim that belief must be based on what is rationally impossible.[13] Rather, unrestrained speculation can only lead to philosophy and
possible error. The actual revelation of God is what really matters to the
believer. And the nature of Christian truth is such that when "we believe,
we desire no further belief." The truth has been given to the *ecclesia* once-
and-for-all in Jesus Christ, and to borrow a Lutheran formula, *theologia non
est habitus demonstrativus sed exhibitivus*: it is meant not for rational demonstration but for proclamation.

The core of the argument in the *Prescription* appears in chapter 15,
where Tertullian maintains that every discussion with heretics on the basis
of Scripture is out of order, for heretics have no right or claim to the sacred
texts:

> I take my stand above all on this point: they are not to be admit-
> ted to any discussion of Scripture at all. If the Scriptures are to be
> their strong point (supposing they can get hold of them), we must
> first discover who are the rightful owners of the Scriptures, in case
> anyone is given access to them without any kind of right to them.
> (*Praescr.* 15 [Greenslade])[14]

From this point on, the focus of the book unfolds. The Scriptures belong
to the *ecclesia,* which only may use them. The Scriptures and true doctrine,
summarized by the *regula fidei,* were given by the apostles to their successors, and so on until they were inherited by the present *ecclesia* (see
13; 36).[15]

Although the heretics may have access to the sacred texts, this in no
way proves ownership. In fact, access to the Scriptures alone cannot be a
self-sufficient authority for certain knowledge of the truth:

> And the Bible is indubitably richer in its resources for every con-
> ceivable subject. Indeed, when I read that heresies must be, I think
> I may say without fear of contradiction that by the will of God the
> Scriptures themselves were so arranged as to furnish matter for the
> heretics. For without Scripture there can be no heresy. (39.6–7
> [Greenslade])[16]

Another theological source, in effect, legitimizes Tertullian's argument against the heretics. They have no right to interpret the Scriptures because to interpret them accurately one must be a Christian, which means one must assent to the *regula fidei*.[17] *Regula*, most scholars believe, does not translate into a fixed creed or baptismal confession, although J. N. D. Kelly may be correct in his contention that Tertullian has some knowledge of a liturgical creed that underlies his formulation.[18] That *regula* does not mean creed for Tertullian, however, can be demonstrated by the fact that he can use the term in different contexts to refer to various concepts. He speaks, for example, of the *regula* of Marcion, as well as the *regulae* of Valentinus and the Valentinians, whom he sees as diverging from Valentinus in their views (*Marc.* 1.1; *Val.* 4.3–4). He speaks of the *regulae philosophiae*, apparently referring to philosophical schools (*Marc.* 5.19). In other words, every identifiable philosophical or theological sect has its own *regula*.[19]

For Tertullian the *regula fidei* is what gives the *ecclesia* its definitive nature, and consequently this *regula* is beyond all questioning and doubt.[20] For example, in *Against the Valentinians* (4.1) Tertullian says that Valentinus cut himself off from the *ecclesia authenticate regulae*, which appears to be a technical way of saying that the *regula* is the constitution of the *ecclesia*. The *regula* is the compendium of the theology of the Christian community and can be used as a manual of instruction to prevent a catechumen from being led astray by heresy. And so, when Tertullian says that the *regula* is *immobilis et irreformabilis*, he means not the formula, which he alters each time he uses it, but the chief points of doctrine that the formula expresses.[21] The *regula* is the absolute norm of the faith. It defines who does and who does not have true faith, who is and who is not a Christian. It is an absolute authority insofar as it is the ground upon which absolute judgments of truth and falsehood may be made. The *regula*, then, is not so much a positive authority, revealing ever-deeper truths, as it is a negative authority, a limiting authority that provides all the truth that is absolutely necessary to identify and define Christian identity.[22]

The heretics cannot prove themselves to be the legitimate successors of the apostles, whereas the *ecclesia* can demonstrate its claim to that inheritance. And since the orthodox can prove this lineage of inheritance as well as a unity of doctrine, they alone can claim the Scriptures as their undivided inheritance. The *ecclesia* that has always made use of the Scriptures is the only one that now has the right to use and interpret them (see *Praescr.* 37). As a consequence, if the heretics have no right to the Scriptures, then they cannot use them in any dialogue with the orthodox, a discourse that may draw the orthodox from the true faith. Through such forensic-type rhetoric Tertullian makes his case for orthodoxy. Essentially an argument about property rights, Tertullian uses such rhetoric with devastating effect.

Adversus Praxean

Tertullian's treatise *Against Praxeas* is significant because some of its phrases and terms foreshadow what will become generally accepted Christian theological formulae centuries later. Barnes highlights the significance of this work ironically: "The *Adversus Praxean* exemplifies a paradox: Tertullian helped to rescue the Catholic Church from heresy precisely because he was a Montanist."[23] In particular, he introduces two terms that the *ecclesia* would continue to use for centuries: *substantia* (substance) and *persona* (person). According to the text, Praxeas came from Asia to Rome while preaching against the new prophecy. His presence was detrimental for Montanism because Praxeas persuaded the bishop of Rome to revoke his prior approval of the movement. To make matters worse, Tertullian says that Praxeas committed heresy by confounding the persons of the Trinity. As he says, "Praxeas did a twofold service for the devil at Rome: he drove away prophecy, and he brought in heresy; he put to flight the Paraclete, and he crucified the Father" (*Prax.* 1). Praxeas was a Monarchian. Only mentioned by one other source outside Tertullian, the *Adversus omnes haereses* (8.4), it is difficult to determine exactly what Praxeas preached. Without question, by opposing Montanism Praxeas guaranteed for himself a less-than-sympathetic hearing from Tertullian. The Carthaginian's ire notwithstanding, *Against Praxeas* establishes the framework for later Western theological discourse on the Trinity.

In this work Tertullian means *substantia* not in its metaphysical but its legal sense. Substance is property and the right that a person has to make use of it.[24] In the context of the principate, for example, the substance of the emperor was the empire. His right over this property is what makes it possible for the emperor to share his substance with his son or rightly designated heir, somewhat simple inheritance law under the Roman system.[25] *Persona*, as a result, is to be understood as "legal person" rather than in its philosophical or commonly accepted sense.[26] A legal person is one who owns or controls a certain substance. Under Roman law, it was possible for several persons to share the same substance, as it was also possible for one person to have more than one substance, and this forms the core of Tertullian's doctrine regarding both the Trinity and the person of Christ.

When one carefully reviews Tertullian's terminology in *Against Praxeas*, what initially appears to be clear and precise becomes somewhat ambiguous. For example, Tertullian tends to overemphasize his distinction between the persons of the Trinity, almost at the expense of their essential unity. Also, in a related text, *Against Hermogenes* (3), he says that there was a time when the Son did not exist, something he essentially argues in *Against Praxeas* (5–6). Although later theologians will label this aspect of Tertullian's view as heterodox, it forms an essential part of his Trinitarian understanding.

Another significant aspect of Tertullian's Trinitarian doctrine is his insistence on the divine *economia*, a word that he prefers to transliterate into Latin rather than to translate. According to Tertullian, God is one, "but under his dispensation, which we call *economia*," God manifests God's self in three forms (2). Such a divine economy is necessary for a proper understanding of Tertullian's doctrine of monarchy, for it is under this economy that Tertullian is able to maintain that God is one. Later theologians have characterized this doctrine as organic monotheism, a form of monotheism understood in terms of an organic relationship.[27] As he says,

> We believe in only one God, yet subject to this dispensation, which is our word for economy, that the one only God has also a Son, His Word, who has issued out of Himself, . . . which Son then sent, according to His promise, the Holy Spirit, the Paraclete, out of the Father, . . . the mystery of the economy, which distributes the unity into Trinity, setting forth Father, Son and Spirit as three. (2)

Scattered throughout his works is a clear interest in affirming the reality of Christ's body. By opposing Monarchianism, Tertullian is forced to pay attention, not only to Christ's humanity, but also to the way in which that humanity is related to his divinity (see 27). Although he affirms the unity of the humanity and divinity in Jesus Christ, Tertullian denies the possibility of distinguishing between the two natures. Just as there are three *personae* and only one *substantia* in God, in Christ there are two substances belonging to a single person. This union is such that the properties of either substances or natures (Tertullian uses both terms) are completely preserved and manifest in the actions of the Savior.

De anima

Another influential aspect of Tertullian's theology is his doctrine of original sin, in which one can see the consequences of his Stoic philosophical outlook and its influence upon subsequent Western theology. Tertullian conceived of the soul (*anima*) as he thought of God, as a corporeal entity. This, in turn, led him to argue that an individual's soul is derived from the souls of one's parents, just as a person's body is derived from the bodies of the parents. Known as traducianisim, this understanding maintains that sin is transmitted in a manner analogous to the transmission of the soul. Thus, original sin becomes an inheritance from parent to child. Although Tertullian derived the material aspect of his doctrine from Roman Stoicism, probably influenced by the concept of the *suum ingenium*, there is an urgency to this theological outlook that betrays his North African context. I will have more to say on this below.

De baptismo

Long considered one of his more practical works, what Tertullian has to say about baptism is important for its doctrinal and liturgical relevance. In *Baptism* he gives us an indication of how the sacrament was administered in the Carthaginian *ecclesia*. Furthermore, it sheds valuable light on Tertullian's ecclesiology.[28] He begins by saying, "Happy is our sacrament of water, in that, by washing away the sins of our early blindness, we are set free and admitted into eternal life!" (*Bapt.* 1). As a *sacramentum regenerationis*, baptism initiates the believer into the community of the faithful, the *communio sanctorum* that regenerates the believer's rational capacity through the *mysteria fidei*. As defined later by Augustine, baptism is a visible sign (*signum*) of an invisible grace. As such, one might expect that Tertullian would limit its administration to those duly authorized to confer participation in such mysteries (*sacramenta*). And, in reality, he does:

> The highest priest, who is the bishop, has of course the right to confer it; then the presbyters and deacons, not, however, without the bishops' authority, out of respect to the Church: when this respect is maintained, peace is secure. But besides, even laymen have the right to baptize; for that which is received alike by all, can be by all alike conferred; unless you argue that the name "disciples" belongs only to bishops or presbyters or deacons. (*Bapt.* 17 [Stevenson])[29]

Since later in this section Tertullian denies women the same right to baptize that he gives to men, some scholars speculate that *Baptism* was written in response to the activities of a woman, who was persuading some in the community that baptism was unnecessary.[30] The validity of this assertion notwithstanding, Tertullian claims, "That which is received alike by all, can be by all alike conferred," thus displaying his tendency to view the ecclesiastical hierarchy as analogous to the civil authorities and not as religious specialists. Tertullian's exclusion of women from conferring baptism may sound odd in light of the traditional Roman notion of a woman's place. Women, like children, were expected to be seen and not heard. As Juvenal makes clear regarding an educated woman,

> Don't marry a woman who speaks like an orator—or knows every history book. There should be some thing in books which she doesn't understand. I hate a woman who reads and rereads Palaemon's treatise on grammar, who always obeys all the laws and rules of correct speech, who quotes verses I've never even heard of, moldy old stuff that a man shouldn't worry about anyway. Let her correct the grammar of her stupid girlfriend! A Husband should be allowed an occasional "I ain't." (*Sat.* 6.456 [Shelton])[31]

At any rate, Tertullian tells his hearers that he has already written a treatise explaining why heretics who join the *ecclesia* need to be rebaptized (*Bapt.* 15.2). This address is of a different sort. It is an instance of cultic exhortation and ecclesiastical catechesis. It is addressed to catechumens and, arguably, seeks to preserve some of the integrity of the ecclesiastical hierarchy, since Tertullian does warn his bearers that disobedience to the bishop causes schism (17.2).

De oratione

A skilled rhetorician, Tertullian's writings display not only his learnedness; they also have identifiable Roman rhetorical structures, at least generally. A few of Tertullian's writings cannot be classified according to the canons of Roman rhetoric. One such treatise is the focus of our concern in this chapter. Robert Sider suggests that writings such as *Prayer* lack the organizational structure usually found in Tertullian's work because they are either published versions of initially oral homilies or deliberate attempts at informality.[32] And although I agree with Sider's assessment, I would push the argument forward by saying that homily, as a rhetorical style, serves a fundamental catechetical function whether its mode is forensic, epideictic, demonstrative, or a mixture of all three. In this case, *Prayer* provides insight into how this second-century Carthaginian perceived and constructed his community's relationship with God.

The content of *Prayer* conforms to the imagined ceremony in which the *traditio* of the LP was passed on to catechumens.[33] "On that day," according to some scholars, "after a brief exhortation, the priest solemnly recited the Lord's Prayer, pausing with each phrase in order to comment on it; finally he extricated the conclusion from it in a short final discourse."[34] And these are exactly the elements one finds in the first part of the treatise.

The first part of *Prayer* offers a phrase-by-phrase exegesis of the LP in the form of notes prepared for such an oral discourse (1–10). Inserted between sections 10 and 29, Tertullian offers some reflections on the problems of conduct and disposition during prayer. The structure of these sections suggests that they were added to the original homily, after its oral presentation, but before its publication. And so, it is observed that as the work proceeds, its scope expands beyond attention to the LP, and comes "to include prayer in general, and private prayers in particular."[35] At the conclusion of the published homily, Tertullian offers a panegyric on the values to be realized by means by prayer (29). And so, while Tertullian's organizational structure defies the canons of Roman rhetorical composition, its rhetorical function is nevertheless clear. It is an ethical exhortation, presented in a homiletical mode, for the purpose of instructing catechumens as to appropriate behavior in the realm of the cult.

Tertullian's Hermeneutics

Up to this point, I have said little regarding Tertullian's hermeneutical method. I do believe, however, that such an understanding is crucial for a proper interpretation of *Prayer*. In general, Tertullian's hermeneutics are characterized by "common sense, realism, and restraint."[36] And yet, two theological categories consistently dominate Tertullian's interpretation of Scripture: the *regula fidei* and the Holy Spirit.

Tertullian's theory of scriptural authority can appear confusing on the surface. Using the resources of the Roman rhetorical tradition, including its treasury of forensic oratory, Tertullian attributes the inspiration of Scripture to God, its author, and the guidance of the Holy Spirit. Drawing on Roman legal reasoning, the Scriptures form the *testamenta* of God mediated through human authors. Although writings from the past, they address believers in the present (*Apol.* 20.1–5). As such, they are the foundation for establishing the nature of God and his moral will.[37] Hence, whatever is found in Scripture is in accordance with the true nature of things (cf. *An.* 21.5). Behind this position, I believe, also stands the Roman concept of *auctoritas*. True doctrine and true moral law must be firmly established by reference to those things that bear *auctoritas*, the ground or basis of certitude. The Scriptures have *auctoritas* as the most ancient source of divine knowledge, operating under the principle that antiquity guarantees veracity (see *Apol.* 47.1). And yet, as we have seen in the *Prescription against Heretics*, the Scriptures by themselves cannot have *auctoritas* because they can be interpreted incorrectly. The sacred texts have *auctoritas* when an individual under the guidance of the Spirit interprets them. In this sense, the *auctoritas* of Scripture is derived from the *auctoritas* of God.[38]

Since Scripture needs the proper method of interpretation to insure that its *auctoritas* shines through, and this is accomplished under the guidance of the Spirit, the *regula fidei* serves as the objective norm against which any interpretation must be judged. Since Tertullian understands the Scriptures to be the *testamenta* of God to those in the present, further elucidation of this concept may assist us in viewing the landscape of Tertullian's hermeneutical portrait. According to *Against Marcion* 3.5, the prophetic announcements of Scripture are of two sorts: (1) future events are announced as if they were already passed, and (2) many events are figuratively predicted by means of enigmas, allegories, and parables and must be understood in a sense different from their literal descriptions. Later, Tertullian builds upon this method:

> And no doubt it was proper that this mystery should be prophetically set forth by types, and indeed chiefly by that method: for in proportion to its incredibility would it be a stumbling-block, if it were set forth in bare prophecy; and in proportion too, to its grandeur, was the need of obscuring it in shadow, that the difficulty of understanding it might lead to prayer for the grace of God. (*Marc.,* 4.18)

Although he will maintain that Scripture should be interpreted primarily in a literal fashion, Tertullian also defends a typological reading of the text, depending on its relationship to one of the sources of Christian truth, the Holy Spirit or the *regula fidei*. Tertullian was wary of using nonliteral types of exegesis because he felt that the heretics used them to evade the clear meaning of Scripture.[39] By contrast to these so-called fanciful interpretations of the text, Tertullian follows the Roman rhetorical tradition that advocates interpreting a text according to the ordinary use of the words (*Marc.*, 4.11, 19; 5.5).[40]

Primary attention in any exegetical enterprise must be given to the *ipsissima verba*, the very words of the text and their inherent logic (*Praescr* 9.1–2).[41] Looking at the context of a passage is one of the ways this is accomplished. Tertullian takes into account the context within which a given scriptural statement is made. Of course, even a casual reader can see that Tertullian does not entirely forego nonliteral readings of Scripture.[42] Under certain circumstances, in fact, he insists upon their use. This is especially true when an interpretation might violate the parameters of the *regula fidei*. For example, Tertullian adopts a nonliteral approach as a way of arguing for the unity of the Old and New Testaments. But even here he limits its use by saying that it is only advisable when the text is not intelligible on any other basis.

According to Heinrich Karpp, Tertullian's normative method of exegesis can be synthesized into eight canons. Although they do not account for all of Tertullian's interpretive practices, they do demonstrate how Tertullian's understanding of the *regula fidei* influenced his reading and interpretation of sacred texts. And so, these canons may be deemed the *regulae interpretationis*:

1. The whole Bible should not be interpreted on the basis of one passage. The many should take precedence over and govern the interpretation of the one. (*Prax.* 20)
2. Scripture must be taken literally. Allegory can only be used where the literal meaning is impossible. (*Scorp.* 11)
3. Those passages that are unclear must be interpreted on the basis of others that are clear. (*Res.* 19.1)
4. The verbal structure and context of each passage must be taken into account. (*Mon.* 11)
5. Biblical authors never contradict each other. When they seem to do so, they may be reconciled by the use of figurative exegesis. (*Res.* 29–32)
6. Clear prescriptions or rules are more binding than figures or examples. (*Mon.* 6)
7. The passage of Scripture must be related to the essence of the Christian faith and the essence of Christian discipline. (*Pud.* 8.10; 9.1, 11; passim)

8. The import of Scripture is clear if it is not confused by human quibblings over its meaning. (*Prax.* 18)[43]

In addition to these canons, Tertullian employs other concepts, also called *regulae*, that include the *regula scriptarum*, the essential meaning of the Scriptures; the *regula sacramenti*, the normative relationship between the law and the gospel; and the *regula sacramentorum*, the content of the preaching of the contemporaries of Paul (*Marc.* 3.17; 1.21; 5.20 respectively). In other places he uses *regula* in connection with a specific doctrine. Thus, the *regula Dei* refers to his doctrine of God while the *regula spei* refers to that of the resurrection (*Marc.* 1.21; 48.2).[44] In all cases the *regula fidei* governs the other *regulae* and limits their abilities to grow and expand on their own. And so, we can see how the *regula fidei*, the fundamental datum of Christian truth, serves as an objective measure that dominates Tertullian's theological vision.

The other dominant theological category for Tertullian is the Holy Spirit. God is the true author of the Scriptures because the Spirit's voice is heard through them. The Spirit clears up possible ambiguities in scriptural interpretation (see *Res.* 63.7–9). The active role of the Spirit in the *ecclesia* is found in the Spirit's protection of it from heresy, to keep it from wandering away from the doctrine of the apostles. Interestingly, however, the only times Tertullian specifically cites apostolic authority is in connection with the authorship of Scripture. This suggests interdependency between the *regula fidei* and the Scriptures; especially since both authorities derive their *auctoritas* from the Holy Spirit (see *Praescr.* 36–37). And so, what we find in Tertullian is a vision permeated by the Spirit. Whether it is the *regula fidei* or Christian sacred texts, the Spirit governs them in their entirety. Even what appears to be an objective measure against which to judge the activity of the Spirit in the life of the *ecclesia* turns out to derive its fundamental *auctoritas* from the Holy Spirit—and if from the Spirit then actually from God.

Looking at Clement and Tertullian Side by Side

Like Clement of Alexandria, Tertullian appeals to an outside theological authority to establish his reading of the biblical text. In Clement, this outside authority is the Logos. And although Clement assents to the *regula fidei*, his idea of the Logos transcends the fundamental nature of the *regula*. As the original voice of God, the Logos is the *principium quo*, the active principle or basis of all that exists. By contrast, Tertullian discovers in his

Prescription against Heretics that the Scriptures cannot guarantee knowledge of the truth. In order for a particular reading of Scripture to be authoritative, it must be guided by the Holy Spirit and confirmed by the *regula fidei*, the historic and somewhat objective compendium of Christian faith authorized by the *auctoritas* of the Spirit. And so, both thinkers appeal to a source of theological authority that stands above and validates all other sources of authority, the Godhead. In this sense they testify to a universal Christian understanding regarding the source of ultimate truth.

By looking at the specific social locations of both writers, one begins to see the differences in their theological visions. Clement of Alexandria is a product of the Greco-Egyptian intellectual culture of Alexandria. As an apologist for Egyptian Christianity, he is a speculative thinker. Writing in the birthplace of Neoplatonism, Clement's writings indicate his willingness to take intellectual risks. His primary audience, Christians in Alexandria, also appears to have appreciated his approach. In contrast, Tertullian reflects the general conservatism of the Romano-African culture of Carthage.[45] An advocate of restrained speculation, Tertullian focuses his intellectual energies on questions that pertain directly to the daily lives of members of the Carthaginian Christian community. Some have characterized Tertullian as an anti-intellectual, an unfair label to place on someone trying to give meaning to the everyday lives of members of a struggling community. Each served as an advocate for his respective constituency, and it is in conjunction with their communal experiences that they construct their theologies. Clement's Alexandria, former seat of the Ptolemaic dynasty, sage of Greco-Egyptian esoterica, cultured queen of the Mediterranean, is reflected in his writings. Tertullian's Carthage, rugged replica of its former Punic self, curious Caesarean creation, inspiration of the Roman world, is abundantly displayed in his writings and vision. Tertullian's view looks toward the mountains and overflowing sunshine of his native Africa. Also a Roman citizen, Tertullian brings Roman philosophy to his theological writings and builds his vision of Christian community on his inherited cultural perspective. Tertullian is brash and outspoken in his views, a mode of being congruous with his African background. An intellectual and forensic orator, Tertullian's writings reflect his interest in ecclesial, christological, anthropological, and doctrinal questions. Tertullian's argument against heretics helped him maintain that the Scriptures belong, as an inheritance, to the orthodox *ecclesia* and it alone. His reflections on the Trinity in *Against Praxeas* further display his legal and philosophical acumen. The argument in *Praxeas* demonstrates his loyalty to Roman thinking and sensibility. His arguments in *The Soul* (*An.*) and *Baptism* represent something else. *The Soul* first is a sustained reflection on the possibilities of Stoic philosophy for Christian theological discourse. By contrast, *Baptism* gives us a special glimpse into the ecclesiological thinking of North Africa. *Prayer* gives us yet another look into the doctrinal lives of African Christians. And yet, we are given more than a view of dusty doctrines; in this treatise we also get a glimpse into the living devotional practices of early African Christians. To this discussion we now turn.

Tertullian's Theology of Prayer

In *The Soul* (5) Tertullian lays out the philosophical basis of his anthropology, Stoicism. His repetitive return to a philosophical position espoused by so many Roman intellectuals further illustrates Tertullian's relationship to Roman patterns of thinking. He defines the soul as a fiery intelligent spirit.[46] This understanding is compatible with the Stoic claim that the soul is corporeal. As he says, "The soul, therefore, is endued with a body; for if it were not corporeal, it could not desert the body" (5). Materiality, also present in Tertullian's doctrine of God, places him on the other end of the philosophical spectrum as compared to Clement, who argued that God was incorporeal and intellectual. Against such a view, Tertullian maintains that even the Gospels understand the soul to be corporeal: "In the Gospel itself they will be found to have the clearest evidence for the corporeal nature of the soul" (7). A few scholars characterize Tertullian's thought as "the unexpunged remnant of classical materialism." Nevertheless, the corporeality of the soul is but one instance in which materialism informs Tertullian's theological view.[47] The starkest example may be found in *The Shows* (*Spect.* 30) where hell is portrayed as an unearthly coliseum providing the faithful with the satisfaction of seeing the physical torment of the damned.

In reflecting on the nature of the soul, Tertullian rejects all theories of the soul's preexistence. Likewise, he questions the belief that the soul is created simultaneously with the body, called creationism. As a traducianist, Tertullian maintains that every soul is derived along with the body from one's parents. The entire human being is produced in one and the same generative act. Inheriting more than their looks from their parents, children also inherit some aspect of their parents' souls. Harking back to the Genesis account, all souls, whether actual or potential, were in a real sense contained in Adam, derived from the original *anima* breathed into Adam by God. Every soul then is a sapling cut from the same root, although it now exists independently (see *An.* 19).

Materialism also strongly influences Tertullian's understanding of original sin.[48] Although a firm believer in free will, an idea he defends against Marcion, Tertullian also believes that human beings are biased toward sin because of Adam (see *Marc.* 1.22; 2.5–7). As a consequence, humans inherit an irrational soul from their prehistoric ancestor (*An.* 16).[49] It is a stain upon the human condition, so that "every soul is counted as being in Adam until it is re-counted as being in Christ, and remains unclean until it is so re-counted" (40). Seeing demonic influence as a secondary agent of evil, Tertullian says, "[The] evil that exists in the soul . . . is antecedent, being derived from the fault of our origin and having become in a way natural to us" (41). Created initially in the image of God, human nature has been transformed from its original integrity into one of rebellion against God (*Spect.* 2). Adam, being deceived into revolt by Satan, "infected the whole race by his seed, making it the channel of damnation" (*Test.* 3). This means that even the children of the faithful are impure until they have been cleansed by water and the Holy Spirit (*An.* 39). To Africans in the second century, this understanding of anthropology functioned as a strong argument for pedobaptism.[50]

In an interesting twist, Clement and Tertullian identify the same condition as the root of human sin: irrationality. In Clement's theology irrationality is overcome by the intervention of the Logos. Being incorporeal and intellectual by nature, the Logos draws the mind of the believer into *gnōsis*. Tertullian finds his solution to the problem of irrationality another way. Although both writers draw from Stoic philosophy, they overcome this problem in almost opposite ways.

Tertullian, with his forensically oriented mind, expounded a soteriology maintaining that good deeds accumulate merit and bad deeds demand satisfaction (e.g., *Paen.* 5; *Exh. cast.* 1; *Scorp.* 6). Such an understanding of atonement has a basic material orientation for the Carthaginian. Thus, he anchors his soteriology in the material sacrifice of Christ (*sacrificium propitiatorium*). It was Christ's purpose, he contends, to be offered as a material sacrifice (see *Carn. Chr.* 6). Nor does he appear to acknowledge any other alternative. Indeed, he says, "neither could our own death have been annulled except by the Lord's passion, nor our life have been restored without his resurrection" (*Bapt.* 11). And since humans could not effect salvation for themselves, "He delivered himself up for our sins" (*Scorp.* 7; see also *Adv. Jud.* 13).

The material character of the *sacrificium propitiatorium* corresponds well to Tertullian's overall theology. The offense of Adam had to be counterbalanced in order for justice to be satisfied and the *pax Dei* to be restored.

Such an understanding can also be explicable according to two legal principles. First, that the party to an action must be a living person.[51] Anything other than a human being, as commonly understood, would fail to fulfill this requirement. Second, that the act had to be in some way material, an *actus reus*.[52] The act of Adam formed an acceptable ground for charging him with a crime against God. And since Adam was a living person, a living person must perform the reparation.

Since the Romans practiced rituals of reparation, the primary form of atonement, sacrifice, was a logical choice for the Latin theologian.[53] Dumézil points out the importance of "material goods" to the Roman cultic process. He says that the fundamental religious act was offering material for a *sacrificium*.[54] The Romans saw sacrifice as an effective means of influencing the deity. According to Ogilvie, in choosing out something special for the gods, the believer concentrated his attention on something animate because the gods' activity required vitality.[55] Jesus' death is, thus, a material act to a material God to address a material problem; it combines two important elements of Roman thinking, the legal and the religious. Through the death of Jesus the transgression of Adam is counterbalanced and the *pax* restored: Tertullian's material solution to a material problem.

Tertullian's Christian ethic proceeds from the *sacrificium propitiatorium* in that Christ has the *auctoritas* to induce obedience.[56] *Auctoritas* is necessary because the soul needs to be transformed from the irrational to the rational. As he says in *The Soul* (41),

> Therefore, when the soul embraces the faith, being renewed in its second birth by water and the power from above, then the veil of its former corruption being taken away, it beholds the light in all its brightness.

Once irrationality is banished, the soul still needs guidance to function properly.[57] Christ and the Holy Spirit provide this guidance. Again, the rationale for this can be understood according to Roman legal philosophy. The idea of guardianship in Roman judicial *praxis* pertained to persons who were *impubis*, not fully matured (see *Dig.* 26.8). Such persons were in need of oversight, guidance, and legal standing. Thus, tutorial authority (*auctoritas tutoris*) strengthened the action of the *pupillus* in order to make his activity legal and binding. Although the *pupillus* enters the legal arena voluntarily, the *tutor*, as *auctor*, strengthens and makes valid the action of the *pupillus*. This same guardianship is exercised in the *ecclesia*.[58] Thus, all those desiring to follow the divine rationality must belong to the established *ecclesia*. As his successor Cyprian will say, *salus extra ecclesiam non est* ("There is no salvation outside the church" [*Ep.* 73.21]).

One aspect of the *ecclesia's* guardianship is grounded in the Roman concept of the *mos maiorum*.[59] As pointed out in chapter 2, the *auctoritas* of the Senate was based on its historical link to the *maiores* of the city. By analogy, the legitimacy of the *ecclesia* is based on its historical link to Jesus Christ and the apostles. The apostolic church is the only institution that can guarantee proper Christian disciplinary practice through adherence to apostolic tradition. Ecclesial guardianship empowers and assists the believer in taking her place as a fully constituted individual in the eyes of God. In short, the *ecclesia* rehabilitates individuals by keeping them to the vision of its founders.

The image of the *ecclesia* as the *corpus Christi* is another way Tertullian connects the present Christian community with its *maior*.[60] Through its foundation and the present activity of the Spirit, God constitutes his *ecclesia*. Clerical officials affirm the validity of the *corpus* through their submission to the dictates of the *maiores* and the Holy Spirit.[61]

Corpus Christi is not the only image Tertullian uses to describe the *ecclesia*. From the world of philosophy and education, he uses *schola* as an ecclesial image. The figure of school serves as a vehicle for making the *ecclesia* intelligible to the larger Carthaginian community.[62] It also performs a function related to legitimacy. Tertullian calls the original disciples a *schola* (*Scorp.* 12.1). In this respect, the church is analogous to the academy. Here Tertullian is calling upon the Greco-Roman educational understanding of succession.[63] A related term also employed by Tertullian is *secta*. According to many scholars, Tertullian's use of educational imagery serves to underline the essential apostolicity of the church.[64]

Tertullian uses educational language to argue that the *ecclesia* is treated unfairly in comparison to other philosophical schools. For example, he links Christian teaching to that of Judaism to contend that Christianity has a continuous teaching tradition stretching back to antiquity (*Apol.* 21.1). Thus, out of respect for its antiquity, Carthaginians should set aside their prejudices against the *ecclesia*. Tertullian's reference to the *pallium*, the philosopher's cloak, and its fellowship with Christianity was designed to analogize not just philosophy and Christianity, but also the Christian community and the larger Carthaginian intellectual enterprise (*Pall.* 6.2). Christianity is not some foreign philosophical sect transplanted on the African shore; it is an expression of Romano-African values inasmuch as Carthaginians transformed other elements of formerly foreign sects to their distinctively African perspective. Like the worship of Ceres, Christianity in Carthage is an expression of an Africanized *Romanitas*.

Holiness is the watchword of Tertullian's vision of church discipline. Although some scholars implicitly criticize his "exclusive sectarian concept of the Church," this vision is at the heart of Tertullian's theology.[65] For example, he lists a number of sins for which "Christ will on longer plead" (*Pud.* 19.26). Certain sins result in automatic exclusion from the *familia Dei*. Even from those facing persecution, Tertullian expects perfection (*Praescr.* 3.6). According to his vision, anything other than holiness is indicative of a lack of ecclesial authenticity (*Mon.* 3.2).[66]

In Tertullian's theological anthropology and ecclesiology we see a synthesis of many strands of Roman legal and religious thought. Rooted in materialism, Tertullian addresses the human situation according to the principles of Roman legal science and religion. Using the idea of the *mos maiorum*, the Carthaginian intellectual provides the *communio sanctorum* legitimacy through its connection to Christ. As we saw in the *regula fidei*, the Holy Spirit authorizes both the historical and contemporary witness of the Christian faith. And so, whether it is doctrine, discipline, or anthropology, Tertullian's distinctive Romano-African perspective informs every aspect of his theological vision. Tertullian's discussion of prayer in *Prayer* more than illustrates the truthfulness of this assertion.

As mentioned earlier, Tertullian ends *Prayer* with a panegyric on its efficacy. He exclaims, "The old prayer, no doubt, brought deliverance from fire and wild beasts and hunger, while yet it had not received its pattern from Christ: then how much more fully operative is the Christian prayer!" (*Or.* 29.3–5). It is clear that Tertullian views the LP as *the* model of how Christians should pray. In fact, Tertullian's treatise is meant to establish a code of cultic behavior that is appropriate to its context. And since proper interpretation only exists within the church, ecclesiology is at the heart of this devotional practice. As he says, "We meet together as an assembly and congregation, that, offering up prayer to God as with united force, we may wrestle with him in our supplications" (*Apol.* 39).

Calling the LP "a new plan of prayer," Tertullian highlights how he views the *ecclesia* as both adhering to and reinterpreting the tradition of prayer (*Or.* 1.3).[67] Primary among his declarations is that Christian prayer has supplanted all other prayer practices. Tertullian makes this clear when he says, "For everything that was aforetime has either been transmuted, like circumcision, or supplemented, like the rest of the Law, or fulfilled like prophecy, or made perfect, like faith itself" (1.8–11). Although prayer under the old dispensation was effective, Christ's teaching on prayer has made it perfect. As a devotional practice for disciples, called an *orandi disciplina* by the African theologian, prayer is more than just a casual act (1.22).

Tertullian addresses the issues I have already highlighted among Greco-Roman intellectuals. For example, he confronts the problem of egoism in prayer:

> [Our] petition is for [the Name of God] to be hallowed in us who are in him, and at the same time also in the rest whom as yet the grace of God is looking out for, so that we obey this precept besides, of prayer for all. . . . We say not "hallowed in us," we say "in all." (*Or.* 3.18–22)

Prayer is not for the sole benefit of Christians. It is both petitionary and intercessory. In Tertullian's view, we ask not only for ourselves, "we [also] ask for his will to be done in all" (4.3–4). In short, the Carthaginian refutes any idea of egoism in his vision of Christian prayer. For example, although Christians pray for an imminent *eschaton*, the benefits of Christ's coming extend far beyond the ranks of their community (see 5.5–17). Christian prayer avoids the problem of egoism, according to Tertullian, because its primary aim is to fulfill the will of God. It thus transcends both personal and corporate egoism and makes the orant an intercessor, even for his persecutors (see *Or.* 29.12–14; as well as *Apol.* 30–34; *Scap.* 4).

Another reason why Tertullian lifts up the LP as the model prayer is that God himself instituted it: "God alone was competent to teach us how he wished to be prayed to" (*Or.* 9.7–8).[68] The proper form of prayer is also indicative of the proper form of divine service (*officium*). Tertullian says that this *officium* has certain characteristics: "[The] prayer instituted by Christ is of three constituents, of word (*sermo*) in that it is clearly spoken, of spirit (*spiritus*) in that it has great power, of reason (*ratio*) in that it reconciles" (1.12–13). These characteristics highlight Christian prayer as a manifestation of the new grace of God, a grace that has moved all things from carnal to spiritual.[69] As such, the entire gospel is summed up in the LP.[70]

Tertullian's recurrent use of the term precept (*praeceptus*) in *Prayer* highlights the gospel as the new law of God. Primary among the gospel's mandates are precepts governing behavior. This line of argumentation is similar to the Roman concept of the *ius* (*jus*) *divinum*.[71] From Tertullian's perspective, these precepts are embodied in the LP. For example, the *ius* underlying the LP prohibits the use of "an army of words," an indication of an immodest prayer (1.30). The proper performance of the *officium* involves a prayer that is "restrained in wording" yet "copious in meaning" (1.31–32). Such a legally oriented model of prayer is at the heart of Tertullian's vision of its practice.[72] He even strengthens the argument by making prayer similar to a divinely instituted and mandated act. As he says, "Even the Lord himself prayed" (29.33). The *disciplina* of prayer means following the pattern laid down by the Lord, the guarantor of the act's propriety. Anything else makes the act potentially illegitimate.[73] In sum, Tertullian views prayer as a component of proper divine worship, and the LP as the prime example of how people should pray. The LP epitomizes the gospel because it is the practical application of theology in word and deed.

Tertullian calls prayer a sacrifice, "an oblation which is God's own and is well pleasing [to him], that in fact which he has sought after, which he has provided for himself" (28.9–10).[74] As a divinely ordained form of worship, prayer replaces animal sacrifice as a primary means of honoring the deity. Prayer then is the Christian form of sacrifice. By contrast to Clement of Alexandria, who also sees prayer as a substitute for sacrificial animals, Tertullian's view has a fundamentally material orientation. Flesh and bone is replaced by words and deeds, the new sacrificial material.[75] Thus, prayer is properly a *meritum fidei*, a work of faith (2.1, 3). It is a mechanism that defines relationships, both human and divine, and cements allegiances among human beings and to God (see 2.11). Tertullian employs sacrificial language most often in sections 27–29. For example, he calls appending psalmic phrases to prayers "a rich oblation, a prayer fattened with all that conduces to setting forth the dignity and honor of God" (27.3–5; see also *Jejun.* 10). Prayer is a spiritual, though not immaterial, sacrifice that dispenses with the necessity for other forms of sacrificial material (*Or.* 28.1).[76]

By alluding to Isa 1 and John 4 in 28.2–8, the Carthaginian Christian further underscores his view of prayer as sacrifice. This, by analogy, means that every orant is a priest, an idea acceptable to Romano-Africans but not to Jews (*Or.* 28.9). In fact, he describes prayer in these terms:

> This [sacrifice], devoted from the whole heart, fattened by faith, prepared by truth, unmutilated in innocency, pure in chastity, garlanded with charity, it is our duty to bring to the altar of God, along with a procession of good works. (28.10–13)

The replacement of animal sacrifice with prayer allows the orant to offer God something costly and noble, which is at the same time material and active (*Apol.* 30). The difference between pagan and Christian sacrifice is a matter of distinguishing true Deity and its proper cult from what is false. He describes the Christian sacrifice: "We therefore sacrifice for the emperor's safety, but to our God and his, and after the manner God has enjoined, in simple prayer. For God, Creator of the universe, has no need of odors or of blood. These things are the food of devils" (*Scap.* 2).

It is not surprising that Tertullian maintains that for prayer to be effective it must be inspired. Under the guidance of the Holy Spirit, prayer becomes efficacious: "For what will God deny to a prayer which proceeds from the Spirit and the Truth?" (*Or.* 29.1). The inspiration of prayer involves both its *sermo* and *ratio*, as Tertullian makes clear:

> As therefore by [God] the sanctity of the prayer was ordained, as it did, at the very time when it was being brought forth of the divine lips, receive life from his Spirit, [so] by its own special right it ascends into heaven, commending to the Father the things the Son has taught. (9.8–10)

Since Christ commands it, the Lord oversees the prayer's *sermo* by having taught it and its *ratio* by acting on the supplicant's behalf. Likewise, the Holy Spirit, in Tertullian's view, initiates prayer through its own guidance (cf. 1.1–2). Again, we see the activity of God as fundamental to Tertullian's theological vision. Even *sermo* and *ratio* describe God's activity. The terms are found most often in Tertullian's account of creation and its maintenance (see, e.g., *Prax.* 5.7; *Apol.* 6.21; *Herm.* 18). They are not static. They are expressions of divine action. Embracing both the historical teaching of Jesus and the contemporary guidance of the Spirit, prayer is the central cultic act that highlights the role of all believers as priests.

In this way prayer is also catechetical; it prepares the orant for participation in the heavenly liturgy. He calls the supplicant an "angel designate" and his earthly *officium* as a preparation for that "glory that is to be" (*Or.* 3.14–15). Unlike Clement, Tertullian believes that prayer influences God. It not only defends the believer from the assaults of evil persons and devil spirits; it also turns aside the wrath of God and conquers Satan (29.13–14, 23–24).

Because of its importance, the *disciplina* of prayer occupies a large section of Tertullian's discussion.[77] Tertullian labels these actions *omnem commemorationem disciplinae* (1.35–36); that is, all the acts that need to be represented in the liturgy. This understanding of *disciplina* is highlighted in his use of the terms *breviarium* and *spiritalia* (1.8, 36). It is also represented in Tertullian's idea that prayer can be done in secret as a sign of self-restraint (1.24–25). Although decidedly at variance with the ancient practice of prayer, Tertullian views silent prayer as a work of faith, a *meritum fidei* (2.1). Of course, the term *meritum* itself raises the idea of reward. Tertullian addresses this: "It is to our advantage to commend to the cognizance of God alone that which God's grace performs, lest we receive from man the recompense we hope for from God" (22.62–64). Merit, if it is to be gained by the Christian at all, must be received from God. And so, we see how the proper cultic activity can improve the orant's standing before God. Silent prayer is a further assurance to the petitioner that the act is rewarded by the deity rather than by members of the community. And although Tertullian understands prayer to be predominantly public act, this concession to private prayer highlights it as a form of *pietas*. It seeks its reward only from God.

Prayer, the Christian sacrifice, cannot be done with an improper temperament. Prayer cannot be performed properly in anger (11.15). As a part of the *disciplina* of the cult, disposition is an important aspect of Christian worship. Or, as the Carthaginian asks, "[What] sense is there in addressing oneself to prayer with washed hands but a dirty spirit?" (13.1–2). As a principle, and since like corresponds to like, prayer cannot be performed correctly by a person with an improper spirit. For it to be effective, like must approach like (12.3–4). Such an emphasis on similarity is characteristic of a Roman religious disposition. As W. Warde Fowler points out,

> [In] order that the worship might be entirely acceptable to the deity invoked, it was essential that the person who conducted it should be also acceptable. . . . [The] principle is perfectly clear—that the person who is to represent the community in worship must be one of whom the *numina* openly expresses approval.[78]

In this way, worship becomes an *imitatio Dei*. The orant's disposition must reflect the divine disposition to make her prayer performance acceptable. This is made clear in *Prayer* 12.1–3: "And not from anger only, but from all and every perturbation of mind, ought the intensity of prayer to be free, being sent forth from such a spirit as is that Spirit to whom it is sent forth." The orant takes her cue regarding prayerful disposition from Jesus Christ and the apostles (15.1–4). Like taking your coat off for prayer, Tertullian rejects any prayer practice that is not based in Christianity's historic past (15.7). Any custom not rooted in that past is not valid since "the apostles, who [gave] instruction concerning demeanor during prayer, would have included it" (15.8–9). For example, Tertullian condemns people who pray too loudly as "shouting down the people next to them" (17.13).

Just as important as disposition is the actual performance of prayer. It should be done with washed hands, lifted up, and spread out (13.1, 3; 14.6).

Cleanliness was an important aspect of Roman worship. Again Fowler says, "There is abundant evidence from historical times that all worshippers, and therefore a fortiori all priests, when sacrificing, had to be personally clean and free from every kind of taint."[79] Tertullian translates this sacrificial behavior into his vision of prayer as sacrifice. In prayer, one represents the passion of Christ (14.5–7). He cautions, however, that hands should not be lifted up too high (17.2–3). Eyes should not be lifted up, as it is presumptuous (17.3). In addition, one's voice should be subdued (17.6). A tone to one's voice is not, in fact, important at all (17.7–8; see also *Scorp.* 7). As he asks, "[Do] God's ears want for a noise?" (*Or.* 17.10). Proper worship is conducted with "restraint and humility" (17.1). By contrast, those without restraint are no better than hypocrites attracting attention on street corners (see 17.13–15). Tertullian labels appropriate ritual activity as *modestiam fidei*, the type of restraint characteristic of Roman religion.[80] As Ogilvie makes clear, "[The] Romans exercised every care to ensure that the whole ceremony was dignified."[81] And so, Tertullian's concern that prayer be done with restraint and humility is certainly representative of a Roman perspective (see 17.1–2).

Although standing was the normal prayer posture, Tertullian advocates kneeling, at last on certain occasions. He comments that prayer should be done on bended knee: "For then we do not only pray, but also make supplication and satisfaction to God our Lord" (23.12–13).[82] Augustine indicates that many North Africans upon entering the church made the sign of the cross and then knelt in prayer (*Serm.* 7). Some even touched their foreheads to the ground (*Serm.* 211). Tertullian associated kneeling with worry and preoccupation with mundane concerns. On solemn fasts it is appropriate to kneel, he believes, as a gesture of humility (*Or.* 23.11–12). The only exceptions to kneeling are prayers of thanksgiving and adoration, or joyous celebrations like Eucharist and Easter (23.5–7). Such acts constitute proper worship of God. In short, prayer is not an act performed solely with the mouth and heart, but with the entire body. It is a total performance in which the ritual elements are just as important as the disposition (see, e.g., *Or.* 3.8–10, 15–16, 18–22, 27; *Apol.* 30.39).

Concerning the times of prayer, Tertullian says, "No rules at all have been laid down, except of course to pray at every time and place" (*Or.* 24.1–2). Yet, he also maintains that Christians should avoid prayer acts that can be considered hypocritical (24.2–3; cf. 17.13–15).[83] And so, Tertullian understands the admonition for continual prayer to mean those places "which propriety or even necessity suggests" (24.3–4). Such a precept, he says, is found in the practice of the apostles (24.4–7). Similarly, Tertullian points to a scriptural custom that prayer was performed during at least three hours of the day (25.1–4). And yet, this does not establish for Tertullian a clear precept of observance (25.9). He opts to follow the practice of Israel, and concludes that prayer should be performed ideally five times a day (25.13–15).[84] In addition, prayer should be said before meals and baths. This *disciplina* is executed as a reminder or indication of Christian priorities: "[For] the refreshment and sustenance of the spirit ought to be given precedence over those of the flesh, because heavenly things have precedence over earthly" (25.17–19). In the same vein, Tertullian counsels that prayer be performed at the departing of a brother (26.1–4). According to Tertullian, such acts when performed appropriately place the orant in harmony with the angels who pray, and in truth with all of creation, since it prays (29.28). To put it another way, a life appropriately governed and punctuated by prayer fulfills the ideal of the life according to nature—understood in Christian terms as a life according to the will of God.

On the subject of petition in the LP, Cyprian once wrote, "There is absolutely nothing passed over pertaining to our petitions and prayers which is not included in this compendium of heavenly teaching" (*Dom. or.* 9.34). Tertullian also views the LP as an epitome of the gospel and so finds within it all the necessary *official* and particular functions proper prayer must fulfill, including that of appropriate petition (*Or.* 1.34).

In 4.20–25 Tertullian uses the image of Christ in Gethsemane as a representation of appropriate petitionary prayer. Although a particular request was made, ultimately the supplicant trusts and submits to the *auctoritas* of the divine will. The divine character, of course, justifies such trust. Tertullian believes that God would provide "for his own even without their asking" (1.30). And so, the purpose of petition is not really to get anything from God, but to align one's will with God's will. This is not only appropriate, but also fundamental to a correct view of petition. As he says, "But whatever it is we choose for ourselves we express with reference to him, and reckon to his account that which we look for from him" (5.3–4). The *voluntas Dei*, which Tertullian defines as "the salvation of those he has made his children," is both the fundamental and ultimate standard against which petition must be measured (4.11). Thus, any request must be tempered in accordance with the divine will. In fact, the sum of Tertullian's statements implies that he considers the primary petition to be the request for salvation. This, above all else, is what is truly good and needed from God. As he says, "We ask then from him to supply us with the substance and effect of his will, that we may be saved both in heaven and in earth" (4.9–10). As he uses it here, the substance of God's will is a joining of its form and matter. It is the *summa*, or main point, of God's activity. All other divine actions are then subordinate to and in assistance of God's primary aim. And since God's will is the salvation of humanity, the ultimate and proper petition for the orant is that God act in accordance with God's will.

Although Tertullian recognizes that human beings have needs, he subsumes them under the *voluntas Dei*, since "[the] Lord [is] the foreseer of human necessities" (10.1). And yet, he acknowledges that "there are things to be asked for according to each man's circumstances"; particular acts or requests that apply to emergency situations in a believer's life (10.3). As in the Gethsemane episode, a supplicant has the right to petition for particular goods, according to her circumstantial need. As Tertullian says, "[We] have the right, after rehearsing the prescribed and regular prayer as a foundation, to make from other sources a superstructure of petitions for additional desires" (10.4–6). On its face, such a statement contradicts the idea that human will should be subordinated to the divine will. However, Tertullian ends his discourse on petition with the words: "yet with mindfulness of the precepts, lest we be as far from the ears of God as we are from the precepts" (10.6–7). In other words, the precepts of submission governs and validates the petitioner's request. Using Gethsemane as a model, the believer is to imitate Christ, which entails preaching, working, and suffering, "even unto death." "And for us to be able to fulfill these," Tertullian says, "there is need [to submit to] God's will" (4.15–17; see also 29.7–11; *Apol.* 31). And so, submission to the *voluntas Dei* assures prayer's efficacy.

Speaking of efficacy, *Prayer* highlights its importance and function in two additional ways. First, Tertullian extols the virtues of the LP and how its components conform to the ideal of Christian worship:

> How many edicts of prophets, Gospels, and apostles, how many discourses, parables, examples, and precepts of the Lord, are touched upon in the brevities of a few short words, how many duties summed up all at once. (*Or.* 9.1–3)

In just a few short lines the LP embodies the entirety of the Lord's teachings, including proper worship; "as it is restrained in wording, so it is copious in meaning" (1.32–33). Such an understanding of worship is characteristic of a Roman theological perspective: restrained dignity following the *traditio* of the ancestors. The structure of the prayer thus corresponds to the Carthaginian's religious sensibility since its brevity is enhanced by its comprehensiveness. As he illustrates,

> In Father the honor of God, in name [our] witness to the faith, in
> will the sacrifice of obedience, in kingdom the commemoration of
> [our] hope, in bread the petition for life, in the prayer for pardon
> the confession of debts, in the request for safeguard wariness
> against temptations. (9.4–7)

According to Tertullian, this structure gives the LP its own special power
so that "by its own special right it ascends into heaven" (9.10).

Second, Tertullian argues that dedication to Christian ethics makes
prayer efficacious: "Mindfulness of the precepts paves for prayers the way
to heaven" (11.1). Chief among these precepts is the cancellation of interpersonal debt and the restoration of peace. He says, "[We] go not up to the
altar of God before we cancel whatever of discord or offence we have contracted with the brethren. For how can one without peace draw nigh to the
peace of God, or to the remission of debts with the retention of them?"
(11.2–5). Operating by analogy, Tertullian believes that ethical infractions
prohibit the efficacy of prayers. In short, if prayer is to be efficacious, then
the orant must somehow imitate God, because only those things alike in
nature can communicate effectively. Prayer must be "sent forth from such
a spirit as is that Spirit to whom it is sent" (12.2–3).

Since submission, proper structure, and moral rectitude are components of efficacious prayer, then this new form of Christian sacrifice "will
obtain for us from God all that we ask for" (28.13–14). The eminence of
this Christian sacrifice is apparent to Tertullian. Prior to Christian practice, prayer "induced plagues, put to flight the hosts of the enemy, withheld
the benefits of rain" (29.11–12). Christian prayer, by contrast, does not take
care of merely physical problems but spiritual ones as well. According to
Tertullian, these are the real problems Christians must confront. And yet,
Tertullian's vision of prayer does not exclude the possibility of suffering;
instead, it prepares the believer for suffering. As he describes it, the power
of Christian prayer, specifically the LP, resides in its ability to affect the
good:

> And so [the LP's] only knowledge is how to call back the souls of
> the deceased from the very highway of death, to straighten the fee-
> ble, to heal the sick, to cleanse the devil-possessed, to open the bars
> of the prison, to loose the bands of the innocent. It absolves sins,
> drives back temptations, quenches persecutions, strengthens the
> weak-hearted, delights the high-minded, brings home wayfarers,
> soothes the waves, astounds robbers, feeds the poor, rules the rich,

lifts up the fallen, supports the unstable, upholds them that stand. (29.17–23)

And yet, the Carthaginian is very careful not to say that prayer can avert suffering. Christian prayer embraces and promotes the good. And even though many would not view suffering as something good, persecution and martyrdom both imitate the actions of Christ and feed the church's growth. And so, the perspective of the *ecclesia* of the martyrs comes through, even in prayer.

In sum, Tertullian envisions prayer in light of his Romano-African context. In that vein, this cultic act is to be done with the greatest dignity and restraint, as befits the honor of God. As the Christian replacement for sacrifice, prayer is a comprehensive act that embraces both the interior and exterior dimensions of the cult. It involves much more than just one's internal disposition. It has to do with the rehabilitation of the soul and the proper representation of acts that accompany that rehabilitation.

As the *sermo* and *ratio* of God, Christian prayer aligns one with the *voluntas Dei*, the activity of God in creation and through the church. Of course, Tertullian views the LP as the model upon which all other prayers must be based. As such, it is valid and binding upon all Christians. Since it comes from the mouth of God, it defines what is truly good. And because the perfect instructor has taught it, it satisfies the conditions raised by Greco-Roman thinkers on the subject.

Tertullian's Reading of the LP

It is now possible to examine Tertullian's reading and exposition of the LP. In our previous discussion in this chapter, we reconstructed Tertullian's theological perspective on prayer, primarily from *Prayer*. This perspective arises from a careful and sometimes imaginative exegesis on Tertullian's part. Using the LP as his starting point, Tertullian constructs a cultic *didachē* appropriate to the North African context. As in chapter 4, this discussion will proceed on three fronts. First, I will give a short reprise of Tertullian's understanding of prayer and its relation to the LP. Second, I will analyze the different elements of the LP and Tertullian's reading of it. In conclusion, I will analyze how Tertullian recontextualizes the LP to fit his Romano-African audience.

Because of his North African worldview, Tertullian does not seem to object to the concept of petitionary prayer as does his Alexandrian counterpart. As I mentioned in chapter 2, Roman prayer was essentially petitionary prayer. By defining prayer as sacrifice, Tertullian tends to focus on the *official* aspect of the act as opposed to the conversational activity that characterizes Clement's view (e.g., *Or.* 27.3–5; 28.1, 9–10; passim). Tertullian would agree with Cicero that "holiness is the science of divine worship" (*Nat. d.* 1.116). In this manner Tertullian understands the work of the true Christian to be priestly. One could say that Tertullian is a precursor of the Reformation concept of the priesthood of all believers. A true Christian knows how to perform correctly the *officia* (services) of this new sacrifice, this new form of prayer. Tertullian also limits the ability of petitions to influence the will of God. To make one's petition conform to the divine will, the orant avoids asking for specific things and instead asks for favorable conditions.

In many ways, Tertullian's view of prayer is distinct from that of our Greco-Roman auditor. For example, our auditor was able to postulate God as having certain needs. Tertullian, by contrast, appears to dismiss the idea that God needs anything, including honor and praise, from human beings: "Not that it is seemly for men to wish God well, as though there were another from whom it were possible to wish him [well], or as though he were in difficulties unless we so wish" (*Or.* 3.6–10). That he has several versions of the prayer available to him is illustrated by his use of the Lukan form in *Against Marcion* 4.26, but another form in *Prayer.* And so, Tertullian's decision to use this particular form of the LP may serve to illustrate a theological perspective, a perspective he may not have been able to access by using Matthew. Let us now turn our attention to Tertullian's reading of the prayer.

The invocation, *Pater qui in caelis es* ("Father who is in heaven"), marks one difference between *Prayer* and Matthew. Recognized as "bearing witness to God" and a "work of faith," the *invocatio* is both a prayer and a confession (*Or.* 2.1–3). In fact, Tertullian says prayer to the Father is part of keeping the divine precepts (2.7). The Carthaginian also invokes the Trinity: "[Even] our mother the church is not omitted, seeing that in 'son' and 'father' there is a recognition of 'mother:' for the name of both father and son has its actuality from her" (2.12–14). In other words, in calling God as Father, the orant recognizes a permanent kinship with God. By discussing this relationship within the framework of the Trinity, Tertullian places the individual in the *familia Dei*. Through birth into the *mater ecclesia*, the believer gains the right to petition God as Father (*Bapt.* 20.5).

The next issue Tertullian raises in the term *Father* is the naming of God: "[When] we say *Father* we also give God a name" (2.10–11). The *cognomen* Father, as explained in chapter 1, was often used to invoke deities in the Greco-Roman world. Roman worshippers, including those in Carthage, understood their gods as performing parental functions. This also coincides with the Roman interest in addressing a god according to his activity. And so, Tertullian sees this appellation as appropriate, since the Christian God is known primarily through his activity in creation (see *Apol.* 17.1–2).

Tertullian also makes what on its face appears to be a puzzling statement: "The name of God the Father has been revealed to no man. . . . [Yet,] to us it has been revealed in the Son" (*Or.* 3.1, 3). What this statement highlights is the difference between a *nomen* and a *cognomen*. Father is a *cognomen* (surname) derived from God's activity in creation. However, the *nomen* of God the Father was presumably not accurately known until its revelation in Christ. Since the Son is of one substance with the Father, the *nomen* of God is identical to that revealed by Christ. As Tertullian says, "[The] Son is the Father's new [*nomen*]" (3.3). As the Son is the manifestation of the *ratio* and *sermo* of God in creation, he becomes the proper subject to name when one seeks to address the deity (cf. *Marc.* 4.26). At this point, a substantial difference exists between Tertullian and our Greco-Roman auditor. Although Greco-Romans saw various gods as manifestations of a single divine power, their understanding of divine monarchy was not synonymous with the Christian Trinity. Calling Caelestis as Juno or Eshmoun as Aesculapius is not the same as the relationship between the Father, Son, and Holy Spirit.

The invocation of God as Father leads to the first petition, "Hallowed be thy name," *sanctificetur nomen tuum* (*Or.* 3.17–18). Tertullian says the Son is the one whose name we ask to be sanctified, since the proper name of God is revealed in Christ (3.6). Tertullian maintains that the purpose behind this petition is to keep humans in "remembrance of [God's] benefits that is always due" (3.9–10). Although he denies that God's name could ever be profaned, which would suggest some deficiency in God, Tertullian reenvisions the petition as pointing to the *eschaton* (3.10–13). In this sense the petition to make God's name holy is a precursor to heavenly worship, a request for the realization of God's holiness; a situation not presently manifest on earth.

However, where the sanctification of God's name is conspicuous in the present is in the *ecclesia*. This petition, in Tertullian's view, is actually two-pronged: (1) to have God's name hallowed by those in the *ecclesia*, and (2) to have God's name hallowed by all (3.18–21). In other words, the sanctification of the divine name is to be carried out by human beings, but presently by those who belong to the *ecclesia*. As the *tutor* of believers, the *ecclesia* oversees, teaches, and validates proper Christian worship. Thus, the sanctification of God's name by the *ecclesia* is a foretaste of the full recognition of the deity that will come at the end of time. By fulfilling the *voluntas Dei*, God will satisfy this petition.

Tertullian's second petition does not conform to any of the extant versions of the LP that scholars have at present. His version of it reads, *fiat voluntas tua in caelis et in terra* (4.1). He has also altered the order of the petitions. In other versions of the prayer the petition for God's will comes after the petition for the coming of God's kingdom. This alteration appears to have had an effect on the meaning of the petition.

In our reading of the petition in chapter 1, we noted that our auditor might understand this request to mean that human beings oppose their wills to God's will. Such a hearing is clearly dismissed in Tertullian's understanding of the request. According to Tertullian, the *voluntas Dei* cannot be opposed in any respect (4.2–3). In fact, he denies any reading of the petition meaning that one is praying for God's will eventually to succeed (4.3). God's omnipotence would be threatened if God's will could be opposed or thwarted. Rather than have the petition focus on God, Tertullian reads the petition figuratively as focusing on human activity: "For by the figurative interpretation of flesh and spirit, heaven and earth means us" (4.5). In this way, Tertullian avoids the sticky issue of divine providence. So the petition does not mean that God is not in control of the cosmos, or that human beings can actively oppose the divine will; instead, the petition asks that the orant's will be harmonized with that of the *voluntas Dei*.

As discussed earlier, Tertullian understands the divine will to be the salvation of humanity (see 4.11). And since the focus of the petition is humanity and not God, the practical application of this petition pertains to the vocation of the disciple. When the disciple acts in accordance with the divine will, she will preach, work, and suffer to bring about its fulfillment (4.16). Of course, this necessitates an uncommon understanding of good and evil (4.18–19). Again, the Gethsemane episode governs Tertullian's hearing and application of this text. In short, Tertullian's reading of this petition places primary emphasis on human adherence to the divine *disciplina* rather than on God's obligation to make human beings obey. Because of Christ's actions at Gethsemane, the precept for the application of this petition is clear to Tertullian. In effect, Christ's acts are part of the Christian *ius divinum*.

In other versions of the LP, this petition is usually the second. Tertullian does not make a functional distinction between the two petitions, however. He says, "Also, *Thy kingdom come* has the same pertinence [as]

Thy will be done—in us, of course" (5.1–2). And yet, he uses the petition to take up an eschatological theme: the final coming of the kingdom of God. According to our Greco-Roman reading, the kingdom petition involves the recognition of God's dignity and the establishment of a just social order. From Tertullian's perspective, this reading is acceptable. The God of justice cannot tolerate a disobedient world indefinitely (5.14). And yet, Tertullian understands the *eschaton* as the consummation of the world (5.8). It is not clear, however, if consummation means conflagration in the Stoic sense or something else.

As the Carthaginian understands it, the fourth petition moves the focus of prayer from heavenly things to earthly things:

> But how gracefully has divine wisdom drawn up the order of the prayer, that after heavenly things, that is, after God's name, God's will, and God's kingdom, it should make place for petition for earthly necessities too: for the Lord has also stated the principle: *Seek ye first the kingdom and then even these things will be added to you. And yet we prefer the spiritual understanding of Give us today our daily bread.* (6.1–6; emphasis added)

This creates an interesting tension. On the one hand, Tertullian says that the fourth petition is for "earthly necessities." And yet, on the other hand, he says that he prefers "the spiritual understanding" of bread. The solution to this conundrum may be explicable by reference to the commentator's Romano-African worldview. For example, the prayer of Scipio Africanus discussed in chapter 2 asked the gods for favorable conditions, not for concrete actions. Romans believed that given the proper circumstances, they themselves could achieve the material goods they sought. The Roman idea of the *pax deorum* emphasized the absence of direct divine intervention in human affairs. Assuming the benevolence of the Deity, Tertullian questions the material reading and application of the petition. Since God gives to each individual according to his needs, this petition for bread is superfluous if taken in its ordinary sense. And so, as Tertullian's *regulae interpretationis* dictate, it must be understood in a figurative or spiritual sense.

And yet, Tertullian offers an alternative reading of the fourth petition. He says, "But even in that this expression has a carnal acceptation, it can with all reverence be made to belong also to spiritual discipline. For it is bread he enjoins us to ask for, which thing alone is what the faithful need: for after the other things do the Gentiles seek" (6.12–14). By making the petition for bread a form of spiritual *disciplina*, Tertullian avoids the pitfall of having the petition contradict the Roman idea of the *pax deorum*. Notice also that he positions bread as a primary representation of material fulfillment, and that he dismisses other material pursuits as those things after which Gentiles seek. Thus, the *disciplina* for bread lets a material need serve a higher, spiritual purpose.

Also in connection with the petition for bread, Tertullian calls Christ our bread: "By asking for daily bread we request continuance in Christ and inseparableness from his body" (6.7, 10–12). As recognized earlier, Tertullian allows for specific requests to be made in prayer as long as they conform to the will of God. And so, by identifying Christ as the bread for which one prays, the request, in effect, becomes a way of asking for the continuance of divine guidance. As he says, even if the request were for actual bread, this would be a form of spiritual discipline that subsumes one's will to the *voluntas Dei* (see 6.13–15). In addition, when Tertullian speaks of this petition as a form of spiritual discipline, he invokes the idea of generosity; both human and divine (see 7.1). Our reading in chapter 1 also highlighted the implicit notion of generosity found in the petition. And as a mechanism for recalling and honoring God's generosity, Tertullian would agree with the necessity of praying the LP on a regular basis.

The fifth petition is a confession of indebtedness. As observed in chapter 1, the language embedded in the petition is legal. And yet, as a social metaphor the request for forgiveness points toward a socially obligatory generosity that permeates justice throughout the social system. Tertullian also understands debt to be a metaphor or *figura* for wrongdoing, and wrongdoing "no less owes a debt to judgment and is avenged by it, and does not escape the justice of restitution" (7.8–9). Such legal terminology resonates with Tertullian's own theological perspective, and he agrees that the remission of debts is an act of mercy. This appears to be the idea behind Tertullian's use of the parable of the unforgiving servant. The orant is required to dispense mercy as she has received mercy. Tertullian understands that if forgiveness is to be meaningful, it must resonate throughout the social order. Justice is the remedy for evil, and the God of justice will call all evildoers to account.

Tertullian places the continuing problem of evil squarely in the hands of Satan. As he says, "[Wickedness] and malice belong to the devil" (8.6). The Carthaginian intellectual dismisses the idea that there could be any evil in the will of God, one of the reasons why we should not fear to pray "Thy will be done." As he clearly states, "[There] is no evil in God's will" [4.18–19). In this, he sounds like Chrysippus. According to Plutarch, "In Chrysippus' view no instance of [vices], small or great, is contrary to the reason, law, justice and providence of Zeus" (Plutarch, *Stoic. rep.* 1050c–d [Long and Sedley]).[85] Tertullian rejects the idea that God is the source of temptation: "God forbid that the Lord should be supposed to tempt, as though he were either ignorant of each man's faith or desirous of overthrowing it" (*Or.* 8.4–6). The tempter is clearly the devil. To further illustrate his argument, Tertullian points to Christ's temptation and says, "[Jesus] himself, being tempted of the devil, showed who is the patron and artificer of temptation" (8.10–11). Temptation involves either (a) being ignorant of a person's faith, something not applicable to an omniscient God, or (b) desiring to overthrow a person's faith, something also inapplicable to the God of justice. Again, a proper understanding of prayer rests on a proper theology. And although Tertullian makes a distinction between being tempted and actually sinning, the idea of God even testing (*peirasmos*) an individual is repugnant to his theological vision. Thus, Tertullian could not blame the problem of evil on anything but human beings and the devil. Cyprian also sums up this entire situation:

> [Nothing] remains beyond this for which we ought to make request, when once we have asked for God's protection against the evil one. For when that is granted we stand secure and safe against all that the devil and the world can do.[86]

In total, Tertullian's reading of the LP shares much with our Greco-Roman auditor. Using both forensic and theological reasoning, Tertullian constructs an understanding of the LP that resonates with his Romano-African audience. He creates a cultic *didachē* for Carthaginian Christians. What sets Tertullian's perspective apart from that of our auditor is his emphasis on prayer as sacrifice and his forensic focus on precepts that constitute a coherent *disciplina*. What is not found directly in his reading of the LP, although it heavily influences it, is Tertullian's emphasis on the presence and guidance of the Holy Spirit. Tertullian's vision permeated by the Spirit is at the heart of not only his ecclesiology but also his cultic understanding.

Notes

1. Timothy David Barnes, *Tertullian: A Historical and Literary Study* (Oxford: Clarendon Press, 1971), 30–56; Stanley Helms Kelley, "*Auctoritas* in Tertullian: The Nature and Order of Authority in His Thought" (PhD diss., Emory University, 1974), 1–23.

2. Barnes, *Tertullian*, 101.

3. Ibid., 27–29.

4. Ibid., 101–2.

5. Ibid., 13–15, 21, 109, 113.

6. Charles de Lisle Shortt, *The Influence of Philosophy on the Mind of Tertullian* (London: Elliot Stock, 1933).

7. Charles Norris Cochrane, *Christianity and Classical Culture: A Study of Thought and Action from Augustus to Augustine* (New York: Oxford University Press, 1957), 40–42.

8. Barnes, *Tertullian*, 120–21.

9. H. F. Jolowicz, *Historical Introduction to the Study of Roman Law* (Cambridge: Cambridge University Press, 1951), 212.

10. Fritz Schulz, *History of Roman Legal Science* (Oxford: Clarendon, 1953), 50.

11. William C. Morey, *Outlines of Roman Law Comprising Its Historical Growth and General Principles* (New York: Putnam's Sons, 1884), 309.

12. James Stevenson, *A New Eusebius: Documents Illustrative of the History of the Church to A.D. 337* (London: SPCK, 1978), 178. Unless otherwise noted, all translations of Tertullian's works come from Alexander Roberts et al., eds., *Ante-Nicene Fathers: The Writings of the Fathers Down to A.D. 325* (Peabody, MA: Hendrickson, 1994). Translations of *De oratione* come from Tertullian, *Tertullian's Tract on the Prayer* (ed. Ernest Evans; London: SPCK, 1953).

13. Vianney Decarie, "Le paradoxe de Tertullien," *VC* 15 (1961); Étienne Gilson, *La philosophie au moyen âge* (2d ed.; Paris: Payot, 1944), 97–98; Justo L. Gonzalez, "Athens and Jerusalem Revisited: Reason and Authority in Tertullian," *CH* 43 (1974): 17–25, D. E. Groh, "Tertullian's Polemic against Social Co-Optation," *CH* 40 (1971): 7–14, F. Refoule, "Tertullien et la philosophie," *RSR* 30 (1956): 42–45.

14. S. L. Greenslade, ed., *Early Latin Theology: Selections from Tertullian, Cyprian, Ambrose, and Jerome* (Library of Christian Classics; Philadelphia: Westminster, 1956), 41.

15. Barnes, *Tertullian*, 66.

16. Greenslade, *Early Latin Theology*, 60.

17. Barnes, *Tertullian*, 64–65; Kelley, "*Auctoritas* in Tertullian," 206–7.

18. For the general scholarly view, see E. Flesseman-Van Leer, *Tradition and Scripture in the Early Church* (Van Gorcum's theologische bibliotheek 26; Assen: Van Gorcum, 1954), 166–67; cf. J. N. D. Kelly, *Early Christian Creeds* (2d ed.; London: Longmans, 1960), 82–88.

19. Damien van den Eynde, *Les normes de l'enseignement chrétien dans la littérature patristique des trois premiers siecles* (Paris: Gabalda et Fils, 1933), 291–93; Kelley, "*Auctoritas* in Tertullian," 208.

20. Alexander Beck, *Römisches Recht bei Tertullian und Cyprian: Eine Studie zur frühen Kirchenrechtsgeschichte* (Halle [Saale]: Niemeyer, 1930), 51–54.

21. Heinrich Karpp, *Schrift und Geist bei Tertullian* (Gutersloh: Bertelsmann, 1955), 36–38.

22. Kelley, "*Auctoritas* in Tertullian," 214–15.

23. Barnes, *Tertullian*, 142.

24. Fritz Schulz, *Classical Roman Law* (Oxford: Clarendon, 1951), 338.

25. On the legal particularities, see Jolowicz, *Roman Law*, 352–55.

26. Not all scholars agree on the importance of legal terminology for a correct interpretation of Tertullian. For more information on the debate, see Michael Joseph Brown, "The Lord's Prayer Reinterpreted: An Analysis of This Cultic *Didachē* by Clement of Alexandria (*Stromateis* VII) and Tertullian (*De oratione*) (PhD diss., University of Chicago, 1998), 182.

27. George L. Prestige, *God in Patristic Thought* (London: Heinemann, 1936), 97–106.

28. Robert E. Roberts, *The Theology of Tertullian* (London: Epworth, 1924), 191–98.

29. Stevenson, *A New Eusebius*, 183.

30. Barnes, *Tertullian*, 118; Robert L. Simpson, *The Interpretation of the Lord's Prayer in the Early Church* (ed. S. L. Greenslade; The Library of History and Doctrine; Philadelphia: Westminster, 1965), 21.

31. Jo-Ann Shelton, *As the Romans Did: A Sourcebook in Roman Social History* (2d ed.; (New York: Oxford University Press, 1998), 299.

32. Robert D. Sider, *Ancient Rhetoric and the Art of Tertullian* (Oxford Theological Monographs; London: Oxford University Press, 1971), 40.

33. Simpson, *Interpretation of the Lord's Prayer*, 83–84.

34. Paul Monceaux, *Histoire littéraire de l'Afrique chrétienne depuis les origines jusqu'à L'invasion arabe* (vol. 1; Paris: Ernest Leroux, 1901), 371.

35. Ibid., 366.

36. R. P. C. Hanson, "Notes on Tertullian's Interpretation of Scripture," *JTS* 12 (1961): 275.

37. David Rankin, *Tertullian and the Church* (Cambridge: Cambridge University Press, 1995), 47.

38. Kelley, "*Auctoritas* in Tertullian," 196.

39. Hanson, "Notes on Tertullian's Interpretation of Scripture," 273–79.

40. Barnes, *Tertullian*, 186–232.

41. Kelley, "*Auctoritas* in Tertullian," 198–99.

42. Ibid., 200.

43. Karpp, *Schrift und Geist*, 22–29.

44. Kelley, "*Auctoritas* in Tertullian," 209.

45. Simpson, *Interpretation of the Lord's Prayer*, 78.

46. Edward Vernon Arnold, *Roman Stoicism: Being Lectures on the History of the Stoic Philosophy with Special Reference to Its Development within the Roman Empire* (London: Routledge & Kegan Paul, 1958), 243 n. 224.

47. Charles Norris Cochrane, *Christianity and Classical Culture: A Study of Thought and Action from Augustus to Augustine* (New York: Oxford University Press 1957), 247.

48. Kelley, "*Auctoritas* in Tertullian," 182.

49. Ibid., 183–84.

50. Ibid., 188.

51. Olivia F. Robinson, *The Criminal Law of Ancient Rome* (London: Duckworth, 1995), 16–17.

52. Ibid., 17.

53. Georges Dumézil, *Archaic Roman Religion, with an Appendix on the Religion of the Etruscans* (2 vols.; Chicago: University of Chicago Press, 1970), 2:556.

54. Ibid., 2:557–58.

55. R. M. Ogilvie, *The Romans and Their Gods in the Age of Augustus* (ed. M. I. Finley; Ancient Culture and Society; London: Chatto & Windus, 1969), 41–42.

56. John N. D. Kelly, *Early Christian Doctrines* (2d ed.; London: A & C Black, 1960), 177.

57. Kelley, "*Auctoritas* in Tertullian," 159, 162.

58. Rankin, *Tertullian and the Church*, 46.

59. Kelley, "*Auctoritas* in Tertullian," 93–94.

60. Rankin, *Tertullian and the Church*, 71.

61. Ibid., 77.

62. Ibid., 86–87.

63. Ibid., 87.

64. Kelley, "*Auctoritas* in Tertullian," 218, 220; Rankin, *Tertullian and the Church*, 88–89.

65. G. W. H. Lampe, "Christian Theology in the Patristic Period," in *A History of Christian Doctrine* (ed. Hubert Cunliffe-Jones; Edinburgh: Clark, 1978), 61.

66. Rankin, *Tertullian and the Church*, 95–97.

67. Simpson, *Interpretation of the Lord's Prayer*, 94.

68. Ibid., 93, 116.

69. Ibid., 117–18.

70. Ibid., 44, 82–83.

71. W. Warde Fowler, *The Religious Experience of the Roman People, from the Earliest Times to the Age of Augustus: The Gifford Lectures, 1909–1910* (London: Macmillan, 1911), 169–70; Ogilvie, *Romans and Their Gods*, 23.

72. Ogilvie, *Romans and Their Gods*, 50–51.

73. Simpson, *Interpretation of the Lord's Prayer*, 113.

74. Fowler, *Religious Experience of the Roman People*, 171; Simpson, *Interpretation of the Lord's Prayer*, 76, 91, 126.

75. On the materiality of words, see A. A. Long, "Language and Thought in Stoicism," in *Problems in Stoicism* (ed. A. A Long; London: Athlone, 1971), 75–113.

76. See the description of the Roman sacrificial ritual in Fowler, *Religious Experience of the Roman People*, 169–222; Ogilvie, *Romans and Their Gods*, 41–52.

77. Fowler, *Religious Experience of the Roman People*, 173–74.

78. Ibid., 174–75.

79. Ibid., 178; Ogilvie, *Romans and Their Gods*, 47.

80. Simpson, *Interpretation of the Lord's Prayer*, 45–46, 80, 141.

81. Ogilvie, *Romans and Their Gods*, 50–51.

82. Bonnie Bowman Thurston, *Spiritual Life in the Early Church: The Witness of Acts and Ephesians* (Minneapolis: Fortress, 1993), 75, 80–81.

83. Simpson, *Interpretation of the Lord's Prayer*, 90.

84. Ibid., 150.

85. Lang and Sedley, 334.

86. Quoted in Simpson, Interpretation, 47–48.

7

Two Visions of Prayer in Early Christian Discourse

> *You cannot have God for your father*
> *unless you have the church for your mother.*
> —Cyprian (*Unit. eccl.* 6)

Like the Rays of the Sun

In his memorable defense of the centrality of episcopal authority, Cyprian wrote, "[The church is] a single whole, though she spreads far and wide into a multitude of churches as her fertility increases" (*Unit. eccl.* 5 [Greenslade]).[1] Using the rays of the sun as a metaphor, Cyprian argues that multiplicity and unity are simultaneously evident in the *ecclesia*: "In the same way the Church, bathed in the light of the Lord, spreads her rays throughout the world, yet the light everywhere diffused is one light and the unity of the body is not broken" (5). Cyprian is pointing to the universal authority of the episcopacy to govern the *ecclesia* as a whole, while also arguing that each bishop is supreme in his own diocese. In a similar manner, theological discourse in the *ecclesia* displays this same multiplicity within an overarching idea of unity.

Chapters 3 through 6 examined the various ethnoreligious influences that affected Clement of Alexandria's and Tertullian of Carthage's visions of prayer. Allowing each intellectual to speak out of his context, we began to appreciate the degree to which social location influences the interpretive enterprise. It would be overly simplistic to say that Clement speaks out of a Greek philosophical context and Tertullian a Roman one, at least without qualification. The significance of the label Greco-Roman comes from the recognition that easy categorization into Greek and Roman is not pos-

255

sible in this period. Take, for example, the governmental position of *strategos* in Egypt. Its roots go back to Alexander's conquest of the region and the replacement of the Persian satraps. Under the Ptolemies a *strategos* had both civil and military authority. Under Rome a *strategos* became a civil functionary. Yet, in times of crisis, such as the Jewish revolt of 115 CE, the military role of the *strategos* was revived. An attempt to categorize this position as something Greek in one period and something Roman in another would rob the office of its social and historical complexity. As a form of governance, the position owes a debt to Hellenistic and Roman notions of proper political structure, but beyond that to Persian and native Egyptian models of population management. The *strategos* was not a simple creation of the Greeks whose function the Romans transformed, but a complex historically situated governmental position growing out of the particular social environment that characterized post-Persian Egypt. Likewise, early Christian attitudes about prayer grew out of distinctive social environments that contained various ethnoreligious influences. What I have attempted to do in this book is tease out some of the more dominant ethnoreligious understandings that influenced Tertullian and Clement. And so, when I say that Tertullian speaks out of a Roman religious sensibility regarding prayer, I am not claiming to have discovered the universal conceptual model that governs the Carthaginian's theological vision. I am highlighting, by contrast, the influence of one ethnoreligious tradition on his thought.

By exposing the influence of one ethnoreligious tradition on Clement's and Tertullian's conceptions of prayer, I believe scholars can better account for the obvious differences in their perspectives. Unlike my generic Greco-Roman auditor, the ethnoreligious environments of the Alexandrian and the Carthaginian influenced their distinctive readings of the LP greatly. In fact, scholars have long recognized differences between Alexandrian and, say, Roman theological discourse. What I have done is push that recognition even further. There is a difference between a Roman theological perspective and a Romano-African one. A Roman provincial, because of the peculiar social environment that developed in North Africa, cultivated a different cultic understanding than his contemporary living in the imperial capital. Of course, there were similarities in their perspectives. Without them, Greco-Roman as a heuristic category would be meaningless. Nevertheless, we cannot ignore the obvious: early Christian thinkers came from distinct ethnoreligious environments that greatly influenced their theological visions. Once we accept this, it becomes possible to trace the inheritance and development of particular patterns of Christian cultic thinking. These traditions of cultic appropriation form the foundation upon which later forms of cultic *didachē* flourished. Robert Simpson points to this: "Among the primary factors that contributed to and helped shape [the fathers'] understanding of prayer in general and their exegesis of the LP in particular is . . . that they were writing in a defined tradition."[2]

Clement of Alexandria wrote out of a Greco-Egyptian philosophical tradition. Drawing upon its resources, he constructed an Alexandrian vision of Christian theology, one appropriate to the cosmopolitan urban environment of the former Ptolemaic capital. For example, Clement adopted the largely Platonic idea of God as *nous*. And although he shared this vision with various Greco-Roman thinkers, Clement extended the Christian understanding of a noetic God into one that is immaterial. God inhabits the world of the intellect. Consequently, a relationship with God comes ideally by means of the Logos and operates primarily in an intellectual fashion. The Unknown can only be known through the grace of the Logos. Although derided as a "cult of intelligence" by some, the Alexandrian's anthropology pointed to irrationality as the basis of sin and enlightenment as its cure.[3] This philosophical orientation fit quite well with a community whose ethnoreligious self-understanding derived from Alexandria's role as a Greco-Roman intellectual center.

In his continuation of the Greek philosophical enterprise, Clement pointed to the gnostic as the ideal exemplar of Christian discipleship. Only a truly rational individual can worship God in a manner befitting God's nature (*Strom.* 7.1.2). Clement's largely therapeutic understanding of Christian discipleship emphasizes cultic activity as both an expression of εὐσέβεια and a form of education. Proper theology leads to proper action (εὐσέβεια), and proper action reinforces orthodox theology. In his arguments against Valentinus and others, Clement will point to the absence of εὐσέβεια among the gnostics as an indication of their flawed theological vision. Since right action is a consequence of right thinking, the heterodox demonstrate that they are such by their rejection of the *regula fidei* and fellowship with the established church. It is through the congregation of souls united by one common voice and mind, the instrument used by the Logos to illuminate and educate the soul, that one can attain "the habit of mind which preserves the fitting attitude toward God" (7.1.3). And so, the Alexandrian's vision of prayer finds its grounding in his distinctive anthropology and ecclesiology. *Stromata* 7 is as much an exercise in apologetics as it is a reflection of Christian devotional practice. As a form of cultic *didachē*, it distinguishes between appropriate and inappropriate manifestations and conceptions of divine worship as an outgrowth of acceptable and unacceptable understandings of the deity. In short, Clement developed his theology of prayer as a means of answering counterclaims made by those within and outside the Alexandrian church concerning the true nature of Christianity and its practices.

Tertullian of Carthage wrote out of a Romano-African philosophical tradition. Like his Alexandrian counterpart, Tertullian was a Roman citizen. Their comparable legal status serves to highlight, however, their different ethnoreligious contexts. Clement's openness to philosophy stands in contrast to Tertullian's reticence regarding speculation. As a potent illustration of his ethnoreligious context, tradition trumps speculation as the primary source of Tertullian's theological reflection (see Tacitus, *Agr.* 4.2–4). God's activity in creation serves as the *proprium* from which Tertullian's vision emerges. Fundamentally materialistic in orientation, the Carthaginian anchors his soteriology in the *sacrificium propitiatorium*, a material solution to a material human problem. Tertullian's strategic use of the Roman rhetorical tradition illustrates his belief in a rational God whose actions have resulted in a rationally oriented universe operating according to rational laws. Thus, Tertullian's frequent application of legal principles and use of forensic rhetoric underscores his belief in divine rationality.

What distinguishes Tertullian's theological vision from that of his Alexandrian counterpart is his doctrine of the Holy Spirit. As the theological authority that oversees and governs all other theological authorities, the Holy Spirit directs the *ecclesia* (and the believer) into truth. *Mater ecclesia* rehabilitates her children, preparing them for participation in the heavenly liturgy. The guardian of believers, the *ecclesia* protects the individual from heresy through apostolicity, the church's own version of the *mos maiorum*. Ecclesial legitimacy resides in its historical link to Jesus and the apostles. The ongoing activity of the Spirit in the life of the *corpus Christi* is the indicator of its true relationship with God and ability to dictate a Christian version of the *ius divinum*.

The differences of emphasis between Clement and Tertullian manifest themselves in many ways. Divergences in their theological visions are manifest, for example, in their understandings of inclusivity and apostolicity. Clement of Alexandria's ecclesiology is inclusive as compared to Tertullian's admittedly sectarian vision. In Clement's vision the ἐκκλησία embraces both the gnostic and the nongnostic. This communal structure, somewhat analogous to the larger Alexandrian community, recognizes that not all Christians will achieve the gnostic ideal. In similar ecclesial visions, like that of the Valentinians, the elitist character of such an organizational model is readily apparent. It is more subdued in Clement's conception of the church, although elitism still exists. In an effort to have it both ways, Clement argues for a basic equality among all believers despite his preference for those with *gnōsis*.

By contrast, Tertullian of Carthage's ecclesial vision excludes any person unable to live up to the ideal of holiness. Anything less than perfection threatens to undermine the *ecclesia*'s legitimacy. Since the Holy Spirit functions as the guardian of the church, a believer's inability to live up to the Spirit's demands demonstrates the absence of the *auctoritas tutoris* in her life, an indication that she was not rehabilitated by the *mysterium* of baptism. This vision was an integral part of the North African Christian self-understanding manifested succinctly in its characterization as the church of the martyrs. Persecution and martyrdom form part of the *traditio* of the *ecclesia*. By confessing Christ and submitting to capital punishment, Perpetua acted in the tradition of Jesus and the apostles. Her veneration was a result of an *imitatio Christi*, and her death legitimized her standing as a Christian and the Carthaginian Christian community as well. In short, whereas Clement's ecclesial vision allows for less than ideal members, Tertullian's vision sacrifices such inclusivity for the sake of legitimacy.

Both early Christian intellectuals agree that the basis of sin is irrationality. In Tertullian's view, irrationality is the consequence of original sin. His traducian perspective allows him to argue that because of the transgression of Adam, all human beings are biased toward sin until they are redeemed in Christ. Under the *auctoritas tutoris* of the church, believers are rehabilitated by adherence to the *regula fidei* and the guidance of the Holy Spirit. It is a soteriological model dramatically different from that espoused by his contemporary in Alexandria. Firmly rooted in the notions of tradition and charismatic guidance, Tertullian's perspective on discipleship looks for precedents for proper conduct.

Since neither Clement nor Tertullian allowed persons outside the established church the possibility of legitimate prayer, the authors' ecclesiologies ring loud and clear. Clement's view of the church carries three characteristics with it: (1) faith and love belong only to the church (7.10.55, 57), (2) *gnōsis* from the Logos comes according to the rule of the church (7.15.90), and (3) proper interpretation of the Scriptures only comes from the rule of the church (7.16.94–96). Since Clement emphasizes the church in such a universal manner, his vision allows for distinctions of better and best to be introduced into the conversation by tacitly acknowledging an internal hierarchy.

The African agrees with his counterpart in two of his three characteristics. First, *mater ecclesia* produces and nurtures children that can properly interpret the Scriptures. Second, the church guards the apostolic tradition and believers through *auctoritas tutoris*. However, he conceives of the church in the life of the believer differently. Because of the Holy Spirit, holiness is the watchword of the church. Holiness is at the heart of Tertullian's concept of the church's legitimacy. Since exclusivity is a dominant feature of his ecclesiology, the outcome is a view that limits efficacious effects to the church's *disciplina*.

Both define prayer as sacrifice. Clearly, Tertullian views prayer as the model sacrifice God has provided for himself (*Or.* 28.9–10). As a *meritum fidei*, prayer dispenses with the necessity of other forms of sacrifice (28.1). The entire prayer act, including its words and deeds, is the material replacement for animals, incense, and grain. When conducted properly, the orant becomes a true priest of God (28.9). Physical performance is just as important as disposition. Proper prayer is a re-presentation of the *sacrificium propitiatorium* (14.5–7).

Prayer for Clement also substitutes for the flesh of animals (*Strom.* 7.6.30–7.7.35). He believes that for prayer to be properly done, one must have a proper view of the Deity. Tertullian allows for this to be enacted through the church's *auctoritas tutoris*. Improper understanding of God results in an economic view of sacrifice. An economic view of the sacrifice only benefits humans and not God: "Sacrifices, I believe, are an invention of mankind to excuse the eating of flesh" (7.6.32). According to Clement, proper theology generates something immaterial, something other than animal flesh. Understood as an act of the church, prayer is an immaterial institution honoring an immaterial God (7.6.32). In this view the scrupulous observance of rituals becomes unnecessary. This understanding draws upon the Greek intellectual critique of sacrifice, a view that privileges the disposition of the individual over her actions.

The category of petition distinguishes the two Africans. Tertullian views the LP as raising appropriate requests that coincide with his understanding of omnipotence. As Carl Jung memorialized it, *Vocatus sed atque non vocatus deus aderit*, "God is present and provides without petition" (*Or.* 1.30). In Tertullian's vision, proper petitions find their ultimate basis in alignment with the *voluntas Dei* (4.9–10).

Clement holds that most petitions arise from "appetites and desires," objects for the body, not the cultivation of the psyche (*Strom.* 7.7.38). The gnostic, in contrast to others, looks toward what benefits the soul. Like his counterpart in Carthage, Clement trusts divine omnipotence and beneficence (7.7.41). The gnostic petitions for *gnōsis*. Although they appear similar, Tertullian and Clement place different emphases in petition. The

Carthaginian accepts the presence of petition as necessary, while the Alexandrian questions the validity of most petitions in themselves.

Clement places his confidence in the power of *gnōsis*, the gift provided by the Logos, which can be trusted to guide the church since *gnōsis* and virtue are synonymous. In somewhat of a contrast, Tertullian puts his trust in the *auctoritas* of the Lord and his apostles, as well as the constant vigilant guidance of the Holy Spirit. In short, the differences between the two rest on their ecclesiologies. Looking at the church from a Greek philosophical perspective, Clement emphasizes the individual work of the Logos. From Tertullian's Romano-African perspective, the Spirit's work in the *ecclesia* as a body of believers is paramount.

Despite these differences, a common trait for both authors was to spiritualize the image of bread. Clement calls the Logos the bread of heaven, using bread as a metaphor for reception of the Logos (*Paed.* 1.6), immaterial nourishment for the believer. Tertullian says, "[We] prefer the spiritual understanding of *Give us today our daily bread*" (*Or.* 6.6). With his Roman outlook, Tertullian seeks what Roman pagans called the *pax deorum*. Although admitting that bread has a "carnal acceptation," Tertullian deemphasizes any relationship between bread and materiality (6.12). He calls the petition for bread a form of spiritual discipline. Both authors spiritualize their understandings of bread based on their visions of the needs of human beings.

The Central Vision of This Book

This book's core has been an examination of the authors' relationship to the LP. Although Clement knew the LP, it does not appear in *Stromata* 7, his treatise on prayer. Requesting anything other than *gnōsis* was unnecessary because God always acts on behalf of the good. Thanksgiving, of course, can be offered for God's generosity. The LP is much more than that. It explicitly, although succinctly, requests the fulfillment of several needs, as if God were unaware of their existence.

Tertullian's knowledge of the LP is evidenced by his commentary. Agreeing with the Alexandrian regarding God's beneficence, Tertullian does make allowance for specific needs according to one's circumstances (*Or.* 1.30). The basic governing authority is God's will. Petitions that fail to correspond to the *voluntas Dei* will not receive the desired response. Since proper prayer can effectively wrestle with the Deity, the true priest always succeeds in his prayer. Petitioning the Deity is not a problem because God only effects the petitions that are in accordance with the *voluntas Dei*. Related to beneficence, Tertullian makes it clear that God stands far above others in honor and power: "Not that it is seemly for men to wish God well, as though . . . he were in difficulties unless we so wish" (3.6–10). Clement supports such a view and, as normal for the Alexandrian, outlines how an improper theological view negatively affects εὐσέβεια. As he says, "Where then there is an unworthy conception of God, passing into base and unseemly thoughts and significations, it is impossible to preserve any sort of devoutness" (*Strom.* 7.7.38).

Two Perspectives on the Lord's Prayer

This issue of divine power also influences how the authors understand the metaphors of the LP. For example, the invocation of God as Father "in the heavens" would not be understood as an indication of God's location, since God is in reality unknowable and uncircumscribable. As Clement says, "Surely it cannot be denied that we are following right and truth when we refuse to circumscribe in a given place him who is incomprehensible, and to confine in temples made with hands that which contains all things" (*Strom.* 7.5.28). The invocation of God through metaphors such as Father "in the heavens" should not be confused with the reality of God's nature. Whereas Clement would see the *invocatio* as a potentially misleading metaphor, Tertullian believes the metaphor actually accentuates God's transcendence. Since God can only be known through his activity, the *cognomen* Father illustrates that God's real nature is incomprehensible (see *Apol.* 17).

Tertullian's rendition of the LP does not contain the Matthean pronoun "our." As I indicated, he may have chosen a particular version of the LP as better reflecting his theological perspective. Simply addressing God as Father posits a relationship between the Deity and humanity. Christians understand this implicitly. God the Father is beyond personal and ethnoreligious egoism. AsTertullian says, "[Our] petition is for [the name of God] to be hallowed in us who are in him, and at the same time also in the rest whom as yet the grace of God is looking out for" (*Or.* 3.18–19). The Alexandrian also wants to transcend egoism. Nongnostics in the church are taught to transcend their egoistic tendencies through continual education. Gnostics avoid egoism by participation in the Logos. They hold the proper theological outlook, one accompanied by ministry to others. Although he frequently calls God Father, Clement understands it to be a metaphor, a perception of God that does not capture the Deity's true nature. Such metaphors benefit those who are not gnostics, those for whom they are necessary. In short, both intellectuals are fully aware of the importance of metaphors like the one found in the invocation of the LP. The both understand them to be symbols or signs pointing to a more potent divine reality. And although they differ on their acceptance of this metaphor in the LP, they recognize the necessity of metaphors in general.

The second and third petitions of the LP present another set of alternative interpretations. The kingdom is a present reality to Clement. One becomes a member of God's kingdom through *gnōsis*. Participation in the kingdom reveals God's activity to the believer. The gnostic then realizes the immutability of God's will. Life in communion with the Logos gives the believer the ability to act in accordance with providence (see *Strom.* 7.2.6). Tertullian also promotes divine immutability. His reading of the LP, however, places emphasis on human activity. Thus, the request for the fulfillment of God's will means that this must be accomplished by human beings. He also makes the kingdom an eschatological symbol. It represents the final act of God's restoration of justice. Since God's will is the salvation of humanity, the arrival of the kingdom would be an indication of fulfillment. Again, this has practical implications for the believer's vocation. Looking at Gethsemane as a paradigm, the focus of Tertullian's reading is on human submission to the *voluntas Dei* rather than any particular activity on God's part.

Another idea evoked by petitions two and three is *disciplina*. It is, likewise, raised in the following petitions. For example, the petition for bread joins *disciplina* to generosity as a Christian act (see *Or.* 7.1). The two are also joined in Tertullian's discussion of the remission of sin (*Or.* 7.8–9). Forgiveness constitutes an act of divine generosity, which must be equaled by a human act of generosity, if it is to be effective. The idea of discipline can also be seen in Tertullian's understanding of the final petition. As we saw, evil is the province of Satan. Humans who have been regenerated in Christ, although they still must confront satanic assault, are able, under the guidance of the divine *disciplina*, to withstand the devil. In fact, Tertullian is confident that they will be victorious.

Clement's view of providence excludes the possibility of requesting material goods. God provides for human material welfare because God is benevolent by nature. And since benevolence is an attribute of God's πρόνοια, the request for bread in the LP is theologically inappropriate, unless it is understood metaphorically. As a metaphor, bread represents *gnōsis* and the church. In this sense, the petition for bread would correspond with Clement's theological perspective. By contrast to Tertullian, the Alexandrian does not view sin as debt. To him, sin is the consequence of the weakness of material corporeal beings. It cannot be eradicated by *disciplina* alone. The "cure" for what ails humanity is *gnōsis*. Denying any real power to Satan, evil is only a perception of God's educational enterprise. Human beings experience what they call evil as an opportunity for growth in godliness.

And so, in Clement and Tertullian we see two visions of prayer as part of the early Christian cult. Situated in two different settings within the Roman Empire, these early Christian intellectuals reflect the ethno-religious diversity that abounded in its borders. In Alexandria, Clement promotes a Christian continuation of the Greco-Roman philosophical tradition and its critique of popular religion. The philosophers wanted cultic acts to reflect the true majesty of deity. In order to accomplish this, they began a thorough analysis of the concept of deity itself. They operated under the mind-set that cultic acts should imitate and correspond to deity's nature. Platonic, Stoic, as well as other philosophical schools developed ideas of divinity that they believed to be appropriate. For example, Platonists argued on behalf of divine perfection. From their perspective perfection meant a maximization of certain attributes. A deity could not change since perfection meant the absence of change, an indication of deficiency, or imperfection. Deity must be omnipotent because it represents a maximum of power. Likewise, a deity must be perfect in knowledge and other desirable attributes.

The Alexandrian Perspective and Its Trajectory

With this renewed concept of deity in place, Greco-Roman philosophers developed a corresponding understanding of εὐσέβεια. Cultic performance had to embrace acts that gave honor to the divine. Interestingly, they purported that this understanding of cultic practice was in line with the intention of the ancestors. In many understandings of εὐσέβεια the ἦθος of the actor was a central concern. Using ideas like purity of mind and absence of emotion in the soul, these philosophers frequently placed a premium on the ability to think correctly. Such an understanding subverted the classical idea of reciprocity in Greco-Roman religion. In that view an individual offered a gift to the deity in order to influence the god to act on his behalf. The Greco-Roman philosophical perspective held that any offering to the deity was solely for the purpose of honoring the god. Influencing the divine was unnecessary. Since god is perfectly good, god always acts on behalf of what benefits the whole.

The end of cultic practice is thus transformed. Formerly, the cult was a way to inform or influence a god regarding something one wanted. The philosophers deemed this to be dangerous. Human beings by definition are deficient in knowledge. Such an imperfection means that humans are incapable of making truly appropriate decisions. For example, Socrates believed it to be dangerous to petition for material things because that could lead to disaster. The wisest course of action is to leave the concrete realization of the good to the gods, who know what is truly good. As in the prayer to Pan, the orant should ask only for what the god deems appropriate (see Plato, *Phaedr.* 279bc).

Like the Greco-Roman philosophers, Clement understood Christian cultic practice in light of his philosophical insight. Drawing upon the philosophers, especially Plato, the Alexandrian imported the notion of divine perfection into his community's practice of prayer. This allows him to deny the possibility of appropriate prayer to all who hold an improper view of God. Unless a prayer accords with providence, it is impious and will not be answered. Only an individual holding a proper view of Deity is capable of pious prayer. He uses the gnostic as the paradigm for the believer who practices true piety. The Christian life (εὐσέβεια) embraces all things that constitute proper service to God. To Clement acceptable divine service means service to others (see *Strom.* 7.3.21). From Clement's perspective such an understanding subverts the possibility of egoism. Since the gnostic serves others, she cannot be egoistic in her daily life or in the cult.

Since proper theology corresponds to true εὐσέβεια, then the source of that perspective must be above reproach. Jesus Christ, the Logos of God, is the mediator of Clement's theological view. As the agent of creation, the Logos guarantees that his dictates are in line with the intention of the ancestors. The *gnōsis* bestowed by the Logos is not mere empiric epistemology. It is divine. Divine *gnōsis* regenerates the believer and gives her the one thing she lacked from birth: the ability to think correctly.

Such an ability, for example, underlies Clement's critique of animal sacrifice. He asks, "And yet, if they hold that the Deity is nourished without needing it, what is the use of nourishment to one who needs it not?" (7.6.31). Offering to God a gift that God does not need is emblematic of the very attitude the Greco-Roman philosophers criticized. One cannot know how to serve God properly (εὐσέβεια) unless one knows the nature of the deity's being and activity. As sacrifice demonstrates, the mere performance of cultic acts without a proper theological underpinning renders such actions illegitimate. And so, the Greco-Roman philosophical perspective on both the Deity and the cult translated into a Christian theology and εὐ-σέβεια that flourished in this metropolis of the Egyptian province.

Origen picks up this philosophical tradition in his commentary *Peri proseuchēs* (*Prayer, Or.*). Origen's treatise on prayer combines Alexandrian theology with his own concern for and practice of scriptural exegesis. Like his predecessor, Origen intends his commentary to be an apology for a true version of Christianity against those who have philosophical reservations concerning the Christian practice of prayer. The contents of his treatise are determined by this purpose. The first part of Origen's *Prayer* addresses prayer in general: its content, limitations, and efficacy. The treatise also explores the various types of prayer and forms of divine address. In short, all the major questions involved in a discussion of prayer are canvassed here. The second part of the treatise discusses the LP in particular, offering the reader a detailed and highly allegorized exegesis of each petition. The final part of the treatise is an appendix. Discussing the orant's disposition, the place and orientation of prayer, as well as containing a final statement on the content of prayer, Origen's work is a good example of an intellectual disciple building upon the insights of his predecessor.

One can detect the intellectual handprint of Alexandrian theology throughout Origen's work. For example, paralleling Clement in *Stromata* 7.3.19, Origen says, "[God] no longer wishes to be their lord, but becomes the friend of those whose lord he formerly was" (*Or.* 1.1 [O'Meara]).[4] Clement calls prayer a sacrifice in *Stromata* (7.6.32). The younger Alexandrian says, "Indeed, what greater gift could be offered to God by a rational being than a prayer of fragrant words offered by one whose conscience is free from the stench of sin?" (Origen, *Or.* 2.2). Clement sees prayer as a participation in the divine mysteries, an experience with the ineffable reality of God. As such, the acts surrounding prayer must correspond to the divine nature. Origen says, "[One] does not pray as one ought unless one performs the duty of the ineffable mysteries of marriage also with reverence, with restraint, and without passion" (2.2). Finally, Origen echoes Clement's disdain for those who reject prayer: "The protagonists of [not praying] are they who do away with all sense perception, and practice neither baptism nor the Eucharist. They quibble about the Scriptures as not even recommending the prayer of which we speak, but as teaching something else quite different from it" (5.1). Interestingly, the last part of Origen's statement could also be directed at Clement, who neglected the LP in *Stromata* 7.

Origen's famous dual conception of prayer also appears to correspond to Clement's views. Origen says, "He prays without ceasing who joins prayer to works that are of obligation, and good works to his prayer. For virtuous works, or the carrying out of what is enjoined, form part of prayer. . . . We regard the whole life of the saint as one great continuous prayer" (Origen, *Or.* 12.2). Clement deems the entirety of gnostic piety as a religious festival. Origen also champions this conception of prayer for the gnostic. Unlike his predecessor in *Stromata* 7, he spends considerable time on the prayer life of the nongnostic. In this way, Origen builds upon Clement's understanding and vision of prayer.

The Greek philosophical tradition can also be seen in Gregory of Nyssa's homilies on the LP. As Endre Ivánka once said, "It is quite correct that [the Cappadocian fathers] endeavored to maintain and preserve for Christian theology everything valuable and Christian in the thought of Origen that they could."[5] In Gregory's hands, the philosophical tradition that began in Alexandria continued well into the Nicene era. Gregory's five homilies *On the Lord's Prayer* (*De oratione dominica*) are an important statement on the application of the Greek philosophical tradition to the daily devotional lives of believers. In his first homily, Gregory calls Christians from their materialistic busyness to participation in a more appropriate life center, Christian prayer. Unlike Clement's *Stromata* 7 and Tertullian's *Prayer*, Gregory's homily is a deft application of Christian theology to the average believer. He manifests a line of progression from Clement not only in his use of Platonic categories, but also in his emphasis on the importance of receiving *gnōsis*. Upon examination, one can trace a clear development from Clement to Origen to Gregory. Each of them relies heavily on Platonic philosophy to structure their understandings of the world and the way cultic practice functions in it. They each define prayer as *homilia* and describe its content in a similar spiritualizing manner (see Origen, *Or.* 9.2; Gregory of Nyssa, *Or.* 1.1124d). Drawing upon Origen, Gregory also wrestles with a dual conception of prayer. In Gregory of Nyssa one finds the Greek philosophical tradition advanced on three fronts: (1) the continued interplay between Greek philosophical conceptions of prayer and biblical ones, (2) the continued influence of Platonic presuppositions upon their exegeses of the LP, and (3) the ongoing modification of this tradition as these intellectuals seek to define orthodox Christianity in contrast to its intellectual contenders and in relationship to their ethnoreligious settings. In sum, although each theologian adjusts the tradition to reflect his particular ethnoreligious context, one can detect a clear trajectory from Clement's treatise on prayer to Gregory's homilies. This tradition continues even into the modern world.

The Carthaginian Perspective and Its Trajectory

In Tertullian of Carthage one can trace a line of development that begins with the Roman religious perspective. Although conservative, Roman religion not only preserved ancient ritual practices but also adapted new ones. As we saw in North Africa, the conception of *Romanitas* varied according to one's environment. Carthaginians saw themselves as Romans as well as Africans. Of course, this dual perspective influenced their ethnoreligious allegiances, which in turn influenced their religious practices. For persons from their tradition, *cultus* was as important as disposition, practice as important as belief.

Although Jo-Ann Shelton was correct in saying, "[Roman religion] was . . . concerned with material success rather than ethical behavior," the ethical was represented in the concept of *pietas*.[6] This notion of proper behavior was at the foundation of Roman life. Likewise, the Romans placed great importance on the concept of *auctoritas*. This rested on the concept of the *mos maiorum*, which held that if the Romans were to prosper, they would do so by means of the guidance established by the *maiores*. This link between the founders and the present constitutes *traditio*, the guarantor of appropriate behavior.

Tertullian continues in this Roman tradition. A practical thinker and rhetorician, he promotes an understanding of Christianity that corresponds to his Romano-African environment. A central constituent of this perspective rests on the concept of *traditio*. It forms the core of the argument against the heretics in the *Prescription*. The Scriptures, as well as correct doctrine or the *regula fidei*, belong solely to the established church. They are her inheritance from the apostles. This patrimony forms the living tradition of the church, and adherence to it is the basis of her *auctoritas* and her children's legitimacy.

In addition to its sacred text and tradition, the Holy Spirit guides the church. In short, the legitimacy of the church is grounded in its historical relationship to Jesus Christ and its present relationship with the Holy Spirit. If these were extinguished or removed, then the church would lose its legitimacy, according to Tertullian's clear application of Roman religious thinking. He draws primarily upon the idea of *auctoritas* and uses it as a vehicle to communicate his understanding of Christianity. Tertullian's concern for the proper performance of rituals is an indication of his allegiance to this ethnoreligious view. Thus, he means his treatise *Prayer* to establish a code of cultic behavior for Christians in Carthage that places them in an appropriate relationship with their God. He takes tradition and joins it to the precedents he finds in his reading of Scripture, to construct this cultic *didachē* on prayer.

By emphasizing submission to *auctoritas*, especially that represented in the *voluntas Dei*, Tertullian constructs an understanding of church and discipleship that valorizes his Romano-African milieu. Take, for example, his advocacy of martyrdom. Although Christianized, it reflects a great deal of the Roman and Carthaginian traditions of self-sacrifice. From Aeneas and Dido to Christ and later Perpetua, Carthaginian Christians and particularly Tertullian saw persecution as an opportunity to manifest *pietas*.

Closely related to Tertullian's theological perspective is the work of a later Bishop of Carthage, Cyprian. As chapter 5 showed, Tertullian and Cyprian shared a lot in terms of status and ethnoreligious perspective. Similarly, we noted differences, especially concerning the role and function of the ecclesiastical hierarchy. Tertullian's church of the martyrs was eclipsed by Cyprian's notion of episcopal supremacy. Both drew on Romano-African sources to advance their views. Cyprian exploited Tertullian's emphasis on submission by denying a certain degree of *auctoritas* to martyrs in favor of the episcopacy. Although Tertullian's vision remained alive in the early days of Donatism, it was also amended when Donatism became the dominant Christian institution in North Africa. In sum, the aspect of Tertullian's vision that extolled martyrdom became increasingly unnecessary as the church gained legitimacy in the larger Greco-Roman environment.

Cyprian's treatise *The Lord's Prayer*, like Origen's *Prayer*, was more popular and more widely used by other commentators than was that of his predecessor. For example, Hilary of Poitiers, in his commentary on the Gospel of Matthew, passes over an opportunity to comment on the LP by saying, "Cyprian, that man of holy memory, has freed us from the necessity of commenting upon the sacred mystery of the prayer."[7] By contrast, more recent commentary, influenced by biblical studies' oft-repeated mantra that older is better, has not been as flattering to Cyprian's *Lord's Prayer*. One commentator of the early twentieth century expressed this bias: "[Cyprian's treatise] is flatter than Tertullian's, much less incisive and original, and often diluted with honest commonplaces, but it succeeds in expounding the Prayer with more breadth and with considerable effectiveness of a plain order."[8] Although offering a generally unflattering assessment of Cyprian's commentary on the LP, James Moffatt nevertheless indicates that Cyprian's commentary represents a comparable improvement upon its predecessor in terms of scope and structure. In other words,

Cyprian extended a Romano-African tradition of cultic commentary first manifested by Tertullian's *Prayer*.

Although he generally replicates Tertullian's hermeneutical style, Cyprian differs in his understanding of biblical inspiration, the application of Scripture, and the unity of the Bible.[9] In many ways, these differences represent a development of the tradition. Because of Tertullian's book *Prayer*, Cyprian can concentrate his treatise more on the LP itself. Cyprian's *Lord's Prayer* is longer and more comprehensive than Tertullian's *Prayer*. One can also detect in Cyprian's treatise a marked change in the church's status. No longer a mere persecuted and relatively unknown minority, the church by Cyprian's day had become a formidable social institution. His staff rivaled that of the provincial governor, and his congregation was too large for repeated persecutions to extinguish.

The content of Cyprian's *Lord's Prayer* reflects a Romano-African reflection upon, as well as expansion of, the Carthaginian Christian practice of prayer. Similar to Tertullian's *Prayer* in many ways, Cyprian's treatise aims at the average believer. Eduard von der Goltz said of both works:

> They are practical through and through, scarcely interested in philosophy, and understandable for every Christian. In addition to an interpretation of the LP they provide a code of practical rules for the Christian prayer life, . . . the outer and inner discipline of the Christian life.[10]

In other words, the Romano-African cultic tradition stressed *disciplina* in cultic matters. Such an emphasis on *cultus* is found not only in Tertullian and Cyprian, but also in other North African and later Latin expositions on worship.

Donatist and African Catholic interpretations of Scripture and cult trace their roots to the perspective advanced by Tertullian. As recognized earlier, Donatist interpretations of Scripture relied heavily on Tertullian's idea that persecution was an indication of being the true church.[11] Likewise, in his own homilies and writings Augustine draws upon Tertullian and Cyprian. For example, Augustine valued Cyprian's *Lord's Prayer* highly, especially for what he perceived to be its implicit refutation of Pelagianism. In short, one can trace a trajectory of Romano-African thought from Tertullian to Cyprian to the Donatists and Augustine. Although amended along the way, Romano-African thought continues to influence the present.

From Myopia to Hyperopia

I began this book by calling traditional approaches to the LP myopic (nearsighted). Their emphases upon what the prayer meant to its original Jewish hearers overlooks the reality that Christian sacred text and its interpretation flourished among Greco-Roman adherents to the religion. Traditional interpretive visions of the text played a pivotal role in the development of Christian exegesis and cultic practice. I have expanded the conversation by including the cultic perceptions, both real and imagined, of early Greco-Roman Christians. Needless to say, this book does not constitute a truly hyperopic (farsighted) vision of the cultic practice of prayer. Nevertheless, it urges other scholars to be extended in their discussions and representations of the LP.

Another important concept of this discourse involves the determination of an author's ethnoreligious context. Over the past few years, I have become convinced that one of the most important factors influencing an author's interpretation of text and cult involves his interaction with his surrounding environment. As demonstrated, the Greco-Egyptian tableau of Alexandria influenced Clement's theological vision. An intellectual center of the Roman world, Alexandria played host to Platonists, Stoics, Epicureans, and other budding philosophers. Thus, education was an integral part of the Alexandrian economy. In a similar manner, education influenced the church's development. The Christian Catechetical School there performed an integral role in the community's ongoing self-definition. Through its educational institution, Alexandrian Christians constructed their own understanding of the world around them. Christians in Carthage did something similar in their construction of a Christian vision for the world.

Whether through Clement's treatise in *Stromata* 7 or Tertullian's exposition in *Prayer*, Christianity benefited from these expositions on the cultic practice of prayer. They represent trajectories in early Christian thought that developed, adapted, and present themselves to prayer's modern practitioners. I have not been able to trace the full development of these visions in this work, but this is something I hope to accomplish in a later work. A full exposition of these trajectories would immensely benefit scholarship. Greco-Roman interpretations of the Christian cult constitute a necessary and often-overlooked aspect of early Christian development. Although this book develops the discourse on the Lord's Prayer in one aspect, much more needs to be done.

Notes

1. S. L. Greenslade, *Early Latin Theology: Selections from Tertullian, Cyprian, Ambrose, and Jerome* (Library of Christian Classics: Ichthus Edition; Philadelphia: Westminster Press, 1956), 127.

2. Robert L. Simpson, *The Interpretation of Prayer in the Early Church* (The Library of History and Doctrine; Philadelphia: Westminster, 1965), 19.

3. Christopher Stead, *Philosophy in Christian Antiquity* (New York: Cambridge University Press, 1994), 65.

4. Translations of *Peri proseuches* come from Origen, *Prayer: Exhortation to Martyrdom* (trans. John Joseph O'Meara; ACW 19; Westminster, Md.: Newman Press, 1954).

5. Endre Ivánka, *Hellenisches und Christliches im frühbyzantinischen Geistesleben* (Vienna: Herder, 1948), 28.

6. Jo-Ann Shelton, *As the Romans Did: A Sourcebook in Roman Social History* (2d ed.; New York: Oxford University Press, 1998), 372.

7. As quoted in James Moffatt, "Cyprian on the Lord's Prayer, " *The Expositor* 18 (1919): 176.

8. Ibid., 177.

9. Maureen A. Tilley, *The Bible in Christian North Africa: The Donatist World* (Minneapolis: Fortress, 1997), 31–32.

10. Eduard A. F. von der Goltz, *Das Gebet in der ältesten Christenheit* (Leipzig: J. C. Hinrichs, 1901), 279.

11. See Tilley, *Bible in Christian North Africa*, 41.

Bibliography

Adcock, F. E. *Roman Political Ideas and Practice*. Ann Arbor: University of Michigan Press, 1959.

Adkins, Lesley, and Roy A. Adkins, eds. *Dictionary of Roman Religion*. London: Oxford University Press, 1996.

Agnew, F. "Almsgiving, Prayer, and Fasting." *TBT* 33 (1995): 239–44.

Armstrong, A. H. "The Self-Definition of Christianity in Relation to Later Platonism." In *Jewish and Christian Self-Definition: The Shaping of Christianity in the Second and Third Centuries*. Edited by E. P. Sanders. Philadelphia: Fortress, 1980.

Arnold, Edward Vernon. *Roman Stoicism: Being Lectures on the History of the Stoic Philosophy with Special Reference to Its Development within the Roman Empire*. London: Routledge & Kegan Paul, 1958.

Augustine. *The City of God*. Translated by Marcus Dods. New York: Modern Library, 1950.

Austin, M. M., ed. *The Hellenistic World from Alexander to the Roman Conquest: A Selection of Ancient Sources in Translation*. Cambridge: Cambridge University Press, 1981.

Bagnall, Roger S. *Egypt in Late Antiquity*. Princeton: Princeton University Press, 1993.

Bagnall, Roger S., and Bruce W. Frier. *The Demography of Roman Egypt*. Cambridge Studies in Population, Economy, and Society in Past Time 23. New York: Cambridge University Press, 1994.

Barnes, Timothy David. *Tertullian: A Historical and Literary Study*. Oxford: Clarendon, 1971.

Barr, James. "Abba Isn't Daddy." *JTS* 39 (1988): 28–47.

Beard, Mary, et al. *Religions of Rome*. 2 vols. Cambridge: Cambridge University Press, 1998.

Beck, Alexander. *Römisches Recht bei Tertullian und Cyprian: Eine Studie zur frühen Kirchenrechtsgeschichte*. Halle (Saale): Niemeyer, 1930.

Beckwith, Roger. "The Daily and Weekly Worship of the Primitive Church in Relation to Its Jewish Antecedents." *EvQ* 56 (1984): 65–80.

Beeck, F. J. van. "The Worship of Christians in Pliny's Letter." *Studia liturgica* 18 (1988): 121–29.

Betz, Hans Dieter. *Essays on the Sermon on the Mount*. Philadelphia: Fortress Press, 1984.

———. *The Sermon on the Mount: A Commentary on the Sermon on the Mount, Including the Sermon on the Plain (Matthew 5:3–7:27 and Luke 6:20–49)*. Edited by Adela Yarbro Collins. Hermeneia—A Critical and Historical Commentary on the Bible. Minneapolis: Fortress Press, 1995.

Bevan, Edwin R. *Later Greek Religion*. New York: E. P. Dunn, 1927.

Bianchi, Ugo. "Le Colloque International sur les Origines du Gnosticisme." *Numen* 13 (1966).

———, ed. *The Origins of Gnosticism*. SHR 12. Leiden: Brill, 1967.

Bowersock, G. W. *Greek Sophists in the Roman Empire*. Oxford: Clarendon, 1969.

Bowie, E. L. "Greeks and Their Past in the Second Sophistic." Pages 166–209 in *Studies in Ancient Society*. Edited by M. I. Finley. London: Routledge, 1974.

Bowman, Alan K. *Egypt after the Pharaohs 332 BC–AD 642: From Alexander to the Arab Conquest*. Berkeley: University of California Press, 1986.

Brown, Michael Joseph. "The Lord's Prayer Reinterpreted: An Analysis of This Cultic *Didachē* by Clement of Alexandria (*Stromateis* VII) and Tertullian (*De oratione*)." PhD diss., University of Chicago, 1998.

———. "'Panem nostrum': The Problem of Petition and the Lord's Prayer." *JR* (2000): 595–614.

Brown, Peter Robert Lamont. *Augustine of Hippo: A Biography*. Berkeley: University of California Press, 1967.

———. "Christianity and Local Culture in Late Roman Africa." *JRS* 58 (1968): 85–95.

Burns, Sharon. "The Roots of Christian Prayer and Spirituality in Judaism." In *The Journey of Western Spirituality*. Edited by A. W. Sadler. Chico: Scholars Press, 1980.

Campenhausen, Hans von. *Ecclesiastical Authority and Spiritual Power*. Stanford: Stanford University Press, 1969.

Carabine, Diedre. "A Dark Cloud: Hellenistic Influences on the Scriptural Exegesis of Clement of Alexandria and Pseudo-Dionysius." Pages 61–74 in *Scriptural Interpretation in the Fathers: Letter and Spirit*. Edited by Thomas Finan and Vincent Twomey. Dublin: Four Courts, 1995.

Carr, Edward Hallett. *What Is History?* The George Macaulay Trevelyan Lectures Delivered at the University of Cambridge, January–March, 1961. New York: Random House, 1961.

Casey, Robert. "Clement of Alexandria and the Beginnings of Christian Platonism." In *Studies in Early Christianity: A Collection of Scholarly Essays*. Edited by Everett Ferguson et al. New York: Garland, 1993.

Charlesworth, James. "A Prolegomenon to a New Study of the Jewish Background of the Hymns and Prayers in the New Testament." *JJS* 33 (1982): 265–85.

—— et al., eds. *The Lord's Prayer and Other Prayer Texts from the Greco-Roman Era*. Valley Forge, PA: Trinity, 1994.

Cicero, Marcus Tullius. *De natura deorum; Academica*. Translated by H. Rackham. New York: G. P. Putnam's Sons, 1933.

Clay, D. "Socrates' Prayer to Pan." Pages 345–53 in *Arktouros: Hellenic Studies Presented to Bernard M. W. Knox on the Occasion of His 65th Birthday*. Edited by B. M. W. Knox. Berlin: W. de Gruyter, 1979.

Clemens, Titus Flavius. *Stromateis: Books 1 to 3*. Edited by Thomas P. Halton. Translated by John Ferguson. The Fathers of the Church. Washington, DC: The Catholic University of America Press, 1991.

Cochrane, Charles Norris. *Christianity and Classical Culture: A Study of Thought and Action from Augustus to Augustine*. New York: Oxford University Press, 1957, 1970.

Conn, H. "Luke's Theology of Prayer." *Christianity Today* 17 (1972): 6–8.

Corbier, M. "City, Territory and Taxation." Pages 211–40 in *City and Country in the Ancient World*. Edited by John Rich and Andrew Wallace-Hadrill. London: Routledge, 1991.

Cullmann, Oscar. *Prayer in the New Testament*. Overtures to Biblical Theology. Minneapolis: Fortress, 1995.

Cuming, G. J. "Egyptian Elements in the Jerusalem Liturgy." *JTS* 25 (1975): 117–23.

——. "The New Testament Foundation for Common Prayer." *Studia liturgica* 10 (1974): 88–101.

Cyster, R. F. "The Lord's Prayer in the Exodus Tradition." *Theology* 64 (1961): 377–81.

Davison, James E. "Structural Similarities and Dissimilarities in the Thought of Clement of Alexandria and the Valentinians." *SecCent* 3/4 (1983): 201–44.

Dawson, David. *Allegorical Readers and Cultural Relativism in Ancient Alexandria*. Los Angeles: University of California Press, 1992.

——. "Ancient Alexandrian Interpretation of Scripture." PhD diss., Yale University, 1988.

Decarie, Vianney. "Le paradoxe de Tertullien." *VC* 15 (1961): 23–31.

Dibelius, Martin, and Heinrich Greeven. *A Commentary on the Epistle of*

James. Edited by Helmut Koester. Rev. ed. Hermeneia. Philadelphia: Fortress, 1975.

Dillon, R. J. "On the Christian Obedience of Prayer (Matthew 6:5–13)." *Worship* 59 (1985): 414–20.

Dixon, Suzanne. "Continuity and Change in Roman Social History: Retrieving 'Family Feeling(s)' from Roman Law and Literature." Pages 79–90 in *Inventing Ancient Culture: Historicism, Periodization, and the Ancient World*. Edited by Mark Golden and Peter Toohey. London: Routledge, 1992.

———. *The Roman Family*. Ancient Society and History. Baltimore: John Hopkins University Press, 1992.

Dumézil, Georges. *Archaic Roman Religion, with an Appendix on the Religion of the Etruscans*. Translated by Philip Krapp. 2 vols. Chicago: University of Chicago Press, 1970, 1996.

Epictetus. *The Enchiridion*. Translated by Thomas W. Higginson. Library of Liberal Arts. New York: Macmillan, 1948.

Eusebius. *The History of the Church*. Translated by G. A. Williamson. New York: Penguin, 1965.

Eynde, Damien van den. *Les normes de l'enseignement chrétien dans la littérature patristique des trois premiers siecles*. Paris: Gabalda et Fils, 1933.

Faraone, Christopher A., and Dirk Obbink, eds. *Magika Hiera: Ancient Greek Magic and Religion*. New York: Oxford University Press, 1991.

Ferguson, John. *Clement of Alexandria*. New York: Twayne, 1974.

———, ed. *Greek and Roman Religion: A Sourcebook*. Noyes Classical Studies. Park Ridge, NJ: Noyes, 1980.

Finegan, J. *Encountering New Testament Manuscripts*. Grand Rapids: Eerdmans, 1974.

Fischer, B. "The Common Prayer of Congregation and Family in the Ancient Church." *Studia liturgica* 10 (1974): 106–24.

Flesseman-Van Leer, E. *Tradition and Scripture in the Early Church*. Van Gorcum's theologische bibliotheek 26. Assen: Van Gorcum, 1954.

Fowler, W. Warde. *The Religious Experience of the Roman People, from the Earliest Times to the Age of Augustus: The Gifford Lectures, 1909–1910*. London: Macmillan, 1911.

Frankfurter, David. *Religion in Roman Egypt*. Princeton: Princeton University Press, 1998.

Frend, William Hugh Clifford. *The Early Church*. Philadelphia: Fortress, 1982.

———. *The Rise of Christianity*. Philadelphia: Fortress, 1984.

———. *Saints and Sinners in the Early Church: Differing and Conflicting*

Traditions in the First Six Centuries. Theology and Life Series 11. Wilmington: Michael Glazier, 1985.

Fry, Timothy, ed. *The Rule of St. Benedict in English.* Collegeville, MN: Liturgical Press, 1982.

Garnsey, Peter. *Food and Society in Classical Antiquity.* Key Themes in Ancient History. Cambridge: Cambridge University Press, 1999.

Gatzweiler, K. "Jesus in Prayer: Texts of the Our Father." *Lum* 39 (1984): 148–54.

Giallanza, Thomas Henry. "The Organization and Administration of the Church of Carthage under St. Cyprian: Evidence from the Letters." MA Thesis, University of Virginia, 1988.

Gilson, Étienne. *La philosophie au moyen âge.* 2d ed. Paris: Payot, 1944.

Glazov, G. "The Invocation of Ps. 51:17 in Jewish and Christian Morning Prayer." *JJS* 46 (1995): 167–82.

Glover, T. B. *The Conflict of Religions in the Early Roman Empire.* Boston: Beacon Hill, 1960.

Goltz, Eduard A. F. von der. *Das Gebet in der ältesten Christenheit.* Leipzig: J. C. Hinrichs, 1901.

Gonzalez, Justo L. "Athens and Jerusalem Revisited: Reason and Authority in Tertullian." *CH* 43 (1974): 17–25.

———. *A History of Christian Thought.* Rev. ed. 3 vols. Nashville: Abingdon, 1970.

Goudriaan, Koen. *Ethnicity in Ptolemaic Egypt.* Dutch Monographs on Ancient History and Archaeology 5. Amsterdam: J. C. Gieben, 1988.

Goulder, M. D. "Composition of the Lord's Prayer." *JTS* 14 (1963): 32–45.

Grant, Robert M. *Gods and the One God.* Edited by Wayne A. Meeks. Library of Early Christianity 1. Philadelphia: Westminster, 1986.

Greenslade, S. L., ed. *Early Latin Theology: Selections from Tertullian, Cyprian, Ambrose, and Jerome.* Library of Christian Classics: Ichthus Edition. Philadelphia: Westminster, 1956.

Griggs, C. Wilfred. *Early Egyptian Christianity: From Its Origins to 451 CE.* Rev. ed. Brill's Scholars' List. Leiden: Brill, 2000.

Groh, D. E. "Tertullian's Polemic against Social Co-Optation." *CH* 40 (1971): 7–14.

Haas, Christopher. *Alexandria in Late Antiquity: Topography and Social Conflict.* Ancient Society and History. Baltimore: John Hopkins University Press, 1997.

Haenchen, Ernst. *The Acts of the Apostles: A Commentary.* Translated by Robert McL. Wilson. Philadelphia: Westminster, 1965.

Hammond, M. *The Augustan Principate in Theory and Practice During the Julio-Claudian Period.* Cambridge: Harvard University Press, 1933.

Hanson, R. P. C. "Notes on Tertullian's Interpretation of Scripture." *JTS* NS 12 (1961): 273–79.

Harner, P. B. *Understanding the Lord's Prayer.* Philadelphia: Fortress, 1975.

Hartshorne, Charles. *The Divine Relativity, a Social Conception of God.* New Haven: Yale University Press, 1948.

Heiler, Friedrich. *Prayer: A Study in the History and Psychology of Religion.* Translated and edited by Samuel McComb. 2d ed. New York: Oxford University Press, 1933.

Heinze, Richard. *"Auctoritas."* In *Vom Geist des Römertums: Ausgewählte Aufsätze.* Edited by E. Burck. 3d ed. Stuttgart: Teubner, 1960.

Herodian. *Herodian.* Translated by C. R. Whittaker. 2 vols. LCL. London: Heinemann, 1969.

Hickson, Frances V. *Roman Prayer Language: Livy and the Aneid of Vergil.* Stuttgart: Teubner, 1993.

Hoek, Annewies van den. "How Alexandrian Was Clement of Alexandria? Reflections on Clement and His Alexandrian Background." *HeyJ* 31 (1990): 179–94.

Holleran, J. W. "Christ's Prayer and Christian Prayer." *Worship* 48 (1974): 171–82.

Homer. *The Odyssey of Homer.* Translated by Richard Lattimore. New York: Harper & Row, 1965.

Horst, Pieter W. van der. "Silent Prayer in Antiquity." *Numen* 41 (1994): 1–25.

Irwin, Terence. *Plato's Moral Theory: The Early and Middle Dialogues.* Oxford: Oxford University Press, 1977.

Ivánka, Endre. *Hellenisches und Christliches im frühbyzantinischen Geistesleben.* Vienna: Herder, 1948.

Jeremias, Joachim. "The Lord's Prayer in Modern Research." *ExpTim* 71 (1960): 141–46.

———. *New Testament Theology: The Proclamation of Jesus.* New York: Scribner, 1971.

Johnson, Luke Timothy. *The Letter of James: A New Translation with Introduction and Commentary.* Anchor Bible. New York: Doubleday, 1995.

Jolowicz, H. F. *Historical Introduction to the Study of Roman Law.* Cambridge: Cambridge University Press, 1951.

Jones, Peter, and Keith Sidwell, eds. *The World of Rome: An Introduction to Roman Culture.* Cambridge: Cambridge University Press, 1997.

Kajanto, Iiro. *The Latin Cognomina.* Commentationes humanarum litterarum. Rome: G. Bretschneider Editore, 1982.

Karpp, Heinrich. *Schrift und Geist bei Tertullian.* Gutersloh: Bertelsmann, 1955.

Kelley, Stanley Helms. "*Auctoritas* in Tertullian: The Nature and Order of Authority in His Thought." PhD diss., Emory University, 1974.

Kelly, John N. D. *Early Christian Creeds*. 2d ed. London: Longmans, Green, [1960].

———. *Early Christian Doctrines*. 2d ed. London: A & C Black, 1960.

Kiley, Mark, ed. *Prayer from Alexander to Constantine: A Critical Anthology*. New York: Routledge, 1997.

Koester, Helmut. *History, Culture and Religion of the Hellenistic Age*. 1st ed. Vol. 1 of *Introduction to the New Testament*. New York: Walter de Gruyter, 1982.

Kraemer, C. "Pliny and the Early Church Service: Fresh Light from an Old Source." *CP* 29 (1934): 293–300.

Kyrtatas, Dimitris. *The Social Structure of the Early Christian Communities*. London: Verso, 1988.

Laet, Sigfried J. de. *Portorium: Étude sur l'organisation douanière chez les Romains, surtout à l'époque du Haut-Empire*. Roman History. New York: Arno, 1975.

Lampe, G. W. H. "Christian Theology in the Patristic Period." In *A History of Christian Doctrine*. Edited by Hubert Cunliffe-Jones. Edinburgh: Clark, 1978.

Lang, Bernhard. *Sacred Games: A History of Christian Worship*. New Haven: Yale University Press, 1997.

Lebreton, J. "La prière dans l'église primitive." *RSR* 14 (1924): 105–33.

Lewis, Naphtali. *Greeks in Ptolemaic Egypt: Case Studies in the Social History of the Hellenistic World*. New York: Oxford University Press, 1986.

———. *Life in Egypt under Roman Rule*. Oxford: Oxford University Press, 1983.

Lilla, Salvatore Romano Clemente. *Clement of Alexandria: A Study in Christian Platonism and Gnosticism*. Oxford Theological Monographs. London: Oxford University Press, 1971.

Long, A. A. "Language and Thought in Stoicism." Pages 75–113 in *Problems in Stoicism*. Edited by A. A. Long. London: Athlone, 1971.

Long, A. A., and D. N. Sedley, eds. *The Hellenistic Philosophers*. 2 vols. Cambridge: Cambridge University Press, 1987.

Lüdemann, Gerd. *Early Christianity according to the Traditions in Acts: A Commentary*. Translated by John Bowden. Minneapolis: Fortress, 1987.

MacMullen, Ramsay. *Paganism in the Roman Empire*. New Haven: Yale University Press, 1981.

———. *Roman Social Relations, 50 B.C. to A.D. 284*. New Haven: Yale University Press, 1974.

Malherbe, Abraham J. *Moral Exhortation: A Greco-Roman Sourcebook.* Edited by Wayne A. Meeks. Library of Early Christianity 4. Philadelphia: Westminster, 1986.

Manson, T. W. "The Lord's Prayer." *BJRL* 38 (1955): 99–113.

Markus, R. A. *Saeculum: History and Society in the Theology of St. Augustine.* Cambridge: Cambridge University Press, 1970.

Martin, Dale B. *The Corinthian Body.* New Haven: Yale University Press, 1995.

Martin, R. "Aspects of Worship in the New Testament Church." *VE* 2 (1963): 6–27.

McLelland, Joseph C. *God the Anonymous: A Study in Alexandrian Philosophical Theology.* Patristic Monograph Series 4. Cambridge: Philadelphia Patristic Foundation, 1976.

Meeks, Wayne A. *The First Urban Christians: The Social World of the Apostle Paul.* New Haven: Yale University Press, 1983.

Mellor, Ronald, ed. *The Historians of Ancient Rome: An Anthology of the Major Writings.* London: Routledge, 1997.

Merdinger, Jane E. *Rome and the African Church in the Time of Augustine.* New Haven: Yale University Press, 1997.

Metzger, Bruce M. *A Textual Commentary on the Greek New Testament.* New York: United Bible Societies, 1971.

Mikalson, Jon D. *Athenian Popular Religion.* Chapel Hill: University of North Carolina Press, 1983.

Millar, Fergus. "Local Cultures in the Roman Empire: Libyan, Punic, and Latin in Roman Africa." *JRS* 58 (1968): 126–34.

Modrzejewski, Joseph. *The Jews of Egypt: From Ramses II to Emperor Hadrian.* Translated by Robert Cornman. Princeton: Princeton University Press, 1997.

Moffatt, James. "Cyprian on the Lord's Prayer." *The Expositor* 18 (1919): 176–89.

Monceaux, Paul. *Histoire littéraire de l'Afrique chrétienne depuis les origines jusqu'à l'invasion arabe.* Vol. 1. Paris: Ernest Leroux, 1901.

Morey, William C. *Outlines of Roman Law Comprising Its Historical Growth and General Principles.* New York: Putnam's Sons, 1884.

Mortley, Raoul A. *Connaissance religieuse et herméneutique chez Clément d'Alexandrie.* Leiden: Brill, 1973.

Niebuhr, H. Richard. *Radical Monotheism and Western Civilization.* Montgomery Lectureship on Contemporary Civilization. Lincoln: University of Nebraska Press, 1960.

Noonan, James-Charles. *The Church Visible: The Ceremonial Life and Protocol of the Roman Catholic Church.* New York: Viking, 1996.

Ogden, Schubert M. *The Reality of God and Other Essays.* Dallas: Southern Methodist University Press, 1992.

Ogilvie, R. M. *The Romans and Their Gods in the Age of Augustus.* Edited by M. I. Finley. Ancient Culture and Society. London: Chatto & Windus, 1969.

Origen. *Prayer: Exhortation to Martyrdom.* Translated by John Joseph O'Meara. ACW 19. Westminster, MD: Newman, 1954.

Osborn, Eric. "Clement of Alexandria: A Review of Research, 1958–1982." *SecCent* 3/4 (1983): 219–44.

Pagels, Elaine H. *Adam, Eve, and the Serpent.* 1st Vintage Books ed. New York: Vintage Books, 1989.

———. *The Gnostic Gospels.* 1989 Vintage Books ed. New York: Vintage Books, 1989.

———. *The Gnostic Paul: Gnostic Exegesis of the Pauline Letters.* Philadelphia: Fortress, 1975.

Palmer, W. D. "Atheism, Apologetic, and Negative Theology in the Greek Apologists of the Second Century." *VC* 37 (1983): 234–59.

Patte, Daniel. *The Gospel according to Matthew: A Structural Commentary on Matthew's Faith.* Philadelphia: Fortress, 1987.

Pinsent, John. "Roman Spirituality." In *Classical Mediterranean Spirituality: Egyptian, Greek, Roman.* Edited by A. H. Armstrong. New York: Crossroad, 1986.

Plato. *Five Dialogues: Euthyphro, Apology, Crito, Meno, Phaedo.* Translated by G. M. A. Grube. Indianapolis: Hackett, 1981.

———. *Great Dialogues of Plato.* Edited by Eric H. Warmington and Philip G. Rouse. Translated by W. H. D. Rouse. New York: Penguin, 1956.

Plutarch. *Plutarch's Moralia.* Translated by Frank Cole Babbitt. 15 vols. Loeb Classical Library. New York: Putnam, 1927.

Potter, David S. *Literary Texts and the Roman Historian.* Approaching the Ancient World. London: Routledge, 1999.

———. *Prophets and Emperors: Human and Divine Authority from Augustus to Theodosius.* Revealing Antiquity 7. Cambridge: Harvard University Press, 1994.

Prestige, George L. *God in Patristic Thought.* London: Heinemann, 1936.

Proctor, Everett L. "The Influence of Basilides, Valentinus, and Their Followers on Clement of Alexandria (Egypt)." PhD diss., University of California, 1992.

Pruitt, Dean G., and Jeffrey Z. Rubin. *Social Conflict: Escalation, Stalemate, and Settlement.* Topics in Social Psychology Series. New York: Random House, 1986.

Rankin, David. *Tertullian and the Church*. Cambridge: Cambridge University Press, 1995.

Refoule, F. "Tertullian et la philosophie." *RSR* 30 (1956): 42–45.

Rives, J. B. *Religion and Authority in Roman Carthage: From Augustus to Constantine*. New York: Oxford University Press, 1995.

Robbins, Vernon K. "Divine Dialogue and the Lord's Prayer: Socio-Rhetorical Interpretation of Sacred Texts." *Dialogue* 28 (1995): 117–46.

Roberts, Alexander, James Donaldson, A. Cleveland Coxe, and Allan Menzies, eds. *Ante-Nicene Fathers: The Writings of the Fathers Down to A.D. 325*. Peabody, MA: Hendrickson, 1994.

Roberts, Colin. *Manuscript, Society, and Belief in Early Christian Egypt*. The Schweich Lectures of the British Academy. London: Oxford University Press, 1979.

Roberts, Louise. "The Literary Form of the *Stromateis*." *SecCent* 1 (1981): 211–22.

Roberts, Robert E. *The Theology of Tertullian*. London: Epworth, 1924.

Robinson, Olivia F. *The Criminal Law of Ancient Rome*. London: Duckworth, 1995.

———. *The Sources of Roman Law: Problems and Methods for Ancient Historians*. Edited by Richard Stoneman. Approaching the Ancient World. New York: Routledge, 1997.

Rordorf, W. "The Lord's Prayer in the Light of Its Liturgical Use in the Early Church." *Studia liturgica* 14 (1980–81): 1–19.

Rowlandson, Jane, and Roger S. Bagnall. *Women and Society in Greek and Roman Egypt: A Sourcebook*. Cambridge: Cambridge University Press, 1998.

Rudolph, Kurt. *Gnosis: The Nature and History of Gnosticism*. 1st ed. Translated by R. McL Wilson. San Francisco: Harper & Row, 1984.

Sage, Michael M. *Cyprian*. Patristic Monograph Series 1. Cambridge, MA: Philadelphia Patristic Foundation, 1975.

Salisbury, Joyce E. *Perpetua's Passion: The Death and Memory of a Young Roman Woman*. London: Routledge, 1997.

Schulz, Fritz. *Classical Roman Law*. Oxford: Clarendon, 1953.

———. *History of Roman Legal Science*. Oxford: Clarendon, 1953.

Shaw, Teresa M. *The Burden of the Flesh: Fasting and Sexuality in Early Christianity*. Edited by L. Michael White. Minneapolis: Fortress, 1998.

Shelton, Jo-Ann, ed. *As the Romans Did: A Sourcebook in Roman Social History*. New York: Oxford University Press, 1998.

Shortt, Charles de Lisle. *The Influence of Philosophy on the Mind of Tertullian*. London: Elliot Stock, 1933.

Sider, Robert D. *Ancient Rhetoric and the Art of Tertullian*. Oxford Theological Monographs. London: Oxford University Press, 1971.

Simpson, Robert L. *The Interpretation of Prayer in the Early Church*. Edited by S. L. Greenslade. Library of History and Doctrine. Philadelphia: Westminster, 1965.

Slingerland, H. Dixon. *Claudian Policymaking and the Early Imperial Repression of Judaism*. Edited by Jacob Neusner. South Florida Studies in the History of Judaism 160. Atlanta: Scholars Press, 1997.

Sloyan, G. "Jewish Ritual of the First Century C.E. and Christian Sacramental Behavior." *BTB* 15 (1985): 98–102.

Stalley, R. F. *An Introduction to Plato's Laws*. Indianapolis: Hackett, 1983.

Starr, Chester G. *The Ancient Romans*. New York: Oxford University Press, 1971.

Stead, Christopher. *Philosophy in Christian Antiquity*. New York: Cambridge University Press, 1994.

Stegemann, Ekkehard, and Wolfgang Stegemann. *The Jesus Movement: A Social History of Its First Century*. Minneapolis: Fortress, 1999.

Stevenson, James. *A New Eusebius: Documents Illustrative of the History of the Church to AD 337*. London: SPCK, 1978.

Stowers, Stanley K. *Letter Writing in Greco-Roman Antiquity*. Edited by Wayne A. Meeks. Library of Early Christianity 5. Philadelphia: Westminster, 1986.

Teachers, Joint Association of Classical, ed. *The World of Athens: An Introduction to Classical Athenian Culture*. Cambridge: Cambridge University Press, 1984.

Tertullian. *Tertullian's Tract on the Prayer*. Edited by Ernest Evans. London: SPCK, 1953.

Theophrastus. *Peri eusebeias: Griechischer Text*. Edited, translated, and introduced by W. Pötscher. Leiden: Brill, 1964.

Thurston, Bonnie Bowman. *Spiritual Life in the Early Church: The Witness of Acts and Ephesians*. Minneapolis: Fortress, 1993.

Tilborg, S. V. "Form-Criticism of the Lord's Prayer." *NovT* 14 (1972): 94–105.

Tilley, Maureen A. *The Bible in Christian North Africa: The Donatist World*. Minneapolis: Fortress, 1997.

Trevett, Christine. *Montanism: Gender, Authority and the New Prophecy*. Cambridge: Cambridge University Press, 1996.

Trudinger, P. "The 'Our Father' in Matthew as Apocalyptic Eschatology." *DRev* 107 (1989): 49–54.

Versnel, H. S., ed. *Faith, Hope and Worship: Aspects of Religious Mentality in the Ancient World*. Studies in Greek and Roman Religion 2. Leiden: Brill, 1981.

Walbank, F. W. *The Hellenistic World*. Rev. ed. Cambridge: Harvard University Press, 1992.

Walker, G. S. M. *The Churchmanship of St. Cyprian*. Ecumenical Studies in History 9. London: Lutterworth, 1968.

Wardman, Alan. *Religion and Statecraft among the Romans*. Baltimore: John Hopkins University Press, 1982.

Watson, Alan. *The State, Law, and Religion: Pagan Rome*. Athens, GA: University of Georgia Press, 1992.

Wilkin, Robert L. *The Christians as the Romans Saw Them*. New Haven: Yale University Press, 1984.

Wilson, Robert McL. "Philo of Alexandria and Gnosticism." *Kairos* 14 (1972): 213–19.

Winter, Bruce W. *After Paul Left Corinth: The Influence of Secular Ethics and Social Change*. Grand Rapids: Eerdmans, 2001.

Xenophon. *Xenophon in Seven Volumes*. Edited by G. P. Goold. Translated by E. C. Marchant. Vol. 4. Loeb Classical Library. Cambridge: Harvard University Press, 1929.

Zanker, Paul. *The Power of Images in the Age of Augustus*. Edited by Alan Shapiro. Jerome Lectures 16. Ann Arbor: University of Michigan Press, 1988.

Zeitlin, S. "Prayer in the Apocrypha and Pseudepigrapha." *JQR* 40 (1949–50): 201–3.

Index